RADHASOAMI REALITY

RADHASOAMI REALITY

THE LOGIC OF A MODERN FAITH

Mark Juergensmeyer

Published by Princeton University Press, 41 William Street,
Princeton, New Jersey 08540
In the United Kingdom: Princeton University Press, Chichester,
West Sussex

Library of Congress Cataloging-in-Publication Data

Juergensmeyer, Mark.
Radhasoami reality : the logic of a modern faith /
Mark Juergensmeyer.
p. cm.
Includes bibliographical references and index.
ISBN 0-691-07378-3
ISBN 0-691-01092-7 (pbk.)
1. Radhasoami Satsang. I. Title.
BP605.R33J84 1991
299'.93—dc20 90-23132

This book has been composed in Linotron Sabon

Princeton University Press books are printed
on acid-free paper, and meet the guidelines
for permanence and durability of the Committee
on Production Guidelines for Book Longevity
of the Council on Library Resources

First paperback printing, with corrections and a new preface, 1996

Printed in the United States of America by
Princeton Academic Press

10 9 8 7 6 5 4 3 2

TO MY MOTHER

Clara Johannaber Juergensmeyer

WHO FIRST TAUGHT ME THE SUBJECTS

THAT ARE AT THE HEART OF THIS STUDY,

FAITH, HOPE, AND LOVE

Contents

Illustrations

Unless otherwise indicated, the photographs are by the author.

Preface to the Paperback Edition

In the latter part of the 1990s one is impressed not only by what Radhasoami is, but also by what it is not: a movement for neither religious nationalism, separatism, nor political power. Despite this fact—or perhaps because of it—the various branches of the Radhasoami community (also known as Sant Mat) continue to expand throughout North India and around the globe at what seems to be an exponential rate. Radhasoami continues to be one of the most successful new religions of modern times.

Although seemingly apolitical, Radhasoami fits the profile of a much broader postmodern religious revolt. Like its more political counterparts, the Radhasoami movement embraces the efficiency, organization, and technology of the contemporary world—employing science as both metaphor and model of the spiritual exercise—while rejecting some of the more painful features of modernity. Radhasoami goes to some lengths to overcome what it regards as modernity's dismal legacies: the alienation of individualism, the cynicism of secularity, and the pretensions of rational thought.

Yet the members of Radhasoami are not at war with the secular world in the same way as Christian fundamentalists in the United States, Islamic activists in the Middle East, and Hindu nationalists in India. One reason for this is theological: since Radhasoami theory deems it impossible for an individual's spiritual progress to be seen or known by another, the possibility of judging others is foreclosed. Another reason is social. The Radhasoami communities cohere as fellowships under the direct authority of spiritual masters, rather than as large national entities held together by a politico-religious ideology. Like their political counterparts, Radhasoami members aim to create moral communities and effect social transformation, but unlike them, they want to work through societies that are small and manageable.

Several years have intervened since the first edition of this book was published, and although the Radhasoami communities have grown—especially among uprooted urban populations in India and expatriate Indian societies abroad—they have not substantially changed. They continue to appeal to members of managerial and administrative classes, and to mobile minorities regardless of station or faith. Lower- and upper-caste Indians, Sikhs and Hindus, White Christians and Black South Africans are all included in the Radhasoami fold.

In making the revisions for this paperback edition, I benefited greatly from the assistance of David Christopher Lane and the detailed comments provided by leaders of several branches of the movement. Master Gurinder Singh Dhillon of Beas met with me in Honolulu, discussed various aspects of the book, and subsequently provided me with an extensive set of corrections and clarifications prepared by his staff. At Soamibagh, Madan Gopal Gupta clarified the Soamibagh position and pointed out differences between his interpretations and mine in his book, *Modern Indian Mysticism: Commentary on Western Response to Radhasoami Faith* (Agra: MG Publishers, 1994). I also appreciate the efforts of Shrivatsa Goswami and Dr. Umesh Prasad Sharma, both of Vrindavan, in securing answers to a list of questions I had about the Agra centers. At Dayalbagh, they contacted Surendra Nath Srivastava and Shiv Pujan Sahai; at Soamibagh, Jang Bahadur Mathur and Anand Mishra; and at Pipalmandi, Prof. Agam Prasad Mathur.

Although this edition gives me the opportunity of correcting several errors and updating factual information, I have not changed my analysis or interpretation of Radhasoami tradition since this book was first published. Some readers have urged me to bring my perspective more in line with their own positions, but most have been kind enough to realize that an outsider such as myself will always have "a difference of approach and different views," as Master Gurinder Singh Dhillon said in a letter to me. I continue to be impressed with the tolerance and support that he and most other members of the Radhasoami communities have given to this project, and their acceptance of the fact that I have been motivated only by curiosity and a deep desire to understand the changing role of religion in the modern world.

Santa Barbara, California
July 4, 1995

Acknowledgments

As an outsider to the Radhasoami faith, I am profoundly grateful to those within the Radhasoami communities who have shared their knowledge and insight with me, especially since I suspect that from their point of view anything an outsider might write must seem a bit odd. I have tried to retain a balance, however, between my own critical faculties and my sympathies toward them and to all others in the modern age who attempt to retain a sense of religious faith. Most members of Radhasoami communities with whom I have come in contact have been supportive of this endeavor.

Many of their names appear in the list of interviews at the end of this book. Among those who have been most helpful are, at the Beas center, Janak Raj Puri and Kirpal Singh Narang; the late master of the Beas branch, Maharaj Charan Singh; and the late general secretary at Beas, K. L. Khanna, who first introduced me to Radhasoami ideas and concepts; at the Ruhani Satsang and Sawan-Kirpal centers in Delhi, Vinod Sena and the late Master Darshan Singh; at Peepalmandi in Agra, Prof. Agam Prasad Mathur, Radhasoami historian and himself the master of one branch of the tradition; at Dayalbagh, G. D. Sahgal, Master M. B. Lal, and the late Baba Ram Jadoun, who was for years its general secretary; and at Soamibagh, the late Sant Das Maheshwari. The staff of Mahatta Studio, Delhi, was helpful in providing pictures from Radhasoami archives and in helping me secure permission from Beas for their use in this book. Some of the ideas that appear in this book were first discussed with Malcolm and Kate Tillis, members of the Ruhani Satsang and the Sawan-Kirpal Ruhani Mission, who made available to me their personal library in Landour, India, during the writing of the first draft.

The completed manuscript was read in its entirety by Prof. Arthur Stein, who helped improve its accuracy and balance of interpretation, and by David Lane, who has been my research assistant on this project for many years. At one time, when he was a student of mine at Berkeley, David accompanied me on a research trip to India. Later, as a doctoral candidate in sociology at the University of California, San Diego, he assisted in pursuing references and in creating a comprehensive family tree of the Radhasoami lineages, which is included as an appendix to this book. I am also grateful to Anthony Schlagel for word processing and Donna Wilke for preparing the index.

Others who have read parts of this manuscript and helped see it through to completion include L. A. Babb, Ainslie Embree, Bruce Lawrence, and W. H. McLeod; and Margaret Case of Princeton University Press has pleasantly persevered through several lengthy revisions. Srivatsa Goswamy, by telephone, provided last-minute information on Soamibagh, for which I am grateful. Most of all I am thankful for Jack Hawley, who has read seemingly innumerable versions of this book, patiently reviewing and correcting each as if it were the last. Through his friendship my awareness of Indian religion has greatly expanded, and without his support for this project—conceived years ago while we were hiking in the Himalayan foothills—it would never have been completed. Finally, a special thanks to my friend and spouse, Sucheng Chan, who has also read through parts of the manuscript and supported this undertaking, even though religion has never been a salient aspect of her intellectual life. In a remarkable way, it seems to me, the most intense skeptics and the most intense believers of our age share a common conviction: that beneath all superficial appearances lies a deeper truth.

Berkeley, California

RADHASOAMI REALITY

Introduction

The Rise of a New Religious Tradition

ON THE WALL behind the desk of a high-ranking government official in New Delhi hang various emblems of his identity: the obligatory portrait of the prime minister, a diploma from a distinguished British university, a snapshot of the administrator's handsome family sitting in the garden of his suburban home, and a black and white photograph of an elderly man dressed in traditional clothing, somberly enthroned on a carpeted platform. The latter picture is of his guru, a master in one of the Radhasoami lineages of spiritual guides and teachers.

This evidence of an administrator's devotion to a spiritual master is not by any means an anomaly in modern Indian offices. In recent years there has been a remarkable interest in *guru bhakti*—devotion to a spiritual master—throughout North Indian cities, and among those responding to its appeal have been a considerable number of administrators and office workers in government and business organizations. The Radhasoami movement has flourished in this setting and has become the largest of the new religious communities in North India. All told, in its various branches and under the several names by which it is known, the Radhasoami community can claim over a million initiates in South Asia, and tens of thousands more in other parts of the world.[1]

The emergence of a new religious tradition is a significant event in the history of religions. India, of course, has had more than its fair share of them, beginning with Brahmanical Hinduism, Buddhism and Jainism in the sixth century B.C.E., and including Sikhism, which began to develop into a separate religious tradition in the sixteenth and seventeenth centuries C.E., and Hindu revival movements, which emerged at the end of the nineteenth. The Radhasoami tradition is related to many of these earlier currents, but it has taken on a character of its own.

It began rather simply in Agra in the 1860s with the teachings of Swami Shiv Dayal Singh. These showed a mix of influences —Kabirpanthi, Sikh, Nath yogi, Hindu Vaisnava—and focused on the efficacy of sacred words and the saving power of a spiritual master in transforming the self and achieving access to otherworldly realms beyond. Swami Shiv Dayal advocated a form of yoga that was appropriate for householders as well as ascetics, and his following, largely members of his own urban merchant-

[1] See Appendix C for the sources on which I have based this figure.

caste community, continued to be a lively if increasingly fragmented group after his death. He was succeeded by other spiritual masters, and presently there are at least twenty lineages in the Radhasoami family tree. Some of the branches have prospered. During the 1930s the residential community at Dayalbagh, near Agra, developed an enormous complex of industries, shops, and model farms and dairies; at the same time the colony at Beas, in the Punjab, created something of a utopian city of its own. In the last thirty years Beas has greatly expanded its membership throughout North India, and it and one of its offshoots—the Ruhani Satsang in Delhi—have developed large multicultural networks that are in many ways prototypes for a new kind of international religious organization.

Why has the Radhasoami faith prospered? The question is not easy to answer, for the Radhasoami tradition is a peculiar blend of opposites. On the one hand, its leadership is efficient, progressive, and international; on the other hand, its beliefs and spiritual practices are arcane and esoteric, reviving a certain form of spirituality that reaches back to medieval Hinduism and perhaps beyond. In this book I intend to explore how this apparent contradiction is overcome, and how the juxtaposition of progressive and traditional modes of thought has enabled this new tradition to flourish in the modern age.

Radhasoami as Modern Religion

In raising the issue of the Radhasoami tradition's appeal to modern people, I am concerned with more than just its contemporaneity: I am interested in the way it relates to the conditions of modern life. Although some would deny that there is such a thing as a "modern personality,"[2] the term is often used to describe characteristics that members of Radhasoami share with urban people throughout the world. These cluster together to yield a pattern of identity that is individualistic, organizational and empirical, and that is linked to a cognitive process that Max Weber called rationalization and Daniel Bell described as placing theoretical knowledge at the center.[3] People in the modern age see themselves as atomistic individuals whose identities are not basically tied to groups and commu-

[2] Mary Douglas, for example, rejects most characterizations of modern persons because they stereotype premoderns, some of whom are "as mobile, footloose, and uncommitted as any modern academic" ("The Effects of Modernization on Religious Change," *Daedalus* 111, no. 1 [Winter, 1982]:18).

[3] Daniel Bell, *The Cultural Contradictions of Capitalism* (New York: Basic Books, 1976), p. 20.

nities;[4] their social relationships, especially in their work, are what Ferdinand Toennies has described as conducive to organization (*Gesellschaft*) rather than to community (*Gemeinschaft*);[5] and they seek objective, observable verification of things that they regard as true. This is the kind of outlook that most people would describe as "scientific," extending a mode of analysis appropriate to the natural order into the realm of social and personal truths.[6]

Each of these characteristics—individualism, organization-mindedness, and empiricism—has appeared at various times and places in world history, but the constellation of all three is distinctive to the habit of thought that emerged as a major theme in Europe with the Enlightenment and has become the prevailing paradigm of thinking among educated people throughout the world. Since modernity is a view of reality, it has often come into conflict with other worldviews, especially those provided by religion.

This conflict is clearly visible in European history, where modernity replaced a medieval view of reality in which the Church was the organizing principle of society, and the mysteries of the natural and social order were largely explained as the workings of God. Religion did not disappear in Europe with the rise of modernity, but it did change. Over the course of the last several centuries, new forms of Christianity have developed in response. Most of these fall somewhere between the extremes of traditionalism and reform. The conservative movements within the Catholic and Protestant churches provide an escape from modernity by denying its premises and reasserting those of the past; and the liberal wings of Christianity accommodate themselves to modernity by regarding spiritual development as complementary to modern intellectual and social progress.

In Europe and America these religious responses to the modern view of reality have taken several centuries to develop. In India the confrontation between traditional and modern worldviews has been more recent—

[4] Perhaps the most lively recent discussion of the role of individualism in modern Western society has followed the publication of Robert Bellah et al., *Habits of the Heart: Individualism and Commitment in American Life* (Berkeley: University of California Press, 1986). Following Jurgen Habermas, the authors distinguish between two kinds of individualism in contemporary Western society: utilitarian (directed towards personal acquisition of power, prestige or wealth) and expressive (directed towards individual fulfillment in aesthetic and hedonistic ways).

[5] Ferdinand Toennies, *Community and Society*, trans. and intro. Charles P. Loomis (East Lansing: Michigan State University Press, 1957). Toennies's categories have been refined by subsequent social theorists, but his general distinction is still relevant.

[6] For the way in which scientific thinking displaces an earlier, religious conception of the world, see E. A. Burtt, *The Metaphysical Foundations of Modern Science* (Garden City, N.Y.: Doubleday Anchor, 1954).

mainly since the nineteenth century—but the range of responses is largely the same. There have been right-wing Hindus such as the Sankaracarya of Puri who have vigorously opposed the social effects of what they see as Western influence, while other Hindu intellectuals such as Swami Vivekananda have fashioned progressive forms of religion more commensurate with modern tastes.[7]

The Radhasoami tradition falls somewhere between the two. Although it was born and nurtured in the same nineteenth-century urban society that produced among Hindus the Arya Samaj, the Ramakrishna movement, and the Brahmo Samaj, and among Sikhs, the Singh Sabha, it did not entirely follow their reformist patterns. In its scientific language and progressive social organization, the Radhasoami community made concessions to modern tastes, yet in other areas, such as in its emphasis on personal interaction, transcendence, and trust, it provided more conservative solutions to the spiritual and moral dilemmas of modern life. The Radhasoami form of modern religion is in many ways unique to Indian culture, yet its thorough mix of modern and conservative elements is becoming increasingly popular throughout the world.[8] Similarly hybrid movements have expanded markedly in recent years, while those that are exclusively modern or conservative have tended to wither away.

The Relationship of the Radhasoami Tradition to Hinduism

By speaking of Radhasoami faith as a modern form of Hinduism, I am speaking of Hinduism in the loosest sense, as India's religious heritage. To say anything more than that would be to enter into the debate sometimes heard within Radhasoami circles about whether their faith comprises a sect within Hinduism, a branch of Sikhism, or a religion of its own. Whether one judges the Radhasoami community as the latter or part of another religion depends largely on what one means by the word. Elsewhere I have argued that one would need at least three North Indian terms to translate the word *religion*: *dharma* for religious culture, *qaum* for a large community of religious identity, and *panth* for a fellowship of believers grouped around a specific line of teachers and teachings.[9] The

[7] See, for examples, David Kopf, *The Brahmo Samaj and the Shaping of the Modern Indian Mind* (Princeton: Princeton University Press, 1979) and Kenneth W. Jones, *Arya Dharm: Hindu Consciousness in 19th-Century Punjab* (Berkeley: University of California Press, 1976).

[8] Bruce Lawrence regards this mix of modernity and tradition as a factor in the recent rise of fundamentalism. See his *Defenders of God: Fundamentalist Movements in Christianity, Judaism, and Islam* (San Francisco: Harper and Row, 1989).

[9] Mark Juergensmeyer, *Religion as Social Vision: The Movement Against Untouchability in 20th Century Punjab* (Berkeley: University of California Press, 1982), pp. 2–6.

Radhasoami community probably fits most closely the panthic model of religion, but it has elements of the other two as well.

The term *Hindu* is most often used in a dharmic sense, as a label for the common religious culture of the Indian subcontinent. As such, it is not what those influenced by Christianity and Islam think of as religion: the qaumic pattern of centralized organization accompanied by a unified set of beliefs. If Hinduism is a "religion" in the qaumic sense, this is a fairly recent development associated with efforts to bring together various Hindu groups in causes of national concern. Such efforts have a long way to go: the very term *Hinduism* came into usage only within the last several centuries, and the adjective *Hindu*, an older term, was initially just an appellation given by outsiders from the West to people who lived near or beyond the Indus River.

Members of the Radhasoami community who live in India can be considered Hindu in a dharmic sense: they share the cultural outlooks and practices that are the heritage of most other religious persons in India. For example, they subscribe to such central Hindu notions as *karma*. Yet Radhasoami spiritual teachers have been quite emphatic in rejecting other elements of what is commonly thought of as Hindu belief, including some that are cardinal. According to the first master, Swami Shiv Dayal, "image worship, pilgrimages, or the reading of religious books" is a "waste of time,"[10] "ceremonies and ritual observances are a conceit,"[11] and all Hinduism's traditional religious technicians—"the Rishis, Yogis, Brahmans and Sannyasins"—have "failed."[12] This kind of suspicion of Hindu institutions led another nineteenth-century Radhasoami leader to say that "Radhasoami faith is not built on the basis of scriptures appertaining to Hinduism or any other religion."[13]

In the Punjab, the Radhasoami community is often regarded as an offshoot of Sikhism. This description is largely incorrect, but the Radhasoami tradition does have some connections with the Sikhs. The teachings of the first Radhasoami master were based, in part, on those of Guru Nanak, the Sikhs' founding master. Moreover, the religious culture of medieval Hinduism that provided the background for the rise of Sikhism, which included just the sorts of criticism of Hindu institutions as Swami Shiv Dayal was to make, is regarded by members of the Radhasoami communities as their heritage as well. Yet few within Radhasoami would call their community a Sikh "sect"—there are no ties of any sort between it

[10] Swami Shiv Dayal Singh, *Sar Bachan: Prose*, trans. Sewa Singh (Beas: Radhasoami Satsang, Beas, 1955), p. 46.

[11] Ibid., p. 121.

[12] Ibid., p. 155.

[13] Rai Saligram, *Radhasoami Mat Prakash*, quoted in S. D. Maheshwari, *Thesis on a Thesis* (Agra: Radhasoami Satsang, Soamibagh, n.d.), p. 26.

and Sikh organizations—and most Sikhs would regard the ideas of Radhasoami as separate from their own.

Many Radhasoami leaders choose to avoid the term *religion* altogether. According to Charan Singh, the late spiritual master of the largest branch of the faith, Radhasoami is "no religion at all," but rather an amalgam of "the teachings of the saints; and by saints is not meant a particular saint but all saints of the world."[14] In rejecting the label of religion, Charan Singh holds Radhasoami teachings at some distance from what often passes for religion today: quaint but irrelevant customs, myths and festivals. Charan Singh takes this as the common fate of religion: "Rituals and ceremonies generally come after the saints leave, when the organizations come and society takes over."[15] Those who adopt the Radhasoami perspective see it as vital and new, and are naturally unenthusiastic about what they regard as the dinosaurs of old worldviews—the "religions."

Because the word *religion* is problematic, I have chosen to speak instead of the Radhasoami community and the Radhasoami tradition. In this book I also talk about Radhasoami faith, which is a way of speaking about the community and the tradition from the participant's point of view.[16] Occasionally I will also refer to the Radhasoami movement, but I try to restrict the usage of this term to the Radhasoami community's early years, since the term implies a state of transition from an old worldview to a new one and connotes a community not yet fully formed. In its later years it seems better to call Radhasoami a tradition; that is, a culturally transmitted view of reality with a constituent community of its own. When we speak of movements, we usually have in mind social forms that are linked to a larger tradition and endure for only a limited time; traditions, by contrast, have a great deal of diversity within them and maintain an identity separate from other traditions that persists over many generations. Even though it has clearly emerged from the broader religious culture of Hindu India, the Radhasoami tradition meets these three criteria—diversity, identity and endurance—and may be thought of as a tradition in its own right.

The Radhasoami tradition is young, of course, still feeling its way into maturity. As such, a study of its history presents us with an unusual opportunity to see how religious traditions develop. It is as if we, as observ-

[14] Charan Singh, *The Master Answers to Audiences in America* (Beas: Radhasoami Satsang, Beas, 1966), p. 17.

[15] Ibid., p. 17.

[16] The categories of "tradition," "community," and "faith" are those preferred by Wilfred Cantwell Smith in speaking about "religion," a word he finds so muddled in meaning and so modern in coinage as to be useless for comparative and historical purposes. See his *The Meaning and End of Religion* (New York: Harper and Row, 1962).

ers of the world's religious history, could witness the rise of the Christian community during the time of the early fathers, the emergence of the Buddhist tradition as the teachings of Sakyamuni were passed on to the sangha, or the expansion of Islam under the first caliphate. Of course, there is no assurance that Radhasoami will have as grand a place in history as these older traditions. Yet the Radhasoami community is faced with issues of succession and self-definition that are broadly parallel to those encountered by the early Christian, Buddhist, and Islamic communities. And it has likewise experienced what most religious communities confront in their youths: schisms, organizational fragmentation, and persistent disagreements over theological issues. Whatever their disgreements, however, the various parts of the Radhasoami community share enough of a common outlook on the basic things in life, and have done so for a sufficient number of years, that there is a genuine core to their tradition. This makes it possible to speak of a Radhasoami view of reality, a common Radhasoami worldview.

Studying a New Tradition

I believe that to understand a worldview, one must at some point take seriously the perspective of those who hold that view. Those of us who study a worldview other than our own are always to some extent involved in cross-cultural studies, for we are translating from someone else's frame of reference into our own. To do so, I believe, we cannot be limited to examining the historical factors that "caused" someone else's culture to emerge or the social ones that "impelled" persons to join it (as a more deterministic social scientist might put it); we have to examine the culture that has been constructed, and the spiritual and social vision that makes it attractive to those who join. Studies of religious movements sometimes explain away their appeal by focusing entirely on the members' nonreligious motivations; my own studies, including this one, attempt a more balanced view of factors internal and external to religion.

One could call this a multidisciplinary study, for it employs a variety of academic perspectives, but its primary purpose is singular: to understand the Radhasoami view of reality in relation to its context in the modern world. Such an attempt is, I believe, within the proper domain of the field of studies that originated as *Religionswissenschaft* in nineteenth-century Germany. Today in continental Europe it is often called "phenomenology of religion," and in Great Britain and the United States, "religious studies." This field is dedicated to studying the phenomena of religion not only as expressions of social and cultural factors, but as entities that make sense in their own terms. As Jacques Waardenburg puts it, to study religion in the "phenomenological perspective" requires one "to reconstruct religious meanings."[17] In a similar vein, Wilfred Cantwell Smith argues that the most appropriate subject of religious studies is "the religious life" of a community that knits together the various literary, social, and psychological ways in which that religious life is manifest.[18]

To this way of thinking, religion is not so much a thing—a set of beliefs or an organizational structure—as a way of looking at the world. It is, as Clifford Geertz says in regard to all forms of culture, a "context" for understanding "social events, behaviors, institutions, or processes."[19] Other scholars have described religion as a kind of language through which meaningful events and perceptions are communicated.[20] Both of these metaphors for religion—context and language—are helpful in describing it in a phenomenological way.

But these metaphors also reveal a basic question inherent in the study of religion: does religion point beyond its contextual framework and its religious language to a special, indeed ultimate, aspect of reality, or is it simply a particular way of thinking and talking about the everyday world? This ambiguity about the "reality" towards which religion is oriented is often mirrored in the discourse of religious leaders, where the sacred is sometimes said to be transcendent, sometimes immanent. Radhasoami leaders often seem to be describing—perhaps even creating—remarkable and unexpected areas of reality; yet at other times they seem to be providing a language, a context, for perceiving what is real in the ordinary world. Although I tend to talk about religion more frequently in the latter sense, I will attempt to describe both ways of thinking about Radhasoami's "reality," and to do so without judging the believers' perception of it. Since perceptions are the true subject of every phenomeno-

[17] Jacques Waardenburg, *Reflections on the Study of Religion* (The Hague: Mouton, 1978), p. 94.

[18] See Wilfred Cantwell Smith, "Comparative Religion: Whither—and Why?" in Mircea Eliade and Joseph Kitagawa, eds., *History of Religions: Essays in Methodology* (Chicago: University of Chicago Press, 1959), p. 37.

[19] Clifford Geertz, *The Interpretation of Cultures* (New York: Basic Books, 1973), p. 14.

[20] J. Frits Staal, for instance, has made an interesting comparison between the study of ritual and the study of language; see his *Rules without Meaning: Ritual, Mantras, and the Human Sciences* (New York: Peter Lang, 1989). George Lindbeck describes such theoretical approaches to the study of religion as "cultural-linguistic," for they view religion as a kind of language or symbolic structure for a cultural worldview; it is the approach he prefers (*The Nature of Doctrine: Religion and Theology in a Postliberal Age* [Philadelphia: Westminster Press, 1984], pp. 32–41). For a different perspective, one that rejects the idea that language implies a particular worldview, see James Barr, "The Language of Religion," in Lauri Honko, ed., *The Science of Religion: Studies in Methodology* (The Hague: Mouton, 1979), pp. 436–38.

logical study of religion, my task is to make coherent the internal logic of the perceptions put forward in the Radhasoami faith.

The Logic of Radhasoami Faith

In talking about Radhasoami's "logic," I refer to those central propositions that hold the Radhasoami worldview together. These propositions are not immutable—the way they are understood is affected by historical and cultural conditions and by the different angles of vision provided by varying branches of the community. But each proposition is essential to the total framework of Radhasoami faith. The Radhasoami mind-set is unimaginable without any one of them, and each is indispensable in understanding the others. They are Radhasoami's fundamental categories for describing reality, and as such they buttress one another in a complementary way. In this book I will look at the most important of these concepts—*guru*, *bhajan*, *satsang*, *seva*, *dera*, and *bhandara*—and try to understand how they are connected.

The titles of the chapters that describe these aspects of Radhasoami indicate the particular significance of each within the broader Radhasoami milieu. The chapter "Someone to Trust" looks at the experience of accepting a particular person as *guru*, as the source of absolute authority and the locus of truth and trust in one's life. "The Journey of Light and Sound" deals with the nature of the self and its possibilities for transformation in a process that Radhasoami likens to music, *bhajan*. "The Fellowship of the True" is about *satsang*: notions of community, responses to love, and new forms of family and society. "Selfless Service" explores the notion of *seva*, which establishes a relation between personal and social wholeness, linking the attention that is demanded by the predicament of one's soul to the service that is required by the needs of others. "The Sense of a Center" examines the utopian ideals that are implied in the Radhasoami organizational models, such as *dera*, especially as they are manifested in the great communal gatherings called *bhandaras*. Inherent in such concepts are notions of centeredness and location that are found throughout Radhasoami thought.

The exploration of these interrelated aspects of the Radhasoami world forms the second section of the book. Preceding it is a section examining the origin of the Radhasoami tradition in India's culture and its evolution in the last 130 years, and following it is a section on the social locations of those who have embraced the faith. In the chapters of that section I describe several believers—among them a lower-caste village woman, a high-ranking administrator in India's civil service, and an American surgeon—each of whom represents a significant segment of Radhasoami's present-day following. At the end of the book I return to the issues with which I began: why a religious perception of reality such as Radhasoami's has emerged and flourished in our time, and how it helps a diverse and intercultural following to participate in, and make sense of, the modern world.

Part I

THE EMERGENCE OF A MODERN FAITH

One

Remembering a Hidden Past

THE LATTER HALF of the nineteenth century was a period of religious ferment and rapid social change throughout North India, but perhaps especially so in Agra, a city on the banks of the Jumna river some two hundred miles south of Delhi. Although Agra is an old Moghul city, it began to expand and develop its modern character after the British established it as a major military center in the 1800s. It was then that large numbers of villagers came to Agra in search of employment, and merchants and moneylenders came to service the rapidly expanding population.[1] They came from all areas of the surrounding countryside, but since the British relied heavily on Sikhs from the Punjab to staff the Indian army, many of the newcomers—including the family of Shiv Dayal Singh, the founder of the Radhasoami lineages—were from the Punjab.

The religious consequence of this demographic change was an upsetting of the old order. The Muslim and Brahmanical establishments were not revered by these newcomers to the same degree as they had been by an older clientele. Indians who worked with the British government were particularly susceptible to the attitude that the old religious authority was passé.[2] The Christianity offered by missionaries attracted some of the urban newcomers, but many more preferred to ignore religion altogether or seek out new forms of spiritual identity that provided links with their own religious culture. It was this latter route that appealed to Swami Shiv Dayal.

The Life of Swami Shiv Dayal

Swami Shiv Dayal Singh [3] was born in the Panni Gali section of Agra on August 25, 1818, to Mahamaya and Seth Dilwali Singh, members of a

[1] *Census of the Government of India*, Agra District Tables (Delhi: Government of India, 1880).

[2] C. A. Bayly, *Indian Society and the Making of the British Empire*, vol. 2, part 1 of *The New Cambridge History of India* (Cambridge: Cambridge University Press, 1988), p. 166.

[3] The Radhasoami convention is to transliterate the term *Swami* as *Soami*, and to add the honorific syllable *ji* and the title *Maharaj*. I have chosen to use the noninflected version of his title and name. The earliest biographical data about the Swami is given in the introduction to Swami Shiv Dayal's poetry, published under his honorific name, Param Purush Puran Dhani Soamiji Maharaj, as *Sar Bachan Radhasoami: Poetry* (2 vols.), edited by Rai Sali-

mercantile Khatri subcaste.[4] The family originally emigrated from the Punjab, where Shiv Dayal's grandfather, Seth Malik Chand, was an official in the court of a princely state.[5] His father, Seth Dilwali, settled in Agra and became a moneylender, a common occupation for a member of his caste. The family had been followers of Guru Nanak; this might suggest that they were Sikhs or Nanakpanthis, a term that refers to people who venerate the first Sikh master, Guru Nanak, to the exclusion of the

---

gram (Huzur Maharaj), originally published in Hindi (Allahabad: Rayag Press Company, 1884), and translated into English by S. D. Maheshwari (Agra: Radhasoami Satsang, Soamibagh, 1970). The introduction was written by Rai Saligram in 1884. The first reference to Swami Shiv Dayal in writings other than those from within the movement itself is a brief comment in an article in a Vedantic journal, *Prabuddha Bharata*, in May 1898, to which Max Müller refers in *Ramakrishna—His Life and Sayings* (New York: Charles Scribner's Sons, 1899). Other early reports, these by missionary scholars, are found in H. D. Griswold, *Radha Swami Sect* (Cawnpore: Cawnpore Mission Press, 1907) and J. N. Farquhar, *Modern Religious Movements in India* (Delhi: Munshiram Manoharlal, 1977; orig. pub. 1914). Both of these report the basic outlines of Swami Shiv Dayal's life as I have given it. Farquhar, however, gives a Vaisnava cast to the Swami's teachings, and Griswold says that according to one former member of the movement, he was also known as Tulsi Ram (Hervey DeWitt Griswold, *Insights into Modern Hinduism* [New York: Henry Holt and Co., 1934], p. 131). I find both of these suggestions unlikely and have found no corroborative evidence for either of them.

[4] There are minor variations in some of the published accounts of the Swami's life. For instance, most accounts give the time of his birth as 12:30 A.M. on the morning of August 25, but the anonymous introduction to the Beas translation of *Sar Bachan-Prose* gives the time as 4 A.M. The author of *Sar Bachan-Prose* is listed under Shiv Dayal Singh's honorific name, Purush Puran Dhani Huzur Soamiji Maharaj; it was originally published in Hindi (Allahabad: Rayag Press Company, 1884) with subsequent English translations by S. D. Maheshwari (Agra: Radhasoami Satsang, Soamibagh, 1958); Sewa Singh (Beas: Radhasoami Satsang, Beas, 1934; rev. 1955, 1978); and by an anonymous translator (Agra: Radhasoami Satsang Sabha, Dayalbagh, 1959). The name of Swami Shiv Dayal's mother is not mentioned in Pratap Singh Seth's *Biography of Soamiji Maharaj* (Agra: Radhasoami Satsang, Soamibagh, 1978; orig. pub. in Hindi, 1902) or any of the Agra accounts of the Swami's life; it is given as "Mahamaya," however, in several of the Beas versions, including the introduction to the Beas translation of the *Sar Bachan: Prose* (1964 ed.), p. 1; and in Janak Raj Puri, *Tulsi Sahib: Saint of Hathras* (Beas: Radhasoami Satsang, Beas, 1978), p. 6. Sawan Singh, in his introduction to Jaimal Singh, *Spiritual Letters* (Beas: Radhasoami Satsang, 1967), describes Swami Shiv Dayal's family not as Khatri but as "a well-known family of Baikal Seth Kshatriyas" (pp. 3–4). It should be noted that the term Khatri is derived from Kshatriya, and many members of the Khatri community insist that they should be designated in the higher-ranking Kshatriya (warrior-caste) stratum of the Hindu caste system, rather than in the somewhat lower Vaisha (merchant-caste) stratum where most scholars, following conventional attitudes in India, place them. In this book I adopt the conventional view, and in doing so mean no disrespect to members of the Khatri community.

[5] A reference to the Swami's grandfather as a diwan (prime minister) of the state of Dholpur is found in the Beas accounts, but not in the *Biography* or the Agra accounts. According to Sawan Singh, Shiv Dayal Singh's family "had migrated from Lahore to Delhi about two hundred years previously, and then had moved from Delhi to Agra" (Introduction to Jaimal Singh, *Spiritual Letters*, p. 3). See also the reference to Dholpur in Kirpal Singh, *A Great Saint, Baba Jaimal Singh: His Life and Teachings* (Delhi: Ruhani Satsang, 1973), p. 12.

other nine.[6] Whatever was the case, the family turned in a different direction during Swami Shiv Dayal's childhood—towards the spiritual tutelage of a local holy man named Tulsi Sahib.

The Swami was married at an early age to Naraini Devi, a woman of his caste whose family had settled in the new industrial city of Faridabad, located between Agra and Delhi.[7] Her nephew was a lawyer in the princely state of Jodhpur who had become a disciple of Swami Shiv Dayal. After marriage, Naraini Devi—who became known as Radhaji—learned to read, studied sacred writings, and was eventually regarded as a knowledgeable spiritual leader in her own right.

Whether or not Shiv Dayal ever pursued much of a secular career is unclear. Members of his own and his wife's family persisted in trying to secure employment for him. For a time he agreed to accept part-time work as a teacher of Persian, first in the employ of the government and later as a tutor for the Raja of Ballabhgarh, and after his father died he joined the family moneylending business. But when his brother Rai Bindraban secured a position in the government postal services, this alternative source of income for the family allowed Swami Shiv Dayal to abandon all forms of gainful occupation. From then on he meditated and gave spiritual discourses, drawing on the Sikh scriptures and the writings of Tulsi Sahib and his medieval predecessors. He gradually developed a personal following, initiating his devotees into a yogic practice that did not require strict asceticism. The Swami lived his entire life in Agra; he taught and meditated there, and died there in 1878.

So much is more or less public knowledge, but a great deal more is remembered about Swami Shiv Dayal inside the community of faith. An early account is given by his main disciple, Rai Saligram, and another is given by a master at Beas, Sawan Singh.[8] By far the largest collection of

[6] One of the reasons why it is difficult to determine whether or not Swami Shiv Dayal Singh's family were Sikhs is that the defining boundaries of Sikhism as a religion were imprecise before the end of the nineteenth century, when a reform movement, the Singh Sabha, began to legislate on matters of faith and identity. Kirpal Singh (*A Great Saint*, pp. 12–14) marshals several pieces of evidence to indicate that Shiv Dayal Singh's family were at least devotees of Nanak, if not Sikhs in the Singh Sabha definition of the term: Swami Shiv Dayal's father was devoted to the Sikh scriptures, a copy of which was transcribed by his grandfather and is located in the archives of the Soamibagh branch; the Swami is reported to have recited *gurbani* (Sikh worship) at the time of his father's death; he gave discourses on Guru Nanak's morning prayer, *Japji*, one of which is published as *Elucidation of Japji* (Agra: Radhasoami Satsang, Soamibagh, 1975; orig. pub. in Hindi, 1960, from notes said to have been dictated in 1877); and he is said to have been a frequent speaker at the Sikh shrine of Mai Than in Agra.

[7] Radhaji's name is variously recorded in Radhasoami's English-language publications as Naraini Devi, Narain Devi, or Narayan Dei. I have chosen to use the first and most familiar of these variants.

[8] Rai Saligram, Preface to Shiv Dayal Singh, *Sar Bachan: Poetry*, trans. S. D. Maheshwari, pp. 17–22; Sawan Singh, Introduction to Jaimal Singh, *Spiritual Letters*, pp. ix–xv.

1. Swami Shiv Dayal.

stories is contained in what is regarded as his official biography, a book written by his youngest brother in 1902.[9] This account is so crowded with miracles and reports of remarkable piety that one is tempted to pass it off as mere hagiography, and from the historian's view it may be just that; but if one wants to understand the Radhasoami tradition—and the process of collective recall that is present in all religious traditions—one should be cautious about dismissing these stories quite so easily.

The Remembered Life

The stories may be clustered under four main headings: Swami Shiv Dayal's remarkable childhood, his single-minded adherence to religious practices, the generosity and kindness of his character, and the enthusi-

[9] Pratap Singh Seth, *Biography of Soamiji Maharaj.*

asm with which his greatly varied clientele received his pronouncements. It is remembered that from early childhood he undertook in an interior room of his house, "the practice of merging the soul in the Divine Current of the Supreme Being's Melody and Power," [10] and that his own mother recognized him less as a son than as a miniature holy man. It had been prophesied to her that she would give birth to a remarkable spiritual being.[11] In school it is said that he read the books as if he already knew their contents.[12] In his adult life he would spend days without food or sleep—he would not even feel the "call of nature"[13]—so immersed was he in meditation. He would go off to the fields outside Agra, where he could escape notice and remain in solitude.

Despite his introspective nature he is remembered as being almost omnisciently sensitive to others' needs and thoughts. When a young boy in his wife's family was grievously ill, the Swami knew that the lad would die and that he had the power to save him, but he hesitated to tamper with the economy of nature. He offered his wife a compromise: he would arrange for two days to be added to the boy's life, but only if two days would be taken from his own. His wife, perhaps selfishly, refused.[14] Other stories recall that he could make trees wither and elephants appear.[15] So astonishing were his acts and teachings that people from all stations of life fell under his influence: the very rich and powerful; the poor and feeble; merchants, Brahmans, and laborers; Hindus, Muslims, Christians, and Jains.[16]

All these stories coalesce into a picture of someone who possesses the senses of any other mortal being but is also infused with a divine power. This is no anomaly in the Radhasoami view of history, for in the Radhasoami understanding the physical and metaphysical realms are in some ineffable way interrelated. Swami Shiv Dayal manifests the divine, but he also exhibits worldly traits in their most perfect forms. In doing so he possesses attributes that devotees would like to possess, even though at times these ideals seem to contradict one another. For instance, he is said to have been single-minded about his spiritual practices yet generous and sensitive to other persons, powerful in his appropriation of spiritual energy yet unwilling to use that power for anything but benign purposes, and spiritually accomplished without being socially condescending.

It is this luminous image of Swami Shiv Dayal as much as the central teachings of Radhasoami that unites all adherents of the faith. All agree

[10] Lekh Raj Puri, *Radha Swami Teachings* (Beas: Radhasoami Satsang, Beas, 1965), p. 5.

[11] J. R. Puri, *Tulsi Sahib*, p. 6.

[12] Pratap Singh Seth, *Biography of Soamiji Maharaj*, p. 4.

[13] Rai Saligram, Preface to Shiv Dayal Singh, *Sar Bachan*: *Poetry*, p. 18.

[14] Pratap Singh Seth, *Biography of Soamiji Maharaj*, pp. 43–44.

[15] Ibid., pp. 91–92.

[16] L. R. Puri, *Radha Swami Teachings*, p. 8.

that he was remarkable both as a person and as a point in history: he was the instrument through which the internal history of the tradition links up with the metahistory of cosmic time. Beyond this area of agreement, however, disagreements almost immediately arise. Central to them is the matter of how one should conceive the connection between Swami Shiv Dayal and cosmic history. According to one side of Radhasoami's family tree—the branches located in Agra—Swami Shiv Dayal is to be regarded as a *parmatma satguru*, a term that unites the ideas of "the highest soul," and a "true master." This phrase expresses the conviction that Swami Shiv Dayal was a singular event in human history. According to the Agra branches, "the incarnation of the most exalted, most gracious, most merciful, most munificient and most forgiving Radhasoami Dayal is a memorable event for the entire creation."[17]

One forceful expression of this conviction is taking shape today in the field outside Agra where Swami Shiv Dayal meditated. There, an immense marble and granite building is being constructed as both a place of worship and a tomb. The half-finished edifice is something of an architectural oddity: to the Western eye it looks like a cathedral with minarets encircling a giant turnip-shaped dome. Its builders hope that when finished it will rival the Taj Mahal. Whatever one feels about the aesthetics of its design, it is a dramatic visual demonstration of the centrality of the Swami in the perception of many Agra members of the Radhasoami faith.

Those on the other side of Radhasoami's family tree—the groups in Delhi and the Punjab—are somewhat embarrassed by the construction of this colossal marble tomb, for their view of the Swami is more humble. They too remember Swami Shiv Dayal as a remarkable person—a *satguru*, in fact, a perfect realization of spiritual achievement—but they stop short of declaring him absolutely unique. They believe that although satgurus are rare, there have been a number of them in human history, and none exceeds the others in greatness. According to the late master at Beas, Charan Singh, "The teachings of all of the saints are the same . . . and by saints is not meant a particular saint but all saints of the world."[18] In Charan Singh's view, Swami Shiv Dayal is one link in a sacred chain that includes not only the medieval sants, but their ancient predecessors, figures such as Jesus and the Buddha.[19]

[17] S. D. Maheshwari, *Radhasoami Faith: History and Tenets* (Agra: Soamibagh, 1954), p. 12; see also S. D. Maheshwari, *Truth Unvarnished* (Agra: Radhasoami Satsang, Soamibagh, 1970), vol. 1, p. 114. The leaders of the Peepalmandi branch in Agra tell me that they amend this notion to include the second master, Rai Saligram, as equal to Swami Shiv Dayal in his special importance; together they share the unique role in history that other Agra branches limit to Swami Shiv Dayal (Interview with A. P. Mathur, Peepalmandi, Agra, August 12, 1985).

[18] Charan Singh, *The Master Answers to Audiences in America*, p. 17.

[19] Charan Singh, *Light on St.Matthew* (Beàs: Radhasoami Satsang, Beas, 1978), pp. 3–4. Yet Charan Singh never equates Christ with the highest of the saints, such as Kabir, and

2. The tomb of Swami Shiv Dayal at Soamibagh, under construction.

Many members of the Agra branches find this position offensive; to them it is vital that Swami Shiv Dayal be seen as a phenomenon sui generis, a man without an immediate predecessor, an abrupt intervention of the Divine in history.[20] But both the Agra and Beas branches agree that Swami Shiv Dayal was preceded by some significant religious figures: the medieval sants of India, especially Kabir.[21] In fact, an alternate term for

---

some Radhasoami writers belittle the spiritual accomplishments of Jesus compared with those of Radhasoami masters. See Julian Johnson, *Path of the Masters* (Beas: Radhasoami Satsang, Beas, 1939), pp. 104–7.

[20] See, for instance, the lengthy diatribe and rebuttal to the Beas position in Maheshwari, *Truth Unvarnished*, part 2, pp. 120–83. Maheshwari's argument for the uniqueness of Swami Shiv Dayal is put in a more positive frame in *Truth Unvarnished*, part 1, p. 114.

[21] Swami Shiv Dayal lists his predecessors as "Kabir Sahab, Tulsi Sahab, Jagjiwan Sahab, Garib Das ji, Paltu Sahab, Guru Nanak, Daduji, Tulsi Das ji, Nabha ji, Swami Hari Das ji, Sur Das ji, and Raidas ji; and among Mohammedans, Shams-i-Tabrez, Maulana Rumi, Hafiz, Sarmad and Mujaddid Alifsani" (*Sar Bachan: Prose* [Dayalbagh version], verse 39, pp. 29–30). According to Brahm Sankar Misra, Kabir was the first of the saints and was a manifestation of the highest regions of Radhasoami Dham; others after him were "Guru Nanak, Jagjivan Sahab, Paltu Das, Tulsi Das of Hathras," and of course, Swami Shiv Dayal. Misra places on a somewhat lower level other spiritual adepts, including "Garib Das, Dalam Das, Charan Das, Nabhaji, Darya Saheb, Raidas, Surdas, Shums Tabrez, Mansur, Sarmad, Moinuddin Chisti" (Misra, *Discourses*, [Soamibagh version], p. 92; the spelling of the names are those given in the English translation). The present master at Peepalmandi, A. P.

the Radhasoami tradition that is sometimes used by those within it is *sant mat*—the sant point of view.[22]

The Link with the Sant Tradition

In order to understand why these sants are so important to Radhasoami's conception of its history, one has to have a sense of the role they played in India's religious history.[23] The term *sant* is so close in meaning to the English *saint* that it is frequently assumed that there must be some etymological connection. Actually there is none, for *saint* comes from the Latin *sanctus* (holy), and *sant* is a variant on the Sanskrit *sat*, a term that means both truth and reality, and indicates that the two ultimately converge. A sant is a person who apprehends that convergence and has thereby realized ultimate truth.

The best known of the medieval sants are Kabir and Nanak.[24] The former, said to have been born a Hindu but raised a Muslim in the fifteenth century, composed in a terse, vigorous style that even in English translation has a fresh, modern appeal.[25] Through abrupt, mind-churning con-

---

Mathur, told me in an interview (December 6, 1980) that the sants emanating from Radhasoami Dham prior to Swami Shiv Dayal included the following: first, Kabir; then Nanak, Dadu, and Jagjivan.

[22] The phrase *Sant Mat* is occasionally used in the *Sar Bachan: Poetry* (e.g., p. 184, Soamibagh translation) in a general way to refer to the teachings of saints, and used by Rai Saligram in his preface to specify Radhasoami teachings in particular (p. 18). Janak Raj Puri has suggested that the phrase was an invention of Tulsi Sahib (*Tulsi Sahib*, p. 17). It is to be found, however, in the poetry of Kabir, where it refers to the path of truth, or true teachings.

[23] For a general introduction to the sant literature see Karine Schomer and W. H. McLeod, eds., *The Sants: Studies in a Devotional Tradition of India* (Berkeley: Berkeley Religious Studies Series; Delhi: Motilal Banarsidass, 1986). J. S. Hawley and I have cotranslated selections from the poetry of six of India's medieval saints, and in the introductions to these selections Hawley provides a discussion of the sant tradition in general; the book is entitled *Songs of the Saints of India* (New York: Oxford University Press, 1988). Selections from our translations also appear in the section on *bhakti* literature in Ainslie Embree, ed., *Sources in Indian Tradition*, rev. ed. (New York: Columbia University Press, 1988), vol. 1.

[24] Others from the medieval period who are commonly regarded throughout India as sants are Ravi Das, Nam Dev, and Dadu. Other *bhakti* poets who are often linked with these figures are Mira Bai, Sur Das, and Tulsi Das; their poetry is usually addressed to particular forms of the gods rather than to a formless divinity, which is the usual criterion for demarcating those poets known as sants from writers of sacred devotional poetry in general.

[25] Some excellent translations of Kabir have recently become available to the English-speaking world. See Charlotte Vaudeville, *Kabir* (Oxford: Clarendon Press, 1974); Linda Hess and Sukhdev Singh, *The Bijak of Kabir* (Berkeley: North Point Press, 1983); and V. K. Sethi, *Kabir: The Weaver of God's Name* (Beas: Radhasoami Satsang, Beas, 1984). The translations by Rabindranath Tagore (*Songs of Kabir* [New York: Macmillan Publishing

junctions of images, Kabir would jolt his listeners out of their complacent satisfaction with the exterior realities of life and introduce them to a sharply different, almost indescribable realm within. Nanak was less innovative as a stylist and is remembered more for his concepts, especially his attention to the unknown name of the Lord as the access to spiritual union.[26] Nanak is also remembered by the Sikhs as the first in a lineage of ten masters that extended from the sixteenth to the eighteenth centuries; these ten are collectively esteemed as the founders of the Sikh community.

The sants are regarded by all Hindus as innovators, religious radicals, rebels against prevailing orthodoxies of belief and the social institutions that are related to them.[27] Although it is difficult to identify a definite core of motifs that can be found in the writings of all the sants, the following themes are widely shared:[28] the concept of the absolute as beyond human attributes (*nirguna*, without qualities), and by implication the judgment that the entire Hindu pantheon is insufficient if taken in its own terms; the persuasion that all forms of religious leadership and accomplishment—those claimed by Brahmans, yogis, and the like—are ultimately invalid, save one, that of the devoted follower of the Lord, whose own achievements in spiritual matters enable him or her to serve as a model for others; the conviction that such spirituality is essentially interior rather than bound up with external forms of piety and religiosity; the belief that this interior experience can be invoked through a sacred word or name; and the expectation that those who follow the path of spiritual growth will enjoy a spiritual fellowship (*satsang*) with one another.

Co.], 1915) have been interestingly paraphrased by the American poet Robert Bly in *The Kabir Book* (Boston: Beacon Press, 1971).

[26] Translations of Guru Nanak may be found in Trilochan Singh et al., *Selections from the Sacred Writings of the Sikhs* (London: George Allen and Unwin, 1973); Khushwant Singh, *Hymns of Guru Nanak* (New Delhi: Orient Longman, 1978); J. R. Puri, *Guru Nanak: His Mystic Teachings* (Beas: Radhasoami Satsang, Beas, 1982); Hawley and Juergensmeyer, *Songs of the Saints of India*, pp. 78–88; and W. H. McLeod, *Guru Nanak and the Sikh Religion* (Oxford: Clarendon Press, 1976) and *Textual Sources for the Study of Sikhism* (Manchester: Manchester University Press, 1984). The historical role of Guru Nanak is discussed in McLeod, *Guru Nanak and the Sikh Religion*; J. S. Grewal, *Guru Nanak in History* (Chandigarh: Punjab University, 1969); and Grewal's article, "A Perspective on Early Sikh History," in Mark Juergensmeyer and N. Gerald Barrier, eds., *Sikh Studies: Comparative Perspectives on a Changing Tradition* (Berkeley: Berkeley Religious Studies Series, 1979).

[27] The social role of the sants is praised in V. Raghavan, *The Great Integrators: The Saint-Singers of India*, Patel Memorial Lectures (New Delhi: Government of India, Publications Division, Ministry of Information and Broadcasting, 1966).

[28] I have based this summary of sant teachings on Pitambar Datta Barthwal, *The Nirguna School of Hindi Poetry: An Exposition of Medieval Indian Santa Mysticism* (Benares: Indian Book Shop, 1936), pp. 32–56.

The Radhasoami tradition displays an allegiance to each of these tenets, but each is refracted through a lens peculiar to Radhasoami.[29] The nameless God beyond the gods is given a name: it is *Radhasoami*, according to those who follow the Agra branches of the movement.[30] Repetition of the name (or names) enables the seeker to gain access to their energy and lift his or her own internal energy currents to the higher levels of God-consciousness, the realms of ethereal light and sound. The Radhasoami conception of the interior realm alluded to by the sants is articulated in considerably greater detail than it was by the sants themselves: it has multiple tiers, the discovery of which involves a journey through increasingly rarefied strata of consciousness. To Radhasoami eyes, the most devoted followers of the Lord—especially the Radhasoami masters, who are regarded as the most recent links in the chain of sants—are incarnate forms of the absolute. And the "fellowship of the sants" (satsang), originally an idea that had nothing directly to do with formal initiation, is conceived by the Radhasoami tradition as the gathering of those who have been properly selected by a Radhasoami guru. The *satsang* into which a new member of Radhasoami is ushered is a highly structured and well-organized association.

Although not considered normative sant teachings by those outside Radhasoami, the Radhasoami complex of sant-related concepts bears a coherent and distinctive stamp. Those within the Radhasoami community have not given it a specific name, but it might be called "esoteric santism." It is santism because the concepts are roughly comparable to those taught by the medieval sants, yet it is esoteric, since it makes each of the sant concepts part of a special system of interior spirituality. When and where did this esoteric santism arise?

The Origins of Esoteric Santism

The first clues to answering this question are provided by the writings of Swami Shiv Dayal himself, many of which, fortunately, have survived. The most important are collected in a two volume work, *Sar Bachan* (Essential Teachings). One volume is a collection of utterances in versified Hindi and the other consists of transcriptions of his sermons.[31] Both were

[29] I develop this point further in "The Radhasoami Revival of the Sant Tradition," in Schomer and McLeod, *The Sants*, pp. 329–55.

[30] See, for instance, Sant Das Maheshwari, *Teachings of Radhasoami Faith Based on Babuji Maharaj's Discourses* (Agra: Radhasoami Satsang, Soamibagh), pp. 332–35.

[31] English translations of the *Sar Bachan* volumes have been published by each of the major branches of the tradition. The Soamibagh translation is by S. D. Maheshwari, published in 1958 (prose) and 1970 (poetry). Dayalbagh has published both poetry and prose

compiled and edited posthumously by a chief disciple and successor, Rai Saligram, who appears to have inserted amendments of his own, especially in the poetry volume.[32] The prose volume is regarded as authoritative in all branches of the tradition, and it is therefore the first place to turn in assessing Radhasoami's relation to its sant roots. A close reading reveals two matters of interest. First is the Swami's ambiguity about his own status as a sant or living master. It is certainly possible that others may have regarded him as such, but his own writings are more modestly framed, and only those inside the Radhasoami communities will assume that when he speaks about the powers of the satguru he is speaking about himself. The other matter of interest is that he refers to the whole of the earlier sant tradition as his antecedent,[33] including not just the well-known medieval sants but many who were closer to his own era, in particular the sant named Tulsi Sahib, who lived during his own time in the nearby town of Hathras. The Swami is said to have had with him an association "of great love."[34] According to some, the followers of Tulsi Sahib shifted to Swami Shiv Dayal after the death of their master, which would imply a guru-to-guru succession.[35] There is no record, however, of Tulsi Sahib actually having initiated Swami Shiv Dayal, and other early accounts report someone else as the successor to Tulsi Sahib: one Gir-

---

volumes in Hindi, but has translated only the prose volume into English; that translation, unattributed, was published in 1959. Beas has published only the prose volume; the English translation, by Sewa Singh, was published in 1934, and has been reissued several times since.

[32] A disciple of Sawan Singh, Radha Krishna Khanna, is particularly insistent on claiming that Rai Saligram authored sections of both volumes of the *Sar Bachan* (see his *Truth Eternal: The True Nature of Soamiji's Teachings on Sant Mat, The 'Radhasoami Faith'* (New Delhi: privately published, 1961).

[33] See the list in footnote 21 above.

[34] L. R. Puri, *Radha Swami Teachings*, p. 6. The common account of Tulsi Sahib's life is that he was born into a family of Maharashtrian royalty and renounced his status to wander in search of truth. He found it, apparently, in the town of Hathras, for he established an ashram there that continues to revere his name. His dates are given as 1763–1843 (J. R. Puri, Introduction to *Tulsi Sahib: Saint of Hathras*, pp. 2–3). See also S. D. Maheshwari, *Param Sant Tulsi Saheb* (Agra: Radhasoami Satsang, Soamibagh, 1979). A conversation with a present-day sadhu in the lineage established by Tulsi Sahib is described in Daniel Gold, *The Lord as Guru: Hindi Sants in North Indian Tradition* (New York: Oxford University Press, 1987), pp. 132–34. Gold also reports that a collection of poetry in the Tulsi Sahib tradition, *Bichar Sagar*, written by Gajadhar Das, has been published by Sant Prakash Das at Hathras (p. 132).

[35] Kirpal Singh reports that in the Hindi version of S. D. Maheshwari's *Biography of Babuji Maharaj* (which I have not been able to locate), vol. 3, p. 29, he states that Garib Das, one of Tulsi Sahib's disciples, came to Swami Shiv Dayal after Tulsi Sahib's death, claiming that the mantle of Tulsi Sahib's succession had been passed to Swami Shiv Dayal (Kirpal Singh, *A Great Saint*, p. 11).

dhari Das, whom it is said Swami Shiv Dayal also revered.[36] Other Radhasoami writers turn the matter upside down by making Tulsi Sahib forecast the coming of Swami Shiv Dayal, as John the Baptist preceded Jesus.[37]

The similarities between the teachings of Tulsi Sahib and Swami Shiv Dayal do show some sort of relationship, whatever its nature. Like Swami Shiv Dayal, Tulsi Sahib depicted life as a series of struggles against *kal*—mortality, the negative power—a concept that is personified as a demonic force. He held that the major means of avoiding the ravages of Kal's power was to adhere to an even greater positive force, the words of the satguru, which are hidden within each person as a remarkable interior sound. The seeker is admonished to find that sound, fix on it, and follow its path as it makes its transit through the third, interior eye and through level after level of increasingly higher realms of sound and light. The ultimate moment is described as follows: "The soul hears a wave of sound and rhythm . . . and opens the door—unspeakable, indescribable. Going beyond rhythm and sight, one enters the gate of the tower of emptiness. . . . Then one sees the sound-current issuing forth hundreds of thousands of universes, and sound penetrates to the middle of them all, their crown-jewel, which is tiny as an insect."[38]

This esoteric teaching of Tulsi Sahib had its antecedents. His best known work, *Ghat Ramayana* (which purports to be the essence, or *ghat*, of the great Hindu epic, the *Ramayana*), is a dialogue between Tulsi Sahib and Phul Das, a follower of Dharam Das, who was in turn one of the best known disciples of Kabir. In it references are made to an even earlier dialogue, one between Kabir and Dharam Das.[39] This dialogue is contained

[36] Girdhari Das is described as being the "chief disciple" of Tulsi Sahib, a term that would usually imply he was understood as his designated successor (Pratap Singh Seth, *Biography of Soamiji Maharaj*, p. 108). After Tulsi Sahib's death, Swami Shiv Dayal brought Girdhari Das into his house, "treated him with love, and accorded him respect due a pious Mahatma" (Pratap Singh Seth, *Biography of Soamiji Maharaj*, Soamibagh version, p. 37). Girdhari Das's home was apparently in Lucknow, to which he returned; Swami Shiv Dayal is reported as having made some of his infrequent journeys out of Agra to visit him there (*Souvenir of the Centenary of the Radhasoami Satsang* [Agra: Radhasoami Satsang Sabha, Dayalbagh, 1962], p. 25). It should also be noted that Swami Shiv Dayal probably did not begin giving public *satsang* until after Girdhari Das's death (although his death date is uncertain). But the present Mahant at Tulsi Sahib's tomb in Hathras told me that in his reckoning neither Girdhari Das nor Swami Shiv Dayal was the true successor of Tulsi Sahib. He claims that it was one Sur Swami, and following him, Darshan Das, Mathura Das, and, at present, himself, Sant Prakash Das (Interview with Sant Prakash Das, Hathras, August 9, 1978).

[37] J. R. Puri, *Tulsi Sahib*, p. 6; and Maheshwari, *Param Sant Tulsi Saheb*, p. 3.

[38] Tulsi Sahib, *Ghat Ramayana* (Allahabad: Belvedere Press, 1911). The title could be translated as "The Interior Ramayana" or "The Ramayana within the Bodily Vessel."

[39] Maheshwari, *Param Sant Tulsi Saheb*, p. 96.

in a document entitled *Anurag Sagar* (The Sea of Love), which the *Ghat Ramayana* resembles in style and content and which may be regarded as its precursor. Several Radhasoami masters have acknowledged its relevance for their teachings and have urged their followers to read it.[40]

The main ideas of the *Anurag Sagar* are those we have described as esoteric santism, but particular attention is paid to the remarkable power of a salvific sound that can be transmitted only to appropriate persons, and only through initiation. Behind the *Anurag Sagar* lies an elaborate mythology about a cosmic conflict between the forces of darkness and the forces of good. As in Tulsi Sahib's writing, the former is Kal, and Kabir himself embodies the latter. A particularly dramatic scene has Kabir meeting Kal in combat at the top of the causal plane. According to the *Anurag Sagar*, the public, historical Kabir was only a momentary revelation, a brief glimpse of a much more important reality: a cosmic Kabir-force that originated before creation, entered into human history briefly as Kabir, and is still accessible in the form of a pure sound that resonates through the cosmos and provides liberation from the evil grip of time and mortality.

Although few of these mythological details survive as such within Radhasoami teachings, the grand role that Kabir plays within Radhasoami thought and its view of history is indisputable; one of the Radhasoami masters, for instance, claimed to have recognized Benares on seeing it for the first time because he had been there as Kabir in a previous birth.[41] The general framework of the myth is to be found in Radhasoami notions of the evilness of time (Kal), the creation of religion by Kal as part of a sinister plot, and the saving power of a cosmic guru—incarnate in a living spiritual master—that penetrates Kal's kingdom by a force of light and sound, rescues souls, and guides them toward ascending vistas of reality.[42]

[40] Sawan Singh, for instance, refers to the *Anurag Sagar* in *Philosophy of the Masters* (Beas: Radhasoami Satsang, Beas, 1977), vol. 4, p. 67; and one of Sawan Singh's disciples says that the master advocated that the book be studied diligently (Rai Saheb Munshi Ram, *With the Three Masters* [Beas: Radhasoami Satsang, Beas, 1967], vol. 2, p. 187).

[41] The master was Anand Swarup, founder of Dayalbagh (*Souvenir*, p. 170). Maheshwari calls Kabir "the first harbinger of the message of Dayal Desh" (Shiv Dayal Singh et al., *Holy Epistles*, vol 1, p. 389); A. P. Mathur, leader of the Peepalmandi branch, calls him "a great force" (Interview with Mathur, August 13, 1985); B. L. Gupta, leader of one of the branches at Gwalior, calls Kabir "the first true sant" (Interview with Gupta, Gwalior, August 21, 1985); and followers of Kirpal Singh have called him "the founder of the tradition of Sant Mat" (Russell Perkins, Introduction to *The Ocean of Love: The Anurag Sagar of Kabir*, trans. Raj Kumar Bagga, ed. Russell Perkins [Sanbornton, N. H.: Sant Bani Ashram, 1982], p. xx).

[42] For echoes of the *Anurag Sagar* account see Shiv Dayal Singh, *Sar Bachan: Prose*, Soamibagh version, p. 31.

The *Anurag Sagar* would seem to point to Kabir as the source of esoteric santism. The problem with this conclusion, however, is that although the *Anurag Sagar* is said to have been written by Kabir, its style and content suggest an authorship sometime in the eighteenth or even nineteenth century—several centuries after Kabir's death.[43] Moreover, the ideas of esoteric santism contained in the *Anurag Sagar* are rejected by many of the people who today consider themselves the direct followers of Kabir, the Kabirpanthis.

There is one present-day branch of Kabirpanthis, however, for which these ideas are not at all extreme: the Dharamdasis. The *Anurag Sagar* is indeed one of their principal texts. Their main tenet is that Kabir did not disappear after his earthly death but reappeared in a cosmic form and continues to manifest himself in a lineage of spiritual masters. But for the focus on Kabir, this is an idea quite congenial to Radhasoami itself. Not surprisingly, then, the Dharamdasi community, headquartered in Raipur in the southeastern part of the central Indian state of Madhya Pradesh, shows several points of similarity to the Radhasoami communities.[44] Although there are far more unmarried ascetics (*sadhus*) in the Dharamdasi order than in Radhasoami, the overwhelming majority of members, including the current master, Grindhmuni Nam, are married. Most of its members are from merchant castes. Dharamdasi teachings about the cosmic realms are quite similar to Radhasoami's; like the Beas branch it gives the *panch nam* (five names) as one of its mantras at the time of initiation; Dharmdasi practitioners listen for the sacred sound from the right-hand side, as Radhasoami devotees do; and the Dharamdasi master, like his Radhasoami counterparts, is worshiped as a temple god might be.[45]

[43] It is impossible to date the *Anurag Sagar* precisely, but since it makes reference to disputes over the lines of succession within the Dharamdasi branch of the Kabir panth, it is unlikely that it was written before that branch was firmly established in the eighteenth century. J. S. Hawley tells me that the literary style of the piece also would locate it most probably in that century. Charlotte Vaudeville makes no attempt to date it but simply lists it among "apocryphal works attributed to Kabir" (*Kabir*, p. 338). When I first encountered the *Anurag Sagar* it was available only in Hindi (ed. Swami Sri Nanhelal Murlidhar [Narsinghpur: Sarasvati Vilas Press, n.d.]), but it has since been translated into English, accompanied by color plates of illustrations, and published in paperback in the United States by followers of one of the successors of Kirpal Singh under the title *The Ocean of Love: The Anurag Sagar of Kabir*. In his introduction to the English translation, Russell Perkins vehemently denies Vaudeville's characterization of the work as "apocryphal" and argues for its authenticity "on linguistic and doctrinal grounds" (p. xxxi).

[44] The Dharamdasi ashram is located at village Damkhera near Raipur, where the spiritual master, Grindhmuni Nam, has his residence. I am grateful to Grindhmuni Nam for helping to arrange my visit to his ashram on August 23–24, 1985, and to Jack Hawley for his assistance in translating the conversations. The Dharamdasis are briefly described in Kshitimohan Sen, *Medieval Mysticism of India*, trans. Manmohan Ghosh (New Delhi: Oriental Books Reprint Corp., 1974), pp. 92–93, 106–7.

[45] G. H. Wescott, *Kabir and the Kabir Panth* (Cawnpore: Christ Church Mission Press,

This connection between Dharamdasis and Radhasoamis, to which the *Anurag Sagar* has led us, is confirmed by another set of writings venerated by Radhasoami leaders but little known outside of Radhasoami and Dharamdasi circles: the poetry of Dariya Sahib. Dariya Sahib was an eighteenth-century poet who lived in a Dharamdasi region of Bihar and referred to both Kabir and Dharam Das as his predecessors.[46] Like the author of the *Anurag Sagar*, he viewed Kabir as a divine and mystical force and enumerated aspects of the ascending realms of consciousness in a manner remarkably similar to what one sees in Swami Shiv Dayal's *Sar Bachan*.[47] Dariya Sahib is listed by Brahm Sankar Misra as one of India's great saints, and the Beas branch of Radhasoami has recently published both Hindi and English versions of his poetry.[48]

Dariya Sahib adds another link to the chain that connects the Radhasoami and Dharamdasi traditions, but important differences between the two remain. Dharamdasi teachings are less specific about the higher levels of consciousness than Radhasoami teachings. Furthermore, they require a different kind of initiation and emphasize a spiritual practice that focuses on breathing exercises, at least at the initial stages, rather than listening for an interior sound.[49] Radhasoami spiritual masters consistently and vehemently denounce breathing exercises, distancing their own form of yoga, *surat shabd yoga*, from *hatha yoga*, which emphasizes the control of one's breath and one's internal winds.[50] Hatha yoga is practiced

1907), p. 123. Regarding worship of the Dharamdasi guru: Grindmuni Nam has in his possession a videotape of a festival occasion vividly portraying the reverence of his devotees toward him; and the high point of the evening prayers at the Damkhera ashram is the blowing of a conch shell and the lifting of lighted candles at the tombs of previously departed masters.

[46] K. N. Upadhyaya, *Dariya Sahib: Saint of Bihar* (Beas: Radhasoami Satsang, Beas, 1987), p. 4.

[47] See, for instance, the reference to "the tenth door," and "the whirling cave" in Upadhyaya, *Dariya Sahib*, p. 179.

[48] Misra, *Discourses*, Soamibagh version, p. 92. I am grateful to the translator of the Beas book, K. N. Upadhyaya, a professor of philosophy at the University of Hawaii, for bringing the Dariya connection to my attention.

[49] The Dharamdasis do have a notion of higher regions into which one gradually ascends through meditation practices, but they are not sharply defined, as they are in Radhasoami. In the initiation (*diksha*), the new member receives a necklace of wooden beads and a mantra to chant during meditation, but the mantra has none of the force of the name (or names) given by Radhasoami at the time of initiation. The meditation practice does involve listening to an interior sound (the Vedic term *sohang*) at the advanced stages, but at the initial stages it involves forms of breath control and the repetition of the mantra 108 times each morning and night (Interview with Grindhmuni Nam, Raipur, August 23, 1985).

[50] For the Radhasoami disdain of hatha yoga and its breathing exercises, see Rai Saligram, *Jugat Prakash Radhasoami* (Agra: Radhasoami Satsang, Soamibagh, 1964); Rai Saligram, *Prem Patra Radhasoami* (Agra: Radhasoami, Satsang, Soamibagh, 1960), vol. 1, Bachan 18, pp. 107–11; A. P. Mathur, *Radhasoami Faith* (Delhi: Vikas Publishing House, 1974), p. 65; and Kirpal Singh, *A Great Saint*, p. 46. It should be pointed out, however, that Rai

by a group called the Nath Yogis, whose ideas are in many other ways quite compatible with those of Radhasoami. It is perhaps not surprising to find that the Naths have had a close and formative influence on the Dharamdasis.

The Naths' ideas are linked with the mystical or "tantric" strain in both Hinduism and Mahayana Buddhism. Some scholars trace the origins of these ideas to a time not long after the Buddha's lifetime when theories were developing about a subtle and immortal body that could replace our material bodies through a sort of spiritual alchemy.[51] Nath teachings as we know them today crystalized as early as the ninth and tenth centuries and were shaped into their present form in the fifteenth century by Gorakhnath, who established a lineage that continues to exist in Gorakhpur, northwest of Benares. The goal of Nath practices is to transmute the body into its incorruptible aspect, which eventually disappears in a "Body of Pure Light."[52] The human body, which is called *pinda*, contains within it levels of energy that replicate the cosmic structures of consciousness, and Nath spiritual practices attempt to reverse the downward flow of negative consciousness, turning it in an upward and more positive direction.[53] Ideas parallel to these are found not only in Radhasoami, but in a variety of Buddhist, Vaisnava, and Shaivite tantric sects. They are also found in the Dharma cult of Bengal.[54] The latter is especially relevant since there is a possibility that the Dharma cult influenced the Dharamdasis, who may, in turn, have passed the Dharma cult's ideas on to Radhasoami via Tulsi Sahib.[55]

Saligram himself is said to have been a practitioner of these breathing exercises before becoming an initiate of Swami Shiv Dayal (*Souvenir*, p. 38). There are references to the Naths in *Sar Bachan*, where they appear as advocates for a rival, and inferior, form of yoga (Shiv Dayal Singh, *Sar Bachan: Prose*, Dayalbagh version, p. 110).

[51] According to Shashibhusan Das Gupta, the ancient origins of the Naths can be traced to the pre-Christian Rasayana school of Indian philosophy which advocated a spiritual alchemy said to have been influenced by Chinese Taoists (S. Das Gupta, *Obscure Religious Cults* [Calcutta: Firma K.L.M Private, 1976; orig. pub. 1946], p. 193). See also H. P. Dwivedi, *Natha-sampradaya* (Allahabad: Hindustani Academy, 1950), and Mircea Eliade, *Yoga: Immortality and Freedom*, trans. from the French by Willard R. Trask (Princeton: Princeton University Press, 1969), pp. 301–18.

[52] Das Gupta, *Obscure Religious Cults*, p. 253.

[53] A. K. Banerjea, *Philosophy of Gorakhnath* (Gorakhpur: Mahant Dig Vijai Nath Trust, 1961), p. 92. See also Das Gupta, *Obscure Religious Cults*, p. 230.

[54] See Das Gupta, *Obscure Religious Cults*; he describes the Dharma cult as "crypto-Buddhist" (pp. 262–64).

[55] The suggestion of a connection between the Dharma cult and the Dharamdasis, and between the Dharma cult and Radhasoami, was made to me by Prof. Sukhdev Singh of Banaras Hindu University in a private conversation (Benares, August 19, 1985). A prominent spiritual power in the Dharma cult's perspective is Niranjan—a concept that figures prominently in Radhasoami terminology as well (Das Gupta, *Obscure Religious Cults*, p. 266).

Even if these direct links did not exist, however, the Radhasoami teachings would have been indirectly influenced by Nath ideas through the sayings of Kabir, Nanak, and the other sants. According to Charlotte Vaudeville, Kabir was "so heavily indebted to the Nathpanthi form of Yoga that his sayings can hardly be understood without reference to it."[56] W. H. McLeod says much the same about Nanak, describing the sant teachings as a synthesis between Nath ideas and Vaisnava devotion.[57]

Radhasoami teachings are different from the rest of the sant corpus in that they seem to lean more heavily in the direction of tantric ideas and the Naths; the disagreement over hatha yoga is one of the few issues of consequence that separate the two schools of thought. But how Radhasoami and Nath teachings came to be related is still uncertain. All we know from the circumstantial evidence of the texts is that within Radhasoami writings and concepts are the outlines of an esoteric santism that was prevalent among a certain group of mystical devotees of Kabir during the late eighteenth century and contain practices and ideas that reach back to the Naths and other tantric groups, and to the sants themselves.

The Hidden View of Swami Shiv Dayal

Our attempt to trace the trail of esoteric santism does not, however, solve the Radhasoami dispute about guruship and lineage. We cannot confirm either Agra's claim that Swami Shiv Dayal's message was a unique revelation in human history, or the Beas view that he was part of a lineage that extended to the medieval sants. In a certain sense this is of no great importance. The very fact that Swami Shiv Dayal is conceived as the progenitor and the exemplar of the Radhasoami vision is a more forceful statement about his life than anything that could be said about it on the basis of textual evidence. What is remarkable is that this vision has survived so coherently over the years and despite the differences that divide the Radhasoami tradition. More than a dozen separate lineages of living masters are now current within the Radhasoami fold, but each traces its spiritual genealogy back to Shiv Dayal. Most abruptly halt there.[58]

[56] Charlotte Vaudeville, *Kabir*, p. 120.

[57] W. H. McLeod, *Guru Nanak and the Sikh Religion*, pp. 151–58. See also his *The Evolution of the Sikh Community*, pp. 6–7.

[58] The only significant attempt to trace the lineage before Swami Shiv Dayal is Kirpal Singh's; he suggests a guru-to-guru succession between Swami Shiv Dayal and Tulsi Sahib, and a historical link between Tulsi Sahib and Guru Gobind Singh, the tenth of the Sikh gurus in the lineage established by Guru Nanak, via a ruling family of Peshwas in Maharashtra whom Gobind Singh is said to have visited and who in turn influenced the young Tulsi Sahib when he lived among them (Kirpal Singh, *A Great Saint*, pp. 9–10). The sugges-

Shall we then call Swami Shiv Dayal a founder? To those within the traditions, the question is not whether the "founder" —be it Jesus or Siddhartha Gautama or Shiv Dayal Singh—intended to found a religious tradition, but where he stands within it. Because he is at the intersection between the tradition's internal history and a cosmic one to which it claims connection, Swami Shiv Dayal is remembered with special attention. He is a person who lived in modern times, came from an urban merchant background, and broke free from his family's expectations of what he should become. In those ways he is like many of his followers. Yet he is also remembered as having been touched with a divine grace, and his own past is seen as having antecedents that stretch back to India's medieval heritage, and beyond it to an infinite past, one that is hidden and beyond remembering.

---

tion of a Tulsi Sahib-Gobind Singh connection is not widely accepted, however, by branches of the Radhasoami faith other than Kirpal's own Ruhani Satsang.

Two

Shaping a Tradition

ON JUNE 15, 1878, Swami Shiv Dayal Singh died. He "shuffled off the mortal coil," as Radhasoami biographers, quoting Shakespeare, like to put it.[1] From that moment on, the movement that had formed around him began the process of evolving into a modern tradition and gained the authority granted by history rather than by the immediacy of a charismatic presence. In the life cycle of new religious movements, the death of the original central figure usually signals the beginning of a critical stage, and often spells the end of the movement itself. In the case of Radhasoami, this problem was alleviated by the expansive view the movement took of its own history and destiny. By perceiving its origins as having extended back to the medieval sants it appropriated the past, and by claiming that the founder's spiritual authority could be transmitted to a successor it projected its lease on charisma into the future as well.

Several difficulties, however, lay in the way of a smooth transition from movement to tradition. One concerned the delicate issue of agreeing upon who was to be heir to the collective memory. A second concerned the memory itself: the need to sort out orthodox from heterodox interpretations of the past. A third matter was the challenge of keeping pace with history by assimilating new pasts into the collective memory. Each of these dilemmas was solved in the social and historical contexts specific to it, and these in turn contributed to, and altered, the shape of the emerging tradition.

In the hundred years or so since the death of Swami Shiv Dayal, Radhasoami history has moved through several stages. The first, from 1878 to roughly 1911, was marked by attempts to solidify and stabilize the movement and establish the main lines of its continuity. The second, from 1911 to the time of India's independence in 1947, was a time for the institutionalization of Radhasoami communities. The third, from 1947 to the present, has been an era of expansion and internationalization. These stages describe Radhasoami's social development; theological changes are less easily defined. No branch of the movement is willing to concede that it has altered or deviated from Swami Shiv Dayal's original teachings, but there have been variations from time to time and from branch to branch in how Radhasoami teachings have been interpreted.

[1] The quotation is from *Hamlet*, Act 3, Scene 1.

These variations have resulted in conflicts within the ranks and questions about the community's direction and identity.

The Initial Years after the Death of Swami Shiv Dayal

The decades immediately following the Swami's death presented the community with its first crisis in self-understanding.[2] At the time of the Swami's death, the inner circles of the movement consisted of two groups: a monastic order and a loose association of laypeople. Scores of celibate male mendicant sadhus had set up permanent camp in the Swami's fields a few miles north of Agra near the Jumna River, and a somewhat larger number of married devotees, both men and women, met for worship and instruction at the Swami's house in town.[3] In addition to the Agra groups there was a fellowship in Oudh called the Brindabani sect, established by Swami Shiv Dayal's younger brother, Rai Brindaban; it had turned to Shiv Dayal's leadership after Rai Brindaban's death, which preceded the Swami's.[4] The Oudh satsang was the only one that had ever developed apart from the Swami's own commanding presence. At the time of the

[2] My sources for information about the early days of the Radhasoami movement are Pratap Singh Seth, *Biography of Soamiji Maharaj*; Shiv Dayal Singh (Soamiji Maharaj), *Elucidation of Japji*; Shiv Dayal Singh (Soamiji Maharaj), Rai Saligram (Huzur Maharaj), Brahm Sankar Misra (Maharaj Saheb), and Madhav Prasad Sinha (Babuji Maharaj), *Holy Epistles*, ed. and trans. Sant Das Maheshwari (Agra: Radhasoami Satsang, Soamibagh, 1964); Jaimal Singh (Baba Ji Maharaj), *Spiritual Letters*, which includes letters from Jaimal Singh originally written in Punjabi and Urdu, 1894–1903, and letters to him from Pratap Singh Seth and others; Rai Saligram, Preface to Shiv Dayal Singh, *Sar Bachan Radhasoami: Poetry*; Sant Das Maheshwari, *Bhaktmal of the Radhasoami Faith* (Agra: Radhasoami Satsang, Soamibagh, 1979; orig. pub. in Hindi, 1949); J. N. Farquhar, "Radhasoami Satsang," in James Hastings, ed., *Encyclopedia of Religion and Ethics* (Macmillan, 1919); J. N. Farquhar, *Modern Religious Movements in India*; Max Müller, *Ramakrishna—His Life and Sayings*.

[3] Pratap Singh Seth, *Biography of Soamiji Maharaj*, p. 96. The *Biography* claims that one thousand sadhus and seven to nine thousand married devotees, both men and women, were initiated by Swami Shiv Dayal (p. 40). According to another account, at the time of Swami Dayal's death the number of followers was much fewer: only four hundred celibate sadhus and two thousand married householders (*Souvenir*, p. 19).

[4] There is some question about the relationship between Rai Brindaban's group and Swami Shiv Dayal's. Although many of the teachings were similar, the name regarded as supreme in the Brindabani sect, according to S. D. Maheshwari, was *satgur ram*, a phrase that is not usually associated with Radhasoami. It is Maheshwari's contention that Swami Shiv Dayal, who, he claims, initiated Rai Brindaban, commanded him to use that term (S. D. Maheshwari to Harvey H. Myers, June 18, 1940, in Shiv Dayal Singh et al., *Holy Epistles*, part 1, p. 398). Kirpal Singh holds that Rai Brindaban was not a follower of Swami Shiv Dayal but of a guru at Ayodhya named Baba Madhodas (Kirpal Singh, *A Great Saint*, p. 12). Maheshwari claims that Brindaban joined Swami Shiv Dayal's fellowship in 1872 and remained with it until his death (Maheshwari, *Radhasoami Faith*, p. 31).

Swami's passing, his spiritual reign was so secure and so seemingly endless that he had neither a contender for leadership nor a unanimously accepted heir apparent. Years of uncertainty, therefore, followed.

All branches of the Radhasoami movement remember the Swami as having designated a successor, but they disagree about who it was. It is impossible to resolve this dispute, for the historical documents are scanty and imprecise. The Swami's reputed "last utterances"—recorded by his brother and accepted in all branches of the movement as authentic—were not published until twenty-four years after his death.[5] Moreover, they do not place any one person clearly in charge, nor do they imply that Swami Shiv Dayal conceived himself as occupying an office for which a successor was needed. Instead, a sadhu, Sanmukh Das, was appointed to be leader of the other sadhus; the property rights went to the Swami's younger brother; and the women were admonished to revere and obey the Swami's wife, Radhaji. The Swami's last command was to give her "the same place in your estimation as you gave me."[6] When asked to whom they should direct their questions about spiritual matters, the Swami named Rai Saligram, although he made it clear that Saligram's ideas were different from his own.[7] Thus the final speech of the Swami indicates that he left this world without designating any single person to replace him, although he did call for satsang to continue in his absence.[8]

[5] The "last utterances," a part of the *Biography of Soamiji Maharaj*, should be read with the situation of 1902 in mind. It seems likely that Pratap Singh's memory was stimulated by the desire to mediate among the various contending forces within the community at the time, and, not incidentally, to enhance his own reputation as well. This assessment is not solely my own, but is the opinion of some historians within the Radhasoami tradition, including A. P. Mathur, who says that "after 1902, there was a scramble to protect everyone's interests" (Interview with A. P. Mathur, Peepalmandi, Agra, August 13, 1985).

[6] The Swami also told his followers that they were to "treat . . . Radhaji and Chhoti Mata Ji [the widow of Swami Dayal's brother, Rai Brindaban] alike." ("Last Utterances," in Pratap Singh Seth, *Biography of Soamiji Maharaj*, p. 135).

[7] Ibid., pp. 138–39.

[8] Initiations were conducted by Sanmukh Das after Swami Shiv Dayal's death, but there is no suggestion that he was in any way regarded as a spiritual successor (Maheshwari, *Biography of Huzur Maharaj* [Agra: Radhasoami Satsang, Soamibagh, 1971], p. 190). After the Swami's death, the first event in the Radhasoami community of which we have historical record was the compilation of *Sar Bachan* in 1884 by Rai Saligram and Pratap Singh, neither of whom is described in the frontispiece of the book as the Swami's successor, but as his "chief disciple" and "brother," respectively. The *Biography of Soamiji Maharaj*, written by Pratap Singh in 1902, carefully avoids mentioning a successor to the Swami, describing Rai Saligram only as his "chief and most beloved disciple" (Pratap Singh Seth, *Biography of Soamiji Maharaj*, p. 68); but an anecdote in the biography in which the Swami is described as throwing his shoe at Rai Saligram is related as proof that Saligram was "the perfect Gurmukh" (Ibid., p. 105). (Guru-disciple power is often thought to be transferred through a master's feet, so by touching Saligram with his shoe, even in an act of annoyance, the Swami conveyed to him his greatest blessings.) Rai Saligram was proclaimed guru by B. S.

For a while that was enough. There was a conservative tendency to invest the leadership in his family members, and when his wife died in 1894, the Swami's youngest brother, Pratap Singh [Seth], continued as head of the family line. The size of the following, however, seems to have diminished considerably.[9] For a while the sadhus took care of themselves, but their numbers dwindled in time as well.[10]

There were, however, two vigorous new leaders in the wings. One of these was Rai Saligram, the high official in the government postal service who had been introduced to the Swami by Shiv Dayal's brother, also a postal employee. [11] The other was a soldier, Jaimal Singh. While his army unit, the Twenty-fourth Sikh Regiment, was encamped in Agra he slipped away to worship Swami Shiv Dayal.[12] In the years immediately following the Swami's death, both Rai Saligram and Jaimal Singh were largely preoccupied with their secular careers.[13] But in 1887 Rai Saligram retired

---

Misra, among others, as early as 1885, and in 1887 he returned to Agra to take over leadership of the community in earnest.

[9] Rai Saligram reported that when he retired and came to Agra in 1887, there were only forty sadhus and one hundred lay members of the fellowship—numbers considerably smaller than in the heyday of the Swami's ministry. If we are to accept Dayalbagh's statistics, the size of the original group numbered in the thousands (*Souvenir*, p. 19).

[10] Pratap Singh claims there were still one hundred sadhus at Soamibagh in 1902, at the time he was writing the Swami's biography (Pratap Singh Seth, *Biography of Soamiji Maharaj*, p. 41).

[11] Ibid., pp. 68–70.

[12] According to Kirpal Singh, the first meeting between Jaimal Singh and Swami Shiv Dayal occurred in 1856, when Jaimal Singh was 18 years old, two years before Rai Saligram met the Swami in 1858 and five years before the Swami's message was revealed to the public (*A Great Saint*, p. 42). The Agra accounts, however, date the initiation of Jaimal Singh later: sometime after he encamped in Agra with the Twenty-fourth Sikh Regiment in 1856, and after he attended Swami Shiv Dayal's satsang, which was not established until 1861 (A. P. Mathur, *Radhasoami Faith*, p. 128; and Shiv Dayal Singh et al., *Holy Epistles*, part 1, p. 400). Jaimal Singh's spiritual wanderings prior to meeting the Swami are described by Kirpal Singh, and also by Sawan Singh, in his introduction to Jaimal Singh, *Spiritual Letters*. According to Sawan Singh, Jaimal Singh had for a time been interested in the Namdhari sect of Sikhs (the so-called Kukas), who also believed in a living guru.

[13] In both cases it is not clear when—if at all, during their lifetimes—Rai Saligram and Jaimal Singh began to be regarded as the successors and living incarnations of Swami Shiv Dayal. The first person to be initiated by Rai Saligram is not mentioned by name, nor is a date given. This person is merely identified as someone who refused to be initiated by Sanmukh Das and insisted that Rai Saligram should initiate him instead. After initially refusing, Rai Saligram is said to have agreed (Maheshwari, *Biography of Huzur Maharaj*, p. 190). "Slowly and gradually, [Rai Saligram] began holding satsang at His place and also accepting obeisance from satsangis" (*ibid.*). It is also said that later, in 1885, while Rai Saligram was passing through Benares, he met Brahm Sankar Misra, who insisted on receiving initiation from him. As for Jaimal Singh, Daryai Lal Kapur states that his first initiation was performed in 1877, while Swami Shiv Dayal was still alive, but he gives no source for this assertion. Kapur states that "the name of the first initiate cannot be ascertained, for in the list of initiates later maintained by Baba Ji [Jaimal Singh] the first few names have no dates;

from government service in Allahabad and returned to Agra to take up an active role in the movement; and in 1889 Jaimal Singh also retired, leaving the army and devoting his energies to religious matters. Unlike Rai Saligram, however, Jaimal Singh did not elect to stay in Agra; after a brief visit he returned permanently to his native Punjab.[14] There he developed the nucleus of what was to become the Beas branch of the tradition. The members of that branch assert that he was commissioned by Swami Shiv Dayal to go to the Punjab and establish Radhasoami teachings.[15] The Agra branches claim Rai Saligram to be the sole successor, the one who gave to the movement's scattered following a sense of confident leadership and coherent purpose.

Rai Saligram and the Early Organization

The matter of Rai Saligram's spiritual relationship to Swami Shiv Dayal was never clear, even to his own followers. Was Saligram the incarnation of Swami Shiv Dayal, his successor on a lower spiritual plane, or simply a loyal disciple who was trying to keep the community together after the Swami's death?[16] These questions have not been resolved, but most dev-

---

the first entry is Amir Singh of Jhelum [in 1884], who presumably was in [Jaimal Singh's] regiment" (Daryai Lal Kapur, *Heaven on Earth* [Beas:Radhasoami Satsang, Beas, 1986], p. 23).

[14] I have given the version of what happened to Jaimal Singh after the death of Swami Shiv Dayal that is remembered by his followers in Beas and elsewhere. According to some Agra accounts, however, he is said to have stayed in Agra as a disciple of Rai Saligram. A. P. Mathur claims that Jaimal Singh had a house built in Peepalmandi so that he could live near Saligram "like any other sadhu" (Interview with A. P. Mathur, August 13, 1985). Mathur also says that Jaimal Singh did not go to the Punjab permanently until after Saligram died, on December 6, 1898. Present-day followers of the lineage said to have been established by the Swami's youngest brother, Pratap Singh, claim that Jaimal Singh was a disciple of his, and that Pratap deputed him to go to the Punjab (Interview with B. L. Gupta, Gwalior, August 21, 1985).

[15] In the Beas memory, the charge was as follows: "In October, 1877, when Baba Ji [Jaimal Singh] came on leave, Swami Ji Maharaj said to Him: 'This is our last meeting. Now I shall go away to Param Dham [the eternal home], after completing my life's pilgrimage. I have made you my beloved and my own form.' Bhai Chanda Singh then requested that Satsang be started in the Punjab. Swami ji Maharaj replied: 'This request has been accepted by Akal Purush [the Supreme Being], and this task has been allotted to Baba Jaimal Singh.' Then Swami Ji Maharaj gave His own turban to Baba Ji as prasad [a blessing] and ordered Him to go and preach Nam [the Divine Name] in the Punjab." (Sawan Singh, Introduction to Jaimal Singh, *Spiritual Letters*, pp. xiii–xiv.)

[16] Swami Shiv Dayal's brother, Pratap Singh, chastized Rai Saligram for his spiritual pretensions and for allowing his disciples to worship him and treat him as the Swami's equal. Saligram accepted these criticisms as valid, even though he regarded the manner in which Pratap leveled them as "not good or courteous." He subsequently ordered his followers not

3. A portrait of Rai Saligram, with his wooden sandals in the foreground.

otees agree that Saligram, like his counterpart in the Punjab, provided the genius that held his fledgling community together and gave it the continuity that otherwise it might not have had.

Saligram had already distinguished himself as the first Indian to be appointed postmaster-general of the United Provinces, the largest state in

to kneel in front of him or put garlands of flowers around his neck (Rai Saligram to Prem Anand, March 5, 1889, in Shiv Dayal Singh et al., *Holy Epistles*, part 2, p. 225). Rai Saligram's followers, however, continued to regard him as a satguru. Members of the Dayal-

British India. The nineteenth century Indologist, Max Müller, concluded that Saligram's retreat from the high offices of government bureaucracy to religious obedience under Swami Shiv Dayal was prompted by Saligram's experience of the social chaos that came in the wake of the mutiny of 1857. According to Müller, "He saw thousands of men, women, and children butchered before his eyes, the rich reduced to poverty, the poor raised to unexpected and undeserved wealth, so that the idea of the world's impermanent and transient nature took complete possession of him and estranged him from all that had formerly enlisted his interest and occupied his energies."[17]

Perhaps for these reasons, Saligram was determined to eradicate disorder wherever he encountered it, including the religious movement of which he assumed leadership. Saligram drew up an effective administrative system, formalized the satsang worship services, compiled and edited his master's sayings into book form, and clarified the movement's theology. Saligram's most ardent supporters downplay his originality, however, for if he and the Swami were essentially one, how could his spiritual ideas possibly have been any different from Swami Shiv Dayal's? [18] The debate over Saligram continues to this very day, and at the heart of it is his use of that interesting word, *Radhasoami*.

The word is important not only because it is the name of the movement, but also because adherents of the Agra branches hold it to be the name for God and a conduit for divine force. Beas devotees partially disagree over this matter. They do not think that any worldly name, including *Radhasoami*, carries divine freight, but they do agree with their Agra counterparts that there is an ultimate, unspeakable name that does. They

---

bagh branch regard him as one of their spiritual masters, although not quite equal to Swami Shiv Dayal. Some at Peepalmandi and Soamibagh regard Rai Saligram as an incarnation of Swami Shiv Dayal, and the meeting of the two "on the physical plane" is touted as being the beginning of Radhasoami faith. According to S. D. Maheshwari, that meeting was "the most important event for the entire creation; from that day the work of salvation started" (*Biography of Huzur Maharaj*, p. 44). At Beas, of course, the spiritual claims of Rai Saligram are largely discounted; but the Great Master at Beas, Sawan Singh, has called him a "prominent" disciple of Swami Shiv Dayal (Introduction to Jaimal Singh, *Spiritual Letters*, p. 4). Kirpal Singh allows that Rai Saligram "had been entrusted after him [Swami Dayal] with the work at Agra" (*A Great Saint*, p. 58).

[17] Max Müller, *Ramakrishna*, pp. 20–21. Müller's knowledge of Rai Saligram is based on an article about him in an issue of a Vedantic journal, *Prabuddha Bharata*, that appeared in May 1898.

[18] Maheshwari, *Radhasoami Faith*, p. 34. The present master in Rai Saligram's family lineage, Agam Prasad Mathur, regards Swami Shiv Dayal and Rai Saligram as cofounders of the faith and awaits their reincarnations with anticipation. He admits to some differences of emphasis between Rai Saligram's theology and Swami Shiv Dayal's, however. For instance, Mathur regards Saligram's focus on love as the cardinal spiritual virtue as one of his original contributions (Interview with A. P. Mathur, August 13, 1985).

agree that the most fundamental spiritual energy comes in the form of a sound that is beyond the range of ordinary hearing. This is the eternal Name described as *dhunyatmak* by Swami Shiv Dayal in the *Sar Bachan*; it is the "embodiment" of Truth.[19] Although members of Beas branches think that that Name can never be uttered, Agra members think it can, and the name is *Radhasoami.* No wonder, then, that there is so much interest in how and where it originated.

Saligram used the term ubiquitously in his writings, regarding *Radhasoami* as the only name for the ultimate source of energy that pulses through creation. At first glance, it would appear that in his writings Swami Shiv Dayal used the term with similar frequency and attached to it the same importance; yet the writings of the Swami were compiled and edited some years after his death, and the editor of these volumes was none other than Rai Saligram. The extant letters of Swami Shiv Dayal do not use the term *Radhasoami* even once.[20] Members of the Beas and Ruhani Satsang communities of Radhasoami therefore question whether the name *Radhasoami* is essential to the teachings and whether its frequent appearance in the Swami's writings represents anything more than assiduous interpolation at the hand of Saligram.[21] Members of Saligram's own family, who claim to have the original writings of the first guru in their possession, fervently deny that it is.[22]

The last words of Swami Shiv Dayal, which might settle the matter, serve only to compound the mystery, for he uses the term *Radhasoami* only once in nineteen paragraphs, and that in a puzzling way. The Swami is said to have proclaimed, "The Faith I had expounded was that of Sat Nam and Anami. Radhasoami Faith has been introduced by Rai Saligram. You should let it continue."[23]

Saligram's supporters explain that this statement refers to the way Swami Dayal revealed the word *Radhasoami* to the world—through Saligram.[24] Members of the Punjab branches of the movement tend to take

[19] Shiv Dayal Singh, *Sar Bachan: Prose*, Soamibagh version, p. 128. In Maheshwari's translation the term is transliterated as *dhwanyatmak*. See also Mathur, *Radhasoami Faith*, p. 27.

[20] Maheshwari, *Biography of Huzur Maharaj*, pp. 113–19.

[21] According to Radha Krishna Khanna, a Ruhani Satsang historian, "Only fifty to sixty of the pieces in *Sar Bachan* poetry were really composed by Soamiji himself. The rest were mostly devotional poems written by Hazur Maharaj Salig Ram [Rai Saligram] in praise of his Master whom he addressed as 'Radhasoami'" (Khanna, *Truth Eternal*, p. 11).

[22] Interview with A. P. Mathur, August 13, 1985.

[23] Pratap Singh Seth, *Biography of Soamiji Maharaj*, pp. 138–39.

[24] Mathur, *Radhasoami Faith*, pp. 28–29. Mathur's account of the origins of the name is as follows: "When Huzur Maharaj [Rai Saligram] first saw Soamiji [Shiv Dayal] he said, 'Here is Radhasoami Dham,' and Soamiji agreed" (Interview with A. P. Mathur, August 13, 1985).

the statement at its face value, however. They point out that in one of the few writings accepted as of undoubted authenticity, the Swami calls *sat nam* the "highest and most ancient" of the names for the Divine.[25] The phrase *sat nam* (the true name) is found frequently in the writings of Guru Nanak, and would have been familiar to Shiv Dayal, whose Punjabi family revered Nanak's words.

The Agra leaders admit that Swami Dayal did indeed refer to *sat nam* rather than *Radhasoami* in his writings, but since the latter term referred to the divine force in himself he revealed it only later, through Saligram.[26] The Agra branches use the name *Radhasoami* in their meditation practices and initiation rites, whereas the Beas and Delhi branches use a sequence of five names. None of these is *Radhasoami*, but they use the term as a greeting and a sort of blessing, and of course it also provides the Beas fellowship with its name.[27]

The word *Radhasoami* literally refers to Krishna as lord (*swami*) of his consort, Radha. It would have been natural for Rai Saligram to use this term for the Divine, since members of his family were devotees of Krishna and supporters of the Banke Bihari temple at the Krishna pilgrimage center of Brindavan, near Agra, where Krishna is said to have sported with Radha and his cowherding friends eons ago.[28] Contrary to some early missionary reports, however, there is no evidence that Saligram or anyone else in the movement has used the phrase to refer to Krishna and Radha in their human forms.[29]

Even so, it is possible that a link between the traditional theology of Radha and Krishna and that of Radhasoami is provided by the Vaisnava understanding of Radha as the power or energy of God (*sakti*).[30] "Swami

[25] Shiv Dayal Singh, *Elucidation of Japji*, p. 26.

[26] *Souvenir*, p. 15. Maheshwari's horror at the thought that some branches of the faith were "discarding the Supreme Name" and his account of the differences between Agra and Beas on this point are expressed in Shiv Dayal Singh et al., *Holy Epistles*, part 1, pp. 386–406.

[27] The Dayalbagh branch is under the impression that, at a meeting between Anand Swarup and Sawan Singh in 1932, Beas agreed to abandon its use of the five names at initiation and use the name *Radhasoami* instead (*Souvenir*, pp. 15–17, 220).

[28] It is said that Rai Saligram was initiated by a "Gosain of Mathura Bindraban" when he was a boy, with the condition that he was free to find a more suitable guru when he was of age (Pratap Singh Seth, *Biography of Soamiji Maharaj*, pp. 71–72). Followers of Saligram claim that, although his family members were Vaisnava supporters of a Brindaban temple, Saligram himself was never initiated (Interview with Mathur, August 13, 1985).

[29] I have no idea where Farquhar might have gotten the notion that "the first *guru* and his wife used to dress up as Krsna and Radha" (J. N. Farquhar, "Radha Soamis," in James Hastings, ed., *Encyclopedia of Religion and Ethics*, [1919], p. 559).

[30] For the Vaisnava theology of Radha and her relation to Krishna see J. S. Hawley and Donna Wulff, eds., *The Divine Consort* (Berkeley: Berkeley Religious Studies Series; Delhi: Motilal Banarsidass, 1982), especially pp. xi–xviii, 1–128.

of Radha" could be taken to mean "master of energy." Saligram explains that *Radha* denotes the flow of consciousness in each individual (*dhara*, the inverted form of *Radha*, means "flow"); *swami* describes the cosmic energy source. Together *Radha-swami* is the name of the ultimate union and the highest reality.[31] The peculiar English spelling *Radhasoami* is also said to be an effort to deflect attention from the usual denotation of the words *Radha* and *swami*, and give emphasis to the distinctive sounds contained in the four syllables, *ra-dha-soa-mi*, each of which, according to Rai Saligram, has a certain significance.[32] The Beas group translates *Radhasoami* as "lord of the soul."[33]

Whether Saligram introduced the term *Radhasoami*, then, is not without dispute, but it is clear that he championed it. In other ways, also, he gave clarity to Swami Shiv Dayal's ideas: he systematized the theology and cosmology of *Radhasoami*, compiled lists of moral codes and guidelines for meditation practices, and routinized the criteria for initiation.[34] Given all of this, one can hardly dispute the judgment of J. N. Farquhar in 1918 that "the order and precision which now mark the *Radhasoami* teachings were the fruit of Saligram's vigorous and orderly mind."[35]

Perhaps the most important thing about Saligram, however, was not what he taught or did, but what he was, at least in the minds of many followers of Swami Shiv Dayal: the founder's rightful heir. This idea eventually led to Agra's incarnational doctrine of guruship, the notion that there is always one, and only one, true guru in each generation. Signs of such a theory were already present in the prose volume of Swami Shiv Dayal's *Sar Bachan*, where mention is made of a "succeeding Sat Guru" who will come after the death of a guru; the devotee is admonished to "consider the departed Guru to be present in him."[36] The scriptures go

[31] Rai Saligram, Preface to Shiv Dayal Singh, *Sar Bachan: Poetry*, Soamibagh version, p. 22. This description of the radha-soami union has parallels in the romantic and at times sexual imagery of the love between Radha and Krishna in Vaisnava mythology. Echoes of the Vaisnava theme of *viraha*, soulful longing for a departed lover, may be found in the frequent Radhasoami descriptions of the yearning of the soul for union with the divine current.

[32] Rai Saligram, *Jugat Prakash Radhasoami*, p. 33.

[33] Jaimal Singh, *Spiritual Letters*, p. 171. An early missionary account reports that the movement uses the term *Radhasoami* to mean "Lord of force"; see Hervey DeWitt Griswold, "Radha Swami Sect in India," in *The East and the West* (1908), p. 186.

[34] Rai Saligram's extant writings are by far the most extensive of any of the Agra masters. His discourses were published in a biweekly journal and reissued in the six-volume *Prem Patra Radhasoami*. His collected verse comes to four volumes and is published as *Prem Bani Radhasoami*, trans. S. D. Maheshwari (Agra: Radhasoami Satsang, Soamibagh, 1980). There are several smaller works published as well.

[35] Farquhar, *Modern Religious Movements*, p. 164.

[36] Shiv Dayal Singh, *Sar Bachan:Prose*, Soamibagh version, p. 215.

on to castigate "bigoted devotees" who refuse to "come under the allegiance of the succeeding Sat Guru."[37]

This controversial section of *Sar Bachan* comes from a letter from Rai Saligram to Swami Shiv Dayal Singh's nephew, Sudarshan Singh, that is said to have been written on behalf of Swami Shiv Dayal. The Agra branches claim that it faithfully represents Swami Shiv Dayal's thought, but the Beas branch excises it from its version of the *Sar Bachan*, thinking it unlikely that the Swami would have discussed his own succession.[38]

Whatever one decides about that issue, it seems clear that the actual succession of guruship at the time of a master's death is never as certain and smooth as the theory of spiritual reincarnation implies it should be. There is always the matter of recognizing who the incarnate successor really is. In the years after the death of Swami Shiv Dayal, certainly, the spiritual leadership of the movement was fragmented. In addition to Saligram, the Swami's wife and his youngest brother had their partisans; the head of the sadhus, Sanmukh Das, was giving initiation; Jaimal Singh had garnered his own followers in the Punjab; and other disciples were holding meetings in Delhi and Calcutta.[39] The three main camps, clustered around Saligram, the Swami's family, and Jaimal Singh, formed an uneasy coalition marked by mutual suspicion. From time to time Pratap Singh, the Swami's brother, would use "very intemperate language and harsh words" in speaking about Rai Saligram and his followers.[40] Saligram, for his part, called Pratap Singh "this queer gentleman" whom he "never trusted."[41] Even though Pratap Singh, in his biography of Swami Shiv Dayal, called Saligram the Swami's "chief and most beloved disci-

[37] Ibid., p. 216.

[38] In Agra it is claimed that this verse was written "under the command and instruction of Soamiji" (Maheshwari, *Biography of Huzur Maharaj*, p. 275). For further discussion of the Bachan 250 issue, see Shiv Dayal Singh et al., *Holy Epistles*, part 1, pp. 405–7, and Maheshwari, *Radhasoami Faith*, p. 333.

[39] Another spiritual leader given the power of initiation after Swami Shiv Dayal is Garib Das at Delhi (Mathur, *Radhasoami Faith*, p. 130). Other leaders offering initiation and holding satsang at the time include Baba Chand Singh in the Punjab (Kirpal Singh, *A Great Saint*, p. 63), and Nirmal Chandra Banerji in Calcutta (*Souvenir*, p. 61). Four groups, led by Sanmukh Das, Radhaji, Pratap Singh and Rai Saligram, are mentioned by Rai Saligram in a letter to Madhav Prasad Sinha, Feb. 12, 1889 (Shiv Dayal Singh et al., *Holy Epistles*, part 2, p. 209).

[40] Rai Saligram to Madhav Prasad Sinha, Feb. 12, 1889, in Shiv Dayal Singh et al., *Holy Epistles*, part 2, p. 209. In 1905, Pratap Singh's son, Suchet Singh, refused to take part in a public program because his father was slated to be seated on the dais next to Rai Saligram's son, a position that would seem to equate the two in importance (*Souvenir*, p. 92).

[41] Rai Saligram to Madhav Prasad Sinha, Feb. 12, 1889, in Shiv Dayal Singh et al., *Holy Epistles*, part 2, p. 213. In other writings, Saligram seems to denounce the idea that spiritual authority could be transmitted, as Pratap Singh's presumably had been, through family connections (*Prem Patra Radhasoami*, vol. 1, p. 161).

ple,"[42] Saligram felt that Pratap harbored "a strong spirit of jealousy and venomous rancour."[43] Jaimal Singh, from his distant vantage point in the Punjab, was able to avoid the squabbles among the leaders at Agra. Pratap Singh kept up a correspondence with Beas,[44] but Saligram seems to have ignored Jaimal Singh and his followers. The one person to whom all three of the early leaders gave obeisance was the Swami's widow, Radhaji, who played a neutral role in the controversies among the cliques.[45]

These problems of fragmentation were compounded when Saligram died in 1898. Some disciples followed his son, Ajudhia Prasad, in Agra. Others felt that the legitimate successor was Brahm Sankar Misra, one of Saligram's chief disciples, who served as an official in the accountant general's office of the government in Allahabad.[46] Pratap Singh, the Swami's younger brother, was still around, and some of Saligram's former followers joined his fold.[47] There were branches in outlying regions as well, and each of these was developing its own separate strength and identity.[48] A substantial number of devotees seemed to accord spiritual authority to no one, expecting instead a second coming of Swami Shiv Dayal.[49]

The movement seemed to be splintering apart. Misra had established his headquarters in Allahabad, and it seemed to many that the leadership

[42] Pratap Singh Seth, *Biography of Soamiji Maharaj*, p. 68.

[43] Rai Saligram to Madhav Prasad Sinha, Feb. 12, 1889, in Shiv Dayal Singh et al., *Holy Epistles*, part 2, p. 213. Sudarshan Singh, Pratap Singh's son, seemed to be one link that kept the two leaders on relatively hospitable terms. In his letters, Rai Saligram consistently speaks well of Sudarshan (see, for instance, a letter written on February 2, 1897, in Maheshwari, *Biography of Huzur Maharaj*, pp. 343–44). Sudarshan was also on good terms with the leaders at Beas; in 1933 he wrote to Sawan Singh proposing to build a house at Beas and live there in retirement (Jaimal Singh, *Spiritual Letters*, p. 151).

[44] Jaimal Singh, *Spiritual Letters*, pp. 140–49.

[45] Rai Saligram, for instance, refers to Radhaji as the "supreme mother" (Rai Saligram to Prem Anand, March 5, 1889, in Shiv Dayal Singh et al., *Holy Epistles*, part 2, p. 225).

[46] For information on Misra, see *Souvenir*, chapter 3.

[47] The Dhara Sindhu Pratap Ashram in Gwalior traces its lineage to Pratap Singh but acknowledges that he did not establish a separate community or appoint a successor during his lifetime. He is said to have initiated a number of followers, however, including those who established the Gwalior ashram: Sham Lal Gupta, L. N. Sharma and K. A. Bavnani (Interview with B. L. Gupta, Gwalior, August 12, 1985). Pratap Singh's own son seems to have denounced the notion that his father was a guru (Maheshwari, *Biography of Huzur Maharaj*, p. 347).

[48] In addition to Jaimal Singh's branch in the Punjab, there was one in Delhi led by Garib Das's successor, Ram Behari Lal; there were also fellowships in Calcutta led by N. C. Banerjee and in Benares by Raj Narain. Also in Benares was a new group led by Shiv Brat Lal (who later shifted the headquarters of his movement to Lahore, and then, in time, to Gopiganj). Regarding Shiv Brat Lal, see Mathur, *Radhasoami Faith*, p. 130.

[49] A circular letter that was sent to all members of the Radhasoami branches in 1902 to announce the formation of a Council explained that it would not "in any way interfere with the devotion, service and homage due to the sant satguru *when he makes his advent*" (reprinted in *Souvenir*, pp. 85–87; my italics).

was in exile. Another problem was Misra himself: he was a Brahman in a largely merchant-caste community, and his personality was less than endearing. An American missionary visited him and came away unimpressed. He observed that Misra's style was "didactic or argumentative, but never earnest." He went on to say that Misra "often indulges in a form of wit which does not appeal very strongly to outsiders, and apparently not even to his own disciples."[50]

In 1902, Misra offered a solution to the problem of fragmentation: to contain it through a coalition governed by a ten-member Central Administrative Council.[51] A system of elections was set up to implement this federal system. In the first election—and, as it turned out, the only one—Misra received the highest number of votes. Because his relationship to the founding guru elevated him over factional disputes, Pratap Singh was made president of the board; Saligram's son and Misra were next in command. These three were acknowledged as having the authority to give initiation to new members, a privilege that was soon extended to three leaders of *Radhasoami* fellowships in outlying regions: one in Bengal, another in Benares, and a third—Jaimal Singh—in the Punjab.[52] The power of the Council was administrative and spiritual, and there was a plan to undergird those powers with a financial one: all *Radhasoami* properties were to be pooled under a common trust.

The idea of a Council never really worked. From the outset, Jaimal Singh rejected the authority of Misra to give initiation, balked at the notion of turning over his records to the Council, and refused to be subjected to its judgments.[53] Jaimal Singh's followers, like Saligram's, had become convinced of the continuation of Swami Shiv Dayal's legacy and the importance of a continuing guru-to-guru succession, an idea that had a special credibility to Punjabis familiar with the lineage of the ten Sikh gurus. The differences lay in specifying where that line of spiritual authority went, and Jaimal Singh's followers were not about to relinquish

[50] H. D. Griswold, "The Radha Swami Sect in India," p. 190. According to one current Radhasoami leader, Misra's caste characteristics were part of the problem: he was burdened with "the intellectualism that the Brahmans have" (Interview with A. P. Mathur, August 13, 1985).

[51] The establishment of the council is discussed in Mathur, *Radhasoami Faith*, pp. 101–14.

[52] The extension of the power of initiation to Jaimal Singh, Lala Raj Narain of Benares, and Nirmal Chandra Banerjee of Calcutta was made at the first meeting of the Council, December 25, 1902 (Mathur, *Radhasoami Faith*, p. 112).

[53] Jaimal Singh placed three conditions that had to be met before he would join the Council: (1) Misra's methods of initiation should be rejected, (2) there should be three representatives from Beas chosen by himself, and (3) Beas would not support the Council financially, at least not through soliciting money from its members (*Spiritual Letters*, p. 104).

any of the authority they thought was implicit in his guruship, or to modify their Punjab-oriented approach to suit Agra tastes.

All this meant that when the Council convened in Agra in 1902, Jaimal Singh stayed at home. And in the face of uneasy political maneuvering between different factions in the organization, it took all the leadership talents Misra could muster to hold the rest of the groups together. After Jaimal Singh died in 1903, he was succeeded by Sawan Singh, who continued Jaimal Singh's momentum in steering Beas's course in a direction separate from that of the centers at Agra.

After Misra's death in 1907, the fissures among the Agra groups became more apparent. Much of the tension was between the conservative leadership, enshrined in the family lineages of Swami Shiv Dayal, Saligram, and Misra, and newer members of the movement, such as Kamta Prasad Sinha and Anand Swarup, who were more eager to broaden the base of the community.[54] Pratap Singh continued to have a following until his death in 1911. After that, in 1915, a line of gurus began in Gwalior, claiming to derive their authority from him.[55] Meanwhile his son, Sudarshan Singh, provided leadership for Pratap Singh's fellowship at Soamibagh until his own death in 1935.[56] Similarly at Peepalmandi, at the home of Rai Saligram, Saligram's son Ajudhia Prasad continued to lead the fellowship until his death in 1926, when his son, Gur Prasad ("Kunwar-ji"), took over. Misra was succeeded by no one for a time, and the community was much divided.

Thus the Radhasoami movement moved into the twentieth century as a tradition both strengthened and splintered. Ironically, the sense of coherence that Saligram had infused into the movement also threatened to be its undoing. By elevating the movement's leadership to a level of power and prestige that equaled Swami Shiv Dayal's, and by providing an administrative structure over which his successors could exercise control, Saligram had raised the stakes to be won by any who achieved high status within the fledgling Radhasoami community. As new leaders emerged, the movement fragmented all the more, for each new leader was tied to his flock by spiritual links and by definite instruments of administration. Fissiparous tendencies within each organization would typically come to the fore at the time of an old master's death, with various camps claiming fealty to the possible successors, and the tradition branched out like a family tree. Each new growth sprouted others, until ultimately there arose

[54] *Souvenir*, pp. 136–39.

[55] Shyam Lal, who received initiation from Pratap Singh, established the Dhara Sindhu Pratap Ashram in Gwalior in 1915, and another initiate of Pratap Singh, K. A. Bavnani, served as a spiritual master in Bombay, where he lived after his retirement as an engineer in Gwalior (Interview with B. L. Gupta, Gwalior, August 21, 1985).

[56] Mathur, *Radhasoami Faith*, p. 122.

over a dozen sizable spiritual centers—and many smaller ones—that trace their lineage back to the first master. (See Appendix A: The Radhasoami Family Tree). At each of these centers, however, the pattern of belief and organization set by Saligram, Jaimal Singh, and others in the late nineteenth century endures.

Organization: The Colonies of Beas and Dayalbagh

Radhasoami's early leaders were, by and large, well educated and urbane. Only Swami Shiv Dayal may be described as coming from the traditional rather than modern sectors of Indian society, but even he was well versed in the cultured language of his day: Persian, the literary vehicle of the Moghul courts. His successors were fluent in English, educated in English medium colleges, and familiar with British society. In many cases, their families had long ago detached themselves from the parochial world of rural India and the customs of village Hinduism and had embraced new varieties of reformed Hinduism like the Brahmo Samaj and the Arya Samaj.

So many former members of the Arya Samaj converted to the Radhasoami fold that a rivalry emerged between the two groups in the 1910s and 1920s. Members of the Arya Samaj in Amritsar "gave a disgraceful display of their rowdyism and violent behaviour" when Kamta Prasad Sinha, who founded the branch that became Dayalbagh, visited there in 1911. Later, some Arya Samaj students heckled his speech by "howling and shrieking like jackals and barking like dogs," and in Lahore, leaders of the Samaj put up posters in opposition to the Radhasoami guru.[57] Ironically, Sinha's successor, Anand Swarup, had been a member of the Samaj in his youth, and some members of Radhasoami make the improbable claim that the Arya founder, Swami Dayanand, was initiated by the Radhasoami's Swami Shiv Dayal.[58]

[57] *Souvenir*, pp. 139–40. Other references to the Arya Samaj's attacks on Radhasoami are mentioned by Gurcharandas Mehta in his introduction to Anand Swarup, *Yathartha Prakash* (Agra: Radhasoami Satsang, Dayalbagh, 1954), pp. vi–vii, and by Swarup himself in the 1934 preface to that book, where he refers to the "unrestrained and vulgar criticism" from the Aryas and other groups (p. xvi). Elsewhere in that volume, Swarup quotes Swami Dayanand, leader of the Arya Samaj, as belittling Radhasoami teachings as being "nothing but child's play" (p. 35). Despite this criticism, Anand Swarup was invited in 1931 to speak at meetings in Lahore arranged by the Arya Samaj and by a lower-caste organization related to the Arya Samaj, the Jat Path Thorak Mandal (*Souvenir*, pp. 215–16). The Dayalbagh history credits the persuasive power of Anand Swarup's book, *Yathartha Prakasa*, with dealing "a crushing blow" to the anti-Radhasoami propaganda that had previously been disseminated by the Arya Samaj (*Souvenir*, pp. 223–24).

[58] *Souvenir*, p. 18. Members of the Arya Samaj have demanded proof that would substan-

In the second decade of this century, both the Beas and the Agra centers of Radhasoami began to experiment with a form of progressive spiritual society that went beyond anything envisioned by the Brahmo Samaj or Arya Samaj. Both centers were imbued with the vision of a new society and captivated by the task of creating in their midst a sort of spiritual socialism. Two dates mark the beginning of the shift toward social experimentation: 1911, when Sawan Singh retired from military service to undertake the task of leading his community full-time; and 1913, when in a similar way Anand Swarup gave up his government position to assume full-time the duties of leadership. Both men were relatively young when they took on the mantle of guruhood; Sawan Singh was forty-five, and Anand Swarup was only thirty-two. But both were accomplished administrators, and both succeeded almost single-handedly in designing and creating their own ideal cities.

There were, however, differences between them, and these affected the character of the movements they led and the cities they established. Sawan Singh was a soldier and an engineer. Born a Sikh and a member of the Jat farming caste, Sawan Singh entered the military after college and rose to the position of sub-divisional officer in the Military Engineering Service. It was in the army that he first met Jaimal Singh, also a Jat Sikh, and became his disciple.[59] When he succeeded Jaimal Singh after his death, Sawan Singh created a new colony in the midst of a previously uninhabited wasteland alongside the Beas River where Jaimal Singh had once pitched camp. The place was near Jaimal Singh's home village and had served as a solitary refuge for holy men long before. Sawan Singh dedicated the new city to the memory of his master, calling it the camp (*dera*) of Baba Jaimal Singh.

---

tiate this claim. In a later edition of the *Souvenir*, proof is provided in the form of a photograph of a note written in Urdu by a nephew of Swami Shiv Dayal, Seth Sudarshan Singh, saying that he was present at Swami Shiv Dayal's house in Agra when Swami Dayanand visited in 1872 and received initiation from the original Radhasoami master (*Souvenir*, pp. 367–68).

[59] Biographical information on Sawan Singh is given in Daryai Lal Kapur, *Call of the Great Master* (Beas: Radhasoami Satsang, Beas, 1964), pp. xxx–xliii; Joseph Leeming's introduction to Sawan Singh, *Discourses on Sant Mat* (Beas: Radhasoami Satsang, Beas, 1970); the introduction to Kirpal Singh, *The Way of the Saints* (Sanbornton, N.H.: Sant Bani Ashram), pp. 3–40; and Kirpal Singh, *A Brief Life Sketch of Baba Sawan Singh* (Delhi: Ruhani Satsang, 1960). See also the firsthand accounts of visits with the Great Master in Julian Johnson, *With a Great Master in India* (Beas: Radhasoami Satsang, Beas, 1971); Rai Sahib Munshi Ram, *With the Three Masters*; and the series of reminiscences by Radha Krishna Khanna, "The Master's Master," *Sat Sandesh*, July 1977, and "At the Feet of the Great Hazur," *Sat Sandesh*, April 1978 and July 1978. The Beas branch has produced a large, elaborate volume of original photographs, along with selections of reminiscences about Sawan Singh in Hilda Gill, ed., *Glimpses of the Great Master* (Hong Kong: Cami Moss, 1986).

The centerpiece of Sawan Singh's city is the *satsang ghar*, the worship hall for the community, which he designed himself; its elaborate brick design creates a distinctive landmark on the Punjab plains. The residential community that was built around it has served as headquarters for a constantly expanding organization—some 125,000 devotees were initiated during Sawan Singh's forty-four years of leadership—and Sawan Singh's Dera made a symbolic as well as practical contribution towards the creation of a stable, intimate spiritual community.

Much the same can be said of the Dayalbagh colony created by Sawan Singh's counterpart in Agra, Anand Swarup. Like Sawan Singh, Anand Swarup was a Punjabi; he was born into a middle-class family from the mercantile Ahluwalia caste and raised in the eastern Punjab in the city of Ambala, north of Delhi.[60] His father was a Sikh who had rejected the traditional emblems of that faith, including long hair, turban and beard. When Anand joined the Arya Samaj during his student days, it was split between those interested in educational development and those interested in religious reform. But he soon found another religious movement—Radhasoami—in which one did not have to make a choice. There, spiritual concerns and social progress were not pitted against one another. Eventually, when he created his own Radhasoami colony, Anand Swarup demonstrated how compatible they could be.

The creation of stable residential colonies at Dayalbagh and Soamibagh allowed those two branches to set down roots. The movements' headquarters, such as they were, had followed the residences of the gurus, men whose employment took them first one place and then another. Some in the movement hoped that when they came home to Agra, a single, united community might be created there, but with the collapse of the Central Administrative Council, the two main branches of Radhasoami in Agra entered into an enduring pattern of quiet enmity. The distance in style between the progressive Dayalbagh and the conservative Soamibagh made the narrow road between their two settlements seem like a sea. Ill feeling turned in time to acrimony and resulted in a series of legal actions having to do with the right of the Dayalbagh people to have access to the tomb of Swami Shiv Dayal at Soamibagh.[61]

[60] Biographical information on Anand Swarup may be found in *Souvenir*, pp. 163–65, and in the introduction to *Huzur Sahabji Maharaj—*Sir Anand Sarup—*As Others Saw Him* (Agra: Radhasoami Satsang Sabha, Dayalbagh, 1966), pp. 1–16. His name is sometimes transliterated in Radhasoami writings as Swarup, at other times Sarup. I have followed the convention commonly used in India for transliterating this name; it is also the one adopted by A. P. Mathur in *Radhasoami Faith*, p. 127.

[61] The civil suit, *Radhasoami Satsang Sabha and others v. Shri Amin Adhar Sinha and others*, was decided in 1961, after years of legal intrigue, in favor of the plaintiffs, the Dayalbagh group, which demanded the right of its members to visit and hold services of worship at the tomb of the first master (*Judgement in Civil Suit No.1 of 1943* [*Agra*] (Agra:

From the beginning, Anand Swarup had stated his intent to have a settlement where Radhasoami devotees could take up gainful occupation and be self-supporting and productive.[62] Not all of his devotees moved to Dayalbagh, but those who did provided a core for the spiritual community and gave it definition. The busy colony became a microcosm of what a progressive and prosperous Indian society could achieve and reached its zenith around the time of Anand Swarup's death in 1937.[63] Included in the Dayalbagh industrial complex were the Research Laboratories, which manufactured toilet goods; the Everyday Footwear Factory; a hosiery plant; and, at Amritsar, the Dayalbagh Spinning and Weaving Mills. The community manufactured everything from handkerchiefs and hunting knives to microscopes and toilet soaps, and it created its own banks to handle the investments. The three thousand acres of reclaimed farmland around Dayalbagh were developed into a model of scientific collective agriculture. Several colleges that focused on modern agricultural and industrial techniques were established in and near the colony. The exemplary nature of the undertaking did not go unnoticed by British officials, who visited the colony in a steady stream throughout the 1930s. Through their influence the master was knighted and became Sir Anand Swarup, Kt.

When Anand Swarup died, the momentum he had generated was maintained for a time by his successor, Gurcharandas Mehta, who, like Sawan Singh in the Punjab, was an engineer—Chief of the Public Works Department in the Punjab government. On taking office, Mehta established a five-year industrial program for the Dayalbagh community, and targeted a gross income of ten million rupees annually. In two years he realized this ambitious goal, but by the time India's independence came, the Dayalbagh industrial and agricultural cartel had stagnated, in part because of Mehta's old age. After a lingering illness, he died in 1975, and the

---

Radhasoami Satsang Sabha, Dayalbagh, 1961). Another lawsuit, this one maintaining that certain writings of S. D. Maheshwari published by Soamibagh were slanderous, was brought by the general secretary of Dayalbagh in 1961 and was eventually abandoned in 1982 (S. D. Maheshwari, *Let Them Speak the Truth* [Agra: Radhasoami Satsang, Soamibagh, 1982], pp. 3–4). Yet more legal actions involve a dispute between the Soamibagh and Peepalmandi branches over ownership and rights of access to the original home of Swami Shiv Dayal in the Pannigali district of Agra. This dispute, originating in the early 1980s, has not yet been resolved.

[62] Anand Swarup's reasons for establishing Dayalbagh were given to the Lindsey Commission, an American Christian missionary fact-finding group established in 1931 (quoted in *Souvenir*, p. 200).

[63] *Dayalbagh (Agra): A Brief Description of the Origins, Early History and Development of the Colony and its Institutions* (Agra: Radhasoami Satsang, Dayalbagh, 1984), pp. 26–43.

accession of M. B. Lal to spiritual leadership in 1976 was the occasion for the revival of some of Dayalbagh's earlier enthusiasm.

Critics of Dayalbagh, especially the ones at Soamibagh, said it put worldly aspirations above spiritual ones.[64] And in fact, although Dayalbagh leaders continued to espouse the spiritual teachings of the Radhasoami masters, propagation of the teachings took something of a backseat to economic development. Gurcharandas Mehta, for instance, produced no writings for publication during his lifetime, and when a number of his transcribed comments were published posthumously, they revealed how attentive he was to organizational concerns.[65]

Defenders of Dayalbagh claim that there is a logical connection between spiritual accomplishment and social progress. The key to that connection is the Radhasoami view of science. Rather than fearing science and construing it as the enemy of religion, Radhasoami leaders embraced it and employed the language of science in their spiritual writings. The self was considered to be a laboratory for experiments in higher consciousness, and the proof was provided by experience. According to Brahm Sankar Misra, "There is no conflict between true science and true religion . . . [since] the researchers of the former only confirm and establish all the esoteric and occult principles of the latter."[66] Other Radhasoami teachers, such as Jagat Singh, a chemistry professor, have gone further and argued that Radhasoami is a "science of the soul,"[67] According to another Radhasoami author, his master "extends the scientific method into the areas of moral and spiritual relationships."[68] It was understood, therefore, that such developments as scientific and egalitarian communities were the external signs of internal advancement.

The effects of this way of thinking were to be seen at both Dayalbagh and Beas during the 1930s and 1940s, when they came to serve as twin examplars of the Radhasoami tradition. In the decades following India's independence, however, the emphases of these organizations diverged. While Dayalbagh turned more to developing educational institutions,

[64] S. D. Maheshwari claims that "in trying to increase the wealth of and rehabilitate the material world," Dayalbagh was "acting contrary to the mission of Radhasoami Dayal" (S. D. Maheshwari, *Let Them Speak the Truth*, p. 56; see also pp. 28, 33–34, 37–45, and 51–57.

[65] For instance, he encouraged progress in three things: "Satsang [worship], Charitable societies, and Industries." (Gurcharandas Mehta [Param Guru Huzur Mehtaji Maharaj], *Selected Bachans* [Agra: Radhasoami Satsang Sabha, Dayalbagh, 1984], p. 96.) Radhasoami publications also transliterate his name as Gur Saran Das Mehta.

[66] Brahm Sankar Misra (Maharaj Sahab), *Discourses*, p. v; see also pp. 106 and 119.

[67] Jagat Singh (Maharaj Sardar Bahadur), *Science of the Soul* (Beas: Radhasoami Satsang, Beas, 1972).

[68] John H. Leeming, Jr., Foreword to Sawan Singh, *Philosophy of the Masters*, p. xi.

Beas began spreading its message throughout India and the world, and in the 1960s and 1970s especially, the world seemed ready to respond.

Internationalization: The Global Expansion of Tradition

Foreigners had been attracted to the Radhasoami community's ranks almost from the start: the first was most likely a German Theosophist travelling in India who became an initiate of Rai Saligram in the last decade of the nineteenth century.[69] At about that time an American woman sent her son to India to inquire about visions she had received in her yoga practices; he too found his way to Rai Saligram.[70] Other early followers were British colleagues of Rai Saligram in the postal service and an American lawyer from Philadelphia, who became a resident of Soamibagh in 1913–1914.[71]

Beginning in the 1930s, the records of both the Dayalbagh and the Beas colonies give evidence of a growing number of Westerners coming to settle among them. More than any other Radhasoami masters, however, it has been Sawan Singh's successors who have actively internationalized the faith. One of them, Kirpal Singh, established in 1948 a new organization in Delhi, the Ruhani Satsang (Spiritual Fellowship),[72] and started the practice of going on tours abroad. The number of his foreign initiates increased rapidly in the 1960s and early 1970s. Eventually there were over thirteen thousand comprising some ten percent of the movement's population.[73] At Beas the leadership passed to Jagat Singh, and then in 1951 to Sawan Singh's grandson, Charan Singh, who helped propagate the idea that Radhasoami was a universal faith. He pointed out that the idea of sacred sound is found in many religious traditions, and that various sant concepts are parallel to gnostic philosophy, Taoism, and the *logos* theology of the New Testament. Charan Singh devoted an entire book to the Gospel of St. John, and another to that of St. Matthew, comparing

[69] *Souvenir*, p. 60.

[70] Ibid.

[71] Myron H. Phelps, *Notes of Discourses on Radhasoami Faith Delivered by Babuji Maharaj* (Agra: Radhasoami Satsang, Soamibagh, 1947).

[72] For biographical information about Kirpal Singh, see Russell Perkins's introduction to Kirpal Singh, *The Night is a Jungle and Other Discourses* (Sanbornton, N.H.: Sant Bani Ashram, 1974); and *Portrait of Perfection: A Pictorial Biography of Kirpal Singh*, with text compiled from Kirpal Singh's written and recorded words and introduced by Darshan Singh (Bowling Green, Va. and Delhi: Sawan Kirpal Publications, 1981).

[73] Information on Ruhani Satsang and Sawan-Kirpal Ruhani Mission membership has been supplied in letters to me from J. M. Sethi, secretary, Sawan-Kirpal Ruhani Mission, October 1, 1985; May 7, 1988; May 22, 1988; and November 15, 1988.

4. Sawan Singh and his staff; Jagat Singh is seated at his left and Kirpal Singh is standing behind Jagat Singh.

"the Word made flesh" in the New Testament with *shabd*, the sacred word in Radhasoami.[74]

The medium for many of Charan Singh's writings, and the language into which almost all Radhasoami publications are translated, is English, and it is the medium for the conduct of Beas's and Dayalbagh's organizational affairs. Although the liturgical language in the Agra branches has always been Hindi, and in Beas, Punjabi, the language used to communicate with the outside world has been English, an important choice in internationalizing the faith. At Agra, the preference for English began with the second guru, Rai Saligram; English was the medium in which he and his compeers were intellectually and organizationally most comfortable.[75] The publication program of most branches has expanded enor-

[74] Charan Singh (Maharaj), *St. John, The Great Mystic* (Beas: Radhasoami Satsang, Beas, 1970) and *Light on St. Matthew*.

[75] An example of Rai Saligram's penmanship in English may be seen in a photograph of one of his letters in Shiv Dayal Singh et al., *Holy Epistles*, part 1, p. 36. Photocopies of letters written in English by Misra and Sinha are to be found in the same volume (pp. 153, 155, 220–21, 230–31, 263). At one time the Dayalbagh leaders encouraged their followers to write to the master only in English, according to a notice in their journal, *Prem Pracharak*, Sept 19, 1960, quoted in S. D. Maheshwari, *Truth Unvarnished*, part 1, p. 177.

mously in recent years. Almost all volumes are available in at least one of India's regional languages, but most are also available in English and in a great variety of other international languages as well. At the Ruhani Satsang, for example, the masters' writings have been translated into forty-two languages, including Czech, Hebrew, Swahili, and Indonesian.

The Radhasoami organization has arranged that those who hear its message abroad need not come to India to be initiated into its mysteries. The concept that makes this concession possible is proxy initiation, which seems to have been established as a policy of the Beas branch as early as 1911. In that year Dr. H. M. Brock, a dentist from Port Angeles, Washington, asked for initiation for himself and Mrs. Brock, and a Punjabi immigrant who was a Radhasoami initiate was given the power to initiate them on the guru's behalf.[76] After that the American expansion began. Since the actual initiation takes place in the initiate's own country, where the channel of spiritual authority flows through the master's representatives, the status of some of those local Radhasoami leaders is considerable.

The offices at Beas have become the headquarters of an international organization that boasts more than three hundred centers in India and over two hundred others elsewhere in the world. There are perhaps twenty to thirty thousand active members outside India, and in recent years the rate of new initiations abroad has been approximately a thousand per year, with the largest numbers occurring in the United Kingdom, South Africa, and the United States.[77] The percentage of their financial contribution is even greater than their proportion of the community's membership.[78] More important still is their symbolic contribution. They accord to the movement the prestige of reversing the direction of missionary conquest, and they confirm with their physical presence the conceptual claim that Radhasoami transcends the cultural limitations suggested by its home on Indian soil.

Present-day leaders assure me that today letters written in Hindi and the major regional languages are welcome (Interview with G. D. Sahgal, president, Satsang Sabha, Radhasoami Satsang, Dayalbagh, August 6, 1985).

[76] The Brocks were initiated by Kehr Singh Sasmas, an initiate of Sawan Singh's who emigrated from India in 1904, eventually settling in Oregon and the state of Washington. His own report of his early years in the United States and his attempts to spread the Radhasoami faith is printed as "The Dawn of Spirituality in the West," trans. and intro. Bhadra Sena, *Sat Sandesh* (the English-language magazine of Sawan Kirpal Ashram), April 1977, pp. 23–31. See also Sawan Singh, *The Dawn of Light: Excerpts from Letters, 1911 to 1934* (Beas: Radhasoami Satsang, Beas, 1985).

[77] I have drawn my statistics from the Annual Reports of the Radhasoami Satsang, Beas, 1975–1984.

[78] Although only 3 percent of the membership at Beas is foreign, 17 percent of the income in recent years has come from foreign sources (*Radhasoami Satsang, Beas: Annual Report*, 1983–1984).

The newest masters in the lineage established by Jaimal Singh seem to confirm the internationalizing thrust of the Radhasoami tradition. Gurinder Singh, who succeeded his uncle, Charan Singh, at Beas in 1990, lived much of his adult life in Spain; and Rajinder Singh, who in 1989 succeeded his father, Darshan Singh (the son of Kirpal Singh), as master of the Sawan-Kirpal Ashram in Delhi, worked for many years in a corporation in the United States. Thus the tradition is moving towards the twenty-first century as a multicultural community, one whose leaders have international experience and a global mission.

The Shape of the Tradition

As one looks at the way in which the Radhasoami tradition has developed, one sees a surprisingly familiar pattern. If one sets the Radhasoami tradition alongside the histories of the great religious traditions of the world, it seems a living exhibit of what was encountered by early Christians, Buddhists, Muslims, and Sikhs. These traditions also began with religious movements that were much more modest than what they were later to become; and like members of Radhasoami, they managed to form coherent traditions only after periods of confusion that followed the deaths of the figures around whom they initially gathered. In each case, those who remembered and revered the person regarded as founder were welded into a cohesive community by the strong hands of the founder's successors, and at the same time definite doctrines were distilled out of an initial mélange of teachings. The integrity of these communities and their doctrines persisted in the face of potentially disruptive ideas that arose from each new generation, but at the same time the movements responded to those new stimuli and adapted to them, thus ensuring their survival over the years. Ultimately there came a point, with Radhasoami as with the others, when the movement took wings and provided for persons of diverse cultural backgrounds a sense of universal belonging—a common world of perception that was scarcely less real than what the first circle of disciples had experienced. Thus in the course of time the Radhasoami tradition, like its better-known cousins, provided for its adherents an internally consistent world that depends only marginally on other, earlier traditions. The modern elements of that world reflect both the original impetus of the founding community and the progressive effects of the changes through which that community has lived in its 130-year-old history.

Part II

THE RADHASOAMI WORLD

Three

Someone to Trust

IT IS SAID that for years Jaimal Singh used to "roam about in search of sages" before he met Swami Shiv Dayal.[1] "How many nights had he spent tossing and praying," one of his biographers exclaimed, "wondering if God would ever grant his wishes!" And when he finally did, Jaimal Singh's eyes "brimmed with tears and silently overflowed."[2] Similar stories have been told by countless numbers of Radhasoami devotees. The biographers of Anand Swarup, for instance, claim that long before he began to serve as master of the Dayalbagh community he became frustrated with the limited knowledge of his academic mentors and "grew

5. Sawan Singh bestowing darshan through the window of a railway car.

[1] Sawan Singh, Introduction to Jaimal Singh, *Spiritual Letters*, p. 5.

[2] Kirpal Singh, *A Great Saint*, p. 38. The story of Jaimal Singh's spiritual search begins on p. 24.

desperate" trying to find a spiritual preceptor.[3] He later recalled how his spiritual quest culminated in 1901:

> I was young and simply crazy to find the truth. I asked the trees, the grass, and the sky to enlighten me if truth existed. I sobbed my heart out like a child, with head bent low, begging for light. Finally I could stand the strain no longer. One day I resolved to give up eating and starve to death, unless and until the divine power saw fit to grant me some illumination. I could no longer even work. The next night I had a vivid dream, wherein a master appeared to me and revealed himself. . . . How can I praise my extreme good luck![4]

This master was Brahm Sankar Misra, one of the successors to Rai Saligram, and on seeing his photograph later that year, Swarup recognized him from having seen his face that night in his dream.

Stories such as this underscore the importance of finding a spiritual master who will provide an anchor to what is, in the Radhasoami view, a deeper reality than that revealed through philosophy or science. "The master is absolutely necessary," Anand Swarup insists.[5] "Without a master," another spiritual authority explains, "we are in utter darkness."[6] To understand why a spiritual master is so central to the Radhasoami perception of reality, and how such a person could be so appealing to well-educated modern devotees, we have to begin where many who have joined the community began: with the feeling of uncertainty that they once had about what is ultimately true and real in the world. The hope of overcoming this state of perplexity is the reason that many have turned to religion as "seekers," as those who first come to the Radhasoami community are called.

To those within the community, the perplexity of the newcomers is expected, for a degree of uncertainty is a prerequisite to faith. The limitations of ordinary knowledge are described in some detail in Radhasoami teachings, and the cause of this distortion is kal, personified as Kal, the evil force who embodies both meanings of the term—time and death—and reigns over the whole sphere of temporal understanding, or rather, misunderstanding.[7] From the Radhasoami perspective, we are

[3] Paul Brunton, *A Search in Secret India* (New York: E. P. Dutton and Co., 1935), quoted in *Souvenir*, p. 167.

[4] Brunton, *Search*, quoted in *Souvenir*, p. 167.

[5] Anand Swarup, quoted in *Souvenir*, p. 167.

[6] Kirpal Singh, *Godman: Finding a Spiritual Master* (New Delhi:Ruhani Satsang, 1967), p. 59.

[7] The notion of kal as a person, an evil ruler over the transitory world, appears throughout Radhasoami literature. See, for example, Shiv Dayal Singh, *Sar Bachan: Prose*, trans. Sewa Singh, p. 61, and the glossary definition of *kal*, p. 185. *Sar Bachan: Poetry*, trans. S. D. Maheshwari, part 2, pp. 17–46, includes an extensive discussion of the difference between "Kal Mat and [its opposite] Dayal Mat."

mired in Kal's confusion from birth, and if sensitive people develop a feeling of deep insecurity about ordinary reality, it should come as no surprise. The awareness of that confusion is the first step in the right direction.

But the seekers' path will lead down a blind alley if they continue to trust their rational powers. Indeed, rationality is part of the problem, for the mental processes are under the sway of Kal: the mind is sufficient for ordinary problems, but it cannot fathom the deeper truths of life. It is at this point of despair that Radhasoami offers the seeker what Erik Erikson describes as "basic trust," a sense of self-assurance that comes from a solid relationship with another person. In Erikson's understanding of an individual's psychological development, this bedrock of trust is established in a child's relationship with his or her parents; it is "the first component of a healthy personality."[8] When early bonds of trust are lost or outgrown, they must be supplanted by something else that is trustworthy. "Religion, through the centuries" has provided precisely this; it has "served to restore a sense of trust."[9] Radhasoami restores this trust not only in the way that religion usually does—through scriptural authority and conceptual certainty—but the same way a child learns to trust: through a human form, a spiritual master.

Masters in Modern Times

Radhasoami masters embody the truth they preach; they are both "the way and the truth," as Jesus Christ is said to have described himself (John 14:6). This comment, complete with its allusion to Christ, is one that is frequently made in Radhasoami circles, especially among Western followers. One American devotee said that being near the master was "like being with Jesus in biblical times."[10] Roland deVries, a leading representative of the Beas branch in the United States, regards the Radhasoami master as essentially the same as Christ, except that Jesus has been "caught in a slot of history and frozen there," whereas in Radhasoami the Christ spirit continues to be "a universal spiritual principle" incarnate in each generation.[11]

[8] Erik Erikson, *Identity and the Life Cycle* (New York: Norton, 1980), p. 55.

[9] Ibid., p. 65.

[10] Interview with a devotee at Beas, November 10, 1980. See also the comparisons made between Christ and the Radhasoami masters by Johnson, *With a Great Master in India*, p. 104; Katherine Wason, *The Living Master* (Beas: Radhasoami Satsang, Beas, 1966), p. 257; and Sir Colin Garbett, *The Ringing Radiance* (Beas: Radhasoami Satsang, Beas, 1968), *passim*.

[11] Interview with Roland deVries, Nevada City, California, January 17, 1986.

In meeting present-day Radhasoami masters, however, few outsiders have reported seeing anything Christlike about them. According to Rai Saligram, there is a reason for this: such masters manifest themselves in an unpretentious way to prevent the uninitiated from being overcome by the extraordinary power of their real presence.[12] An American devotee who visited Beas early in this century said that "one of the signs of true greatness is that they do not awe you with their greatness, towering above you, but they inspire in you a subtle peace of mind and soul."[13] In a similar vein, a contemporary devotee wrote these words after having sat beside her master at Beas: "Quietly and modestly He sat there, as would any ordinary man, yet the deliverance of hundreds of thousands of souls rested on His shoulders. Only three feet away from me sat the Living Lord. Ah, it was incomprehensible, this mystery of mysteries."[14]

The master whose presence she could scarcely comprehend was Charan Singh, who, like other Radhasoami masters, is known within his own community not by his given name but by a spiritual honorific, in his case, Maharaj-ji (great respected ruler). Such names not only indicate respect but signal that the persons who become masters have adopted new identities. Rai Saligram, for instance, is Huzur Maharaj (honorable great ruler), and Jaimal Singh is Baba Ji Maharaj (respected elder great ruler). (The titles of each of the masters are listed in Appendix A.) Honorific names are established through popular usage, as one might use a nickname for a familiar and beloved friend.

Charan Singh projected a friendly appearance indeed. When one met him, he seemed very much the gentleman farmer and lawyer that he was trained to be before his religious community prevailed upon him to follow in his grandfather's footsteps and become the spiritual leader of the Radhasoami branch at Beas, a role he performed for almost forty years until his death in 1990.[15] Charan Singh came from the Grewal subcaste of Jats, the dominant rural community in the Punjab, watched television from

[12] Rai Saligram, *Jugat Prakash Radhasoami*, p. 84. The argument is that although the Divine appears in human form, the believer is allowed to perceive the immortal, formless quality that radiates through it.

[13] Johnson, *With a Great Master*, p. 23.

[14] Wason, *The Living Master*, p. 160.

[15] Radhasoami masters usually regard the mundane biographical material about them as being irrelevant to spiritual growth and discourage such biographies from being printed. Daryai Lal, an associate of the Beas master, Charan Singh, says that his master would "never even permit such a biography to be written" (Wason, *The Living Master*, p. 97). Virtually all that is published about Charan Singh's life before he became master is that he was born on December 12, 1916, in the Punjab town of Moga near the present-day border with Pakistan and was initiated into the Radhasoami path by his grandfather, Sawan Singh, in 1933 (Charan Singh, *Spiritual Heritage* [Beas: Radhasoami Satsang, Beas, 1983], p. 118). In addition, some stories of Charan Singh's childhood are told in Kapur, *Heaven on Earth*.

time to time, and was fond of photography. He was married to an active woman who busied herself with the directorship of the nature-cure clinic at the Beas colony, and his two grown sons are well established in business; one assists his uncle in supervising the substantial family farm, and the other has worked in hotel management in Singapore and Hong Kong.[16] When Charan Singh responded to questions about religion, the answers were given with the firm confidence and good humor of one who is sure in his knowledge and at ease with the role to which he has been assigned. Still, he was said to have been reluctant at first to assume his grandfather's exalted spiritual role.

A similar reticence is attributed to M. B. Lal, who ascended to spiritual leadership after much urging from his fellow residents at the Dayalbagh compound. Lal is a quiet, scholarly widower who was once the chief pre-

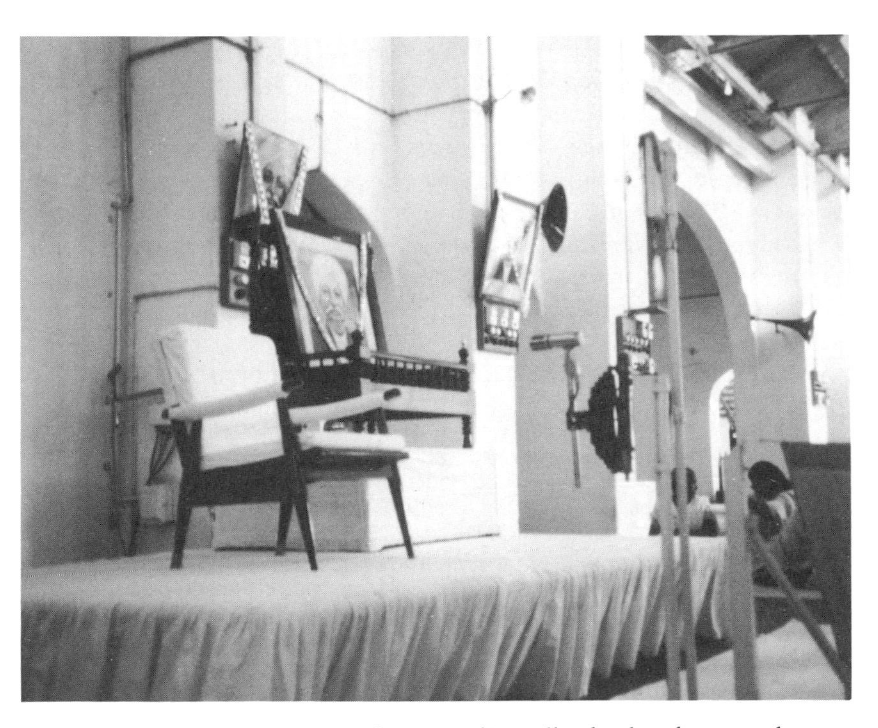

6. Chair of Dr. M. B. Lal, spiritual master of Dayalbagh, placed next to the throne and picture of his predecessor, Gurcharandas Mehta.

[16] Charan Singh's personal income was derived from the family farm near the town of Sirsa, district Hissar, in the state of Haryana adjacent to the Punjab. It was managed by Charan Singh's younger brother, Captain P. S. Grewal (Interview with K. L. Khanna, May 26, 1971).

siding officer of Lucknow University.[17] He is a Kayasth, a merchant-caste Hindu, who lived quietly in retirement at Dayalbagh for some years before being nudged into the colony's leadership in 1975.[18]

Darshan Singh, son of the Ruhani Satsang master, Kirpal Singh, was also reticent about accepting the implications of guruship when he became the new master after his father's death in 1974.[19] A Khatri Sikh, Darshan Singh served as a government official, and his published Urdu verse has won awards. He read one of his own poems at the marriage of a childhood friend, who later became the master at Beas, Charan Singh.[20] Like Charan Singh, he became comfortable in his role as spiritual adviser and ruled effectively until his death in 1989.[21] But although he was willing to take over the reins of leadership during the organizational confusion that followed Kirpal Singh's death, he is said to have been reluctant to be accorded all the honor given his father.[22]

This seemingly universal hesitancy to accept the mantle of guruhood is not merely personal humility. It is almost a matter of spiritual etiquette. Those who are regarded as masters almost invariably deny that the power that works through them is their own. "Pray *through* me, not *to* me," one master urged, claiming that he was only a conduit for his own guru's power.[23] "I know nothing," said another Radhasoami leader, "except what my master wants me to know."[24] Kirpal Singh regards this modesty as one of the true marks of saintliness: "When told they are great, they reply that it is none of their doing; it is the kindness and mercy of their Master."[25]

Writings by Radhasoami teachers are frequently prefaced by praise for

[17] Interviews with M. B. Lal, Dayalbagh, August 9, 1978; December 5, 1980; August 10, 1983; and August 12, 1985. His devotees call him Lal-sahib.

[18] Interview with V. Sadyanarayana, Dayalbagh, August 13, 1985.

[19] Interview with Kate Tillis, October 28, 1980. Others who have been proclaimed the successor to Kirpal Singh include Ajaib Singh and Thakar Singh.

[20] A picture of Darshan Singh reading his poetry at a wedding is to be found in Darshan Singh's published poems, *Talash-e Nur* (The search for light; in Urdu) (New Delhi: Sawan Kirpal Ruhani Mission, 1980; orig. pub. 1965), opposite p. 53. The picture shows Darshan Singh standing beside Sawan Singh; the groom has his back to the camera. The caption explains that Darshan Singh is reciting a poem on the occasion of the marriage of Charan Singh, grandson of his spiritual master, Sant Baba Sawan Singh, at village Pisawa in district Bulandshahar, Uttar Pradesh, November 25, 1944.

[21] Interview with Darshan Singh, Kirpal Ashram, New Delhi, August 16, 1985.

[22] Darshan Singh's willingness to become his father's successor soon after Kirpal Singh's death is expressed in a letter from Darshan Singh to T. S. Khanna, September 26, 1974, reprinted in *Truth Uncovered: Re—Successor to Great Master Kirpal Singh Ji*, privately circulated booklet, n.p.: November, 1974.

[23] Speech given by Thakar Singh in Berkeley, California, January 3, 1981.

[24] Interview with A. P. Mathur, Peepalmandi, Agra, August 12, 1985.

[25] Kirpal Singh, *The Way of the Saints*, p. 139f.

former masters, and pictures of their predecessors may appear as the frontispiece of their books. Behind such modesty is the notion that guruship is conferred from on high and should be assumed almost unwillingly. But it cannot be refused; the person designated must assume the role. For without a living master Radhasoami communities could not exist.[26] Only two branches presently survive without one—Soamibagh and Dhara Sindu Pratap Ashram—and at both places the leaders have declared an interregnum between masters. They await the coming of the next with a certain degree of impatience, and at both places rumors abound that the sacred current has descended into a new master whose identity has been kept secret.

Sant Das Maheshwari, the controversial head of the publications office at Soamibagh, was said to have been one of these hidden gurus. Maheshwari maintained that he was only an author and a modest disciple of the last master at Soamibagh, Madhav Prasad Sinha, but with his air of knowledge and authority it is not surprising that some would revere him as a master, a fact that was revealed only after his death in 1983.[27] Maheshwari's last volume, published posthumously, is prefaced by the comment that "inner revelations mentioned in the letters [published in the book] . . . show what Sant Das Ji was,"[28] and that Maheshwari's writings "conclusively establish the *continued presence of the Supreme Current even today*."[29] In 1990, Maheshwari's followers proclaimed that his son had succeeded him, and the interregnum was over.

At another branch of Radhasoami—Manavta Mandir in Hoshiarpur, Punjab—the idea of a living master is somewhat discredited, for the master of that branch, Faqir Chand, has claimed that the True Guru cannot be known. Having a vision of a guru within can be deceptive, he explained, and persons who play the role of guru are useful only as teachers and guides; they are not manifestations of the Ultimate. But even as Faqir excoriated the pretensions of guruship, his earnest devotees would kneel before him, faithfully preserving his words.[30] After his death in 1981,

[26] Kirpal Singh, *Godman*, p. 59. See also Anand Swarup, "The Necessity of a Living Satguru," in *Yathartha Prakasa*, pp. 88–100.

[27] Visions of Maheshwari as master were experienced by Nirmal Das (Maheshwari's son), Wazir Chand Prabhakar, and P. S. Sharma (Interview with P. S. Sharma, Soamibagh, August 13, 1985).

[28] Preface to S. D. Maheshwari, *R.S. Correspondence*, vol. 6, (Agra: Radhasoami Satsang, Soamibagh, 1985). The authorship of the preface is unattributed, but it was probably written by Nirmal Das Maheshwari, S. D. Maheshwari's son.

[29] Ibid. (Italics in the original.)

[30] Interview with Faqir Chand, Hoshiarpur, August 19, 1978. My interview, and one conducted by David Lane, my graduate assistant at the time, have without our permission been published as a booklet: Faqir Chand, *The Master Speaks to the Foreigners: Seekers from Abroad*, ed. B. R. Kamal (Hoshiarpur: Faqir Library Charitable Trust, n.d. [c. 1979]). David

transcriptions of these tape recordings were published as sacred texts. His successor, Ishwar Chandra Sharma, a scholar of Indian philosophy who has taught in the United States, is more willing to acknowledge his own guruship.[31]

Like Faqir Chand, other Radhasoami masters have also insisted that the True Guru is beyond human imagination. The human form is just an outer symbol or manifestation of something that is to some degree present within each person. When M. B. Lal finally acceded to the guruship at Dayalbagh, he wondered at the miraculousness of the force he felt must be working through him.[32] But even though the external, human guru may not represent the guru's true nature, it is still essential, for according to Radhasoami teachings souls mired in human existence need another human to extract them from it. One guru in human history is not enough; a living chain of authority must be formed to enable the power of salvation to continue.

That line of authority sometimes runs through the previous master's own family. Charan Singh, who was the grandson of Sawan Singh, was succeeded by his nephew, Gurinder Singh. Darshan Singh, son of Kirpal Singh, was succeeded by his son Rajinder. Another master, A. P. Mathur at Agra, is the great-great-grandson of Rai Saligram. Mathur, a forceful administrator and teacher, has served as head of the history department at Agra College and is vice chancellor of Agra University.[33] Yet ultimately the academic achievements and family connections of a master are beside the point; what counts is the spiritual authority that is verified by those who are mastered by him.

Lane has characterized Faqir Chand's refusal to acknowledge his guruship as an "unknowing hierophany" in "The Hierarchical Structure of Religious Visions," *Journal of Transpersonal Psychology* 15, no. 1 (1983): 51–60. Lane has described him as a "reluctant guru" in "The Reluctant Guru: The Life and Work of Baba Faqir Chand," *The Laughing Man*, vol. 3, no. 1, pp. 70–77. See also his discussion of Faqir Chand in "The Enchanted Land, Part I," *Fate*, October 1984; and Daniel Gold's discussion of Faqir Chand as "the Holy Man who would not be a guru" in *The Lord as Guru*, p. 165.

[31] I. C. Sharma is the author of *Cayce, Karma and Reincarnation* (New York: Harper and Row, 1975); *Ethical Philosophies of India*, ed. and rev. by Stanley M. Daugert (London: Allen and Unwin, 1965; reprint. Harper and Row, 1970); and *India's Democracy and the Communist Challenge* (Lincoln, Nebr: Johnson Publishing Co., 1967). He is listed as a professor of philosophy in Christopher Newport College, Newport News, Virginia, in the *1971 National Faculty Directory* (Detroit: Gale Research Co., 1971), vol. 2, p. 1639; he also taught in Cleveland.

[32] Interview with M. B. Lal, August 13, 1985.

[33] Interviews with Agam Prasad Mathur, Peepalmandi, Agra, August 8, 1978; December 6, 1980; August 10, 1983; August 13, 1985. A number of Mathur's spiritual writings have been published in Hindi, and his Ph.D. dissertation for Agra University has appeared in English as *Radhasoami Faith: A Historical Study*.

The Idea of a Spiritual Master

Charan Singh once suggested that a Radhasoami master could be understood as "a favorite teacher . . . someone you have learned more from than the subject itself."[34] The term *guru* is indeed often aptly translated as "teacher." If that word suggests a European or American model of education, however, it is inadequate, for no such thing exists in traditional India, where there are many knowledges and many truths. The good teacher is not only one who knows true things but one who knows how to discriminate one truth from another. Rather than first choosing a subject and then looking for a teacher who can teach it, as one might in the West, someone searching for knowledge in the time-honored Indian method must first establish a relationship with a teacher worthy of trust and then find out what that teacher has to teach.

The word *guru* literally means "heavy," and suggests someone burgeoning with knowledge, a spiritual heavyweight. It is less a title than a term of respect that is thrust upon one person by others. The term arises out of a relationship, and the designation for the other half of the bond—*chela* (disciple)—is often used together with it to describe a linkage of learning and devotion. Perhaps the happiest solution to the problem of translation is the one in Radhasoami circles: to call a guru "master." This suggests mastery over a skill or a body of knowledge, while at the same time connoting a position of authority with a distinctly personal component. The Radhasoami use of the term, however, implies even more: a supreme mastery of the world. In Radhasoami the master is "Godman."[35] As the intermediary between the highest planes of divine consciousness and our own worldly level, he can be viewed both as a manifestation of God and as a human being endowed with divine powers.

The Radhasoami notion of the guru as God-man is unusual, even in India, but not beyond the Indian imagination. The Indian notion of *avatar*—the physical manifestation of God—comes close to the Radhasoami idea, but the term is seldom used in Radhasoami circles, for in the Hindu frame of reference it applies only to the mythical incarnations of gods such as Vishnu, Krishna, and Ram. Even so, some followers worship the Radhasoami masters just as Hindus worship the images of gods in temples. There are reports that devotees of Swami Shiv Dayal would stand in front of him, slowly waving a lamp as one would in a temple.[36] Such

[34] Interview with Charan Singh, Beas, November 11, 1980. The Sanskrit *guruh* is "heaviness"; in Radhasoami circles the syllable *gu* is interpreted as "darkness," and *ru* as "dispeller," so the term is also defined as "the light in the darkness" (Charan Singh, answer given to a question posed by a devotee, Beas, December 5, 1986).

[35] Kirpal Singh, *Godman*, p. 69.

[36] *Souvenir*, p. 55.

devotion sometimes took even more extreme forms. A letter from Rai Saligram to Swami Shiv Dayal reports that he received in the mail dust from the Swami's feet so that he might ingest it and thereby worship him.[37] Rai Saligram was similarly revered by his own disciples, some of whom kept bits of his hair and fingernails as relics and regarded even the touch of his clothing as imparting spiritual power.[38] Water that he had used for gargling was said to cure wounds and salve sore eyes.[39] A missionary scholar early in this century observed that devotees would drink the water that had been used to wash the master's feet.[40] His study went on to say that after the master's death his ashes were mixed with water and consumed, and that during his life devotees would eat "certain products of his body."[41]

Often the least desirable elements of the guru's body are singled out as being of spiritual value: hair and nail clippings, for example, and anything associated with the feet.[42] The most common representation of a departed master is his sandals, often placed prominently on the throne where he once sat. By the same token the feet of living masters also merit special attention; songs celebrate their beauty and saving power. A striking passage in Swami Shiv Dayal's biography describes how two women devotees would sit beside him and adoringly stroke his feet and suck his toes.[43] The logic of this foot-worship—common throughout the Hindu and Buddhist world—is straightforward: the lowest level of an exalted figure, such as a deity, is the point at which the less exalted can make contact. For humans, then, as L. A. Babb points out, the most significant parts of a divine figure are the feet, fingernails, and on occasion even the spittle or urine.[44] Babb observes that in the interaction between master and disciple, the energy that flows downward and out of the master is

[37] Maheshwari, *Biography of Huzur Maharaj*, p. 101.

[38] Ibid., p. 194.

[39] Ibid.

[40] Hervey DeWitt Griswold, *Insights into Modern Hinduism*, p. 139.

[41] Ibid.

[42] Madhav Prasad Sinha, "Questions and Answers," in Shiv Dayal Singh et al., *Holy Epistles*, p. 472. In Rai Saligram's letters to Swami Shiv Dayal, he requests that *charanamrit* and *prasad* be sent to him (ibid., p. 101). *Charanamrit*, "the nectar of feet," in this context appears to be water in which the Swami had bathed his feet or perhaps his whole body (see also *ibid.*, p. 194, and Griswold, *Insights*, p. 139). It is less clear what *prasad* (sacred food) refers to, but presumably it would be a more solid substance.

[43] Pratap Singh Seth, *Biography of Soamiji Maharaj*, p. 117, and S. D. Maheshwari, *Bhaktmal of the Radhasoami Faith*, pp. 50–53.

[44] Lawrence A. Babb makes much of the role of the feet in his analysis of the fluid interaction between disciple and Radhasoami master in his article, "The Physiology of Redemption," *History of Religions* 22, no. 4 (May 1983): 294–95; and in his book, *Redemptive Encounters: Three Styles in the Hindu Tradition* (Berkeley: University of California Press, 1987).

often regarded as energy of the purest form.[45] Ingesting or being in close contact with that energy, then, gives one access to salvific power. In present-day Radhasoami communities this language of physical veneration is understood in the symbolic sense; very few traces of the literal practices remain, and those only in Soamibagh. There S. D. Maheshwari has kept a shelf full of strange bottles labeled as fingernails, hair, and other relics of the original masters. In the other Radhasoami communities one only finds literary references to the "master's gracious feet," yet the wonder that such an exalted being should be present at the lowly level of humanity persists.

This is the central paradox of Radhasoami theology—that the Divine can be present in human form. The master's physical features are for that reason important; as it is sometimes put, his "astral form is exactly like [his] physical form," only "much more beautiful, luminous and magnetic."[46] Ordinarily, then, before one beholds the cosmic image of the guru, one must first be aware of and concentrate upon the human. The physical figure of the master stands at the juncture between two realities, the cosmic and the mundane, and is able to provide access from one to the other. No wonder, then, that the master's physical presence is regarded as a "source of immense benefit" for the spiritual progress of the devoted.[47]

In most Radhasoami interpretations masters are not thought to be born as superhuman beings, but to receive that state of grace at some point in their lives. This means they have reached one of the highest planes of spiritual consciousness. Terms for Indian holy men are applied to those who have achieved specific levels: a *yogi*, for example, is someone who has reached only the first level; a *yogeshwar* has reached the next; a *sadh* has ascended to the one after that; and a *sant* has gained access to the highest regions.[48] A guru is therefore a sant, but of a special kind: like the *bodhisattva* in Buddhism, he is thought to be an ethereal being who resides on our mundane plane in order to help others escape their plight.[49] Among sants, a further distinction is made. Someone who has attained the absolutely highest stage is a *param sant satguru* (most holy true guru) or *swateh sant guru* (self-revealed holy guru), and has been born into the highest states of consciousness rather than acquiring them during his lifetime. If such consciousness is acquired, the term Radhasoami teachings

[45] Babb, "The Physiology of Redemption," p. 310.

[46] Kirpal Singh, *Godman*, p. 93.

[47] Misra, *Discourses*, p. 101.

[48] Ibid., pp. 82–83.

[49] Russell Perkins, in his notes to *The Ocean of Love: The Anurag Sagar of Kabir*, compares the three terms for master in the Radhasoami tradition—*satguru*, *gurudev*, and *guru*—to the three bodies of the Buddha.

apply to those on the path to mastership is *gurmukh* (the mouth of, or face towards, the guru).[50]

Any mention of distinctions relating to types of gurus is a delicate subject. In general, the two major branches of Radhasoami regard their spiritual masters as having gone through the gurmukh stage, but there is a difference of opinion when it comes to the status of Swami Dayal and Rai Saligram. The Agra view, that the Swami was a special event in human history, makes him a param sant, one who required no previous guru to instruct him.[51] The Peepalmandi and Soamibagh branches (but not Dayalbagh) maintain this was true of Saligram as well.[52] Agra's incarnational theory posits that the divine current rises and ebbs.[53] When it is present, it exists only in one person, the satguru of that generation; when it is not, the current has temporarily withdrawn. According to the Beas teachings only a few param sants have appeared in world history—Kabir and Swami Shiv Dayal, for example.[54] But there are many gurmukhs. At least one must be present in the world at all times, and there may be several: "There may be many Masters living in different parts of the world."[55] Beas even accepts that Rai Saligram was an authentic gurmukh, though it does not believe that his lineage has continued.[56] The differences between the Beas and Agra points of view have surfaced in disputes about Swami Dayal's writings. Beas claims that one section of the Agra versions of *Sar Bachan: Prose* has been altered to exclude reference to previous sants. Agra leaders, in turn, claim that Beas has "mutilated" the original.[57]

The Flow of Succession

The first time that the *nij dhar*, the divine current, was thought to have withdrawn and created a vacuum of spiritual presence was after the death of Rai Saligram. One of Saligram's chief disciples advocated patience in a

[50] See Kirpal Singh, *Godman*, pp. 15–16; and Wason, *The Living Master*, pp. 162–63.

[51] Misra, *Discourses*, p. 117.

[52] Interview with A. P. Mathur, Peepalmandi, December 6, 1980; Maheshwari, *Radhasoami Faith*, p. 34.

[53] Brahm Sankar Misra, *A Solace to Satsangis*, 2d. ed. (Agra: Radhasoami Satsang, Soamibagh, 1952), pp. 12–13.

[54] But even a "born saint," a param sant, must have a guru, according to Beas teachings (Charan Singh, quoted in Wason, *The Living Master*, p. 162).

[55] Charan Singh, quoted in Wason, *The Living Master*, p. 163. See also Sawan Singh, *Philosophy of the Masters*, abr. ed., p. 223; and Stanley White, *Liberation of the Soul*, 3d ed. rev. (Beas: Radhasoami Satsang, Beas, 1975), p. 67.

[56] L. R. Puri, *Radha Swami Teachings*, pp. 126–27.

[57] S. D. Maheshwari, "Correspondence Exchanged Between the Secretary, Soamibagh, Agra (India) and a Follower of the Beas Group, Mr. Harvey H. Myers, California, U.S.A.," in Shiv Dayal Singh et al., *Holy Epistles*, part 1, p. 407.

letter written at the time to his grieving colleagues. "I know nothing," he explained, "about the rumour relating to the declaration of a Sant Satguru in the end of this or beginning of next year. But I do not suppose He will declare Himself in a formal way on some day appointed for the purpose. I believe his manifestation will be gradual."[58]

The author of this letter, which was later published as *A Solace to Satsangis*, turned out to be prophetic, for it was Brahm Sankar Misra, and it was he who was later declared to be Saligram's successor. A short interregnum often occurs after a master's death, but when the hiatus in spiritual leadership is longer, it is usually explained in one of two ways: the spiritual leader may be present, but hidden[59] or the nij dhar has withdrawn from the earthly plane altogether. If this happens, says Brahm Sankar Misra, the divine sound current continues to reverberate in this earthly plane, not only for the benefit of devotees who want to be in contact with it through their meditation practices, but for the world, for without it, "the whole creation would collapse."[60]

Agra teaching is less clear about how the transfer of power takes place when the nij dhar becomes manifest. Descriptions of guru succession sometimes sound like the Tibetan conception of how spiritual power is transferred from one Dalai Lama to another: it makes an immediate leap. When Agam Prasad Mathur received the power of spiritual authority from his grandfather, Kunwar-ji, for instance, the transfer was said to have begun even before the latter's death. According to one of Mathur's chief disciples, shortly before Kunwar-ji died Mathur lay down beside him with their bodies touching head to toe, "so that the *dhar* could enter Dadaji [Mathur] through every portal—all nine openings of the body."[61] It was only after that, the disciple explained, that he and others began having internal experiences of Mathur's spiritual presence. At Dayalbagh, a somewhat similar story is told of M. B. Lal's receipt of the nij dhar. In his case, an elder member of the community explained, the dhar lept into the body of Lal a few hours before the death of Gurcharandas Mehta. This was experienced by Lal as "the opening of the curtain to reality; all nine doors opened, and the old personality disappeared."[62] For this reason, the elder explained, "Lal as we knew him before has disappeared. We now see only Mehta in him."[63]

There is no satisfactory explanation of what happens to someone's old

[58] Misra, *A Solace to Satsangis*, p. 37.

[59] This is the theory supported by followers of Maheshwari in Soamibagh. The "hidden guru" theory was suggested by Maheshwari himself. See, for instance, his comments in S. D. Maheshwari, *Truth Unvarnished*, part 2, pp. 184–95.

[60] Misra, *A Solace to Satsangis*, p. 26.

[61] Interview with Brajendra Singh, private secretary to A. P. Mathur, Peepalmandi, Agra, August 12, 1985.

[62] Interview with V. Sadyanarayana, Dayalbagh, August 13, 1985.

[63] Ibid.

personality when he becomes the master, however. Ordinarily the masters are reluctant to describe their own experiences of the transition. M. B. Lal, for instance, told me there was nothing to describe, and Charan Singh explained that the matter was too personal to discuss.[64] Some have reasoned that after becoming a guru the previous being is for all practical purposes dead; the shell of the body has been occupied by the eternal Spirit.[65] Others insist that the previous soul and personality of the new master persist even after the transition. According to one of the Beas leaders, even though "the Saint merges his being in God," his identity does not disappear, for "*his distinct existence as a soul also remains*."[66] Even so, Beas devotees can continue to meditate on the form of the old guru even after his death, a practice that is discouraged in the Agra branches.[67]

Since the new masters usually do not reveal their anointment immediately, an old master's death is the occasion for what is sometimes a massive search to find where—in whose body—the supreme force has been energized. In all branches of Radhasoami there is agreement on who makes the real decision regarding succession: the Supreme Reality, through the *mauj*, or will, of the divine master. Locating where the mauj has newly assigned the spiritual force is what a search is about, and the instrument by which that discernment is made is the internal experience of the members themselves. In Dayalbagh, a meeting is convened after the death of the old master, not for purposes of an election but for a public airing of such experiences. At the conclusion of the meeting, ideally, one person will be proclaimed the successor. At Beas, the rules of the organization provide for the election of a caretaker of the secular aspects of administration, but the true spiritual successor is to be named in the previous master's will and manifested in the spiritual inspiration of the group.[68]

[64] Interview with M. B. Lal, August 12, 1985; interview with Charan Singh, August 11, 1979.

[65] Misra, *A Solace to Satsangis*, p. 13 and *Discourses*, p. 117.

[66] L. R. Puri, *Radha Swami Teachings*, p. 124; italics in the original.

[67] The Agra view is that the spiritual efficacy of the living master is greater than that of a master who has departed this life. The power of the old master is felt to withdraw to the higher reaches and be unobtainable after his death, so it is important to focus on the figure of the new master. The spiritual content of the new master, however, is the same as the old one. (Misra, *A Solace to Satsangis*, p. 13.)

[68] *Constitution of Radhasoami Satsang Sabha, Dayalbagh*, n.p. and "Rules and Regulations," reprinted in *Radha Soami Satsang, Beas: Origin and Growth* (Beas: Radhasoami Satsang, Beas, n.d.), pp. 38–39. L. A. Babb makes a distinction between two ways of validating a new master: through "prior designation" and "present recognition" (Babb, *Redemptive Encounters*, p. 83). Babb suggests that the Soamibagh branch observes the latter method, whereas the Dayalbagh and Beas branches lean toward the former (ibid., p. 85). The Dayalbagh and Beas leaders would probably not accept Babb's conclusions, how-

One indication of the new master comes during meditation, when the devotee sees a new master in place of the old one. The most dramatic revelations, however, have been reported in dreams, and at moments during the day when an ephemeral but recognizable figure suddenly appears to the mind's eye.[69] Some claim that the physical appearance of the true master is always distinctive. According to S. D. Maheshwari, one can "always recognize Him by His forehead and eyes, which the counterfeit gurus would never be able to imitate."[70] Kirpal Singh claims that a devotee is able to experience the sensory current "withdrawing upwards" when in a master's presence, and that the master always has three vertical veins on his forehead.[71] Other members of Kirpal Singh's fellowship have insisted that a distinctive mole will be found on his cheek as well.[72] According to Brahm Sankar Misra the face of the new master will be similar to the old one;[73] others focus on the similarities of the eyes.[74] Some Radhasoami devotees have claimed to see the actual face of the old master transposed onto the new one at the time of an old master's death.[75] This means, of course, that those with the closest physical resemblance to the old master are the most apt to be seen as successors, a tendency that favors members of the guru's own family. Yet a family succession is controversial, for it implies one of two notions that Radhasoami theology will not allow: the possibility of a spiritual heredity or the idea that masters are chosen for other than spiritual reasons.[76]

The Crises of Succession

Several of the more difficult cases of succession illustrate the complexity of the problem. One of these followed the death of Brahm Sankar Misra, the third master at Agra, in 1907. The community was already badly divided at that time, and Misra had failed to clearly indicate who his successor would be. Initially there seemed to be none at all. Some said that the supreme current had withdrawn to heavenly regions and would not

---

ever, since despite their organizational methods, their means of selecting a new master are also grounded in the "present recognition" of a master in the members' spiritual life.

[69] This information is based on my interviews with members of the Beas, Delhi, Soamibagh and Dayalbagh colonies.

[70] Maheshwari, *Truth Unvarnished*, part 1, p. 8.

[71] Kirpal Singh, *Way of the Saints*, pp. 142–43.

[72] Interview with Kate Tillis, Landaur, October 24, 1980. Some have insisted that the mole be found specifically on the left cheek.

[73] Misra, *A Solace to Satsangis*, p. 20.

[74] Kirpal Singh, *Way of the Saints*, p. 142.

[75] Interview with Kate Tillis, Landaur, October 24, 1980.

[76] See Maheshwari, *A Thesis on a Thesis*.

return for hundreds of years; others claimed that Misra himself had prophesied a thirty-year interregnum; still others announced that the current had found its home on another plane in the cosmos and was ruling from there.[77] Nonetheless there was sufficient hope that the current was still pulsing on earth that the leaders of the community launched a concerted effort to find it. A process that contemporaries described as "hideous canvassing" was initiated, but no clear candidate emerged.[78]

One member of Misra's family might easily have stepped into the spiritual vacuum had there not been a problem: she was a woman. Maheshwari Devi, Misra's sister, had helped him organize and lead both the Allahabad and Benares centers of the faith, especially in the years of illness preceding his death. The theory of guruship does not necessarily prohibit women from assuming that role, but the issue is unsettled. Some say Brahm Sankar Misra himself said that "a female cannot attain the status of a Saint."[79] Leaders at Soamibagh who favored Maheshwari Devi's accession, however, claimed that Misra prophesied a month before his departure that his successor would be female.[80] They also accused the opposing group at Dayalbagh of doctoring its English versions of the *Sar Bachan: Poetry* by deliberately translating into masculine terminology Hindi terms for the divine whose gender is actually unspecified.[81]

Some of Maheshwari Devi's contemporaries regarded her as an acceptable successor, others did not; and still others regarded her as a sort of quasi-guru whose power was shared with her brother's chief disciple, Madhav Prasad Sinha.[82] Her status remained ambiguous, in part because she stayed in purdah and was concealed from any contact with men. As a result, many of the day-to-day tasks of administering the community were left in Sinha's hands, a role he had also performed for Misra, who had been his friend since childhood. Madhav Prasad Sinha was also the grandson of Swami Shiv Dayal's sister, but even with all these credentials he was not immediately proclaimed a master. For one thing, Sinha himself seemed at first uncertain about where the dhar had gone, and for another, there was a third contender for Misra's mantle: Kamta Prasad Sinha (no relation to Madhav Prasad), a lawyer who was leader of the Ghazipur branch of the fellowship. Rumors had begun to circulate about Kamta

[77] *Souvenir*, p. 124.

[78] *Constitutional Principles Underlying the Inauguration of the System of Administration of the Radhasoami Satsang Affairs by an Elected Council* (Ghazipur: Radhasoami Satsang Sabha, 1910), p. 17.

[79] *Souvenir*, p. 91.

[80] S. D. Maheshwari, *Biography of Buaji Saheba* (Agra: Mrs. S. D. Maheshwari, Publisher, 1983): pp. 54–55.

[81] Maheshwari, *Truth Unvarnished*, part 1, p. 165.

[82] Maheshwari, *Biography of Buaji Saheba*, p. 85.

Prasad's spiritual appearances during meditation practices and dreams; others claimed that during a meeting Kamta Prasad's face suddenly turned into Misra's.[83] Hearing these reports, Madhav Prasad Sinha traveled to Ghazipur to investigate, but was unimpressed with what he saw. In a letter written at the time, he showed his uncertainty about Kamta Prasad Sinha's role in the drama and gave no hints about what he might later conceive to be his own. "I have myself had no internal or external experiences indicative of the manifestation of the Supreme Father in the person of Babu Kamta Prasad Sinha," Madhav Prasad Sinha explained. "There are undoubtedly some persons who hold this belief," he went on to say, "but I am unable to say how far they are justified in it."[84]

Initially Kamta Prasad seemed to agree. His own letters at the time rejected the suggestion that the mantle had fallen on him, and claimed that he was "not aware of any authoritative directions." He simply hoped that the dhar had not withdrawn forever.[85] Apparently it had not, for in 1910 he was proclaimed the new master, a proclamation that was immediately rejected at Soamibagh. The movement split apart. When Kamta Prasad died three years later, his friends and family rejected the successor chosen by most of his community, Anand Swarup, and, like Kamta Prasad before him, Swarup had to proceed in opposition to the family of his master.[86] In 1914 he purchased land across the road from Soamibagh, moved his community there, and named it Dayalbagh.

When Maheshwari Devi died in 1913 in Benares, Madhav Prasad Sinha became recognized as her successor, making his home at Allahabad the headquarters of his following. When Swami Shiv Dayal's nephew, Sudarshan Singh, died in 1935, his group merged with Madhav Prasad Sinha's, and Sinha moved to Soamibagh where he reigned until his death in 1949 with an authority that has not been succeeded. Thus the strong leaders of the two main lines of the Agra branch emerged out of what was initially a vacuum of leadership. At Soamibagh, Madhav Prasad Sinha established himself largely on the basis of family connections, and at Dayalbagh it was first Kamta Prasad Sinha's, and then Anand Swarup's, personal popularity and commanding spiritual power that held sway.

Some of the same dynamics that attended the Soamibagh-Dayalbagh schism may be found in the transition that occurred at Beas after the

[83] *Souvenir*, pp. 119–21.

[84] Quoted in *Souvenir*, p. 128.

[85] Kamta Prasad Sinha (Sarkar Sahab), *Four Letters from the Pen of His Holiness Huzur Sarkar Sahab* (Agra: Radhasoami Satsang Sabha, Dayalbagh, 1983), p. 30.

[86] The irony continued in the next generation, when Prem Swarup and Shanti Swarup, Anand Swarup's sons, refused to accept Gurcharandas Mehta as guru even though he was the choice of most of the members of the Dayalbagh community; they sided with Gur Das instead (*Souvenir*, p. 258, and *Truth Unvarnished*, part 1, p. 175).

death of Sawan Singh, popularly known as the Great Master, on April 2, 1948. This schism led to the creation of the Ruhani Satsang by Kirpal Singh, who moved from Beas to Delhi. As one of the most active disciples of the Great Master, Kirpal had led services and preached sermons, and was responsible for some of the Beas publications. He is said to have been the real author of Sawan Singh's best-known work, *Gurmat Siddhant*, translated as *Philosophy of the Masters*.[87] But after Sawan Singh's death, the leadership passed to another disciple, a former chemistry professor named Jagat Singh, who had headed the colony's three main committees and had charge of the property and finances.[88] At Beas it is claimed he was chosen by the Great Master shortly before his death. One of his other disciples, a former judge, Munshi Ram, describes the moment in his diary on March 20, 1948:

> I received a message from Huzur [Sawan Singh] today, saying that I should prepare a Will on His behalf in favour of Jagat Singh. I prepared the necessary document and took it to Huzur. He put on His glasses and read the entire Will twice. Sardar Bahadur Jagat Singh Ji was sitting in one corner, all covered up, as if in meditation. Dr. Schmidt, Sardar Bachint Singh (the elder son of Huzur), and Sardar Charan Singh (Huzur's grandson) were present. . . . Huzur then affixed His signatures with Dr. Schmidt's pen, and the Doctor then countersigned the paper. Huzur checked the paper and passed it on to me. Now His soul does not like to return to the body.[89]

A week after Sawan Singh's death his eldest son placed a turban on Jagat Singh's head, and he was proclaimed the new master. Jagat Singh refused to sit in the chairs that Sawan Singh had previously occupied, however, including Sawan Singh's place in the official car. On some occasions his devotees would make sure that the only chair not occupied

[87] Kirpal Singh, *Portrait of Perfection: A Pictorial Biography of Kirpal Singh*, p. 30. Leaders at Beas, however, point out that the earliest version of *Gurmant Siddhant* was published before Kirpal Singh was even initiated into the fellowship. Kirpal Singh's role at Beas is mentioned in *Radha Soami Satsang, Beas: Origins and Growth*, p. 21.

[88] There are no written records of how the decision was made, but I am told that there were meetings among the leaders of the Beas organization after Sawan Singh's death, at which time the choice of Jagat Singh—said to have been made by Sawan Singh himself—was affirmed. The text of the will naming Jagat Singh his spiritual successor, dated March 20, 1948, is in *Radha Soami Satsang, Beas: Origins and Growth*, p. 24.

[89] Ram, *With the Three Masters*, vol. 2, p. 266. Followers of Kirpal Singh find this account suspiciously legalistic in its description—it does not sound like a normal diary entry—and note that there are two entries for April 6, 1948, the first entries after Sawan Singh's death on April 2. The first, at the end of vol. 2 of the diary, describes the situation surrounding the Great Master's death, with no reference to Jagat Singh; the second, at the beginning of the third volume, is a paean of praise to Jagat Singh.

when Jagat Singh came into a room would be the Master's; but when Jagat Singh saw it, he would insist on sitting on the floor.[90]

Meanwhile Kirpal Singh was convinced that he, not Jagat Singh, had been chosen by the Great Master to be his rightful heir, and that the master had done so unambiguously. According to Kirpal Singh's own memory, on October 12, 1947 the Great Master called him to his room:

> When I was in his august presence he said: 'Kirpal Singh! I have allotted all other work but have not entrusted my task of Naam-initiation and spiritual work to anyone. That I entrust to you today so that this holy and sacred science may flourish.' My eyes were filled with tears, and afflicted as I was, I beseeched: 'Hazur! The peace and security that I have in sitting at your feet cannot be had in higher planes. . . .' My heart was filled with anguish, I could not speak any more and sat staring—Hazur encouraging and caressing me all the time.[91]

Kirpal Singh added that from then on, whenever he met privately with the Great Master he would talk about "the interior affairs of Dera" and instruct Kirpal Singh "how to act when he departed forever."[92] That moment came half a year after the October encounter. The day before Sawan Singh died, Kirpal visited him alone in his room, and in this remarkable account by Kirpal Singh himself, the spiritual power is said to have been transmitted through the eyes:

> Hazur's forehead was shining resplendently. He opened his mercy-showering lovely eyes intoxicated by God's divine love and cast a glance at my humble self—both eyes gleaming with a radiance like a lion's eyes. I bowed my head in solemn and silent adoration and said, 'It is all Hazur's own benignity.'
>
> Hazur steadily kept gazing for three or four minutes into my eyes, and I, in silent wonderment, experienced an indescribable delight which infused a beverage-like intoxication down to the remotest corners of my entire body—such as was never before experienced in my whole life. Then those mercy-showering eyes closed not to open again. In his last moments Hazur was in peace.[93]

Things were not so peaceful in the Beas community, however, for the followers of Kirpal Singh and Jagat Singh both claimed to have received internal visitations. One supporter of Kirpal Singh said she saw Kirpal in dreams, and when she looked at his eyes he was transformed into the Great Master.[94] She was in the minority, however, and Kirpal left Beas forever, going first to Delhi, then Rishikesh (a Hindu pilgrimage place in

[90] Dev Prakash, quoted in Charan Singh, *Spiritual Heritage*, p. 98.

[91] Kirpal Singh, *Portrait of Perfection*, p. 42.

[92] Ibid.

[93] Ibid., pp. 44–45.

[94] Mata Sheila Dhir, "How the Master Revealed Himself," in Bhadra Sena, ed., *The Ocean of Grace Divine* (Delhi: Ruhani Satsang, 1976), pp. 31–32.

the Himalayas), and then again to Delhi where, in December 1948, he began the organization known as Ruhani Satsang (Spiritual Fellowship).

Meanwhile, at Beas, Jagat Singh died three years after becoming the guru, and was succeeded by the grandson of the Great Master, Charan Singh. Once again a will was produced, this one testifying that Jagat Singh had intended Charan Singh to be his successor. Since then a procedure has been established for determining what to do in the absence of a will.[95] Kirpal Singh established no such procedure, however, so when he died in 1974 there was a profusion of claims about who should succeed him.[96] The majority of his followers affirmed that the true successor was Kirpal's son, Darshan Singh. Because this and other periods of succession had been so turbulent, Radhasoami leaders made certain that recent successions, those following the deaths of Charan Singh and Darshan Singh, came off quite smoothly.

The most recent transfers of spiritual leadership at Dayalbagh, in 1976, went smoothly as well, in marked contrast to both the Beas and Ruhani Satsang successions in 1948 and 1974. The system established at Dayalbagh stipulates that the Dayalbagh Sabha, a self-perpetuating group of fifty leaders of the community, is legally responsible for deciding upon an appropriate successor when the guru dies. But the Sabha, in turn, has to base its decision upon the wishes of the entire membership, which are made public at an open meeting to be held within eighteen months of the master's death.[97]

In the months following Gurcharandas Mehta's death on February 17, 1975, the tension began to mount. The community was teeming with rumors about whose image had been seen by whom, and a number of candidates began to surface. From the beginning M. B. Lal was considered a logical choice, since he had had a distinguished career as a zoologist, capped by his appointment as head of Lucknow University. At Dayalbagh, he was director of education and played an active role on committees and on special assignments given to him by Mehta. But there were some obstacles. Lal was a convert to Radhasoami relatively late in life—in 1943, when he was thirty-six years old—and his family had not previously kept a strict vegetarian diet. Even so, several members of the community began to report having internal experiences of Lal on what one described as "the television inside."[98] On hearing these reports Lal de-

[95] See "Rules and Regulations," in *Radha Soami Satsang, Beas: Origins and Growth*, pp. 38–39.

[96] See Malcolm Tillis, *Emergence of a New Master, Darshan Singh* (Delhi: Kirpal Printing Press, 1975), part 1.

[97] *Constitution of the Radhasoami Satsang Sabha, Dayalbagh* (Agra: Radhasoami Satsang Sabha, Dayalbagh, n.p., n.d.).

[98] Interview with G. S. Bhatnagar, Dayalbagh, August 13, 1985.

murred and told those who had received them to "revise your opinion."[99] As rumors mounted, Lal countered even more explicitly. He let it be known that he himself was not capable of achieving high spiritual experiences, so he could hardly appear in other people's spiritual visions. He attempted to bar a written report of his internal appearances to a devotee from being circulated, saying that it contained "nonsense."[100] But it was all to no avail. Some older members recalled that Mehta before him had made the same sorts of disclaimers, and Lal's protests only fueled the feeling that he was the rightful heir. "Suddenly," one of his old colleagues said, "we began to change our attitudes toward Lal-Sahib and see him in a different light; we all began acting reverently."[101]

Finally, on March 15, 1976, the great day arrived, and some fifteen thousand members of the branch converged on the Dayalbagh grounds. According to some observers, less than five percent of those attending claimed to have had internal experiences of a new master, but many who did were quite vocal about them.[102] They gave personal testimonies, and letters were read from others who were not able to attend the gathering. Some eighteen names were mentioned, and ten of the most frequently cited candidates were asked to come forward. Each of them, including Lal, denied that he was the recipient of the divine current, but the mere reading of Lal's name created a great roar of acclamation from the crowd. It was an electric moment, and there could be no doubt as to who would be installed as the rightful leader.

The only major reservation on that day came from Lal himself: he told the hushed crowd that he was definitely not the master. The president of the Sabha, G. D. Sahgal, responded by explaining that Lal had no choice. "The rules give us the right to acclaim," the president told Lal, "but it doesn't give you the right to disclaim."[103] Lal then told the delighted throng he would be willing to lead the organization, but without accepting any spiritual authority. He closed by saying that he would try to do what his master would want him to do, and this the crowd took as final confirmation that he was indeed the new master.

In the years since, Lal has continued to demur. He still refuses to sit in Mehta's chair on the dais: an ornate, carved throne that occupies center stage in Dayalbagh Satsang Hall, decorated with a glittering gold necklace and a large picture of Mehta. At its side is a simple wooden chair

[99] Interview with P. Sitaramayya, Dayalbagh, August 13, 1985.

[100] Interview with V. Sadyanarayana, Dayalbagh, August 13, 1985.

[101] Interview with Shri Ram Singh, Dayalbagh, August 13, 1985.

[102] My information about this extraordinary gathering comes from several who were present at it, including the president of the Sabha, G. D. Sahgal, and the general secretary, T. Nath (Interviews at Dayalbagh, August 12, 1985).

[103] Interview with G. D. Sahgal, Dayalbagh, August 12, 1985.

with a white cushion. This is where Lal sits. Initially, he refused to appear alone in front of the community, for he felt that would imply more spiritual authority than he was willing to admit. But one by one the other members of the executive committee would slip away from the stage until only Lal remained.[104] Although he has played an active role in establishing a new university at Dayalbagh, Lal still seems shy when it comes to the spiritual side, claiming that he would rather be kneeling with the devout than sitting on his throne.[105] He seldom gives public discourses, choosing to sit quietly while others conduct the readings in Radhasoami worship. Yet Dayalbagh residents claim that his mere presence is a spiritual benefit—"just knowing that the *dhar* is here."[106]

Falling in Love with a Lord

Despite the appearances of public selection in the Dayalbagh case, the choice of a new master is not, in Radhasoami thinking, primarily a social or organizational event, but a personal one. The intimate bond between master and disciple is experienced first and foremost as an internal presence. Much is made in Radhasoami writings of finding "the guru within," the master who is beyond human form and able to touch each disciple on the inner plane.[107] When the entrapped spirit begins to leave this worldly realm on its spiritual journey, the master's luminous, subtle form "meets and greets the spirit" as it crosses over the border into the next realm.[108] The master is enabled to perform this guiding function because it is assumed that, the denials of masters such as M. B. Lal notwithstanding, he has traveled the road before and serves as a beacon of light from the ultimate source. Yet initially he appears as an ordinary, accessible mortal, and for that reason, as one Radhasoami author states, the human form of the master "is dearer to us than all other forms of God."[109]

Establishing this intimate relationship with the master may be compared with the act of falling in love. One submits fully, as a lover does, sometimes with great suddenness but always in absolute trust. "As soon as I saw a picture of him, and looked into his eyes," a woman from England explained in telling me about her first encounter with Kirpal Singh, "I knew that this was the master destined for me."[110] An American disci-

[104] Interview with V. Sadyanarayana, Dayalbagh, August 13, 1985.

[105] Interview with M. B. Lal, Dayalbagh, August 12, 1985.

[106] Interview with G. S. Bhatnagar, Dayalbagh, August 13, 1985.

[107] See, for example, the discussion of the formlessness of the inner guru in Rai Saligram, *Jugat Prakash Radhasoami*, pp. 84–85.

[108] Kirpal Singh, *Godman*, p. 93.

[109] L. R. Puri, *Radhasoami Teachings*, p. 95.

[110] Interview with Kate Tillis, Landour, India, October 28, 1980.

ple of the Great Master at Beas writes that when he first met his guru he was "unable to speak; scarcely able to think."[111] At Dayalbagh, a young man from Gwalior told me that his moment of commitment came at an unsuspected time: "One day it hit me—an indescribable feeling of my own weakness and his power, and I immediately cried out for initiation and surrendered to his grace."[112]

As in a love affair that matures over time, most relationships between new devotees and their master seem to follow a familiar course. In the initial cathartic experience of overwhelming, complete surrender the devotee is surrounded by thoughts of his or her new master. After some time, perhaps a year or two, critical judgment returns and the devotee's fresh love is increasingly seasoned with doubts as to the certainty of the reality to which he or she had become so deeply and unquestioningly committed. At this stage, devotees may express anger and frustration toward the master and construct tests for him. "If he is who he says he is," said one disenchanted follower of Charan Singh at the guest house of the Beas colony, "he will appear to me in some sort of vision and clear up these doubts."[113] At this stage of disillusioned affection, some devotees become disheartened and search for new masters. Others discount the possibility of ever finding a Lord again. Still others discover their conviction anew, sometimes in miraculous ways, and their faith is made stronger by having weathered a storm of doubts. Those who regain their trust and enter a new stage of affection for the master find that, like mature love, this stage allows for an integration between the reality of the critical, rational world and the uncritical, submissive realm of love.

Not all believers follow the same pattern of aging in the faith. Some pass from fresh love to mature trust without ever suffering the assaults of doubt, and others seem to retain the dizzy ardor of fresh devotion for many years. Then too, the analogy of a courtship is not a perfect one, for the master is always seen as ultimately beyond knowing. Yet there is interaction—the master is experienced as loving as much or more than he is loved—and Radhasoami teachings insist that the act of accepting and being accepted by a master is fundamentally an act of love.[114] It involves loving compassion on the part of the master and loving submission on the part of the devotee, and without both, a relationship with a master would be inconceivable.[115]

[111] Johnson, *With a Great Master in India,* p. 23.

[112] Interview with Kripal Naryanan, Dayalbagh, August 13, 1985.

[113] Interview with Lowell Carter, Beas, August 11, 1979.

[114] Discussions of the role of love in Radhasoami teachings may be found in Sawan Singh, *Philosophy of the Masters*, abr. ed., pp. 165–70, 315–54.

[115] Ibid., p. 170.

The Miraculous Presence

Although the master is most frequently known through love, his power is most dramatically revealed through miracles. There is some controversy within Radhasoami over whether the masters are really capable of such acts and whether, even if they are capable, they actually perform them. Some argue that masters prefer not to meddle with the laws of nature and frown on those whose faith is so fragile that they need supernatural assurance. "The eminence of a saint," a leader at Beas insisted, is not "built on miracles that he has worked."[116] One master, Faqir Chand, denied the existence of such miracles outright. "There are so many miracles attributed to me," Faqir Chand explained, "but I say upon my honor, that I do none of these."[117]

Yet reports of miracles persist. Although seldom witnessed by more than one person at a time, there are accounts of hundreds of them, including moments when the masters demonstrate supremacy over the laws of nature, special knowledge of future and distant events, or the ability to project themselves into the experiences of their devotees. The last is quite frequent: a master may appear in one's dreams, for instance, or in one's room at night, or as a face in the clouds.[118] A vision of Charan Singh to a disciple in Hong Kong is said to have preceded the master's visit there; the Russian woman who saw it claimed never to have met him before.[119]

Miracles that demonstrate the master's supremacy over the laws of nature often involve physical healings, although there are also reports of masters performing supernatural acts for their own sake, as when Swami Shiv Dayal caused a tree to wither by casting his powerful gaze in its direction.[120] This story is reminiscent of the powers ascribed to Jesus, as is the account of how Sawan Singh, faced with an unusually large gathering of followers, multiplied the food at hand so that all could be fed.[121] Anand Swarup explains that once he had to produce a miraculous feat of strength in order to persuade a group of skeptics that he indeed had the power of a guru.[122] Still other stories testify to the masters' omniscience and omnipresence, and many devotees will apologize to their masters for telling them about incidents in their lives with which the masters must

[116] Letter to me from J. R. Puri, October 1, 1985.

[117] Interview with Faqir Chand, August 19, 1978; published in Chand, *The Master Speaks to the Foreigners*, p. 26.

[118] Many such accounts of Kirpal Singh's visits to his disciples on a cosmic plane are recalled in Sena, *Ocean of Grace Divine*.

[119] Wason, *The Living Master*, p. 256.

[120] Pratap Singh Seth, *Biography of Soamiji Maharaj*, p. 127.

[121] Wason, *The Living Master*, p. 251.

[122] Quoted in *Souvenir*, p. 186.

already be acquainted. Rai Saligram is said to have answered his mail without opening the letters.[123] One devotee attests to having seen her master in two places at the same time: while giving a discourse inside a meeting hall, he was also seen entering another building some yards away.[124] And at least one master, Brahm Sankar Misra, was forthright in affirming that miracles like these do indeed take place. He explained that they are the result of higher laws than those science knows, laws to which only the masters have access.[125]

Less miraculous, but still remarkable, is the ability of a master to transmit his or her power through *darshan*. This word, "vision," refers to seeing and being seen by the master and the benefits thought to be transmitted in that exchange. In the wider Hindu tradition, darshan refers to the visual interaction between devotees and temple gods but is also sometimes applied to the sight of holy people.[126] This is especially so in Radha-

7. Devotees at a large rally in Delhi receiving the blessing of Charan Singh's appearance through scores of televisions placed throughout the tent.

[123] *Souvenir*, p. 48.

[124] Interview with Kate Tillis, Landaur, October 28, 1980. This experience convinced her that the master who accomplished the feat, Darshan Singh, was indeed the rightful successor to his father, Kirpal.

[125] Misra, *Discourses*, p. 83.

[126] For a good discussion of the concept of darsan in Indian culture see Diana Eck, *Darsan: Seeing the Divine Image* (Chambersburg, Pa.:Anima Press, 1982).

soami, for its teachings maintain that the eyes are energy centers and energy transmitters; hence the meeting of eyes between master and devotee is a moment of dramatic spiritual interaction. One Radhasoami writer described it as the ultimate aesthetic experience. "On beholding the Guru," he claimed, "there is an indescribable ecstasy which is spontaneous and permeates every pore of the body."[127] Darshan might also be regarded as a sort of spiritual ingestion, and with that comparison in mind, L. A. Babb has suggested that the principle behind it is "You become what you see."[128] The physical sight of the master helps the devotee to appropriate the master within and fashion a true internal image of the guru.

Sant and Sikh Notions of *Guru-Bhakti*

Many of the Radhasoami ideas about the guru are elaborations of themes found in writings of the medieval sants, where the concept of the divine guru, the satguru, helps to resolve a paradox that lies at the heart of sant religiosity. The sants held two central but contradictory truths: that the Absolute has no true form—it is "without quality" (*nirguna*)—and that the appropriate response to the Absolute is loving devotion (*bhakti*).[129] These two truths are at odds, for if the Absolute has no personal qualities, there is no object toward which one's love may be directed. One resolution of this dilemma is to say that *nirguna bhakti* is love for the sake of love; another resolution is to hold that love ought to be directed toward the teacher of nirguna bhakti, the guru. He is a visible symbol of what is ultimate and unseen. The guru gives form to the formless, and nirguna bhakti becomes in effect *guru-bhakti*: devotion to God as guru.

In Radhasoami thinking, also, the traditional gods of Hinduism are rejected, and the guru is affirmed as the only worthy object of one's love.[130] What makes the Radhasoami interpretation unusual is its insistence on a living guru. For most who revere the sant teachings, the guru is not immediately accessible. He is an historical entity—a figure from the past—or a transhistorical, abstract guru within one's own soul: the "voice of God mystically uttered within," as one scholar describes it.[131]

[127] Sawan Singh, *Philosophy of the Masters*, abr., p. 45.

[128] Babb, *Redemptive Encounters*, p. 79.

[129] The standard scholarly reference for nirguna bhakti teachings is P. D. Barthwal, *The Nirguna School of Hindi Poetry*. It should be noted, however, that Barthwal seems to be influenced by the Radhasoami interpretation of the nirguna tradition and places Swami Dayal on the same plane as the medieval sants.

[130] Anand Swarup is said to have even rejected Lord Krishna himself when he manifested himself before him (*Souvenir*, pp. 163–64).

[131] McLeod, *Guru Nanak and the Sikh Religion*, p. 150.

These are precisely the ways the guru is viewed in the Sikh community, the largest and most tightly organized of any group to have evolved from the medieval sant tradition. Nanak and the other nine gurus in the Sikh lineage are historical personages, but most Sikhs regard them also as bearers of a divine, supraphysical existence.[132] The tenth in their line, Guru Gobind Singh, proclaimed that after him the spiritual energy of guruship would be transferred to the sacred book (the *Adi Granth*, a compilation of medieval sant poetry) and the Sikh community. Since the book is guru, some pious Sikhs treat it in an anthropomorphized way: it is sometimes fanned to provide relief from the heat, laid to rest under gentle silks, and awakened to tinkling bells and soft voices. The Radhasoami devotees, of course, have no need for such obeisance to a book, for they have access to the living guru, whom they worship with many of the gestures that Sikhs reserve for their scriptures. This marks Radhasoami as distinctly different from the Sikhs, and it is potentially a source of tension between them.[133]

In the early years of the Beas colony, Jaimal Singh is said to have removed the word *hukka*, water pipe, and any reference to Swami Shiv Dayal using it from *Sar Bachan: Poetry*, for fear that these references would offend Sikhs, to whom the use of tobacco is anathema.[134] In the 1930s, during the time of Sawan Singh, the Great Master at Beas, the community again had to deal with Sikh hostility: a group of Sikhs blocked the entrance to a Radhasoami gathering and police were called to restore order.[135] In the 1960s and 1970s, according to some, such disruptions recurred and Sikh activists erected loudspeakers outside the Beas colony walls. Beas leaders deny that there were ever any tensions. But the rise of Sikh fundamentalism in the 1980s presented a new threat. One of the main camps of the Sikh militants was only a few miles down the road from Beas.

Because the idea of latter-day gurus is offensive to many Sikhs, Radhasoami leaders are careful to downplay this aspect of their beliefs and their connections with Sikhism when they speak in public. Even though they recite from the Sikh *Adi Granth* in their worship, they do not replicate the Sikh view toward the book, a point the Beas branch made when

[132] See McLeod, *Guru Nanak*, and his *Evolution of the Sikh Community* (Oxford: Clarendon Press, 1975).

[133] For an attempt to put Radhasoami-Sikh relations into a larger framework of minority/majority relationships see my "Patterns of Pluralism: Sikh Relations with Radhasoami," in Joseph O'Connell et al., eds., *Sikh History and Religion in the Twentieth Century* (Toronto: Centre for South Asia Studies, University of Toronto, 1988), pp. 52–69.

[134] Maheshwari, *Truth Unvarnished*, part 1, p. 110.

[135] Johnson, *With a Great Master*, p. 44.

it published its own selection of the sayings of Guru Nanak in 1982.[136] Although some within the Radhasoami community regard the Sikh tradition as its precursor, most do not.[137] And although at Beas roughly half of the congregation, and the master himself, dress in the distinctive garb of Sikhs, these external signs are regarded as matters of custom, not religious partisanship.

Another religious movement in the Punjab, the Sant Nirankaris, has not been so cautious in its relations with the Sikhs, and Radhasoami has learned from its mistakes. The Nirankari sect's claim that its present-day guru superseded the Sikh lineage prompted a spiral of acrimonious exchanges, culminating in 1979 in the brutal assassination of the Nirankari guru, Gurbachan Singh.[138] Charan Singh is therefore careful to assert that Radhasoami-Sikh relations are of a different order; he and his followers are not so brazen as to claim a direct association with the Sikh tradition.[139] Yet in the mid-1980s, in the turmoil that climaxed in the Indian government's invasion of the Golden Temple and the subsequent assassination of Mrs. Gandhi, threats were made against Charan Singh's life, and his appearances outside the dera became rare. When he did appear, he was surrounded by bodyguards, and because the government banned foreigners from the Punjab, they could not visit the dera. For two years Charan Singh stayed at Beas, venturing to Delhi and Bombay only in the last months of 1985.[140] When Sant Jarnail Singh Bhindranwale and other militant Sikhs made threatening remarks about Radhasoami, the leaders of the Beas community made every effort not to respond in kind.[141] By doing so, they were protecting not just a person, but a concept crucial to everything Radhasoami stands for; for without a living master, or the hope that one will soon be in their midst, the Radhasoami community would lose much that is distinctive to their faith.

In reviving the idea common in medieval India (and, for that matter, in

[136] J. R. Puri, *Guru Nanak: His Mystic Teachings.*

[137] Kirpal Singh, *A Great Saint*, pp. 9–10.

[138] An account of the anti-Nirankari movement in Sikhism and its role in the development of Sikh extremism in the 1980s may be found in Kuldip Nayar and Khushwant Singh, *Tragedy of Punjab* (New Delhi: Vision Books, 1984).

[139] Interview with Charan Singh, Beas, August 4, 1978.

[140] According to one leader of the community, Charan Singh stayed in Beas "not for safety reasons but because his presence there was essential for the community's support" (Interview with Dalat Ram, Delhi, August 15, 1985). During the period of unrest in the Punjab the bhandara festivals continued as usual, and the crowds were said to have been bigger than ever (Interview with R. N. Mehta, Delhi, August 15, 1985). On a visit to Beas in January, 1991, I was impressed with the extremely tight security measures.

[141] One Radhasoami member responded to Bhindranwale in a letter to the editor printed in a Delhi newspaper and was reprimanded by Beas leaders for having done so (Interview with R. N. Mehta, August 15, 1985). New threats were made in 1990 and 1991.

medieval Europe) that truth is ultimately not embodied in logical propositions but in remarkable persons, the Radhasoami teachers are able to strike at the heart of a modern problem: the limits of knowledge. The great advances of modern science stretch the imagination not only with regard to what is known but also with regard to what cannot easily be known. In the deep uncertainty that comes with this awareness, the Radhasoami teachers offer the calm and security of a relationship: a bond with those who have mastered knowledge far beyond the reach of any conventional mind.

Four

The Journey of Light and Sound

WHEN PAUL BRUNTON, the author of *A Search in Secret India*, visited Dayalbagh in the 1930s, he was attracted to what he described as the "suavely-spoken flow of subtle, recondite ideas" that came from the Great Master of Dayalbagh, Anand Swarup. Brunton saw in them the perfect blend of science and spirituality he was seeking. Still, he had doubts. "You say that the only way to verify these statements is to practise your Sound-Yoga exercises," Brunton said to the Dayalbagh master. "Can you not give me some personal experience first, some convincing proof at first hand?"

Anand Swarup assured him that he could not, that the proof was in the practice. "I am sorry," Brunton replied. "I am built in such a way that it is difficult to give belief before proof." Swarup then turned up his hands in what Brunton described as "a helpless gesture."[1]

The Dayalbagh master's gesture expressed a genuine dilemma in Radhasoami's compromise with modern thought, for its truth is a matter not only of knowledge gained through experience, but of a state of mind, a level of truthfulness. This true consciousness comes about not just as a result of Radhasoami spiritual exercises but because the practitioner develops a trusting relationship with the master. These two aspects of Radhasoami are related, for the yoga practices are the means by which the master transforms the self. Ultimately the practices make sense only as part of the master's process for redeeming and transforming the world.

Of course, all this is not immediately apparent, and it is not surprising that initially an outsider like Brunton would see Radhasoami's *surat shabd yoga* as being much like any other technique of meditation. The routine follows a daily pattern that usually begins at 3 A.M. One is expected to meditate two to four hours daily, the early hours before dawn being preferred. "The night is a jungle," one master remarked to his devotees, admonishing them to tiptoe away from ordinary consciousness at a time when it is least able to defend itself and control the soul.[2] As the

[1] Paul Brunton, *A Search in Secret India*, p. 245.

[2] The phrase is the title of Kirpal Singh's, *The Night is a Jungle*. Sawan Singh also regarded dawn and dusk as the best times for meditation (*Philosophy of the Masters*, abr., pp. 134–35). Rai Saligram is reported to have held *satsang* with his disciples virtually all night, but he warned them against meditating on their own in the darkest hours, from twelve to

yoga begins, the devotees close their eyes, and repeat the name or names of the Lord that were given to them at the time of initiation. They may also close their left ear in an attempt to block any sound coming from that direction and listen only for sound coming from the right and from above.[3] In their minds they attempt to shut out all thoughts and images save one: a mental portrait of the face of their master, which they attempt to project onto an internal screen between and slightly above the eyes. They focus on this image, repeat the divine names, and listen for the sound, and as they do, they may see the form of the master glow as if excited by an electrical current. Then it radiates a brilliant light, and the sound, distant at first, becomes close and clear like the rushing of many winds. The body goes numb. The journey has begun.

At least that is what is supposed to happen, but the experiences of any two devotees are never exactly alike, and the instructions sometimes vary. Kirpal Singh, for instance, advised against deliberately creating an internal image of the master in one's mind, saying it should come on its own accord.[4] Some form of *surat shabd yoga* practices are essential to all followers, however, and most devotees will try them again and again, for these simple exercises are only the beginning. An extraordinary journey lies beyond, and experiencing it is the great promise of Radhasoami faith. The activity that enables one to undertake that journey is called *abhyas*, literally "practices," which include the initial exercises, *simran* (repetition) and *dhyan* (contemplation)—repeating the names of the Lord and visualizing (or waiting for) the master's image. These are prerequisities to *bhajan*, which means "song" but is also etymologically linked to "love." In the Radhasoami context it is the spiritual exercise of riding the divine current through interior realms until one reaches one's ultimate home.

Reaching that home is what salvation in the Radhasoami sense is all about. It is granted through the grace of the divine master, but by arduously following the instructions for *surat shabd yoga*, followers have the opportunity of participating in their own salvation. Initiation into these practices is tantamount to baptism into the faith, and the day that they were first made public is remembered as the founding date of the tradition. Swami Shiv Dayal is said to have proclaimed on that day that the reason the Supreme Being manifested himself in the form of a master was

---

three A.M., when "the evils are most free" (Maheshwari, *Biography of Huzur Maharaj*, p. 201). In Sikhism too the early morning hours are preferred for meditation, following Guru Nanak's injunction to worship during what is often called the "ambrosial hour before dawn."

[3] Rai Saligram, *Jugat Prakash Radhasoami*, pp. 53–54.

[4] See Darshan Singh, *Spiritual Awakening* (Bowling Green, Va.: Sawan Kirpal Publications, 1978), pp. 26–31.

to "explain the secret of His Original Abode and teach the method of attaining the Abode by means of the *Surat Sabda Marga*."[5]

Surat Shabd Yoga

Surat shabd yoga (or *surat sabda marga*) is the discipline (*yoga*) or way (*marga*) that unites the spirit (*surat*) with the spiritual sound (*shabd*).[6] These terms are central to the teachings of Radhasoami leaders, but they were not coined by them, and their origins indicate something about Radhasoami's spiritual ancestry. The word *shabd*, for instance, plays a prominent role in the literature of the medieval sants, especially Guru Nanak and Kabir. It literally means "word," but in a mystical, almost gnostic sense. In Nanak's writings, *shabd* is virtually synonymous with *nam*, the "indwelling Name" of God.[7] "Meditate on the *shabd*," admonishes Nanak, "repeat the Name of God."[8] Kabir also speaks of shabd, making a distinction between the word that can be heard and the word that cannot. The latter is the *anahad shabd*, the unheard word, which one scholar describes as "a mystical vibration audible only to the adept."[9] This way of thinking about shabd, which is much like Radhasoami's, has origins even earlier than Kabir; according to some scholars Kabir's views on shabd are informed by the esoteric thought of the Nath yogis. The Naths regarded the unheard shabd as a mystical manifestation of the divine guru; those who hear it experience "a sudden illumination within the soul."[10]

Unlike *shabd*, the term *surat* is unfamiliar to most Indians. It is seldom found in the writings of the sants—or most other religious teachers in India, for that matter—but like *shabd* it is frequently found in the teachings of the Nath yogis. Although it is not certain how the Naths used the word, it seems to have something to do with hearing (the terms *surat* and *shabd* are sometimes linked in Nath literature, as they are in Radhasoami), suggesting that the word's proper etymology relates it to the Sanskrit *sruti* (that which is heard).[11] Another group using this term, the

[5] "Proclamation" in Shiv Dayal Singh, *Sar Bachan: Poetry*, quoted in *Souvenir*, p. 7. The date of Swami Shiv Dayal's first public discourse is Basant Panchami Day, February 15, 1861 (Pratap Singh Seth, *Biography of Soamiji Maharaj*, p. 39).

[6] *Souvenir*, p. 7; see also L. R. Puri, *Radha Swami Teachings*, p. 8; and Kirpal Singh, *Naam or Word* (Bowling Green, Va.: Sawan Kirpal Publications, 1981; orig. pub. 1960), *passim*.

[7] McLeod, *Guru Nanak and the Sikh Religion*, p. 148.

[8] *Adi Granth* [*Guru Granth Sahib*], Gauri 6, p. 152.

[9] McLeod, *Guru Nanak and the Sikh Religion*, p. 191.

[10] Vaudeville, *Kabir*, p.137.

[11] H. P. Dwivedi, *Kabir*, pp. 247–48; Vaudeville, *Kabir*, p. 135.

Vajrayana Siddha yogis, give it a sexual connotation: *su-rati* (good passion).[12] In Radhasoami circles it is frequently translated as "spirit"; one Radhasoami writer describes it as "self-absorbed intelligent energy," reasoning that the term comes from the Sanskrit roots *swa* (self) and *rat* (absorbed).[13] The Radhasoami interpretation of shabd and surat is essentially similar to the Naths', even though Swami Shiv Dayal denounced the Nath yogis' practice of breath control as an ugly relic of the past and claimed that the advantages of surat shabd yoga are "much greater."[14] He maintained that the discipline of listening to a sound—especially the unheard word—in order to unite with it brings one into contact with the eternal sound of God.

Actually the Radhasoami teachers seldom use the English word *God* or any of its Hindi and Sanskrit analogues. In the Radhasoami view, any name is a form of sound and contains energy; a divine name contains energy in an extraordinary degree. Names such as God, the Supreme Being, and Ram hint at the power of ultimate reality, but its proper name, Radhasoami (according to the Agra branches), or hidden name (according to the Beas branches) contains the full power of godliness.[15] Through Radhasoami practices one can create a sort of assonance between that name, whether manifest or hidden, and the godliness within oneself. Their effect is to draw out the divine particles of sound and liberate them from their mortal shell.

Divine consciousness exists within each person, and the Radhasoami attempts to surmount the limitations of the self are therefore introspective. As one Radhasoami writer put it, "the way out is in."[16] This connection between the external cosmos and the internal self is found in all aspects of Radhasoami thinking: "If you want to know about macrocosm, you must first know about microcosm," one Radhasoami master advised his disciples.[17] The self appears to be in the world, but in another sense the world is in oneself. In order to lose one's false attachment to oneself, then, one has to journey inside—at least initially, until one is freed from the bonds of ordinary consciousness altogether and travels to realms beyond imagining.

[12] Vaudeville, *Kabir*, p. 135.

[13] S. D. Maheshwari, *Glossary of Radhasoami Faith* (Agra: Radhasoami Satsang, Soamibagh, 1967), p. 245.

[14] Swami Shiv Dayal Singh, *Sar Bachan: Prose*, Soamibagh version, p. 41.

[15] For the Beas distinction between *dhunatmak* and *varnatmak* names, see L. R. Puri, *Radhasoami Teachings*, pp. 29–32; and Radhasoami Satsang, Beas, *Teachings and Brief History* (Beas, 1977), p. 5. For a vigorous rebuttal from an Agra point of view see Maheshwari, *Truth Unvarnished*, part 2, pp. 26–65.

[16] Ram Behari Lal, *The Way Out—Is In* (Oak Grove, Calif.: Grove Press, 1958).

[17] Kirpal Singh, *The Jap Ji: The Message of Guru Nanak* (Delhi: Ruhani Satsang, Sawan Ashram, 1964), p. 46.

The Tranformative Self

According to Radhasoami teachings, the self, like all of creation, is a mixture of different forms of matter, extending from the grossest to the most subtle. Before the world began, there was only a concentrated form of pure energy. Then an "original outburst" occurred, an unleashing of spiritual force not unlike the "big bang."[18] According to the Radhasoami account, this cosmic explosion pulsed out—indeed, the currents are still pulsing outward and downward—and the finer elements fell back towards the center. The heaviest and least refined elements precipitated themselves as matter and are controlled and delimited by time. These heavy aspects of energy cannot return to the generating source. Finer forms of energy—dazzling lights and sounds and forms more radiant than humans can imagine—returned, or are returning, to the ultimate realm. They are unfettered by time and unencumbered by matter; these higher forms have virtually no shred of materiality in them at all.

At the dreg end of the scale is our material, temporal world, the dung heap of creation. The fact that it has any structure at all is due to the negative force in the cosmos, Kal, who desired to create his own kingdom in imitation of the pure realm of Radhasoami and fashioned it out of the distant remains of the original effusion. His realm includes the world as we know it and the regions that are called spiritual in ordinary religion, such as heaven and hell.

Ordinarily, humans are firmly entrapped in Kal's material world. Yet they have one redeeming feature: they possess elements of spirituality that really belong—and long to return—to the higher realms. One of the early Radhasoami masters explained how this could happen: "When gold is extracted from crushed ore the greater part will be drawn to the mercury and go into the ingot; but there will be a great number of very fine grains still embedded in the matrix."[19] By analogy, he inferred, bits of purity remain in that living refuse of creation, humanity, even after most of the spirituality has returned to the highest realms.[20] The subtle essence that we humans have within us is the pure sound that still resonates from the time of creation. But since it is trapped, the task of Radhasoami practices is to liberate it through an almost alchemical process aimed at transforming gross matter into subtle. It involves a sort of nuclear fusion that releases pure energy from matter.[21]

[18] Misra, *Discourses*, p. 77. The Radhasoami account presaged the astronomers' big-bang theory by half a century. The most extensive description of creation from the Radhasoami point of view is in Rai Saligram, *Prem Patra Radhasoami*, vol. 1, pp. 210–16.

[19] Phelps, *Notes of Discourses on Radhasoami Faith*, p. 49.

[20] Ibid.

[21] See Babb, "The Physiology of Redemption." Babb describes the "cosmic physiology"

The divine energy that has been inside ourselves emanates from what we commonly call a "soul." The term for soul that Radhasoami writers use is not the familiar Hindu term, *atman*, however, but *surat* or *jiva*, words that in the Radhasoami context may be translated as life force, or living being. This jiva, this heart of ourselves, is a nonmaterial entity that radiates its own special form of energy. We experience our own jiva the way we experience all forms of energy: as warmth, light, and sound. Undifferentiated by space and time, it has no individuality, and is made of the same substance that lies at the core of the universe. It is sometimes described as a drop of water from the divine ocean that yearns to be reunited with its source.[22] It wants to go home.

The first move in that direction is to gather up what fragments of divine energy already exist within. At birth, according to one Radhasoami teacher, the *surat* that is the spiritual essence of the jiva locates itself at a point beneath the center of the forehead and then is diffused downward through the body.[23] It tends to concentrate in six internal regions, each of which has its own focal point. These are the six *chakras*, "wheels" of spiritual energy that are commonly found in hatha yoga and other traditional Indian portrayals of the spiritual anatomy.[24] The lowest of these is located in the bowels, the next in the genitals, and then come the centers of the stomach, the heart, the throat, and the special one above and between the eyes. This "eye center," as it is usually described in Radhasoami literature, is sometimes identified with the pineal gland.[25] It is the point at which the Radhasoami devotee attempts, through meditation, to concentrate the surat, the soul-consciousness that has become diffused elsewhere throughout the body. It is from there that the soul can flee the body into higher (though still interior) realms.

Even if it does, however, the soul is not yet fully free. Once it has left the body, through death or through techniques of soul projection during its earthly life, the soul can lodge itself in other forms of selfhood. But these ethereal bodies are also spiritually insufficient. They are snares in the path of true spirituality, and the soul must extricate itself from them

---

of Radhasoami, locates the Radhasoami guru as the link between coarse physical and subtle spiritual planes, and highlights the "hydraulic" aspects of Radhasoami cosmology: its upward and downward flows of energy.

[22] Sawan Singh, *Discourses on Sant Mat*, p. 30.

[23] Phelps, *Notes*, p. 68.

[24] Brahm Sankar Misra describes the spiritual anatomy in terms quite similar to those of hatha yoga. In addition to the six chakras, Misra describes three channels that run up and down the body and allow the spiritual energy to flow. These are named *irra*, *sushumna* and *pingala*, for the left, center, and right channels respectively (Misra, *Discourses*, p. 210). Hatha yoga texts mention these channels as well, in precisely these terms (see McLeod, *Guru Nanak and the Sikh Religion*, p. 191n).

[25] Anand Swarup, quoted in Brunton, *A Search in Secret India*, p. 244.

as well. One of these forms is called astral and another is called causal, and the soul may be burdened with each in turn before it can disencumber itself of the need to be attached to any form at all and reunite with its parent cosmic soul.

In traditional Hindu thought, the moral weight that keeps the soul from fleeing its mortal limitations comes from the law of karma—literally, "action"—that makes each soul accountable for its deeds in this or in previous lives. The way one lives one's life (or rather, one's many lives) determines whether one gains the opportunity to escape this mortal world or not. Radhasoami teachings accept the notions of karma and the karmic cycles of birth and rebirth, but with a significant difference. According to Radhasoami, there is an "original karma," somewhat like the Christian idea of original sin, that so taints the soul that it can never find release (*moksha*) if it follows the ordinary Hindu prescription: righteous living and ritual observances.[26] Only the power of the Radhasoami master and surat shabd yoga will allow the soul to break the hold of original karma so that, as one Radhasoami publication puts it, "the karmic garbage is consumed."[27] The Radhasoami antidote permits the soul to find release in what is by Hindu standards a relatively short period of time: some teachers have mentioned that release might be only four lifetimes away.[28] Others suggest the possibility of release at the end of one's present lifetime.[29]

In the common Hindu view, one's caste is a factor in determining how long one must wait for release from this world. Brahmans—unless they squander the karmic opportunity—can expect that moksha is not far off; mercantile Khatri castes are well down the karmic ladder, and Untouchables are at the bottom. Not surprisingly, Swami Shiv Dayal's message of equal salvation has been especially appealing to his Khatri caste fellows

[26] Phelps, *Notes*, p. 69.

[27] Radhasoami Satsang, Beas, *Teachings and Brief History*, p. 5.

[28] Rai Saligram claims that for those who practice surat shabd yoga, redemption is possible within "one, two, or three lives" (*Prem Patra Radhasoami*, vol. 3, p. 340). S. D. Maheshwari concurs, citing Shiv Dayal Singh, *Sar Bachan: Poetry*, section 8, verse 1, line 68, and chides the Beas groups for saying that moksha can be attained at the end of one's present lifetime. But I find no evidence that any of the main teachers in the Beas lineages have made that claim.

[29] At Dayalbagh I was introduced to an old man who, it was whispered, had reached the highest realm and would soon, at death, be relieved of the burden of having to live any further lives. One modern master, a successor to Kirpal Singh, claims that "God-realization" is possible in only five years of meditation (Thakar Singh, Lecture at YMCA, Berkeley, California, January 3, 1981). Followers of the Dhara Sindhu Pratap Ashram are told that release is possible at the conclusion of this lifetime (Interview with B. L. Gupta, Gwalior, August 21, 1985). Similarly, Brahm Sankar Misra assured his followers that "spiritual success" is possible after thirty years of meditation, and that release will be granted when this life ends (Misra, *Solace to Satsangis*, p. 55).

and to those farther down the traditional hierarchy, but it has not been received with the same enthusiasm by Brahmans. Radhasoami teachings explain that they are in the grip of illusions spread by Kal, who presents false religious practices as if they were true and lures people into thinking that caste, rituals, gods, and the like will lead to the liberation of the soul, when in fact such practices will enslave it all the more. Nor can one turn to rational solutions, for the mind is also the servant of Kal.

Once it has rejected the physical, spiritual and mental artifices of Kal, the soul is ready to slough off this world and begin its ascent. But how should it proceed? The first words in the Radhasoami answer to that question are "not alone," for one must have a guide, a master to beckon and befriend the soul both in the physical plane and in the higher, interior planes. We have already seen that the Radhasoami notion of salvation requires trust in the master, and now we can see why: the passage out of the material realm requires a master skill in navigation, for the deceptions of Kal make an independent voyage virtually impossible. As one Radhasoami writer puts it, the master "steers [the spirit] safely from plane to plane and explains on the way . . . the dangers of the unknown."[30] In time, master and soul become "joyful riders together" through cosmic seas.[31]

Initiation into the Path

The link between master and disciple, greater soul and lesser soul, is established at the time of initiation. It is a marriage of an extraordinary sort, an enduring union meant to last a lifetime and more. Through the initiation rite, the master transmits the technique of surat shabd yoga to the devotee and, what is more important, imparts the power to utilize it. The high point of the initiation event is reached when the two come together, master and disciple, in what is described by one Radhasoami master as a magnetic attraction.[32] In some cases the initiate experiences this as the sudden awareness of remarkable sound and light within. The Ruhani Satsang master, Kirpal Singh, would quiz his initiates to determine whether they had, indeed, received some unusual experience, and most would affirm that they had.[33]

The verbal links between master and devotee are the words that are given to the initiate—five in the Beas branch, one in the Agra groups. The names given at Beas (and by the Ruhani Satsang) are secret in the sense

30 Kirpal Singh, *Godman*, p. 39.

31 Ibid.

32 Misra, *Discourses*, p. 72.

33 Letter to me from Kate Tillis, an initiate of Kirpal Singh, February 4, 1982.

that noninitiates are not supposed to be told them, but the same names are given to all initiates, and at least in the Indian religious context they are familiar terms. In the Radhasoami context they are the names of the lords of the five regions of consciousness. Their special power comes from the spiritual charge that the words are given by the master at the time of initiation.

In addition to the transmission of spiritual names, initiation includes vows of moral purity and advice on how one should engage in surat shabd yoga. The precise techniques are kept secret, but it is widely known that they involve ways of listening for the sound and looking for the light. In the Beas branches not much is made of this aspect of initiation, but it is very important in the Agra branches, where initiation is done in two stages. The first involves imparting the "devotional practices" of simran and dhyan, which allow the initiate to "gain sufficient control over desires pertaining to his body and senses" so that meditation can begin in earnest.[34] This happens at the second stage, a year or more after the first, when the initiate is inducted into the practice of bhajan, listening for the higher sounds. At the Dayalbagh initiations, the master need not be physically present: two elder members of the fellowship have been empowered to initiate on his behalf.

At Beas, initiation is often a mass event; thousands of people file past the master in multiple lines to be selected, and they later form small groups to receive the charged names from the master's assistants. Masters who have smaller followings can afford to be more intimate. Thakar Singh, for instance, meets with initiates in small groups on three separate occasions. In the first, instructions are given; in the second, sittings are held to impart the light and the sound; and in the third, the initiate's progress since the second session is reviewed.[35] Followers of Beas who live outside India receive an intimate initiation from the master's representatives; Roland deVries, one of his chief representatives in the United States, says he tries to create "a ceremony of tremendous beauty."[36]

Radhasoami branches in which there is no living guru also have initiations, but their leaders feel compelled to explain how a spirit that has withdrawn from the world for a time can come back temporarily to grace an initiation. At Soamibagh, this was said to be achieved when the divine current, which, in the absence of a guru to incarnate it, exists in a sort of suspended animation, stirs into action at the initiation event.[37] At the

[34] Anand Swarup, *Yathartha Prakasa*, p. 4.

[35] From an instruction sheet handed out at a public lecture by Thakar Singh at Berkeley, California, January 3, 1981.

[36] Interview with Roland deVries, Nevada City, California, January 17, 1986.

[37] S. D. Maheshwari, *Correspondence with Certain Americans During Interregnum Fol-*

Dhara Sindhu Pratap Ashram, the spirit of the departed master, Shyam Lal, is said actually to make a temporary return.[38] Regardless of how initiation is received, it has immediate implications: once initiated, followers are empowered to exercise their spiritual practices in earnest. In doing so, they set out upon a complex and arduous journey, and the first stage is among the hardest.

Leaving the Body

At the outset, the object is to concentrate the soul's scattered energy and bring it to the eye center, the portal from which it can flee the physical form. Only when the soul is free from the body may the higher stages of meditation be accomplished. After a time, the soul returns to the body so that the initiate can go about his or her daily tasks; spiritual masters, however, are thought to be constantly in the higher realms, no matter what activities they are externally pursuing.

The ideas of soul travel, astral projection, and out-of-body experiences are fundamental to Radhasoami, for they are related to Radhasoami's perception of the self as a fluid, malleable entity unbound by the physical limitations of time and space. But the idea of soul travel is not unique to Radhasoami, of course. The literatures of ancient India and many other traditions are filled with such accounts;[39] and, as Mircea Eliade has noted, the goal of much of Indian yoga is to transmute ordinary time and experience into a nonphysical, nontemporal state.[40] Even in the West there is an enormous literature testifying to the veracity of out-of-body experiences.[41]

Numbered among those veterans of soul flight are some who have hoped to find in Radhasoami teachings an understanding and a refine-

---

lowing the Departure of Balryi Maharaj, 6 vols. (Agra: Radhasoami Satsang, Soamibagh, 1960–1985), vol. 1, p. 212.

[38] Interview with B. L. Gupta, Dhara Sindhu Pratap Ashram, Gwalior, August 21, 1985.

[39] See, for instance, the essays in Frank E. Reynolds and Earle H. Waugh, eds., *Religious Encounters with Death: Insights from the History and Anthropology of Religions* (University Park, Pa.: Pennsylvania State University Press, 1977); and Allen W. Thrasher, "Magical Journeys in Classical Sanskrit Literature," paper presented to the annual meeting of the American Academy of Religion, San Francisco, December 1977.

[40] Eliade, *Yoga: Immortality and Freedom*, p. 99.

[41] An extensive bibliography on soul travel in near-death experiences may be found in Carol Zaleski, *Other World Journeys: Accounts of Near-Death Experience in Medieval and Modern Times* (New York: Oxford University Press, 1988), pp. 257–66. My thanks to Josh Maddox for his research support in developing my own bibliography relating to this topic.

ment of these remarkable adventures.[42] Those who claim to have had out-of-body experiences state that they are not necessarily pleasant: terrible creatures are encountered—spirits of the dead, for instance—and one must put up with the sensation of being totally at sea. Some say that those who leave the body through the heart chakra rather than the eye center are more likely to experience negative things.[43] Even those who exit the body properly may encounter difficulty, and for that reason Radhasoami masters give advice about what the soul should avoid—e.g., images of houses, gardens and people—and what it should seek.[44] In the latter category are certain sounds. "Stick to the bells," Charan Singh once advised, "and put your attention into that deep, melodious gong sound."[45]

Hearing the sound of a bell is often said to be one of the first signs that the soul is moving out of the body.[46] According to one Radhasoami master, the cue comes when a rather ordinary metallic sound begins to change into the pure tone of a bell.[47] The wife of Darshan Singh tells a charming story about how, shortly after she was married but before she was formally initiated, she was in the presence of Kirpal Singh and heard the sound of bells without knowing where they came from or what they meant.[48] Ordinarily, however, practitioners know what the light and bells mean because they have been looking and listening for them intently during their meditation. The main activities of meditation are to sit quietly—not necessarily in the familiar lotus position but in any comfortable posture—and listen for a sound coming from the right and above, and to block out all thoughts. In the Agra branches, where meditation practices include visualization of the master's face, pictures of the masters are a popular sales item. At Beas, however, the popularity of these pictures is in defiance of the Master's warning that such external images are not to be used as an aid to meditation.[49] Only the internal picture avails.

There are, however, other physical aids to meditation. In addition to

[42] In a near-death experience, an American reported encountering the figures of two white-bearded persons. One he recognized as Jesus; the other, an unknown man on Jesus' right, was able to describe incidents in the American's own childhood. Later, after recovering from the accident and coming to India, the American recognized the second figure as the master at Beas. (Interview with Phoenix Salisbury, Beas, November 11, 1980.)

[43] Interview with Kate Tillis, October 28, 1980.

[44] Rai Saligram, *Jugat Prakash Radhasoami*, p. 26.

[45] Charan Singh, *Light on Sant Mat*, 4th ed., trans. J. Lal, J. R. Puri, and S. D. Lal (Punjab: Radhasoami Satsang, Beas, 1974), p. 320.

[46] Rai Saligram, *Jugat Prakash Radhasoami*, p. 13.

[47] Misra, *A Solace to Satsangis*, pp. 22–23, 55.

[48] Interview with Harbhajan Kaur, wife of Master Darshan Singh, Alexandria, Virginia, July 22, 1986. See also her account of this incident, "The Sound of Naam" in *Ruhani Newsletter*, September–October 1975, p. 50.

[49] According to Charan Singh, a photograph of the master is "only to look at now and then as you come and go." It is not for the purpose of *dhyan* (*Light on Sant Mat*, p. 321).

simran and dhyan are attempts to block the "nine windows of the body,"[50] a practice similar to the spiritual exercises of Nath yogis.[51] These "windows" include the eyes, ears, and nostrils, the anal and genital openings, and the mouth. The point is to discourage the soul from continuing to search outward for sensual pleasures and encourage it to turn inwards and upwards toward the tenth opening of the body, the invisible third eye. The precise way in which the eyes and ears are blocked and the body attuned is secret, but Rai Saligram's published instructions advise initiates to hold a finger over their left ear, thus turning away from the direction where Shiva and Shakti reign.[52] An early missionary account by Hervey Griswold describes a somewhat different pose: the little fingers of each hand are placed in the center of the forehead, with the thumbs pressing each ear shut.[53] Griswold also mentions that a flame may be visualized in addition to the form of the master.

Eventually the practitioner not only hears the bell but sees a vision in which the master's physical form takes on a luminous, radiant appearance. "When the spirit is withdrawn from the body you will see a steady light and, of course, hear sound too," Charan Singh explained to his disciples.[54] This is a signal that the soul has been gathered at the eye center and is ready to proceed. At this point the soul is supposed to make a dramatic departure, take flight, and abandon the physical body altogether. According to some, one sign that this process is taking place is that the body grows cold and numb. Brahm Sankar Misra explains that since the soul is latching onto an upward flow of energy, one feels "an inward stress of great intensity."[55] Other masters explain that at such times one may feel a creeping sensation or a pain in the forehead.[56] One might also experience leg cramps.[57] The body might actually appear to be dead.[58] Those who experience the transition sometimes feel as if they are indeed dying, a sensation explained by an older member of the Soamibagh branch to one of the new initiates as the "abrupt feeling of disjuncture as the soul changes from a solid state to a viscous one."[59]

The experience of dying during meditation is not altogether unexpected, since those who meditate are, in effect, rehearsing death—"dying

[50] L. R. Puri, *Radha Swami Teachings*, p. 202.

[51] Vaudeville, *Kabir*, p. 140.

[52] Rai Saligram, *Jugat Prakash Radhasoami*, pp. 53–54; and interview with Bansi Lal Gupta, Gwalior, August 21, 1985.

[53] Griswold, *Insights into Modern Hinduism*, p. 138.

[54] Charan Singh, *Light on Sant Mat*, p. 321.

[55] Misra, *Discourses*, p. 77.

[56] Rai Saligram, *Jugat Prakash Radhasoami*, pp. 57, 59.

[57] Ibid., p. 55.

[58] Wason, *The Living Master*, p. 263.

[59] Interview with P. S. Sharma, Soamibagh, August 13, 1985.

before death," as one master put it.[60] At the body's last moment the soul sheds its gross physical form, but surat shabd yoga provides opportunities for the soul to do that while the body is still alive. When death does come, the initiate is prepared. "I have no fear of dying," a woman from England told me, "for when the time comes I will know exactly what to do and where to go."[61] After death, she will not need to return to the limitations of the physical form. She will continue on to the grand vistas where Radhasoami masters have gone before, on a route they have charted in meticulous detail. The most complete description of this sojourn—and the most authoritative—is that given by the first guru, Swami Shiv Dayal. The Swami's teachings on the matter are not laid out systematically, but there have been various attempts subsequently to give a more precise and succinct form to what he said. The account that follows relies on several of these, especially the description offered by Lekh Raj Puri in *Radha Swami Teachings*.[62]

A Great Journey

The first abode that the soul discovers after it leaves the physical realm is the astral plane, which it enters by means of the third eye, through an opening provided by the radiant form of the master. That is to say, the soul leaps into the opening and goes beyond it to the vista on the other side. At this point the soul has shed its physical body, but it is now clothed in a new form—an astral form rather than a physical one. It is a strange new world, and Charan Singh offers this advice to those who enter it: "Nothing is to be anticipated. Nothing is to be feared. Whenever you feel any disturbing or frightening effect turn your thoughts loving to the Master and repeat the five Holy Names."[63]

The names are "tests to challenge the spirits that may appear,"[64] and there are a good many spirits to be encountered. Souls of various sorts go to the astral planes after death, and many yogis are able to arrive simply by practicing breath control and exercising their powers of concentration. But they depart from the body via the heart chakra rather than through the third eye, and they lack the sound and the light of the master to guide them. As a result they wander about pitiably, lost and confused.

[60] Sawan Singh, quoted in D. L. Kapur, *Call of the Great Master*, p. xliv. Radhasoami masters are fond of quoting St. Paul's characterization of himself as dying "every day" (I Cor. 15:31).

[61] Interview with Sheila Harris, Beas, November 12, 1980.

[62] L. R. Puri, *Radha Swami Teachings*. pp. 169–223.

[63] Charan Singh, *Light on Sant Mat*, p. 321.

[64] Kirpal Singh, Circular Letter, June 6, 1971.

This is not the fate of the soul led by the Radhasoami master, however; for such a soul the journey has just begun.

The initial technique of simran is less important once a soul attains the astral plane, and dhyan changes its character. The master is now present in his astral form, so there is no need to envision his physical appearance, or to repeat the sacred names in order to center the soul. Still, the sacred names are useful as a shield against the powrs of Kal; they are the only things in the human vocabulary that Kal cannot penetrate and as such they are armor for the upward path. Replacing simran and dhyan in importance is bhajan (song), which in Radhasoami usage refers to listening to a melody—or rather, several melodies, one for each region of consciousness—to which the soul should repair for protection and guidance along the way. Concomitant with the distinctive sound is a particular light (again a different one for each region), which illuminates and directs the passage of the soul. In general, the soul is advised to steer towards bright light, the five colors, and astronomical bodies like the stars, moon and sun.[65] But as one's practice advances, one is encouraged to attend to sounds rather than light, because sounds are thought to contain a purer form of energy. According to Radhasoami teachings, the sense of hearing is "subtler" than the sense of sight.[66] The sounds and lights one perceives as one ascends on one's spiritual journey are thought to be beacons from the highest regions, showing weary souls their way home.

The Higher Regions

One's passage into the astral plane is aided by the sound of a deeply resonant bell. A dazzle of colors immediately emerges, subsiding into a deep blue, like the blue of a late afternoon sky. Subsequently a light appears in the blue, intense but diffused, as if veiled by a gauze screen. The soul aims for the light, penetrates the gauze, and arrives at a brilliant flame surrounded by a dense blue-black sky. That area, a higher realm within the astral plane, is called *shyam kunj* (the thicket of darkness), and it is regarded as the divine headquarters for managing both the physical and astral realms. It is controlled, of course, by Kal; here he appears as Niranjan, the Lord of the astral realm. The soul should not be satisfied with attaining this realm, however, but focus on the flame, which replaces the blue-black sky with an intense bright white. This enables the soul to bypass all the supernatural regions referred to in the literature of other reli-

[65] Rai Saligram, *Jugat Prakash Radhasoami*, p. 26.

[66] Misra, *Discourses*, p. 219. See also Sawan Singh, *Philosophy of the Masters*, vol. 4, pp. 132–33.

gions: the Christians' heaven and hell, the Hindus' *svarga* and *naraka*, the Muslims' *dozakh* and *bahisht*. These all exist at the level of shyam kunj, but there is no ultimate advantage to being lodged in one rather than another. Heaven may be filled with "comfortable rooms" and hell with "painful cells," but in the last analysis all who live in either are trapped "in the same jail."[67] The fortunate soul, however, has a way out. The Radhasoami master guides it to a dark spot in the light and a sound similar to that of a conch shell, which it hears at first only distantly from a tunnel high above. The tunnel is called banknal (the crooked path). Upon following the sound into the tunnel, the soul turns around and then enters the next plane.

This second region is called the causal plane, for it is from here that the phenomenal world is ultimately generated. At one spot, for example, is a four-petaled lotus from which emerge utterances that eventually issue as the four Vedic scriptures of Hinduism. The world was created in this region as a subtle, invisible form, and here karmic burdens are dispatched and reclaimed. Thus cause and effect, both material and moral, begin and end here. Brahm, the creator, sustainer and dissolver of the universe, is considered the Lord of this region, but he too is an agent of Kal, so this world, like the astral, holds its perils for the wary Radhasoami soul.

The soul, forewarned, enters the causal plane with care, listening again for the guardian sound, which in this region reverberates like the sound of large drums or rolling thunder, and which may also sound like the rumbling chant of the Hindus' *om, om,* or the Muslims' *hu, hu*. The light that the soul looks for to guide it takes on a brilliant reddish color in this realm, like that of the sun in a summer sunrise. The soul fixes on these aural and visual guides, and passes by locations where the things of our physical world were created. Within the landscape are also vistas that are well known from Hindu mythology—Mount Kailasa, for example, where Lord Shiva is thought to dwell, or the forests and gardens said to have been inhabited by Krishna. The light that the soul has followed, already brighter than many suns, becomes ever brighter as the wayfarer proceeds upward, bursting through the pyramidically shaped causal realm.

At that point the soul moves beyond the arena in which causation has meaning and transcends the last shreds of materiality. It leaves behind realms referred to by Hindus as "the three worlds" (*trilok*), i.e., the known universe, and moves into what Radhasoami calculates as the third spiritual plane: Daswan Dwar (the tenth door), also known as Sunn (emptiness). This transition is more decisive than any other, and is second in importance only to the initial shift from the physical to the spiritual plane, for it marks the point beyond which the soul no longer inhabits

[67] L. R. Puri, *Radha Swami Teachings*, p. 202.

form, whether physical, astral, or causal. From here onward, the soul exists purely in spirit. It passes beyond the karmic cycle, breaking free of the bondage that forced it to shuttle from one physical life to another. The soul has now achieved moksha (release), in the Hindu reckoning, and is "rid of all covers of matter and mind, and shines forth in its naked glory with the radiance of twelve suns."[68] It has a new name, too. It is called *hamsa*, the high-flying goose that in Indian mythology is invested with almost magical properties; in Radhasoami writings it is usually described as a swan and is sometimes identified with the phoenix. Having passed beyond the realms governed by Kal, the soul is free to revel in divine bliss and enjoy an ambiance suffused by a pleasant light and a divine sound. The light resembles that of the full moon in a clear sky, shimmering in all directions, and the sound is like that of a guitar, lute, or harp.

There are interesting places for the soul to visit on this plane: Maha Sunn, for example, "great emptiness," a vast expanse of utter darkness located above Sunn, where hidden spiritual secrets are revealed and where five new universes, each with its own Brahm, may be observed. Or the soul may rest in Achint Dip, an "inconceivable island" of spirituality in the midst of the void. The Lord of this region is called Parbrahm, "super Brahm." He has the power to direct the soul either downward or upward to an even higher region, and with the assistance of the master, the Radhasoami soul can make the further ascent.

When the soul leaves the third realm and ascends to the fourth, penultimate level, it finds itself in a medium that at first seems strange. The fourth realm whirls in dizzy delight and is called Bhanwar Gupha (the rotating cave). Its central sound is like that of a flute or the sound of the Vedic mantra *soham* (I am that), and the Lord of the region receives his name from that term: Soham Purush (the person of soham). The light is like that of the sun at midday, radiating in all directions. There are lovely islands where souls dwell and have fellowship together, but the Radhasoami soul hastens on to the fifth and final region.

This ultimate level is called Sach Khand, or Sat Lok (both meaning "the realm of truth"), and Radhasoami writers expend countless superlatives attempting to describe it: "an ecstasy of Divine Love," "intense bliss," "a beatitude indescribable."[69] When it approaches this highest state, the soul encounters the transcendent condition of *sahaj* (spontaneous, intuitive consciousness).[70] If it passes beyond sahaj, it is ushered

[68] Ibid., p. 183.

[69] Ibid., p. 180, 181.

[70] One finds *sahaj* also in the final stages of the Buddhist and Nath yoga journeys of consciousness. It is the "mysterious state" that is the goal of hatha yoga as practiced by the Naths (Vaudeville, *Kabir*, p. 125), and their idea has influenced Kabir, who speaks of *sahaj*

into the entrance, which is like a garden or like a courtyard in a golden palace. One is surrounded by flowers of charming fragrance and fountains flowing with nectar. The sound that circulates in this ultimate realm is that of the *bin*, a wooden musical instrument that produces an oboelike tone and is often played by snakecharmers. Some Radhasoami writers, however, claim that the word that is intended here is actually *vina*, which refers to a classical stringed instrument that one Radhasoami author translates as "harp."[71] The words *sat, sat* or *haq, haq* (the Sanskrit and Persian words for "truth," respectively) may be heard intertwined with the tones that emanate from the bin. The light is as strong as sixteen suns, but even with that brilliance it is scarcely able to compete with the radiance emitted from the luminous form of the Lord of the highest realm; his name is Sat Purush (the true person) or Sat Nam (the true name). The soul presently enters into the very chambers of the ultimate Lord, and the meeting that ensues is described by Swami Shiv Dayal as involving a sort of password given in response to the Lord's command. As the soul "pushes forward," it "beholds Sat Nam smiling in bliss. Out of his lotuslike appearance comes a voice: 'Who are you, and why did you come here?' The soul replies, 'A true guru instructed me in the secrets. By his graciousness I have received the grace of your presence, O Lord.' And as the soul beholds the sight of the Lord it becomes greatly enraptured."[72]

After that brief encounter, the soul rushes directly into the form of the highest Lord and "becomes one with Him in an ecstasy of Divine Love and intense bliss."[73] The soul has finally reached its home. The journey is over.

The Varieties of Regions

Despite the importance of the soul journey in Radhasoami belief, or perhaps because of it, there is no unanimity among Radhasoami writers as to how many regions there are, what their names are, or how they should be described. For instance, in the Beas branches the fifth and highest realm is described as having four divisions: Sat Lok (the realm of truth), Alakh (the formless realm), Agam Lok (the inaccessible realm), and Anami Lok

---

as a "spontaneous experience of truth" (Hawley and Juergensmeyer, *Songs of the Saints of India*, p. 44).

[71] Maheshwari, *Truth Unvarnished*, part 2, pp. 35, 107–8. The leader of another Radhasoami branch confirms that the *bin* is the snake charmer's oboe (Interview with Bansi Lal Gupta, Gwalior, August 21, 1985).

[72] L. R. Puri, *Radha Swami Teachings*, p. 180.

[73] Ibid.

(the nameless realm). In addition to these, the Agra branches include Bhanwar Gupha as one of the higher stages and calls the highest realm Radhasoami Dham (the home of Radhasoami), using the term Anami not only for that realm but for the third of its six highest regions as well. It is in the highest of these stages that the spiritual journey ends in the union of the individual soul with the ultimate cosmic reality.

The Agra interpretations are based on the schema worked out by the second master at Agra, Rai Saligram.[74] According to him there were eighteen divisions of consciousness: six, corresponding to the six chakras in the body, were internal and of a purely material nature; five were a mixture of material and spiritual substance and could be experienced only out of the body or at some spiritual distance from it; and the highest seven, purely spiritual, were beyond any physical experience at all.[75] Other Agra versions separated the eighteen into two sets of nine, each of which was further subdivided into three groups of three stages each. One set of nine could be found within the physical body; the second set, which corresponded to it stage by stage, was located in the cosmos at large. Many present-day Agra accounts take little interest in this first set, grouping them all in a single stage, and thereby come out with a total of ten regions instead of eighteen.[76] The Beas version formulated by the Great Master, Sawan Singh, differs from all the Agra accounts, and lists only eight ascending regions.[77] Table 1 is a schematic comparison of the versions that have become standard at Agra and Beas.

The description of regions of consciousness set forth in Swami Shiv Dayal's *Sar Bachan* could be taken to support these and many other schematizations.[78] The main point of the *Sar Bachan* account is that there are three ascending groups of regions, a pattern affirmed in both the Agra and the Beas lists. The Agra version was influenced by Brahm Sankar Misra's attempt to make a physiological connection with each set of regions. He associated the six ganglia of the nervous system with the lowest level, the six areas of gray matter in the brain with the next, and the

[74] Rai Saligram's description of the higher realms appears in *Prem Patra Radhasoami*, vol. 1, pp. 98ff.

[75] Griswold, *Insights into Modern Hinduism*, p. 134.

[76] For an extensive discussion of the regions and how the various versions differ, see Maheshwari, *Truth Unvarnished*, part 2, p. 112; and *Correspondence with Certain Americans*, vol. 5, pp. 364–70. Maheshwari's criticism of A. P. Mathur's exposition of the regions may be found in *Thesis on a Thesis*, p. 22.

[77] Sawan Singh, *Philosophy of the Masters*, abr. ed., pp. 7–11. See also Lekh Raj Puri, *Mysticism: The Spiritual Path* (Punjab: Radha Soami Satsang, Beas, 1964), vol. 2, pp. 14–56.

[78] Swami Shiv Dayal Singh, *Sar Bachan: Prose*, Soamibagh version, part 1, 107–8, 127–146, and *passim*.

TABLE 1
Levels of Cosmic Consciousness

Agra Version	*Beas Version*
Pind (purely material):	*Pind* (purely material):
1. Pind, or And Desh Sometimes described as having 3 divisions corresponding to the three great Hindu gods: Brahma, Vishnu and Mahesh (Shiva). Six chakras.	1. Pind Includes Sahas-dal-Kanwal. Six chakras.
Brahmand (material and spiritual): Sometimes the 3 levels called "And" are inserted here.	*Brahmand* (material and spiritual): The Soamibagh branch locates Suksham Jagat here.
2. Sahas-dal-Kanwal	
3. Trikuti	2. Trikuti
4. Sunn Maha Sunn is listed sometimes as a division within this region, sometimes as a separate region.	3. Daswan Dwar, or Sunn Includes Maha Sunn.
	4. Bhanwar Gupha
Dayal Desh (purely spiritual):	*Sat Desh* or *Sach Khand* (purely spiritual):
5. Bhanwar Gupha	
6. Sat Lok	5. Sat Lok
7. Anami Pad	6. Alakh Lok
8. Alakh Lok	7. Agam Lok
9. Agam Lok	8. Anami Lok, or Radhasoami Dham
10. Radhasoami Dham or Pad	

six areas of white matter within the brain with the highest.[79] At Beas, the eighteen stages, first reduced to eight, were later condensed to five. According to L. R. Puri, this latter formulation was made to avoid repetition, but it also provides a correspondence between the cosmic regions and the five names given out at initiation.[80] Five is also the number of cosmic regions identified by Guru Nanak.[81] The consolidation of eight

[79] Misra, *Discourses*, p. 313.

[80] L. R. Puri, *Radha Swami Teachings*, p. 219. Another Beas version has two groups of six regions: one internal to the body and one beyond it; see D. L. Kapur, *Call of the Great Master*, chart following p. 174.

[81] The five stages according to Guru Nanak are Dharam Khand, Gian Khand, Saram Khand, Karam Khand, and Sach Khand. See McLeod, *Guru Nanak and the Sikh Religion*, pp. 221–26, and Hawley and Juergensmeyer, *Songs of the Saints*, pp. 193–94. Occasionally

regions into five was made possible by collapsing the highest four into one. This annoyed some of the Agra leaders, who felt that it was yet another attempt by Beas to belittle the Radhasoami name, depriving it of its status as the sole title of the ultimate region.[82] Furthermore, S. D. Maheshwari and others at Agra objected to shifting the region of Bhanwar Gupha (the whirling cave) from the bottom of the highest tier to the top of the middle tier.[83] Among other things, this change destroys the imagery implied in the name *Bhanwar Gupha*, which L. A. Babb describes as an anal access to the highest realm. This "dark vestibule" is a significant feature of the Agra cosmology.[84]

Despite such controversies, what is common to all these versions is more striking than the differences. All affirm that there is life beyond this life, that it is obtainable, and that it is discovered in ascending stages. Outsiders may wonder how much of this account the followers of the movement actually accept, but the answer is simple: all of it. If one accepts the premise that there are internal regions to which a fluid, malleable soul may travel, then all else is possible as well.[85] This account, like the mythology found in other religious traditions, gives insight into what the spiritual realm is actually about; like ritual, it facilitates a person's movement from one stage of life to another, or from the physical plane to spiritual ones; and as symbol, it expresses the marvelous potential of the self. To reject it would be to deny that potential and, by implication, much of what is hopeful about the Radhasoami view of human existence.

The Solace for Those Who Fail

Considering the importance that Radhasoami places upon the triumphant journey of the soul, it seems a pity that for many followers the time-consuming, lonely, repetitive hours of intense interior practice produce nothing, at least nothing resembling what the glamorous descriptions of fabulous realms have led them to expect. It is impossible to calculate just how successful the thousands and thousands of attempts at surat shabd yoga have been, for Radhasoami masters forbid their disciples to discuss

---

Guru Nanak describes these stages in language strikingly similar to Radhasoami's. In Gian Khand, for instance, Nanak speaks of beholding "sounds of music, past times, pleasures and joys" (Nanak, *Japu* 36, in *Adi Granth*, p. 12).

[82] Maheshwari, *Truth Unvarnished*, part 2, pp. 26–119. See also the discussion of this controversy in Babb, *Redemptive Encounters*, pp. 46–48.

[83] Maheshwari, *Truth Unvarnished*, part 2, pp. 91ff.

[84] Babb, *Redemptive Encounters*, p. 42.

[85] The fluid nature of the self is a major theme in Babb's interpretation of Radhasoami ideas. According to Babb, this notion is one of the features that links Radhasoami with other movements in modern Hindu culture (*Redemptive Encounters*, pp. 34–61, 205–25).

such matters either among themselves or with outsiders. Among those adherents who have been willing to talk about what happens during meditation, only a few claim to have experienced anything remarkable. During a gathering of some seven hundred foreign devotees at Delhi, a middle-aged American angrily confronted Master Charan Singh and complained that his eighteen years of arduous simran and dhyan had produced absolutely nothing. Charan Singh sympathized but offered only the suggestion that he should try again.[86] Not everyone who tries, he explained, will be privileged to see the higher regions during this lifetime.[87]

This dismal prognosis is not as devastating as one might suspect. Many followers of Radhasoami seem quite content to travel life's road without being dazzled by special experiences, and others seem to have little interest in even trying. "I know I should do my *abhyas* more frequently," a woman at Dayalbagh said, "but I haven't the patience or the time, and to tell the truth I don't think I'm much good at it." For her, and for the many who try but fail, the grand dimensions of the soul's journey must be taken on faith. Those most determined to achieve spiritual success are devotees from Europe and America. Many of their Indian peers, by contrast, are satisfied with whatever level of spiritual achievement has been allotted them, reflecting a traditional Indian acceptance of the idea that some people in this world are more skilled in spiritual matters than others. Nevertheless all are encouraged to try to reach the higher realms, so many who try no doubt fail.

If this leads to frustration, Radhasoami teachings provide a salve: a parallel path to god-realization that shortcuts the way through ascending realms to the ultimate reality. This path is bhakti, loving devotion. Some Radhasoami teachers put it on a par with surat shabd yoga;[88] others rank it even higher. "Love," the Great Master at Beas explained, "is the most powerful and effective of all practices to meet the Lord."[89] His own master, Jaimal Singh, put the matter even more dramatically in a letter written to the young Sawan Singh. "Even after a hundred years of Bhajan," he wrote to his youthful disciple, "one does not get so purified as by an intense longing for Darshan, provided that longing is real and true, and that the love for the Sat Guru is from the innermost heart."[90]

[86] Bhandara at the Bhatti Mines meeting grounds, Delhi, November 29, 1986.

[87] One devotee explained the patience of unsuccessful meditators this way: "The seed of Nam once sown will fructify, if not in this life then in others" (Correspondence from Kate Tillis, February 4, 1982).

[88] According to A. P. Mathur, the master in Rai Saligram's family lineage at Peepalmandi, "Radhasoami has only two things: *surat shabd yoga* and love" (Interview with A. P. Mathur, August 12, 1985.

[89] Sawan Singh, *Philosophy of the Masters*, abr. ed., p. 170.

[90] Jaimal Singh, *Spiritual Letters*, p. 36.

Love is remarkably efficacious, according to Radhasoami teachings, because it assists one's meditation efforts; it allows one to latch onto a current flowing upward towards the divine source, rather than downward towards Kal, as energy in our world ordinarily does.[91] Furthermore, love can replace the need for meditation altogether, by making it possible for a devotee to merge directly with the master, who, in turn, is perfectly attuned to the Absolute. In that way, the act of devotion can serve as a sort of poetic paraphrase of meditation. Through devotion as through meditation the mind can be conquered, the radiant form of the master realized, and the soul of the devotee sent out of its body and on its way to the higher regions—all without consciously thinking about, or working toward, the journey at all.

The devotional shortcut sounds easy, but it is not always so. Simple folk, such as the many villagers who flock to the presence of the master, are thought to be better candidates for it than their educated, urban counterparts, since they are less subject to the deviousness of the intellect. "Those villagers are lucky," one American devotee said enviously. "The master simply tells them to concentrate their thoughts here"—pointing to her forehead—"and think of him, and they're on their way to Sach Khand."[92] The more sophisticated devotees cannot rely on devotion alone, for the power of their minds is too great for love to conquer directly; hence the need for hours of introspective mind control.

Even if those hours do not produce results, one reassurance remains: such devotees are still in touch with a master who resonates with the energy of the higher realms and who can intercede on their behalf. Their love for him may still prove to be their salvation. And even if the soul's journey to Sach Khand may appear so arduous as to be impossible, still it serves for the Radhasoami adherent as a symbol of ultimate optimism. By ennobling and giving meaning to the journey that each person undertakes in life, the cosmic journey affirms the possibilities of human experience. It clarifies who the would-be journeyer is, the nature of the world through which he or she journeys, the marvelous end that is possible, and the cause of any pitfalls along the way. It provides a cognitively satisfying road map, even if one is unable to make the trip. Since the modern world succeeds so dismally in giving a pattern to any of these matters, the Radhasoami view is, for those who accept it, a wonder indeed.

[91] Rai Saligram, *Jugat Prakash Radhasoami*, p. 74. Rai Saligram prescribes hymns of love to be sung during meditation when *dhyan* and *simran* fail (p. 32).

[92] Interview with Sheila Harris, Beas, November 12, 1980.

Five

The Fellowship of the True

Two main forms of spiritual activity—lonely individualistic strivings for mystical union and collective acts of worship—divide almost every religious tradition. These two approaches to the spiritual life answer to differences of religious temperament that are profound, and in some cases they cause schisms within religious communities, especially in the modern age when individualism and community are often at odds with one an-

8. A large crowd surrounding Sawan Singh as he leaves the Satsang Ghar, Beas. The young Charan Singh is on the running board, on the right.

other. In the Radhasoami case, however, both are essential, and they are compatible.

When I asked one devotee whether he could survive on meditation alone without *satsang* (which in this case refers to communal worship), he responded with skepticism: "I don't think it is possible."[1] The reason he gave was pragmatic: the community helped to discipline the mind, and it fostered and exemplified love for the master. One might think of satsang as a sort of spiritual factory, he explained; it produces with greater efficiency the love energy that is created in spiritual exercises. According to Sawan Singh, the connection between love and the soul journey is direct: "The currents of God's love" that are created in worship help the worshiper to "see light inside." Sometimes the light is "in the form of lightning, sometimes stars are seen, and sometimes the stars burst and the sun and moon are visible."[2]

For this reason, Sawan Singh explains, "the singing of praise to the Lord does not interfere with the concentration of the soul," but rather "refreshes our remembrance" and "keeps alive the current."[3] Even when the master is not physically present at the satsang gatherings, his spiritual energy is thought to be manifest; it combines with that of earlier saints in creating an atmosphere potent enough to stave off the negative forces of Kal. "There is a special spiritual charge during satsang," another devotee affirmed.[4]

Radhasoami teachings mention two kinds of satsang, an interior and an exterior one, each of which buttresses the other. One of the earliest Radhasoami publications, in listing satsang as one of the four essentials of the faith, insists that it be practiced in both forms.[5] The interior one is the devotee's soul-meeting with the master during meditation. Even remembering the master for a moment or seeing his picture on the wall is satsang in this sense, and as such it encourages the ascent of the soul, if ever so minutely. The external satsang is also a meeting with the master; ideally it occurs in his physical presence, but if that is not possible, then where he is spiritually present among those gathered in his name. Satsang in the external sense usually refers to a group event, and by extension it refers to the group itself.

Satsang has the multivalent meaning of a word like *church*. It refers simultaneously to a pattern of relationships, an entity, and an event. Followers of the faith are linked to the master and to one another in bonds

[1] Interview with Anil Marwa, Gwalior, August 21, 1985.

[2] Sawan Singh, *Philosophy of the Masters*, vol. 2, p. 137.

[3] Ibid., p. 63.

[4] Interview with Kate Tillis, November 20, 1980.

[5] Pratap Singh Seth, *Biography of Soamiji Maharaj*, p. 27. The other three essentials mentioned are love, perfect Guru, and the secrets of Nam.

9. Sawan Singh leading satsang at Beas.

of satsang; satsang fellowships hold satsang services; and the entire community of followers of a particular master—or even of a particular lineage of masters—is known as a satsang. The Beas Satsang, for example, is distinguished from the Satsangs of Dayalbagh and Soamibagh. Anyone who has been initiated by a master has also entered into the membership of the satsang for which that master is the spiritual head. From that time forth the devotee is known as a *satsangi*, the term that Radhasoami followers use to refer to themselves and to one another.

Becoming a satsangi—identifying oneself with a specific religious community—is so fundamental to the Radhasoami spiritual commitment that allegiance to the faith is unthinkable without it, and this sets the Radhasoami form of religion at some distance from what we usually think of as normative Hinduism. One cannot belong to a Hindu temple in the same way one belongs to a Radhasoami satsang, since a Hindu temple is not a congregational reality. But a Radhasoami satsang is, in much the same way that Christians constitute churches and Muslims participate in communal worship. The precedents for Radhasoami's notion of satsang are not Christian or Muslim, however; they are definitely Hindu.[6]

[6] Since Agra has a large and thriving Muslim community, the similarities between Radhasoami and Islam are most apparent in this city where Radhasoami originated. The two are marked by congregational forms of worship, an abjuring of imagery, and a view of the

The word *satsang* is formed by linking the Sanskrit words *sangha*, meaning group, community, or fellowship; and *sat*, meaning true. The conjoined term can thus mean a "true fellowship."[7] It is also possible for the word *sat* to be a form of *sant* and therefore refer to a "true person" or "a person filled with truth." *Satsang*, then, would mean "the fellowship of the true," something like what Christians call "the communion of saints."[8] Finally, since the compound *satsang* allows for no distinction between singular and plural forms of *sat* (or *sant*), *satsang* may also be interpreted as the fellowship that is created around a particular *sant*.

In the medieval sant tradition, where the term *satsang* came into common usage, it was usually taken in its simplest, least qualified sense. In that context, *satsang* meant "true fellowship" in the most direct sense—"good company"—and any devoted person was regarded as a sant. [9] Later there was a tendency for only the major figures of the tradition to be regarded as "true" or "good," and the concept of *satsang* came to denote the fellowships that were created when two or more persons came together as followers of the same master. The term is used in Radhasoami in various ways: *satsang* continues to mean a true fellowship, or a fellowship of persons who are true, or a fellowship formed around a true master.[10] It also means worship.

Satsang as Worship

The pattern of worship in Radhasoami's fellowship was established very early in its tradition. An Anglican missionary serving in Allahabad in 1908 described a satsang in words that could easily be used to portray a Radhasoami worship service today.[11] Paul Brunton's description of satsang at Dayalbagh in 1935 was equally commonplace. The first thing to

---

divine that rejects anthropomorphism. Swami Shiv Dayal and Rai Saligram are sometimes pictured in Muslim dress. The writings of Muslim as well as Hindu saints are discussed in Sawan Singh, *Philosophy of the Masters*, vol. 4, p. 88.

[7] Kirpal Singh defines satsang as "association with truth" (*Instructions for Holding Satsang*, Circular Letter No. 4, December 1956, p. 1).

[8] The expression comes from the Apostles' Creed.

[9] According to Vaudeville, the term came into sant usage from the Naths, where it referred to a circle of devotees, or "saints," who performed religious music (*kirtan*); *satsang* is thus "the presence and proximity of 'the Saints' " (Vaudeville, *Kabir*, p. 141). In our translations of sant poetry, J. S. Hawley and I have used the phrase "the gathering of the good" or "the company of the saints" for *satsang* (*Songs of the Saints*, pp. 115, 125–29). See also the discussion of the meaning of *satsang* in the poetry of Sur Das in J. S. Hawley, "The Sant in Sur Das," in Schomer and McLeod, *The Sants*, p. 203.

[10] For a description of satsang in modern Sikhism see McLeod, "The Meaning of 'Sant' in Sikh Usage," in Schomer and McLeod, *The Sants*, pp. 251 and 254.

[11] Griswold, *Insights into Modern Hinduism*, p. 139.

greet his eye was a raised platform at the center of the hall. Soon, two men stood up at the rear of the hall and their voices broke out into a slow chant. Although the words were in Hindi, which he did not understand, Brunton described the rhythm as "extremely agreeable to one's ears." After some fifteen minutes, he claimed that "the strange, sacred words" had lulled him "into a peaceful mood," and then the master gave an exposition of the meaning of the words.[12]

An example of modern satsang is to be found in Nabha, a busy, dirty market town in the middle of Punjab.[13] Among the few new buildings in Nabha is a small structure at the outskirts of town that adjoins a large, walled open-air meeting space; the brightly painted sign above the gate announces it as the Nabha location of "Radhasoami Satsang, Beas." Inside the compound are a small office building and an even smaller shed used to store microphones, amplifying equipment, and a tent. The congregation of perhaps two hundred gathers on a large mat beside a shady tree at the far corner as verses from sant poetry are sung into a microphone by a thin, bearded man with a lovely tenor voice. His amplified recitation is projected throughout Nabha for at least a half an hour before the service, imparting a vicarious grace to those who stay at home. The speaker, a local cloth merchant, positions himself on the carpeted podium behind which is a large picture of Charan Singh, whose sayings, along with those of Sawan Singh, Kabir and other sants, form the basis of his remarks. After the singer recites a verse or two in a simple, unaccompanied tune, the leader gives a brief exposition of its message. These paired sets of recitation and exposition take five to ten minutes each, and an average service will have five or six such cycles. The whole event is over in less than an hour.

The peaceful, Spartan simplicity of Radhasoami satsang—so different from Hindu worship—is suggested by the buildings that house it. Hindu temples are dizzyingly ornate; but with rare exceptions, such as the tomb of the first master, Radhasoami buildings are austere. From the outside they look like modern office buildings. The inside is graced only with plain concrete and marble. At the front of the meeting halls is a raised podium for a speaker, or with luck, a master; a picture hanging on the wall behind the podium reminds the faithful that even when he is not physically present he is, in a sense, there.

One of the things that makes the simple liturgy special is the beauty with which the verses are chanted. In satsangs held outside of India, the

[12] Brunton, *A Search in Secret India*, pp. 239–40.

[13] My information on the Nabha satsang comes from an interview with Prof. Surjit Singh Narang, Department of Political Science, Guru Nanak Dev University, Amritsar, August 10, 1979, and from my field trip to Nabha on August 14, 1979. Prof. Narang is the son of Dayal Singh Narang, leader of the Nabha satsang.

verses are read without musical intonation, but in India, satsangis prefer to hear the medieval sant texts in the musical form for which they were written. "Music consoles and silences the mind," one master explained, "and it leads to hearing the music inside."[14] The person who sings the verses is chosen primarily for his musical abilities and is called a *pathi* (reader). He moves from satsang to satsang on a semiannual circuit, and like a cantor in Judaism or a *granthi* in Sikh services of worship, is likely to stay an anonymous and powerless functionary in the local religious communities.[15]

In satsangs connected with the Beas branch the scriptures used are frequently the Sikhs' sacred text, the *Adi Granth*, a compilation of poetry from the medieval sants, including Nanak, Ravi Das, and Kabir. Additional sant poetry may also be used, as are verses from the *Sar Bachan* of the first guru and the *Ghat Ramayana* of Tulsi Sahib. At satsangs held by the Agra branches, the readings are not selected from so wide a field. In the Agra satsangs, the services follow a set pattern of roughly fifteen minutes of recitations from the first master's *Sar Bachan*, fifteen minutes from the *Prem Patra* and other writings of Rai Saligram, and fifteen minutes of verses from more recent Radhasoami masters. The verses of the sants, especially Kabir, are referred to in the Agra masters' writings and discourses but are not used liturgically as they are at Beas. The sayings of present-day masters, at both Agra and Beas, are relegated to the end and used sparingly, if at all. A distinction is made in practice between those sayings that are regarded as scriptural—old, poetic, and easily rendered into song—and those that are didactic in nature and arise from a more recent revelation.

At most satsangs held by Beas or Ruhani Satsang, the exposition comes as a brief homily given by one of the satsang leaders after the verses are sung or read. At Agra, however, the privilege of giving a discourse is exclusively reserved for the master. This means that at Soamibagh, where there has been an interregnum between gurus, there is no discourse at all; and at Dayalbagh, where Lal-sahib has only reluctantly accepted the mantle of guruship, the discourse is often a reading of something written by his predecessor, while he sits quietly on the podium. Members of the Beas satsangs would also prefer to have the master give the exposition of the text, but the master cannot be everywhere, so many satsangs make do with the leaders who are appointed for that task, known simply as "preachers" or "the ones who hold the satsang." In Delhi, these preachers

[14] Thakar Singh, public lecture at Berkeley, California, January 3, 1981.

[15] My information on the pattern and organization of Radhasoami satsang services comes from interviews with R. N. Mehta, head of the Delhi satsangs of the Beas branch, Delhi, August 15, 1985; and with C. L. Kapur, president of one of the local Delhi branches, the Punjabi Bagh Satsang Ghar, Delhi, November 29, 1986.

rotate from one satsang to another, just as the pathis do; there are eighteen of them for the sixteen centers in the city.[16] They choose the text that the pathi will chant and interpret it in light of the master's teachings, using quotations from the writings or sayings of the master as liberally as possible. Sometimes the need for quoting the master at length is satisfied by a modern spiritual resource: a cassette tape recorder projecting the master's own voice. This is particularly popular in meetings held abroad, as are televised satsangs through videotape cassettes and VCRs.

The homilies of both preachers and masters are devotional; they urge followers to love the master, accept his love of them, and radiate that love in the service, righteousness, and humanity of daily life. Some theological concepts are discussed—such as nam, "the Name," which is the ultimate revelation of the Absolute—but allusions to the soul journey and the higher regions are made only in the most general way, in references to the spiritual dimension of the self or the promise of the world to come. Particulars about the mystical path of meditation are left to the writings of the masters and their special discourses; and although the congregation will usually meditate together prior to the readings, satsang is primarily the time when the other path to spiritual achievement—devotion—receives its due.

The Radhasoami Family and the Question of Caste

The Radhasoami fellowship is bound together in a familial love—not necessarily love for one another, at least initially, but love for and from the master. The parental role that the master plays enhances this familial image, and in Indian religious culture in general the terms used to designate the followers of a single master are familial ones: *guru-bhai* and *guru-bahin*, "brothers and sisters in the guru." In the Radhasoami fellowship this sense of camaraderie is even more pronounced; "greater than ties of blood," claims one Radhasoami leader, "are the ties of kinship uniting those who serve the same master."[17]

The contrast between the Radhasoami family and biological families is not usually stressed by Radhasoami teachers, however, most of whom are husbands and householders themselves.[18] To prevent dissension, married women whose husbands are opposed to Radhasoami teachings are often denied initiation. (If it is the husband whose wife is hostile to the teach-

[16] Interview with R. N. Mehta, Delhi, August 15, 1985.

[17] Interview with K. L. Khanna, May 25, 1971.

[18] There are only a few exceptions: most of the masters in the Tarn Taran line have been bachelors, as was Jaimal Singh, founder of the Beas branch. M. B. Lal, present master at Dayalbagh, has been a widower for many years and has no children.

ings, however, he is usually accepted, since it is assumed that in a traditional Indian family the wife will eventually bend to the husband's wishes.[19]) The masters regret any incidents of family discord caused by Radhasoami membership and counsel their devotees to "win your estranged family members over to your side with love."[20]

Most Indian devotees are spared these tensions since they join in family units, but the Radhasoami fellowship often poses a different sort of social problem for them: the problem of caste. Radhasoami's community challenges the traditional Indian notion of social order, that is, the linkage of family networks in a caste hierarchy. In the traditional Hindu scheme of things, salvation is closely bound up with one's respect for dharma, the moral system of caste-defined duties that is based upon a religious principle of inequality separating those who have been born into this world pure from those born impure.[21] To be saved the soul must rise to levels of greater and greater purity through a succession of lives, and at last be released from the social order altogether. One's social role thus plays an integral part in the Hindu scheme of salvation, and any theory that alters that view of salvation is apt to have an effect on social organization. Conversely, any movement for social change in India has to deal with, and alter, the religious rationale for caste.[22]

Radhasoami has that revolutionary potential. Its soteriology does not rely on dharmic purity, so its own society has no need to bear the marks of hierarchical inequality that are so important to most Hindus. In this respect the contemporary Radhasoami satsangis are much like their forebears, whose social backgrounds were diverse; one of the medieval sants was an Untouchable leatherworker, another was a low-caste Hindu weaver who had been adopted by Muslims, others were women, and one was blind. They are often touted in modern Indian writings as India's "first social reformers,"[23] and although it is unclear whether they ever intended their ideas of spiritual equality to extend to social relationships,[24] the religious associations that have been established in their names continue to have a reputation for social equality and are sought

[19] Interview with K. L. Khanna, May 25, 1971.

[20] Charan Singh, discourse to foreign satsangis, Beas, November 12, 1980.

[21] The fundamentally religious nature of caste is argued by Louis Dumont, *Homo Hierarchicus: The Caste System and Its Implications* (Chicago: University of Chicago Press, 1970), p. 47.

[22] See my *Religion as Social Vision*, p. 4.

[23] The thesis that the sants were democratic reformers is put forth in Raghavan, *The Great Integrators*, p. 32.

[24] The issue of whether the spiritual equality of the sants was intended to have implications for social equality is discussed in Hawley and Juergensmeyer, *Songs of the Saints*, pp. 16–17.

out by the less privileged.[25] The modern Radhasoami movement, in holding equality a virtue, keeps this sant idea alive.

Caste is not altogether absent in the social divisions within Radhasoami fellowships, but its more oppressive features are largely negated, and there have even been instances of remarkable alliances forged between members of the lowest castes and those much higher. In Nabha, for example, the leader is a Khatri, and as the fellowship developed in the 1950s, most of the new initiates were also Khatri, with one major exception: a man named Sundar Ram, a Chamar.[26] Khatris, mostly merchants, are considered to be among the twice-born and are allowed to wear the sacred thread; Chamars, however, are traditionally leatherworkers and are regarded as untouchable. But Sundar Ram was unusual: he had left his traditional caste occupation behind, and by becoming a cloth merchant was a sort of Khatri by association. He also encouraged many upwardly mobile members of his family and caste to join the Radhasoami fold along with him. Sundar Ram and his castemates have continued to be staunch pillars of the Nabha satsang since those early years: they contributed the land on which the Satsang compound now stands, and one may occasionally see Sundar Ram himself on the podium, seated on the flowered carpet in front of the picture of the master, expounding the tenets of the faith.

Not all of Nabha's proper society approves of this intercaste conviviality, and the disdain that it elicits exemplifies a familiar theme in Radhasoami history. At the beginning, Swami Dayal became embroiled in a brouhaha with the local Brahmans.[27] According to one account, the Swami allowed everyone who came to his quarters to drink the same water, all of it brought from a well on the banks of the Jumna River nearby. The Brahmans were displeased: not only were persons from different castes drinking from the same source, but the well was drawing water from a sacred source. The Brahmans physically attempted to prevent the Swami's assistants from carrying the water to him, but the Swami commanded them to persist, Brahmans or no. In telling this incident, the Swami's brother followed with a diatribe of his own against the absurdities of Brahmanic rules and the injustices of caste.[28]

[25] Kabir and Ravi Das, especially, have been brought forth as exponents of lower-caste social protest movements. For a discription of the movements that have been established in their names, see David Lorenzen, "The Kabir Panth and Social Protest," in Schomer and McLeod, *The Sants*, pp. 281–303; and his "Traditions of Non-Caste Hinduism," in *Contributions to Indian Sociology* 21, no. 2 (Spring 1987), pp. 263–83. See also Hawley and Juergensmeyer, *Songs of the Saints*, pp. 9–23, 35–49; and my *Religion as Social Vision*, pp. 83–91.

[26] This account is based on my field visit to Nabha, August 15, 1983, and my interview with Sundar Ram, Nabha, August 15, 1983.

[27] Pratap Singh Seth, *Biography of Soamiji Maharaj*, pp. 106–8.

[28] Ibid., pp. 110–20.

Swami Shiv Dayal's disdain for caste is also said to have gotten him into trouble with his own people: the caste leaders of the Khatris tried to excommunicate him.[29] Stories similar to this are also told about Rai Saligram, who is said to have been threatened with excommunication by the leaders of his Kayastha caste for consorting with the Khatri Swami;[30] and Brahm Sankar Misra was damned by his Brahman caste fellows for associating with a religious community that was populated largely by members of merchant castes.[31]

Some of that same spirit of defying caste is to be found in present-day Radhasoami satsangs, where the right to worship, to be initiated, or to assume a leadership role is open to anyone. But this stance does not mean that there is a true balance of caste representation. At Dayalbagh, for instance, there are virtually no lower-caste residents except for a few non-initiates, who in 1960 embarked on an embarrassingly public strike for higher wages.[32] Until 1957 separate eating places for lower and upper castes were maintained at the Beas Dera.[33] Much is made in Radhasoami writings about how the late master at Beas, Charan Singh, created "a significant social reform" when he abolished this practice.[34] It is said that when, even after the pronouncement, the untouchable satsangis huddled together at one side of the dining area, Charan Singh sat down and ate among them, thus establishing forever the precedent of intercaste commensality at the Beas Dera.[35] The master's egalitarian sentiments are undoubtedly the most important factor in shaping the attitude toward caste at Beas, but it is also true that the Indian government attempts to discourage caste through regulations prohibiting caste prejudice at religious places and through the threat that tax-exempt status will be denied to institutions that fail to abide by these rules.

Even so, a kind of status inequality continues to persist in many Radhasoami centers. At Beas, for instance, certain eating arrangements are still separate, for in addition to the large free eating grounds there are other, more pleasant restaurants on the premises that offer a finer fare for a small cost. No caste distinctions are made regarding entrance to one or the other, but the mere fact of the choice allows for a de facto separation between poorer low-caste devotees and richer high-caste and foreign ones. A similar distinction is made in sleeping quarters: the more luxurious ones are assigned to those who are accustomed to higher standards. These inequalities are based on economic position rather than caste, how-

[29] Ibid., p. 89.

[30] *Souvenir*, p. 43.

[31] *Souvenir*, pp. 79–80, 93.

[32] Interview with Baba Ram Jadoun, November 9, 1973.

[33] Interview with K. L. Khanna, Beas, May 25, 1971.

[34] Kapur, *Heaven on Earth*, p. 326.

[35] Ibid., p. 328.

ever, and many satsangis regard the emphasis on merit rather than birth as an improvement on traditional Indian social norms.

Equality Challenged: Gender and Physical Handicaps

Since Radhasoami society is unlike traditional Indian society in its attitude towards social equality, one would expect that its attitude toward gender and physical condition would be different as well. To a large extent that is correct. Women fare relatively better in Radhasoami society than in the power networks of traditional India. The Beas branch recently listed a "lady doctor" as chairman of its governing society,[36] and the head of Dayalbagh's new university is a woman. At least two Radhasoami masters have been women, as have some of the most loyal and spiritually exalted disciples of other masters. Yet it is also true that these women are rare and very special cases. The "lady doctor" who chaired the Beas governing society was Rani Lakshmibai Rajwade, member of the royal family of a former princely state, and the head of the Dayalbagh university, Mrs. G. P. Sherry, is the daughter of the former master, Gurcharandas Mehta. The annual reports of the Beas satsang from 1969 through 1984 list only one other woman to have served on the seventeen-member governing society,[37] and there have never been more than two or three women among the fifty members of the managing committee of Dayalbagh.[38] The two women who became masters have done so under unusual circumstances and not entirely with success.[39] One of the most recent women to be considered for guruship was the Ruhani Satsang's Bibi Hardevi, known as Taiji, "respected aunt."[40] She was never acclaimed Kirpal Singh's successor, however, and some said that the reason was that she was a woman: Kirpal Singh had once said that a woman could never become a sant satguru.[41]

[36] *Radhasoami Satsang, Beas: Origin and Growth* (Beas: Radhasoami Satsang, Beas, 1972), p. 8.

[37] The other prominent woman at Beas is Sheila Bharatram, whose profession is listed as "housewife" (Ibid., p. 9). She became president of the Society in 1979 (Radhasoami Satsang, Beas, *Annual Report*, 1979).

[38] G. D. Sahgal, president, Radhasoami Satsang Sabha, Dayalbagh, August 12, 1985.

[39] The brief and uncertain reign of Maheshwari Devi, the sister of Brahm Sankar Misra, is recounted in chapter 3. The only other woman to be proclaimed a master was Bibi Rani, the daughter of J. N. Hazra; she succeeded her father in 1966 as leader of a small offshoot of the Soamibagh line. Radhaji, wife of Swami Shiv Dayal Singh, was assigned to be a sort of spiritual counselor to the female devotees after the Swami's death, but it is not clear whether she was ever regarded as his successor.

[40] Interview with Kate Tillis, Landaur, November 30, 1980.

[41] Kirpal Singh, *Spiritual Elixir* (Delhi: Ruhani Satsang, 1972), vol. 2, p. 33.

Although the numbers of women in Radhasoami leadership are small, women are often in the majority at Radhasoami events. They also provide an army of workers to feed the thousands who come to Beas's rallies, and at Dayalbagh, the Mahila Cooperative Association, a women's organization, provides much of the community's income.[42] Radhasoami women are also regarded as stalwarts of spirituality. Perhaps best known are the curious trio—Shibboji, Bukkiji, and Vishnoji— who were devoted followers of the first master. Vishnoji was "in constant attendance" on Swami Shiv Dayal,[43] and when he delivered discourses and explained sacred texts "Bukkiji's eyes would become red and tears would flow." While he smoked the *hukka* (water pipe) or sat silently reading the scriptures, Bukkiji would "suck His toes for hours and enjoy the nectar of His Feet," which she described as being "like mother's milk."[44] As for Shibboji, she became "so over-powered" in yearning for the Swami's darshan that "she became stark naked" and ran through the marketplace oblivious to the crowds, explaining that she had not noticed anyone aware of her nakedness except Swami Shiv Dayal, in whose eyes there were no secrets.[45] A later telling of this story provides a different rationale for her nudity. According to this account, Shibboji's husband had tried to keep her from leaving her wifely duties and running off to become a devotee of Swami Shiv Dayal. As she strained to leave him, he held on to what he could—her sari—and the garment ripped from her body as she lunged out of the house, through the marketplace, and up to the satsang of her spiritual master.[46] This version of the story makes Shibboji a modern-day version of the medieval sant Mirabai, who is said to have also torn free from her earthly husband to join her real husband, Lord Krishna.[47]

The Great Master at Beas also had three women attending him—Bibi Lajjo, Bibi Rakhi, and Bibi Ralli—who were also model devotees. One contemporary account reported that they rendered "a great service to the Master by preparing his food, doing his laundry, pressing his clothes, and doing his sewing, mending, etc." The report affirmed that these women were "all spiritually-minded, advanced souls, and serve with a loving devotion that is rare on this earth." It quickly added, "Of course, they get no financial pay." The explanation for their generosity was that "they consider that they are serving the King of Kings."[48]

[42] *Souvenir*, p. 330.

[43] Pratap Singh Seth, *Biography of Soamiji Maharaj*, p. 83.

[44] Ibid., p. 81.

[45] Ibid., p. 79.

[46] Maheshwari, *Bhaktmal of Radhasoami Faith*, pp. 50–53.

[47] For stories about Mira, see the introduction to the translations of her poetry in Hawley and Juergensmeyer, *Songs of the Saints*, pp. 119–33.

[48] Johnson, *With a Great Master in India*, pp. 126–27.

Bibi Rakhi was particularly famous for giving detailed accounts of her spiritual experiences—"what she saw and heard during her journey through the First, Second and Third regions."[49] It is said that "one could see the light of Truth and joy shining in her face as she told in simple language of the marvels she had seen."[50]

The Radhasoami attitude toward gender is complex. On the one hand, its organizations are aggressive, rational, powerful, and efficient and exhibit what are often thought of as male virtues. On the other hand, what is ultimately valued for spiritual purposes are traits of submission, innocence, subtlety, and love, virtues that are often ascribed particularly to women. It is no surprise, then, that Radhasoami men should praise women for doing what men think women do well, and should want in some sense to emulate them. This compliment paid to women has its roots in Vaisnava bhakti, where devotees seek to be like Krishna's lady friends, especially his favorite, Radha, and mimic their love for the handsome Lord.[51] Of course, some people may regard the very premise of this compliment as demeaning to women: the notion that women are inherently less capable of spiritual achievement than men.

The validity of the traditional Indian view that women are born with a heavier karmic burden than men is a matter of some debate in Radhasoami circles. Some masters say that spiritual achievement is a private matter between oneself and one's master, and that gender is irrelevant; others deny that women have a capacity for spiritual greatness; and still others are circumspect. Charan Singh, for instance, says that women are sometimes less able to progress spiritually because they are "tied down to the world" by the "instinct of devotion," but he notes that the same instinct gives them the ability to move more rapidly in meditation in the initial stages. A man takes longer because "his approach is through logic and reasoning," while "a woman's approach is primarily devotional; she does not bother very much to analyse things."[52] Even so, he affirms that it is possible for women to reach a high level of spirituality—the sant, Mirabai, is given as an example—and even the pronoun used to refer to the Absolute could be "He or She, or One."[53] Other masters are more

[49] Ibid., p. 30.

[50] Ibid.

[51] See an interesting exploration of the gender issue in Vaisnava devotion in the essays in Hawley and Wulff, *The Divine Consort*; in Hawley's *Sur Das: Singer, Poet, Saint* (Seattle: University of Washington Press, 1984), pp. 113–18; and his article, "Images of Gender in the Poetry of Krishna," in Caroline Bynum et al., eds., *Gender and Religion: On the Complexity of Symbols* (Boston: Beacon Press, 1986).

[52] Charan Singh, *Spiritual Heritage*, p. 186.

[53] Charan Singh, *The Master Answers*, p. 16.

pessimistic about the ability of women to overcome their heavy burden of karma.[54] "On principle," said Anand Swarup, "a female cannot attain the status of a Saint."[55]

Much the same is said about the physically handicapped. The blind especially are regarded throughout India as having suffered an enormous weight of bad karma, and as a result some within Radhasoami have thought it impossible for the blind to achieve a high degree of spiritual achievement. It is said that once when Kirpal Singh took pity on a blind man and initiated him, the trauma of his assuming the weight of the blind man's karma was so great that the master became physically ill.[56]

The spiritual progress of the blind is also impaired by their inability to visualize the physical form of the master. "The nature of our spiritual practices excludes them," one of the leaders at Dayalbagh explained.[57] For these reasons, some Radhasoami masters have regarded it as futile to initiate the blind at all. Once a British devotee wrote to the Great Master at Beas and urged him to initiate a blind man who earned his living playing the piano and who "loved him very much." His love failed to persuade the master, however, who responded that initiation was out of the question "because a blind man cannot have the Darshan or sight of the Satguru."[58] The barrier against initiation does not apply to persons who, through accident, have gone blind after birth, however, and the Great Master at Beas is said to have restored eyesight to a satsangi who had temporarily gone blind.[59] One successor of Swami Shiv Dayal Singh, Garib Das, was said to have been blind, but he presumably lost his sight through old age rather than as a condition of birth. Because sight is regarded as such a precious gift, Radhasoami leaders have made special efforts to alleviate the problems of those afflicted with eye diseases. At Beas a huge "eye camp" is sponsored each year in order to provide free operations for those whose sight is impaired. But even though it is claimed that true blindness is "not in the loss of eyes, but in keeping away from God," those whose eyesight has been lost from birth continue to be excluded from most of the Radhasoami fellowships.[60]

[54] Interview with Kate Tillis, November 30, 1980.

[55] *Souvenir*, p. 91.

[56] Interview with Kate Tillis, November 30, 1980. Charan Singh is said to have told an audience in London that he would not initiate anyone who did not have the potential of reaching the highest regions within this lifetime, and this excluded the blind, whose karmic weight precluded this possibility.

[57] Interview with G. D. Sahgal, Dayalbagh, August 12, 1985. A similar explanation has been given to me by initiates at the Beas, Ruhani Satsang, and Soamibagh branches.

[58] Ram, *With the Three Masters*, vol. 2, p. 17.

[59] Johnson, *With a Great Master in India*, p. 31.

[60] Kirpal Singh, *Godman*, p. 47.

Radhasoami Customs

Even with these inequities, the Radhasoami fellowships are fairly egalitarian communuties. In fact, their meritocratic societies are somewhat out of phase with traditional Indian social values. For the sake of ecumenical relations, however, Radhasoami teachers want to downplay these differences, and initiates are encouraged to retain their old religious customs.[61] In keeping with this policy of multiculturalism, Radhasoami leaders have avoided establishing their own rituals for the major events in an individual's life. Devotees sometimes fail to abide by this canon, however, and the rudiments of a Radhasoami culture have begun to emerge.

After a Radhasoami couple solemnize their marriage in a traditional Hindu or Sikh ceremony they sometimes will come to the master for his blessings, or they will have a satsang held in honor of the occasion. The preferred marriage is a secular one, but if the marriage follows Hindu rites, it is kept simple: no dowry, no priest, and no lavish feasts.[62] At Dayalbagh lists are kept of available prospects to help in making the match, and there has been a marriage committee (a *panchayat*) at Dayalbagh since 1940 to facilitate these matters.[63] Special satsangs and blessings are also frequently sought at the time of the birth of a child.

New customs and ceremonies have also grown up in Radhasoami communities to deal with death. If there is some indication in advance that a Radhasoami devotee is near death, satsangis will minister to the dying person by reading passages from the writings of the masters. In some cases, at the very moment of death the ears and the eyes of the dying person will be covered to hasten the soul's departure through its proper portal, the eye center in the forehead.[64] After death, a special satsang may be held. The ashes of loved ones have been sent to Dayalbagh or Beas to be ceremonially deposited in the Jumna or Beas Rivers, respectively, but the practice is discouraged by Radhasoami leaders.[65] An American satsangi who wanted to have last rites for his pet cat packed the dead animal in ice and sent it to Beas with the request that it be given "all your ceremonies and traditions"[66] Months later, when the parcel finally arrived, an

[61] Kirpal Singh, "Way of the Saints" (unpublished circular), p. 3.

[62] Interview with Ram Jadoun, Dayalbagh, November 9, 1973.

[63] *Souvenir*, p. 254. In 1977, a Vivah Sangam was established at Dayalbagh in 1977 "to assist Satsangi parents to find amongst Satsangi families suitable matches for their marriageable wards" (*Review of Progress Made by Satsang Institutions During the Last Ten Years [1975–1984]*, supplement to *Dayalbagh Herald*, August 13, 1985, p. 4).

[64] Interview with Kate Tillis, Landaur, October 24, 1980. Beas officials deny that this custom is practiced there.

[65] Interview with K. L. Khanna, May 25, 1971.

[66] Charan Singh, *Spiritual Heritage*, pp. 133–34.

unfortunate general secretary opened the box, and this has made Beas leaders even more resolute in discouraging the practice of sending the remains of departed loved ones to the central satsang. The custom of cremating bodies on the banks of the Beas was common in the time of the Great Master, however,[67] and Dayalbagh also has its cremation grounds, reserved for residents of the Dayalbagh colony.[68] A few deaths have achieved historical significance within the Radhasoami tradition—those of the masters—and their death anniversaries have become great commemorative and pilgrimage occasions. They are celebrated in public events at Agra, Beas, and Delhi and also privately in the home of satsangis.

The Social Significance of Satsang

It would appear, then, that Radhasoami society has two dimensions. On one hand it is intimately linked with the religious cultures around it, to the point that when one of his American initiates asked Charan Singh whether he should leave Christianity behind, it was natural for the Beas master to assure him that since Radhasoami was itself the truest form of Christianity, he should embrace the Church with new enthusiasm.[69] On the other hand, Radhasoami retains a certain suspicion of these traditional cultures, and the same master cautioned his American devotee not to take seriously all of the "dogmas, rituals and ceremonies" of the Church, for the "priestly class" was out to "exploit" the unwary with its rituals and such.[70] Ultimately, he said, such customs held "no significance"; they paled before the deeper truths of the spiritual life.[71]

Most Radhasoami devotees agree with this assessment, but they also have no difficulty with the notion that they can be good Christians, Hindus, or Sikhs and good satsangis at the same time, since they regard Radhasoami as something different from the society around it. Yet they do not think of Radhasoami as being so far beyond ordinary religion that it has no social form at all. In a survey questionnaire I administered to a hundred residents of a Punjabi village, I found that Radhasoami members consistently identified with the social aspects of their religion more strongly than did those who were not satsangis. They said that in times of trouble they would look toward their satsangi comrades, whereas the

[67] Johnson, *With a Great Master*, p. 35.
[68] Interview with G. D. Sahgal, August 12, 1985.
[69] Charan Singh, *Spiritual Heritage*, p. 213.
[70] Ibid.
[71] Charan Singh, *The Master Answers*, p. 499.

others said they would turn to government agencies or caste associations.[72]

Dayalbagh has tried to capitalize on these feelings of social separation; Beas and the Ruhani Satsang have been more cautious. "We are not here to transform society," Charan Singh told his followers, "but to transcend it."[73] When this statement was made at a gathering of Western followers, some were displeased, others felt it reflected a realistically cautious attitude toward Indian society, and still others accepted his statement as fact: that social issues are irrelevant to religion. In an essentially religious society like India, however, religious values have social implications, and Radhasoami continues to be what most panthic movements in Indian history have always been: counterstructures that exist in symbiotic relation to the religious culture of the dominant societies around them.[74]

The panthic model is also one that fits comfortably in a modern secular society. Both dharmic Hinduism and qaumic Islam and Sikhism have recently been at odds with the secular nation-state. These traditional religious communities feel that the secular society intrudes on what had been their domain—a public order for which they provided basic social, spiritual, and political values. But as self-contained societies, the Radhasoami groups are able to exist as islands in a sea of secularity. As Ainslie Embree points out, one of the greatest challenges of a modern religious organization is to find ways of surviving in, and providing a counterbalance to, the secular nation-state.[75] By creating their own ideal fellowships, protected from the rest of the society, the Radhasoami communities insulate themselves from the defects of the broader collectivity and offer a new religious alternative to it.

[72] The results of this poll, and an explanation of how it was conducted, are to be found in an appendix to my dissertation, "Political Hope: Scheduled Caste Social Movements in the Punjab, 1900–1970," Department of Political Science, University of California, Berkeley, 1974. It should be noted that this survey was taken long before the current rise of Sikh militarism and the polarization of religious sentiments in the Punjab.

[73] Charan Singh, discourse to foreign guests, Beas, November 12, 1980.

[74] I explore further the notion of social movements as counterstructures in *Religion as Social Vision*, pp. 278–82.

[75] Embree borrows the phrase "ideology of transition" from the sociologist Thomas O'Dea to describe how religion in a secular society can "work to stabilize social institutions" and at the same time "become a vehicle for changing and transforming society" (Ainslie T. Embree, *Utopias in Conflict: Religion and Nationalism in Modern India* [Berkeley: University of California Press, 1990], p. 10).

Six

Selfless Service

It is said that when the chief disciple of the first master entrusted his spiritual destiny to the master's hands, he immediately began doing "*abyas* [spiritual practices] and *seva* [service] with great devotion."[1] Pictures of Rai Saligram show him standing beside Swami Shiv Dayal with a fly whisk in his hand, looking as selfless as the lowliest servant, apparently ready to dispatch the tiniest insect from his master's presence. Saligram's servile attitude was significant, for in the Radhasoami context, seva is prerequisite to all other spiritual accomplishments, and it gives moral meaning to all outward deeds.

This link between the moral and the spiritual, found in virtually every religious tradition, helps to explain the classic conundrum of why people do good when they receive no obvious and direct benefit from doing so.

10. Devotees at Beas undertaking *mitti seva* by carrying loads of dirt on their heads.

[1] Pratap Singh Seth, *Biography of Soamiji Maharaj*, p. 73.

This puzzle has exercised some of the greatest minds of ethical theory, and the answer they have often given is that people live moral lives because of religious obligation or because of a commitment to a moral order of such a profound and universal character that it approaches religious conviction.[2] One of the reasons why modern persons have difficulty clarifying moral issues is that they must live with a lack of consensus about whether that profound moral order exists or, if it does, what it consists of.

The traditional Hindu explanation is to be found in the concepts of karma and dharma. The theory of karma gives the soteriological reason for doing good—your soul will not be born into a higher form and ultimately leave this mortal plane unless you are virtuous—and the obligations of dharma let you know what the virtues should be. Many modern persons, however, find the metempsychosis of karma to be untenable and the nonegalitarianism of dharma to be unacceptable, and regard both concepts as based on a notion of scriptural authority that is antiquated.

In Radhasoami, the limitations of karma are alleviated by spiritual practices that allow a soul to bypass the cycles of birth and rebirth, and dharmic social order is supplanted by the more egalitarian satsang. The concepts of karma and dharma are not absent from Radhasoami thought, but they have been adapted to the Radhasoami scheme of things. Karma, for instance, was interpreted by the Great Master at Beas as being of three kinds: "store" karma that has burdened souls for eons, "fate" karma that determines how one was born into this world, and "fruit" karma that a person creates day by day.[3] The grace of a master enables one initially to "clear accounts" of all previous karma by inculcating "the spirit of doing actions without any thought of reward."[4] Radhasoami spiritual practices enable a person to continue in a spirit of nonattached action so that no new negative karma will be created.[5]

Thus Radhasoami provides a solution to a modern person's impatience with the theory of karma, but in doing so it seems to revive the classic problem: justifying social responsibility and moral acts. Without the fear of failing to amass sufficient merit to enable one to escape the karmic cycle, why would the Radhasoami devotee want to do good? The answers

[2] Kant's categorical imperative and Rawls's theory of justice, for instance, both envisage an ultimate moral order that makes one willing to sacrifice immediate personal gains. Ronald Green has recently argued that Kant's ethics were not just covertly religious: he presumed that people who make sacrifices for the sake of morality have a faith that provides an ultimate reward for their virtue; see Ronald Green, *Religious Reason* (New York: Oxford University Press, 1978) and *Religion and Moral Reason* (New York: Oxford University Press, 1988).

[3] Sawan Singh, *Philosophy of the Masters*, vol. 1, p. 21.

[4] Ibid., p. 22.

[5] Ibid., pp. 22–23.

to this question are to be found in the Radhasoami practices that are used to counter the deleterious effects of karma. Meditation stimulates the sort of self-discipline that leads to a host of personal virtues, and devotion gives a reason for serving someone in this world besides oneself. On these two foundations—discipline and humility—stand the whole edifice of Radhasoami ethics.

Food, Sex, and Moral Purity

Discipline begins with control of physical cravings. "The journey of the soul begins in the body," explains one Radhasoami master, "so the body must be pure and honorably directed."[6] The nine doors of the body are particularly dangerous zones, and Radhasoami leaders encourage their devotees to control them, to "detach the mind from unnecessary thoughts of the world and concentrate within."[7] The mind can then lead the soul toward the tenth opening, the invisible central eye.

At the time of Radhasoami initiation, candidates are questioned about their capacity for detachment and control. Special attention is paid to their habits regarding the use of drugs and alcohol, the eating of meat, and sex.[8] From a Western point of view, the seriousness with which diet is regarded is the most unusual feature of Radhasoami requirements. Radhasoami teachings insist on strict vegetarianism, forbidding even the eating of eggs. Initiates are not allowed "even an occasional plate of soup containing eggs, fish, fowl or meat or meat broth."[9]

One reason given for Radhasoami vegetarianism is the conviction that all forms of life are to be respected. Then too, there is the concern about the act of killing that is necessary to transform calves into veal and steers into steak: it produces bad karma, not just to those who perform it, but to those who encourage it by their consumption of the products of the slaughter.[10] Yet there are other, even more basic reasons why Radhasoami members avoid meat, and those are revealed in the controversy over eggs.

[6] Interview with Darshan Singh, Delhi, August 16, 1985.

[7] Rai Saligram, *Prem Patra Radhasoami*, vol. 1, p. 229.

[8] These are the Beas and Ruhani Satsang requirements; similar moral strictures are required at other branches. At Dayalbagh, for example, the five vows taken at initiation oblige satsangis to avoid intoxicants, refrain from eating meat, be financially self-supporting, accept *Radhasoami* as the true name of God, and not divulge the secrets of the meditation practices (*Souvenir*, p. 304).

[9] Charan Singh, *Light on Sant Mat*, p. 176.

[10] Charan Singh regards anything that one does to encourage the slaughter of animals as implicating one in their deaths and rebukes the argument given by some Buddhists that eating meat is acceptable as long as one is not engaged in the act of killing (Charan Singh, quoted in Wason, *The Living Master*, pp. 168–71).

From time to time some Western satsangis raise the point that eggs available in American supermarkets are unfertilized, and that an unfertilized egg is not an animal in the technical sense. Nothing is killed, they say, by eating eggs, just as no form of life is destroyed in drinking the milk of cows. Charan Singh responded to these objections by saying that the egg is essentially a fetus, whether it is fertilized or not, and he cautioned that to waver from vegetarianism even minutely "might lead to a possible misuse and thus defeat the purpose."[11] Furthermore, the master argued, "eggs are known to incite animal instincts which, in turn, are not conducive to a calm and peaceful mind."[12]

The concluding point is interesting, for few Americans or Europeans would take for granted that eggs incite "animal instincts." In India, however, it is a matter of common knowledge. Every Indian knows that certain kinds of foods, meat and eggs among them, arouse the passions, and for that reason vegetarianism is one of the marks of Brahmans and others who occupy high spiritual office or aspire to it.

One might infer, then, that when Radhasoami leaders advocate vegetarianism they are showing that they and their followers are as cultured as Brahmans: they are "sanskritizing," as sociologists call the practice of adopting the manners of higher-caste people in order to elevate one's own social status.[13] The fact that the first master was engaged in some sort of rivalry with local Brahmans might give credence to this view,[14] but the historical evidence is too scanty to be sure, and there is nothing in Swami Shiv Dayal's writings that directly supports it. Moreover, none of the Radhasoami teachers following him suggest that one should be vegetarian simply because it is Brahmanic, even though their insistence upon it is extreme. Rai Saligram, for instance, lists proper diet as one of five moral remedies for bad karma,[15] and Darshan Singh mentions it as one of the three chief components of a decent life.[16]

Perhaps the Radhasoami teachers agree with the Brahmanic restriction on eating eggs and meat not because it is Brahmanic, but because they share the major premise that underlies it: that is, that moral attitudes are affected by food. The traditional Indian designation of foods as hot, cold,

[11] Charan Singh, *Light on Sant Mat*, p. 329.

[12] Ibid.

[13] M. N. Srinivas, *Caste in Modern India and Other Essays* (Bombay: Asia Publishing House, 1962) and *Social Change in Modern India* (Berkeley: University of California Press, 1966).

[14] Pratap Singh Seth, *Biography of Soamiji Maharaj*, pp.106–20. See also the discussion in chapter 5 concerning Swami Shiv Dayal's quarrels with Brahmans.

[15] Rai Saligram, *Jugat Prakash Radhasoami*, p. 61. The other remedies are right conduct, a well-behaved mind, good thoughts, devotion, and avoiding bad people.

[16] Darshan Singh, *Spiritual Aspects of Vegetarian Diet*, Ruhani Satsang circular, n.p., n.d.

or neutral, for instance, does not refer to the actual temperature of foods but to their alleged effects on the body and its emotions.[17] Yogurt and milk are said to cool the bodily organs, while meat and eggs excite and heat them. By arousing the passions, hot foods stimulate the baser appetites and impair one's spiritual purity. Echoing the common view, the Great Master at Beas described foods as *sattvik*, which produce "pure feelings"; *rajsik*, which have a "heating effect on the system"; and *tamsik*, which are virtually flammable.[18] Foods placed in each category by Sawan Singh are found in Table 2.[19]

Hot foods, according to Radhasoami teachers, "incite animal instincts" and "generate outward activity and energy" that is detrimental to "the exaltation of the spiritual current."[20] They "excite the body and mind to unnecessary and undesirable activities."[21] These "animal instincts" that are "excited" by hot foods are, of course, sexual feelings.

With only rare exceptions, Radhasoami masters have been united in their condemnation of sex.[22] "Sex is not only sinful," one master ex-

TABLE 2
The Spiritual Significance of Food

Satvik Foods	*Rajsik Foods*	*Tamsik Foods*
butter	food served with pungent spices	stale, raw, over-ripe food
milk		eggs
rice		meat
pulses		fish
vegetables		wine
		any other food, including *satvik* food, taken to excess

[17] For a discussion of the spiritual significance of food in India see R. S. Khare, *Food, Society and Culture*: Durham, N.C.: Carolina Academic Press, 1986), *passim*.

[18] Sawan Singh, *Philosophy of the Masters*, vol. 3, p. 227. In a letter to Sawan Singh, Jaimal Singh advocated drinking milk and *ghi* (butter oil) to "purify the blood" (*Spiritual Letters*, p. 38).

[19] Sawan Singh, *Philosophy of the Masters*, vol. 3, p. 227.

[20] Misra, *Discourses*, Appendix A, p. 309.

[21] Anand Swarup, *Yathartha Prakasa*, part 1, p. 3.

[22] A. P. Mathur is one of the exceptions. He says that sexual relations should have a normal place in the lives of devotees (Interview with A. P. Mathur, Agra, August 10, 1983). According to one of his disciples, Mathur further claims that "deprivation of sex is not

plained, "it is a serious impediment on the Holy Path."[23] Sexual feelings cause one to focus attention on the lower energy centers within the body and discourage the soul from rising higher, and the genitals provide an aperture through which the soul's attention may escape its bodily channel. Moreover, sexual activity causes a male to lose a vital source of spiritual energy: his semen, which traditionally in India has been thought to have spiritual as well as physical potential. The retention of semen is considered an important spiritual discipline for those attempting to build up spiritual strength, such as students and sadhus.[24] One Radhasoami master initiated a conversation with an American student by asking whether the student had been losing his semen.[25] The master, Faqir Chand, despaired that modern people "indulge too much in sex," and went on to explain that "40 drops of blood form one drop of marrow (*ojus*) and 40 drops of marrow form one drop of semen." Those who "waste their semen unnecessarily" will be exploited by doctors or "sadhus of my type."[26] Faqir Chand explained that seminal fluid was identified with the highest spiritual energy: "Semen in man is the only visible God in human body. No Mahatma, no Guru, not even God can grant peace of mind to a person who does not learn to master his instinct of sex. That is the reason I advise young men and women to lead their lives in celebacy [*sic*]."[27]

Few Radhasoami teachers are as direct as Faqir Chand in describing the spiritual value of semen, but some do refer obliquely to "the vital fluid of life,"[28] and Rai Saligram urged young people to "control the desires arising in the mind and the vehemence of sensual pleasures."[29]

---

necessary nor even helpful" for the spiritual path (Interview with Paul Hogguel, Agra, December 6, 1980). See also the interview with Hogguel in Malcolm Tillis, *Turning East*.

[23] Kirpal Singh, *The Teachings of Kirpal Singh*, p. 44.

[24] Regarding the spiritual significance of semen see Lilian Silburn, *Kundalini: Energy of the Depths*, trans. Jacques Gontier (Albany: State University of New York Press, 1988), pp. 160–61; and Wendy Doniger O'Flaherty, *Siva: The Erotic Ascetic* (originally *Asceticism and Eroticism in the Mythology of Siva*) (Oxford: Oxford University Press, 1973), pp. 4–11 and *passim*. On the correspondence of a woman's milk to a man's semen, see Wendy Doniger O'Flaherty, *Women, Androgynes, and Other Mythical Beasts* (Chicago: University of Chicago Press, 1980), pp. 43–48.

[25] Faqir Chand, *The Master Speaks to the Foreigners: Seekers from Abroad*, ed. B. R. Kamal (Hosiarpur: Faqir Library Charitable Trust, 1978), p. 8.

[26] Faqir Chand, *The Master Speaks*, p. 35.

[27] Faqir Chand, *Autobiography of Faqir* (unpublished ms., c. Fall, 1980), p. 15. See also David Lane, *The Unknowing Sage: The Life and Work of Baba Faqir Chand* (Del Mar, Calif.: Del Mar Press, 1989).

[28] Kirpal Singh, *The Teachings of Kirpal Singh*, vol. 2, p. 44. The term Kirpal Singh sometimes uses for power of sexuality is *ojas*.

[29] Rai Saligram, *Prem Patra Radhasoami*, vol. 1, pp. 48–49.

The Radhasoami concern about sex is not simply a matter of prudishness, but a concern over the indiscipline of mind and body that is implied in allowing sexual energy to be squandered foolishly. According to the present master at Beas, "Sex energy is very useful if it is transmuted, that is, turned inwards and utilized by Bhajan and Simran."[30] But although Radhasoami masters find continence and celibacy "admirable" and "proper"[31] and forbid premarital experimentation and sexual relations between members of the same sex,[32] they recognize that householders, including themselves, have a responsibility to indulge in at least as much sexual activity as it takes to bear children. In fact, one young man at Dayalbagh said that he felt that he was positively required to get married in order to stay on the spiritual path. He was expected, he said, to "make himself fulfilled."[33]

In traditional Indian culture, the contradiction embedded in this now positive, now negative attitude to sex is resolved by taking a different view of sex in each stage of life. But Radhasoami teachings deal with this contradiction simultaneously rather than sequentially, by positing a double set of obligations: to one's family and to one's spiritual discipline. "I have to try to be perfect in a worldly as well as a spiritual way," the young man at Dayalbagh explained. "There should be a balance."[34] What makes the two compatible is a sense of self-control. If sex is in its place—if it serves the soul rather than mastering it—then it is permissible. It is only when it gets out of control that sex poses a problem.

This attitude is applied to other moral matters as well. Lust is but the first of five temptations; the others are anger, greed, attachment, and pride.[35] They are sometimes identified with the five sense organs of the eyes, ears, and mouth.[36] It would be a bit misleading to call these the five deadly sins, for the simplistic idea of sin—the notion that some acts are immoral in and of themselves—does not occur in Radhasoami. The only real sin, from the Radhasoami point of view, is humanity's inability to control and discipline itself. It is an original sin, in that such a disposition is congenital to the human condition, and only the grace of a spiritual

[30] Charan Singh, *Light on Sant Mat*, pp. 213–14.

[31] Kirpal Singh, circular letter, July 3, 1972; and Rai Saligram, *Prem Patra Radhasoami*, vol. 2, p. 40.

[32] Interview with Roland deVries, Nevada City, California, January 18, 1986.

[33] Interview with Kirpal Narayan, Dayalbagh, August 13, 1985.

[34] Ibid.

[35] Rai Saligram, *Jugat Prakash Radhasoami*, p. 22. See also idem, *Prem Patra Radhasoami*, vol. 2, pp. 36–48.

[36] Rai Saligram, *Jugat Prakash Radhasoami*, pp. 19–20.

master is a force of sufficient strength to give one freedom from, and power over, one's own intemperate mind.

The Proper Person

The habits of mind that are most highly prized in Radhasoami morality are those that reflect the virtue of self-discipline. The ideal Radhasoami demeanor is upright, responsible, chaste, clearheaded and self-sufficient: what one observer of Radhasoami called "a type of Hindu puritanism."[37] As with Christian Puritanism, the patterns of simple, honest living are not just products of spiritual achievement, they are the prerequisites for it. "An ethical life," counseled Kirpal Singh, "is the stepping stone to spirituality,"[38] and a Radhasoami author at Beas claimed that morality was "the foundation for the superstructure of scientific spirituality."[39]

In comparison with most modern life-styles the preferred Radhasoami demeanor seems downright dull. Charan Singh cautioned his followers to "control the gossiping habit" and discouraged them from watching movies and television too frequently because they "distract the attention."[40] Rai Saligram proposed a fifteen-point rule of conduct, including the avoidance of "jealousy, enmity and anger"; behaving "politely, meekly and affectionately"; not harming anyone; refraining from being "excessively pleased" if good fortune comes one's way; enduring "taunts, criticisms, etc., so far as may be appropriate"; and "not deceiving anybody" for personal gain.[41] One's professional duties, furthermore, should be performed "properly and carefully."[42]

The Radhasoami emphasis on fairness and honesty is especially noticeable in the area of business relations. In India as elsewhere, where shopkeepers are known to haggle and cut corners, Radhasoami businessmen are often scrupulous in the extreme. The horsecart drivers that taxi between the Beas railway station and the dera, for example, accept only a low fixed price for their service and refuse to take a rupee more. Shopkeepers at Dayalbagh have been known to run after customers to make certain they have received the proper change from their purchases, and the books, meals, and other items offered for sale at the Radhasoami cen-

[37] Griswold, *Insights into Modern Hinduism*, p. 139.
[38] Kirpal Singh, *The Teachings of Kirpal Singh*, vol. 3, p. 3.
[39] Johnson, *With a Great Master*, p. 138.
[40] Charan Singh, *Light on Sant Mat*, p. 319.
[41] Rai Saligram, *Prem Patra Radhasoami*, vol. 1, pp. 63–68.
[42] Ibid., p. 64.

ters are available virtually at cost. Anand Swarup, in talking about the effect of Radhasoami teachings on one's daily life, compared them with the curative medicine that neutralizes the poison of a snake bite; the higher calling of Radhasoami protects someone "living in the world and taking part in the struggle for earning his livelihood" from what Swarup regarded as "the poisonous effects of the unrestrained activities he may have to indulge in."[43]

Perhaps the Radhasoami work ethic is also a way of reviving one aspect of traditional Hindu dharma: the notion that one's occupation has intrinsic meaning. Dharmic obligations traditionally included the honorable fulfillment of the duties that went with one's caste, whether one was a potter, a tanner, a peddler, a priest, or any other caste-defined role. In modern urban India many of these jobs no longer exist; the network of personal relationships provided by the caste system has begun to lapse, and the moral duties implied by new occupations are often unclear. Radhasoami teachings help provide an ethical framework for new economic roles and infuse ordinary, often bureaucratic, tasks with a sense of moral purpose.

Because one's work itself has value, there is little impetus to seek jobs for excitement or even personal fulfillment. Instead, satsangis are encouraged to adopt lines of work that will provide financial independence and serve the public good. Devotees seeking initiation may be denied it until they can demonstrate some means of support.

The masters have set an example by being wage earners themselves. They have typically refused to take on full-time positions of spiritual leadership until retiring from their secular occupations. Such recent masters as M. B. Lal, I. C. Sharma, Darshan Singh, and Thakar Singh have been retired university or government workers. A. P. Mathur, Gurinder Singh, and Rajinder Singh took on their duties as spiritual masters at relatively young ages, but continued to earn their living: Mathur was a professor of history at Agra College, Gurinder Singh was a businessman in Spain, and Rajinder Singh was an engineer for AT & T in Chicago. Some of them eventually quit their jobs, as did Charan Singh, who was trained as a lawyer. He had large landholdings, however, and was said to live off their proceeds rather than accepting his devotees' largesse. The Beas branch of the movement, like the others, is proud of the fact that its spiritual leader is not dependent for his livelihood on the movement itself.

[43] Anand Swarup, *Yathartha Prakasa*, p. 108.

Soldiers, Sadhus and Worldly Ascetics

The ideal Radhasoami occupation is a mean between the extremes of being engaged too much in worldly affairs and too little. In the middle are responsible tasks: bureaucratic, mercantile, and agrarian occupations that are much admired in Radhasoami circles. But it is not always clear when an occupation has veered too far in one direction or the other. Military occupations are an interesting case in point, especially since the first two masters at Beas, Jaimal Singh and Sawan Singh, were soldiers. On the whole, Radhasoami teachings oppose violence: "We do not kill birds or animals for food, nor are we to kill anything for sport," says Charan Singh, Sawan Singh's grandson. "We practise nonviolence."[44] Yet Charan Singh concedes that it is a soldier's task to take up arms in battle: "If it is your duty, you have to do it."[45] At the same time he counsels that "if you are really sincere and you do not want to kill . . . there is a guiding force behind you which saves you from such situations."[46] As examples, he can point to his predecessors, who, though soldiers, were never given an order to shoot. The main complaint of Sawan Singh was that army life left little time to meditate, [47] and Jaimal Singh expressed some displeasure with military housing. "You have to live like Europeans," he said in one of his letters, "otherwise the cantonment is good and the air is pure."[48]

At the other extreme from a soldier's way of life is one that is looked upon with even more suspicion in Radhasoami circles: asceticism. Even so, several Radhasoami masters have lived as renunciants for extensive periods of time. Swami Shiv Dayal meditated alone for years, and when the bachelor Jaimal Singh retired from the army, he went to a site along the banks of the Beas River frequented by sadhus and became "a recluse."[49] Whatever he might do himself, however, Jaimal Singh cautioned Sawan Singh against adopting a similar career.[50] He was particularly incensed over rumors that Sawan Singh was accepting offerings like a mendicant sadhu and warned that "nothing should be put to your personal use unless it comes out of your own earnings." He even accused Sawan Singh of "accepting eatables" and told him "this is very, very improper and should never be done."[51]

The Radhasoami ambivalence towards asceticism began early. Al-

[44] Charan Singh, *The Master Answers*, p. 466.
[45] Ibid., p. 465.
[46] Ibid.
[47] Jaimal Singh, *Spiritual Letters*, p. 77.
[48] Ibid., p. 97.
[49] Maheshwari, *Truth Unvarnished*, part 2, p. 233.
[50] Jaimal Singh, *Spiritual Letters*, p. 48.
[51] Ibid., p. 63.

though sadhus comprised a major force in the original community that encamped on the grounds that became Soamibagh,[52] most of Shiv Dayal's followers were householders, and so were the masters. "Redeemer sants always live as householders," the original master proclaimed.[53] Brahm Sankar Misra refused to let the sadhus in his following beg, and in 1905 rules were made at Soamibagh vastly limiting their activities. They were "not to use ochre-colored clothes, not to accept cash presents from Satsangis and not to move about without a pass."[54] At Dayalbagh they had to fill out forms and be approved before they could be permitted to reside there. Today only a few sadhus remain at the Radhasoami centers in Agra, and since 1959 they are no longer ensconced in caves along the Beas riverbank where Jaimal Singh took refuge.

Yet there are a number of sadhus who play an active role at various Radhasoami centers. These men have renounced worldly life—possessions, family, and ordinary occupations—but do not wear saffron robes or go begging. One of these "hidden sadhus"—the term is his own—is Brajendra Singh, who lives at Peepalmandi in Agra and acts as the personal secretary to his master, Agam Prasad Mathur. As an undergraduate student at Agra College from 1957–1959, he became drawn to Mathur, his history professor, and in 1961 he renounced his job and his family life, sent his wife and children to live with his parents, and came to live with Mathur and provide "continuous seva to him."[55] Brajendra Singh, who wears a business suit and works at a typewriter for much of the day, receives only the smallest remuneration for his work. Another inconspicuous sadhu at Mathur's household is Baba Abhay Das, who left his family responsibilities in 1965 and became a Vaisnava sadhu for two years before coming to Mathur's side, where he does a variety of household chores and meditates much of the day. According to Baba Abhay Das, "You have to have had attachment before you can be unattached," or, as he elsewhere expresses it, "You can't be a renouncer without having had something to renounce."[56]

For most Radhasoami followers, however, the ideal is to live out the ascetic and worldly sides of one's existence simultaneously rather than sequentially. Jaimal Singh described the relationship as being like that between a tree and its fruit, each connected to the other.[57] Anand Swarup claimed that at Dayalbagh he was attempting to show "that a man can be perfectly spiritual without running away to caves, and that he can

[52] Pratap Singh Seth, *Biography of Soamiji Maharaj*, pp. 40–41.

[53] Swami Shiv Dayal Singh, *Sar Bachan: Prose*, Soamibagh version, part 2, verse 66.

[54] *Souvenir*, p. 89.

[55] Interview with Brajendra Singh, Peepalmandi, August 12, 1985.

[56] Interview with Baba Abhya Das, Peepalmandi, August 12, 1985.

[57] Jaimal Singh, *Spiritual Letters*, p. 48.

reach the highest attainments in yoga while carrying on with worldly avocations."[58] His interviewer observed that Swarup thinks "it is time for the yogi to descend into the factory, the office and the school and attempt to spiritualize them."[59]

The Radhasoami ideal is the one described by Max Weber as that of the "rational reformer" or "worldly ascetic."[60] This fusion of stringent morality and worldly economic activity is found primarily in the Protestant West, with occasional exceptions in other parts of the world, including the Lingayat sect in South India, a religious community of businessmen that is in some ways similar to Radhasoami.[61] On the whole, however, as Weber observed, worldly asceticism is not the Hindu norm; a Hindu cannot easily renounce the world and live by its standards at the same time.

The Radhasoami understanding of seva, however, helps one do both, mediating between extremes of asceticism and worldliness. True seva is said to be like the attitude of poor servants who work in a luxurious mansion: while they live in riches, they do not pretend to possess them or feel as if they have a right to the luxury in which they live. The feelings of humility—sometimes even humiliation—that servitude entails are important, for they remind servants how little they really own.

Servants of Love

One of the most dramatic examples of ritual humiliation in Radhasoami is *mitti seva*, the service of dirt. At Beas, when thousands take part, the scene looks like something out of a biblical epic: thousands trudging over a levee with wicker baskets on their heads filled with mud, marching in orderly lines to the edge, where they dump their loads and return for more. The dust in the air gives a gauzy, surreal quality to the panorama, especially from the vantage point of a nearby cliff, where Master Charan Singh sits, dressed in immaculate white and shielded by a temporary awning as he oversees the whole affair. The devotees carrying the dirt—in-

[58] Brunton, *A Search in Secret India*, p. 230.

[59] Ibid., p. 248.

[60] Max Weber, "Asceticism, Mysticism and Salvation," in *Economy and Society*, ed. Guenther Roth and Claus Wittich (Berkeley: University of California Press, 1978), p. 542.

[61] Max Weber, *Religion of India: The Sociology of Hinduism and Buddhism*, trans. Hans H. Gerth and Don Martindale (New York: The Free Press, 1958, pp. 19–20). See also Louis Dumont, "World Renunciation in Indian Religions," Appendix B of his *Homo Hierarchicus, The Caste System and Its Implications*, trans. Mark Sainsbury, Louis Dumont, and Basia Gulati (Delhi: Oxford University Press, 1988), pp. 267–86; and T. N. Madan, *Non-Renunciation: Themes and Interpretations of Hindu Culture* (Delhi: Oxford University Press, 1987).

cluding businessmen in smudged white shirts and housewives in soiled saris—affirm that they are not only helping the master's construction projects; they are learning something about submission, humility, and service.

In India, the most common word for someone in servitude is *das*, which means both "servant" and "slave." Oddly (to Western preconceptions) many dases actually cherish being called a slave, but servitude of a certain sort is valued precisely because hierarchy is taken so seriously. It is a great honor to be placed on a hierarchical scale with God, even if only as his servant. And in Radhasoami, one is given ample opportunity to serve the Lord directly, since He is close at hand.

The act of becoming a servant of a Radhasoami master can be expressed quite literally. At each of the Radhasoami centers there are devotees who have given up all their worldly connections to come to the feet of the master and attend to his daily needs. Whole books have been written about the extremely devout, especially women devotees.[62] In addition to those I have mentioned earlier—Bibi Rukko, who served Baba Jaimal Singh at Beas, and Shibboji, Bukkiji, and Vishnoji, who attended Swami Shiv Dayal—the books have described others, such as Prem Pyari Ji, who

11. Women doing seva at Beas by preparing chapattis to feed the thousands attending a bhandara.

[62] See, for example, Maheshwari, *Bhaktmal of the Radhasoami Faith*.

tended constantly to the needs of Rai Saligram, whether he was "sitting or standing or walking."[63] While accompanying him she would "hold his hand or fingers," and after his death her devotion was transferred to his successor, Brahm Sankar Misra, whom she would look at with the gaze of a "chakor bird looking steadfastly at the moon."[64] This image of the chakor bird, frequently found in the literature of Vaisnava devotion, where it symbolizes the love elicited from Radha and her cowherd friends by Lord Krishna, is an expression of undying passion.[65]

The love expressed by some of the male devotees has a similar, intimate intensity. "You are my own darling," Jaimal Singh said to his favorite disciple, Sawan Singh. "Wherever the satguru may be pleased to send you, you will always be with me. Outwardly or physically we might be separated, but inwardly we are always together, wherever you might be."[66] Sawan Singh, in turn, had several disciples who served him with a passionate exclusivity. In addition to Bibi Rukko, there was a bachelor named Shadi who "could not stand women," but who was a "very loving devotee" of Sawan Singh.[67] He looked after the master constantly and reserved for himself the special tasks of preparing the master's bed and removing the socks from his feet.[68] At Peepalmandi in Agra, a young European devotee lived in the household of his master, A. P. Mathur, whom he served "spiritually, mentally and physically,"[69] in order to love Mathur the way Rai Saligram was said to have loved his master: "as Radha loved Krishna."[70] These metaphors of love are strong, for they point toward the ultimate union between the souls of disciple and master that is the goal of Radhasoami spirituality.

A special disciple who is destined to become a master after his own master's death is thought to have merged souls with his master long before the latter's physical demise, so an unusually intimate affection between the two is natural. The editor of the published letters between Jaimal Singh and Sawan Singh assures the reader that "every one was full of love," and reports that each would begin with a salutation such as "to the most Precious One in my whole life."[71]

[63] Ibid., p. 79.

[64] Ibid., p. 80.

[65] See, for example, the chakor bird images in the poetry of Sur Das in Hawley, *Sur Das*, pp. 82, 189; and in Hawley and Juergensmeyer, *Songs of the Saints*, p. 107. For the theological significance of such symbolism, see Shrivatsa Goswami, "Radha: The Play and Perfection of *Rasa*," in Hawley and Wulff, eds., *The Divine Consort*, pp. 72–88.

[66] Jaimal Singh, *Spiritual Letters*, p. 57.

[67] Charan Singh, *Spiritual Heritage*, p. 147.

[68] Ibid., p. 144.

[69] Interview with Paul Hogguel, Agra, December 6, 1980.

[70] Ibid.

[71] Jaimal Singh, *Spiritual Letters*, p. 16.

The younger partner in such a special relationship expresses his love in return in the language of seva. One proof of the bona fides of a master's successor is the humility and devotion of the servant toward the master while the master is still alive. For this reason stories of Sawan Singh's devotion to Jaimal Singh are legendary in Beas, and the picture of Rai Saligram holding the fly whisk beside his enthroned master is ubiquitous in the Agra branches. Dayalbagh publications claim that Saligram was "an ideal disciple," serving his master with his body, mind, wealth and spirit.[72] The bodily service included "pressing the feet, pulling the ceiling fan, sweeping and leeping the floor, dusting the furniture, bringing tooth sticks and clay for cleaning hands daily, cleaning the bathroom and the drain, cleaning utensils, bringing rations from the bazaar, grinding corn, bringing sweet well water, cooking food, offering spittoon and the like, carrying the palanquin and running along with it and carrying Soamiji Maharaj on His back."[73] It is no wonder, after all this, that Rai Saligram was so beloved by his master.

With such evidence of devoted service and servile love, it is also no wonder that Radhasoami devotees would think of love and seva as united. Love is considered an act of seva, and seva the expression of love. Anand Swarup regarded the two as equal and used a metaphor from science to describe this equation:

> If you are given a piece of iron and are asked to make it fly into the air, you shall have to employ either of the two methods, *viz* either you will grind it so fine that, reduced to smallest particles, it may fly into the air, or you will heat it on fire until it is converted into gas and mixes with the air. Exactly the same two methods are employed to refine the mind, that is, either it is purified or made tender by self-mortification or it is made extremely fine and pure through the fire of divine love.[74]

Other masters have claimed that self-mortification is not an alternative to devotion but a complement to it. "Real love demands complete surrender," Sawan Singh explained, for in the eyes of a true lover "all worldly things are dead."[75] The implication is that ardent feelings of devotion are not enough, and that true devotees will give their all.

Seva must be done humbly to deserve the name. When a devotee does seva for the guru, he or she must act with as little ostentation as possible, just as one might send a secret valentine to a very special love. Modesty is sometimes expressed as anonymity: cash gifts are sent without any identification of the donor, professional services go unrecorded, and writ-

[72] *Souvenir*, p. 40.

[73] Ibid.

[74] Anand Swarup, *Yathartha Prakasa*, p. 8.

[75] Sawan Singh, *Philosophy of the Masters*, vol. 2, p. 162.

ers prepare books for the master without receiving credit in the printed volume. On other occasions, however, such as moving dirt, seva can be performed openly. The only requirement is that the service at hand must allow one to diminish the grip of one's own ego and lose oneself completely in the master's love.

The Logic of Generosity

Seva to the master is the Radhasoami analogue to the sort of seva one sees in a Hindu temple, where priests make offerings and sacrifices to the gods. Like the givers of these oblations, the Radhasoami devotee offers seva as worship and praise, and perhaps hopes for blessings in return. Often enough such seva in itself brings blessings as it contributes to the development of the community's projects. Most of the money and labor that is contributed in the name of the master is used to build up the Radhasoami organization. The effort of helping to move piles of dirt from one place to another may seem a token gesture, but when multiplied by the efforts of thousands of devotees it leads to the creation of new dams, roads, and fields that are a tangible benefit to the whole community.

Administrative work is also done as an unpaid act of seva, often by retired executives. The organization that coordinates it is known as the Seva Samiti (service society), which one administrator described as "the grandest of ideas."[76] In Radhasoami organizations, unlike their secular counterparts, administrators are able to steer their agencies towards the noble purposes for which they were founded without any concern for profits or competitors. Even at Dayalbagh's factories, the purpose is not to yield a profit but "to engage in seva as much as possible."[77] At Beas, volunteer workers are called *sevadars* (providers of service), and during festival occasions vast networks of them do everything from managing tea stalls to keeping the queues at bus stands in proper order. They wear armbands with the word *sevadar* emblazoned in red, and receive a special satsang from the master as a reward for their labors.

Finally, there is "money seva": cash offerings and pledges that are expected to average a tenth of the devotee's salary. There is no attempt to enforce this tithe, however, and appeals for funds are seldom heard at Radhasoami gatherings. Instead, some people have had to be restrained from giving too much.[78] Rai Saligram, it is said, "placed His entire monthly salary at the Lotus Feet of Soamiji Maharaj."[79] In most cases the money is not placed at the master's feet, however, but in a trust fund

[76] K. L. Khanna, written answers to my questions, May 25, 1971.

[77] *Review of Progress*, p. 12.

[78] Interview with K. L. Khanna, Beas, May 25, 1971.

[79] *Souvenir*, p. 41.

12. Headquarters of the Sewa Samiti at Beas.

maintained by his organization. Even though it does not go directly to the master, this money is still considered seva because it is given in the master's name and for purposes he has designated.[80] Moreover, it helps to sustain the satsang, the family of the master. As one master explained, "love and service to the devotees of the Lord is love and service to the Lord Himself."[81]

Some of the money goes to projects that serve the wider society. Dayalbagh runs educational institutions, and Beas, hospitals; Kirpal Ashram undertakes flood and refugee relief projects. In addition to the annual eye camp, with its free operations and follow-up care, Beas has recently built

[80] In 1975, the last year that the Beas organization published its receipts and expenditures in its *Annual Report* (after which the practice was discontinued), total receipts were over 9,829,000 rupees, including 1,697,000 attributed to foreign contributions and sales, roughly 17 percent of the total. Yearly income from foreign exchange has steadily grown from 83,000 rupees in 1963 to 6,294,000 in 1984 (Radhasoami Satsang, Beas: Annual Reports, 1963–1984). Ten to twenty percent of that income is from the sale of books and the remainder, presumably, from donations. As of December 31, 1984, the latest date for which I have statistics on foreign initiates at Beas, they comprised no more than 3 percent of what was then the total number of initiates: 939,923. As of July 1990, the Beas organization reported a total of over 1,400,000 initiates; almost all of the recent growth is in urban India.

[81] Sawan Singh, *Philosophy of the Masters*, abr. ed., p. 173.

a three-hundred bed hospital with an outpatient department equipped to handle a thousand patients a day. Like the eye camp, the services of the hospital are available at no cost to satsangis and non-satsangis alike. Said to be the largest charitable hospital in India, its construction costs alone came to over 120 million rupees.[82] Such an expenditure was made possible by an increase in contributions in recent years, especially from abroad, which had led to a financial surplus.[83] Since the Indian government requires nonprofit religious institutions to divest themselves of their income on a regular basis, spending it for social or religious purposes if they are to keep their tax-exempt status, the organization had to do something with its money. There are many ways such funds might have been used, however, and one might ask why Radhasoami would want to give its money away.

The cynical answer is that such charity is undertaken to garner favorable publicity, but the amount of money that is given away seems vastly disproportionate to the publicity value that it actually receives, and members of Radhasoami give a different explanation for their corporate generosity. They say it is an extension of the master's love. His paternal concern extends outside his own family to all who are in need, and Radhasoami acts of charity are examples of his openness to all. They are hints of the vastness of his spiritual domain.

Each devotee also has opportunities to extend the master's love in his or her own way. The little acts of kindness, generosity, and good will that one is able to offer others in the course of an ordinary day are all regarded as deeds performed in the master's name and, in a sense, by him. "The master provided a seva for me today," one devotee explained while recounting an incident in which he was able to assist a bewildered elderly woman at an airport.[84] Such opportunities also allow the devotee the chance to take on a humble servant's role and thus abjure worldly attachments. One of the masters explained the necessity for acts of service in the words of the *Bhagavad Gita*: they purify because they can be done "without any desire for reward."[85]

The Social Ethic of Guru-Dharma

It has been a Christian prejudice since the time of the first cultural contacts between India and the West that Hinduism does not possess a sig-

[82] "Pride of Beas," a United News of India report published in *The Tribune*, Chandigarh, January 25, 1988.

[83] Radhasoami Satsang, Beas: Annual Reports, 1971–1984.

[84] Roland deVries, homily in satsang services held at Menlo Park, California, August 22, 1972.

[85] Sawan Singh, *Philosophy of the Masters*, vol. 1, p. 20.

nificant social ethic. We know now that this is not the case: the notion of dharma infuses all of India's social values with a religious dimension. Yet the old Christian attitude has some justification, for Hindu values do not require most people to attend to acts of public service, which are the special obligation of rulers charged with fostering and protecting the commonwealth. As a result there has not been much of a tradition of social idealism in Hindu thought. And this, as Max Weber once observed, has prevented India from developing much more than the rudiments of social revolution and utopianism.[86]

The Radhasoami social attitude is a significant modern departure from the Hindu norm. It is utopian, it is revolutionary in its way, and it is committed to social reform. The very first page of Sawan Singh's five-volume *Philosophy of the Masters* begins with an appeal for social service: "Those who render no service to mankind," proclaims the Great Master, "cannot hope to achieve anything in this world or hereafter. One who does not serve his fellow beings is worthless."[87] Other masters have been just as forthright. To receive blessings, Rai Saligram advised, a person should look for the "genuinely starving" and feed "one, two or more" of them.[88]

In its broad concept of seva, the Radhasoami movement has generated a substantial inclination toward social service. This is not what one might have expected in a movement whose teachings emphasize the soul's estrangement from the world, and some masters have indeed been skeptical about the possibility of transforming or reforming society in a fundamental way. Charan Singh, for instance, has discouraged his followers from engaging in political and social activity with this end in mind.[89] On the other hand, the theology of Radhasoami discourages an attitude that would wholly ignore the world, for the guru himself is present in it, and seva provides opportunities to put the needs of the world before oneself as a form of self-denial. For that reason, one Radhasoami master claimed, "Our motto should be 'Service before self.' "[90]

These motives for social service are considerably different from the familiar Christian notion of loving and serving other people because they are God's creation, and almost equally distant from the Hindu notion of dharmic obligation. True, one might call this modern Radhasoami ethic "guru-dharma," for it posits a system of personal morality and social responsibility that parallels and replaces the dharmic adherence to social values that one finds in traditional Hindu ethics. But this modern guru-

[86] Max Weber, *The Sociology of Religion*, trans. Ephraim Fischoff (Boston: Beacon Press, 1963), p. 43.

[87] Sawan Singh, *Philosophy of the Masters*, vol. 1, p. 1.

[88] Rai Saligram, *Jugat Prakash Radhasoami*, p. 45.

[89] Charan Singh, discourse to foreign guests, Beas, November 12, 1980.

[90] Kirpal Singh, "Instructions for Holding Satsang," Circular Letter no. 4, December 1956, p. 4.

dharma, unlike the more general Hindu concept of dharma, does not require adherence to the mores of traditional society. And unlike Christian ethical thinking, it does not require one to attach ultimate or even penultimate significance to the transformation of this world. Instead, humility, altruism, and the virtue of social responsibility follow purely as a moral reflex from the guru's love. They are the obligations that are his due. As such they provide an ethical base for persons who are culturally uprooted, mobile, and chary of conventional religious rules.

Seven

The Sense of a Center

To PEOPLE on the move—a category that includes most modern persons—the search for a home base and the reorienting of oneself that is often called "centering" can be significant parts of the spiritual experience. This search and reorientation have been major themes in the Radhasoami tradition from its earliest days. For instance, when Jaimal Singh, the founding master of Beas, retired from military service, he "longed to be at a quiet place suitable for meditation."[1] After searching far and wide, he found a "lonely spot on the banks of the Beas river," where, according to one chronicler of Beas history, dangers lurked on every side: "Snakes, scorpions, jackals, vultures, and other wild animals roamed freely, and the river was infested with crocodiles; small thorny shrubs abounded, and some of the few large trees were believed to be haunted by ghosts and evil spirits. . . . Skeletons of cattle and other animals, as well as of humans, had been found there, and most people avoided passing through this area even during the daytime."[2]

Jaimal Singh was undaunted. He thought the spot would serve as "an ideal place to sit undisturbed."[3] There, in time, he and his followers created Dera Baba Jaimal Singh, a place the chronicler calls a "heaven on earth."

Dayalbagh, like Beas, was created to anchor a floating community and establish a home. Anand Swarup wanted to bring his branch of the movement back to Agra after it had broken from the Soamibagh command, and his colleagues "set out in search for land."[4] They found a location near Soamibagh, but it was nothing but "mounds of sand and large pits," and it was "cxtremely filthy."[5] Despite that, they prophesied that some day "the land would be converted into a garden,"[6] so they called it Dayalbagh, "the garden of Swami Dayal."

Geography has always been important in India's religious imagination. In traditional Hinduism the whole of the landscape is a sacred place, and those who travel to the four ends of the subcontinent are thereby able to

[1] D. L. Kapur, *Heaven on Earth*, p. 28.
[2] Ibid., p. 30.
[3] Ibid., p. 29.
[4] *Souvenir*, p. 197.
[5] Ibid., p. 198.
[6] Ibid.

13. Main entrance, Soamibagh.

achieve merit the way one would in circumambulating a sacred temple. Pilgrimage places, such as Vrindaban or Benares, provide centers of spiritual activity; they are often located in places that are in some way unusual and offer extremes of either excitement or calm.[7] To traditional Indian villagers, it is the busy, bustling pilgrimage places that most appeal.

In the noisy, crowded conditions in which most modern Indians live,

[7] For the spiritual significance of the geographical location of Benares, see Diana Eck, *Benares: City of Light* (New York: Knopf, 1982), pp. 34–42; regarding Vrindaban, see John Stratton Hawley, *At Play with Krishna: Five Pilgrimage Dramas from Brindavan* (Princeton: Princeton University Press, 1982), pp. 3–51. See also Surinder Mohan Bhardwaj, *Hindu Places of Pilgrimage in India: A Study in Cultural Geography* (Berkeley: University of California Press, 1973).

however, an exceptionally quiet place is more to be valued than a lively one. Virtually all Radhasoami ashrams and colonies are to be found in suburban or rural locations and are constructed so as to suggest what an ideal Indian village should be; they are urban visions of rural life. Like Krishna's Vrindaban, the pastoral setting that is contrasted in Vaisnava legends with crass, crude cities, Radhasoami's centers provide places of rest and renewal to people mired in urban society.

The centers also alter the role that temporal locations play in India's religious imagination. In the traditional view, one moves through four stages of life until one comes to the final stage, when classically one becomes a *sannyasin* or a *vanaprasthin* and wanders about in search of truth. If one is a follower of Radhasoami, however, there is no need to wait until old age before one searches for truth, nor must one wander to find it. Truth is to be found in a definite place, in Beas or Dayalbagh or Kirpal Ashram or any of the other centers where a living master resides. Though the median age of long-term residents of these centers—the present-day sannyasins and vanaprasthins—is fairly high, they are open to all. And indeed, just as the entire Radhasoami community is a sort of spiritual family, the Radhasoami centers are distant homes to which all satsangis long to return.

The charisma of any society, argues Clifford Geertz, is conveyed not only through its leaders but through a sense of a center. Geertz describes such centers as "concentrated loci of serious acts."[8] They are the "arenas" in a society, "where its leading ideas come together with its leading institutions" and where "momentous events" are thought to occur. These centers, Geertz suggests, are a vital part of the charisma of leadership, for they convey a sense of "being near the heart of things."[9] At the heart of Radhasoami is the master, and the place where he lives becomes the Greenwich that supplies the mean for the rest of the world. That place becomes the intersection where sacred and mundane orders of reality meet, a sort of *axis mundi*.[10]

For these reasons, the Radhasoami colonies have often been created with utopian visions, as experiments in social living. There are a great many differences among them, however. Many of the colonies are small, but several are sizable: Dayalbagh at one time occupied over three thousand acres of land, and Beas is sufficiently large to be declared a township

[8] Clifford Geertz, "Centers, Kings, and Charisma: Reflections on the Symbolics of Power," in Joseph Ben-David and Terry Nichols Clark, eds., *Culture and its Creators: Essays in Honor of Edward Shils* (Chicago: University of Chicago Press, 1977), p. 151. This essay is also to be found in Clifford Geertz, *Local Knowledge: Further Essays in Interpretive Anthropology* (New York: Basic Books, 1983), pp. 121–46.

[9] Geertz "Centers, Kings, and Charisma," p. 151.

[10] Eliade, *Yoga*, pp. 115–16.

in its own right.[11] Nowadays the various centers have scarcely any official contact with one another. At one time leaders of five of the branches, including Beas, Soamibagh and Dayalbagh, would meet and sit together on a single dais in Agra to commemorate annually the death of Swami Shiv Dayal;[12] and on occasion there have been additional conciliatory gestures: the master at Peepalmandi has visited Beas,[13] and the Beas master, in turn, has visited Peepalmandi, Dayalbagh, and other centers.[14] But since the collapse of the Council in 1910, there has been no attempt to bring the branches together under one organizational umbrella, and the ideal of a united Radhasoami is a distant dream.[15] Even the term that is used to describe their centers differs from one quarter of Radhasoami to another. Dayalbagh and Soamibagh call their communities "colonies"; the Beas branch uses the term *dera*, which literally means a camp; and many of the other branches have adopted the traditional Indian term for such a community, *ashram*. Despite these differences in style and organization, however, there are also important similarities between the centers. In almost all cases Radhasoami communities are larger than traditional ashrams, are meant for married couples rather than celibates, and provide most of the comforts of a modern, middle-class home.

Ashrams for Householders

In the beginning Swami Shiv Dayal had only his own house to shelter the occasional visitor and a field some distance away where the sadhus en-

[11] Prior to 1952, Dayalbagh had owned 3,357 acres of land in the Agra area, but land legislation in that year required the colony to relinquish 1,611 acres which had been rented out to tenants (*Souvenir*, p. 321).

[12] According to one account, from 1918 to 1926 Ajudhia Prasad of Peepalmandi, Madhav Prasad Sinha of Soamibagh, Anand Swarup of Dayalbagh, Sawan Singh of Beas, and Seth Sudarshan Singh, who had his own following, sat together on the dais at Soamibagh on the memorial day celebrations marking the death of Swami Shiv Dayal (Interview with A. P. Mathur, August 12, 1985). After 1926, apparently, the enmity over property rights made such shows of solidarity inappropriate.

[13] A. P. Mathur visited Beas in 1973 (Interview with A. P. Mathur, August 12, 1985). Mathur keeps a picture of Charan Singh on his living-room wall.

[14] Charan Singh made a tour through Agra in 1978, visiting Soamibagh, Peepalmandi, Dayalbagh and Hathras. Expressions of friendship have been exchanged between Sawan Singh and two successive masters at Dayalbagh: Anand Swarup and G. D. Mehta (*Souvenir*, pp. 220, 254).

[15] One of A. P. Mathur's disciples said that Mathur once had an apocalyptic vision in which the various factions of the Radhasoami community finally united, but under dire circumstances: the threat of the extinction of the world following a great calamity, perhaps a nuclear holocaust. At this time, according to Mathur's prophecy, there were new incarnations of Swami Shiv Dayal and Rai Saligram. I was led to believe that Mathur envisaged himself as Swami Shiv Dayal and the disciple as Rai Saligram. (Interview with Paul Hogguel, Agra, December 6, 1980.)

camped.[16] Saligram purchased a house in Agra to be near him, and later others purchased homes to be near Saligram. Thus an urban colony began to arise.[17] Later the sadhu grounds were appropriated to build the colony called Soamibagh, but in the beginning, Radhasoami was an urban ashram.

Ashram has two major meanings, one associated with space and the other with time. It denotes a place of refuge or spiritual relaxation, but can also be used to refer to any one of the four stages of life. Both senses of the word were relevant in traditional forms of religious instruction in which a student—in the first stage of life—was expected to seek out a spiritual teacher at his place of retreat and live with him for a period of education and enlightenment. More recently, ashrams have become associated with spiritual retreats where a renunciant or a group of renunciants resides for an extended period of time. Radhasoami ashrams differ somewhat from both these traditional models. In the first place, there is only one holy man at the core of the community; no circle of renunciants intervenes between him and an outer circle of lay devotees. Second, he is not a celibate.[18] The other permanent residents of the Radhasoami communities and most of the visitors, aside from the few remaining sadhus, are also householders. The fact that Radhasoami ashrams are householder communities has implications for the way the quarters are arranged: the large communal sleeping quarters that one usually finds in traditional ashrams are replaced by separate rooms for couples and rows of townhouses for families. Moreover, those who have not retired from their labors need to earn money. One reason given for the establishment of factories and commercial ventures at Dayalbagh was that it would provide "employment to satsangis to earn their living through honest labor."[19]

The idea of living in a Radhasoami community has increased in popularity over the years. The size of the Dera at Beas has more than doubled since 1960, and some Radhasoami colonies have begun to be established even where the masters do not live. On the outskirts of New Delhi a new residential community called Soaminagar was created in the 1970s by Dayalbagh, and similar colonies are being constructed elsewhere.[20] Those who live at the centers receive not only the social benefit of being with

[16] Pratap Singh Seth, *Biography of Soamiji Maharaj*, p. 41.

[17] *Souvenir*, p. 57.

[18] Some claim that masters practice celibacy after they assume the mantle of guruship, even if they stay married.

[19] *Souvenir*, p. 200. The quote comes from an interview with Anand Swarup by the Lindsey Commission of American Christian missionaries in 1931.

[20] Interview with G. D. Sahgal, Dayalbagh, August 12, 1985. My information on Soaminagar comes from an interview with J. N. Moudgill, Soaminagar, New Delhi, December 5, 1980.

their own kind, but the spiritual benefit of being near the master. "We want to be forever in his company," a resident of Beas explained.[21] This feeling persists even in the new colonies that are built far from the master's primary residence, for a guest house is prominently placed in each for the master's visits. At least symbolically, he is always present.

The concept of a householder ashram is an innovation in Indian spiritual practices, as remarkable in its way as Swami Dayal's conception of surat shabd yoga as a yoga suitable for ordinary daily life; and the two are connected. From a traditional Indian point of view, it seems quite impossible that one could renounce the world and continue to live in it. The Radhasoami ashrams, however, provide locations where the old ways of living can be renounced, yet "the world" is by no means altogether left behind.

The Intimate Ashrams: Huzuri Bhavan, Manavta Mandir, and the Ashram of Dhara Sindhu Pratap

Today the house of the first master stands empty, and the Pannigali area of Agra in which it is located enjoys less than the best of reputations. The house has been kept as a sort of museum. It is large and multistoried, with family rooms, guest rooms, and large halls for satsang. A half mile away in the more respectable Peepalmandi section of Agra is the home of Rai Saligram, built in 1896; called Huzuri Bhavan, "the house of the honorable [Rai Saligram]," it continues to function as a spiritual center.

Huzuri Bhavan is located on a small lane off the main street. Beyond its large double gates is an inner courtyard where a grey Ambassador car is parked, and on three sides is a mansion rising now to two, now to three, stories. The stairs on the side lead to the main sitting room, guarded by a cluster of attendants. The only decorations in this formal room are large portraits of the Peepalmandi lineage: Swami Shiv Dayal; Rai Saligram; Saligram's son, Ajudhia Prasad; and his grandson, Gur Prasad. Because of the early death of Gur Prasad's son, Anand Prasad, the guru succession passed to his grandson—Saligram's great great grandson—Agam Prasad Mathur, the present master. He is portrayed wearing red academic robes and a tassled cap and holding a doctoral scroll. The only other pictures are one of Mathur standing beside Charan Singh, and one of the Buddha. The master himself is usually to be found up another flight of stairs in a sort of combination bedroom and throne room, which is crowded with attendants and visitors. The master, who wears an Indian shirt and horn-

[21] Interview with Janak Raj Puri, Beas, July 12, 1979. A similar sentiment has been voiced about the spiritual value of Dayalbagh (*Souvenir*, p. 200).

rimmed glasses and chews betel, gives discourses from time to time on the power of love.[22] On special days, in the large satsang chambers located on the ground floor of the manse, he speaks to followers from faraway cities such as Meerut, Patiala, and Bhopal. Others journey from Bihar and Bengal,[23] and still others come from no farther than across the street, since several houses nearby are occupied by Mathur's disciples.

The purchase of these houses by Saligram's devotees in 1896 is often regarded as the beginning of the Radhasoami colonies.[24] In 1898 the first meeting hall was built at Beas, and around the same time Swami Dayal's younger brother set up a small center at Soamibagh. Soon thereafter several of Rai Saligram's disciples established their own communities: Brahm Sankar Misra's house in Allahabad was turned into an ashram, Anukul Thakar Chand established Pabna Devghar Satsang in what is now Bangladesh,[25] and in 1904 Shiv Brat Lal established a headquarters at his home in Lahore. None of these latter three ashrams is still functioning in its original location. Misra returned to the family home in Benares near Kabir Chaura; it is now called Radhasoami Bagh, and satsang is held there under deputation of the Council leaders at Soamibagh.[26] After Shiv Brat Lal died, the Lahore ashram was disbanded, and two of his disciples set up centers of their own: Bhai Nandu Singh in Andhra Pradesh, and Faqir Chand in Hoshiarpur.[27] The Hoshiarpur ashram continues to thrive.

Faqir Chand's ashram was created in 1962 after his retirement from government service (he had served as a station master for railroads in

[22] A retired engineer, I. C. Gupta, has transcribed and privately published one volume of Mathur's discourses (in Hindi) entitled *Amrit Bachan Radhasoami* (Agra: Huzuri Bavan, Peepalmandi, 1980).

[23] Interview with A. P. Mathur, August 12, 1985.

[24] *Souvenir*, p. 57.

[25] For information on the Pabna Devghar Satsang see Ram Rijhand Rasulpuri, *Yug Purush aur Yug Dharam* (in Hindi) (Muzufurnagar: Swastiprakashand, 1956); and Saralkumari, *Radhaswami Sampraday aur Sahitya* (in Hindi) Delhi: Oriental Publishers, 1971, pp. 42–44. A biography of Anukul Thakar has appeared in English, entitled *An Ocean in a Teacup*. His headquarters are at Deogarh, Bihar; a branch at Delhi is near Jawaharlal Nehru University.

[26] Misra's grandson, S. S. Misra, a professor at Pratabhgahr College, represents the family's interests at Radhasoami Bagh, and once a year, in October, a large bhandara is held in Misra's memory (Interview with S. C. Mukerji, manager of Radhasoami Bagh, Benares, August 19, 1985).

[27] Bhai Nandu Singh, a forest contractor from Nizamabad, Andhra Pradesh, led a small group of followers in Secunderabad and Hyderabad, A.P., and after his death was succeeded by Anand Rao, an official with the government revenue department in Secunderabad. For a brief biography of Nandu, see Faqir Chand, *Key to Freedom by a True Faqir*, trans. R.S.S.N. Mathur (Dayal Compound, Aligarh: Be Man Hindi Monthly, 1963), pp. 89–94. Other disciples of Shiv Brat Lal who had followings included Divan Chand and Sheri-boa Dutt, both in Delhi; Dutt was a singer and a music teacher who lived in the Patelnagar section of Delhi (Interview with Faqir Chand, August 19, 1978, Hoshiarpur).

India and, for a time, in Iraq). His pleasant ashram, located on the outskirts of Hoshiarpur near the foothills of the Himalayas, consists of several modern hotel-like buildings that accommodate perhaps a hundred or so on special occasions. Large signs at the entrance announce the name of the community in two languages: "Manavta Mandir" (The Temple of Humanity) and "Be Man Ashram." According to Faqir Chand, the English phrase *Be Man* refers to the purpose of his teachings, which is to enable his followers to "be a man who has got correct understanding," and is not bound to "anything or anyone."[28] It was a philosophy Faqir Chand expounded at length from his position on the carpeted dais of the meeting room for almost twenty years, until his death in 1981. Faqir Chand would often carry on a rambling discourse and dialogue with his disciples and visitors that would last for much of the day. His disavowal of any claim to divinity or guruship has had implications for the character of his ashram, since it never actually became his home. He claimed no greater proprietary right to it than anyone else and refused to stay there overnight, preferring to retire to his own residence nearby. Once when he was ill and was forced to remain in the ashram for several days, he paid the ashram management forty-five rupees in rent for his room and board.[29] After his death in Pittsburgh in 1981 during a world tour, Faqir Chand was succeeded by I.C. Sharma, a scholar of Indian philosophy who taught for some years in the United States. Sharma has exerted a much stronger command over the ashram.[30] Not all followers are pleased with this, and the dissidents have refused to accept Sharma's spiritual counsel, preferring either to follow one of the other spiritual leaders appointed by Faqir Chand or to play old audio tapes of his discourses.[31]

Several hundred miles south of Faqir Chand's ashram is one that is in many ways similar. Like the Be Man ashram, Dhara Sindu Pratap ashram near the city of Gwalior began on a relatively small scale and is located in a magnificent rural setting—beneath the high bluffs on which sit an old palace and fort. As at Be Man, the guru's household is kept separate from the ashram itself. The person regarded as founding master of the Dhara Sindu Pratap ashram, in fact, never lived in Gwalior. It was founded in 1915 to honor Pratap Singh, the younger brother of Swami Shiv Dayal, for a good number of the Swami's disciples suspected that it was he, rather than Rai Saligram or Jaimal Singh, who had actually received the authority of guruship from his brother. Pratap Singh died in 1911, but

[28] Faqir Chand, *The Master Speaks to the Foreigners*, p. 35.

[29] Ibid., p. 32.

[30] Interview with Sudhir Bhatnagar, San Jose, California, August 9, 1987.

[31] Leaders appointed by Faqir Chand include M. R. Bhagat of Hoshiarpur, and a woman called Yogini Mataji, also of Hoshiarpur (David Lane, field research in Hoshiarpur, December 1981).

Shyam Lal and other disciples in Gwalior claimed that his spiritual power reappeared there four years later. In a visitation from his spirit, Shyam Lal received the phrase *dhara sindhu* (an ocean of current), which he was told was even more powerful than *Radhasoami*.[32] Shyam Lal, the principal of Sindia High School in the old Gwalior fort, was proclaimed Pratap Singh's successor, and he and his disciples established a residential colony near the ashram, bringing the ashes of Pratap Singh to rest in a tomb they constructed at the site in 1935. The colony managed to hold together even after Shyam Lal's death in 1940, when his supporters were unable to agree on a successor. An estimated six hundred people still live there, led by Shyam Lal's grandson, Sant Prakash Gupta, and his grandnephew, Bansi Lal Gupta.[33] Neither of them claims the status of guru, but scarcely a mile away from the Dhara Sindhu Pratap ashram is a much smaller ashram that was established in 1940 by several of Shyam Lal's disciples who felt that his spiritual power had indeed returned after his death and was to be found in the person of K. S. Thakur Mansingh.

Thakur Mansingh's ashram, Adhyatam Niketan (Spiritual Home), also known as Sant Mansingh Mandir (The Temple of Holy Mansingh), is located on a five-acre plot of farmland that serves as the home of Mansingh's family and a few devotees and provides room for the occasional pilgrim. After Thakur Mansingh's death in 1983, his son, Kripal Singh, was acknowledged as the new master. What is distinctive about the ashram is the eclectic nature of its teachings. Thakur Mansingh and his son teach hatha yoga as well as surat shabd yoga, and they worship images of Siva and Krishna as well as the formless name of God.[34]

Soamibagh: A Community of Memories and Intrigue

The Soamibagh community, with some justification, claims to be the oldest of Radhasoami colonies.[35] Its centerpiece is the cathedral-like marble edifice that will serve as a tomb and memorial for Swami Shiv Dayal Singh. Work on the structure began in 1904, was abandoned for lack of funds from 1911 to 1923, and is now half-finished. Although it has be-

[32] Sham Lal's biography is to be found in *Huzur Data Dyal: Pavitra Jivan Charitra* (in Hindi), Gwalior, n. d.

[33] Interview with Bansi Lal Gupta, Gwalior, August 21, 1985.

[34] Interview with Yogesh Sharma, Gwalior, August 21, 1985. The biography of Thakar Mansingh (known as "Malik-sahib") is to be found in Pitambar Misra, *Divya Charitamrit* (in Hindi) (New Delhi: Architect Sudarshan Kumar Chopra, 1973).

[35] Soamibagh is oldest by virtue of its location in Swami Shiv Dayal's original meditation fields. It could be argued that the community that presently lives there was not founded until 1937, however, when Madhav Prasad Sinha and his followers encamped on the site and developed it into a residential community.

come a tourist attraction, the thousand or so residents of the colony adjacent to the tomb have mixed feelings about whether the structure benefits the spiritual life of their community or detracts from it.

In the Swami's own time the fields on which Soamibagh is now located were a sadhu camp; after his death only a small circle of his relatives and a few other devotees set up residence there.[36] They were led by Swami Shiv Dayal's younger brother, Pratap Singh; after his death in 1911 the leadership passed to his son, Sudarshan Singh Seth. The colony did not develop until after Sudarshan's death in 1935, however, when in 1937 Madhav Prasad Sinha brought his Allahabad group to Soamibagh and took control. His predecessor, Brahm Sankar Misra, had initiated the practice of going from Allahabad to distant regions on tour, and from 1906 on a good number of initiates were garnered from such far-flung places as Sindh, Gujarat and Western Punjab. After Misra's death, some of these initiates became loyal to Soamibagh's rivals at Dayalbagh, but others acknowledged Sinha's leadership and moved to Soamibagh. The colony took on a multiregional character, with a section for Sindhis and Marwaris from Rajasthan, one for Gujaratis, another for Punjabis, and yet another for Bengalis. By 1940, the colony had fifteen hundred residents, a size it has since maintained. Most of the Soamibagh residents come to the colony in their retirement years, but those who come earlier set up shops and stores nearby in Agra, often giving these enterprises Radhasoami names.

In the interregnum that prevailed after Sinha's death in 1949, the colony has given all the outward appearances of being in a terminal state of torpor. Several small offices provide supervision over the work on the tomb and administer the paperwork of the administrative council, which governs a network of perhaps ten thousand members throughout India. There is also an office for publications. For many years this was the liveliest area of the colony, owing to the energies of Sant Das Maheshwari, the former private secretary to Madhav Prasad Sinha. In his lifetime, Maheshwari published over one hundred volumes of writings—his own and those of the Radhasoami masters—and he has proven to be a stubborn defender of the Soamibagh position on matters of faith and property. He was able to speak on behalf of the whole Soamibagh community, since the divisive issue of his guruship did not arise until after his death in 1983.[37]

The controversy over whether Maheshwari was a guru—and who his successor might be—is one of several issues that enliven Soamibagh's oth-

[36] Apparently the leader of the sadhus, Sanmukh Das, tried to gain control of the Soamibagh grounds after Swami Shiv Dayal's death, but it eventually ended up in the hands of the Swami's brother, Pratap Singh (Maheshwari, *Correspondence*, vol. 1, pp. 194–95).

[37] For a further discussion of the claim that Maheshwari was a guru, see chapter 3.

erwise placid atmosphere. Many of these issues revolve around power. In addition to Maheshwari's camp, there is a rival group led by the surviving family members of Maheshwari's master, Madhav Prasad Sinha. They influence the administrative council—the same body that Brahm Sankar Misra established in 1902, hoping to unite all Radhasoami factions. Today the Council, headed by B. K. Patel, oversees Soamibagh's finances and appoints persons authorized to hold initiations into the faith. The tension between the two camps has come to the surface since Maheshwari's death. In a touching biography of his father, Nirmal Das Maheshwari praises the man for his agreeable manner, unlike "the big wigs" who would stand around after satsang and discuss the political affairs of the colony. The elder Maheshwari, his son explained, would "return home in pious silence."[38]

One might wonder why the pious Maheshwari was not proclaimed master during his own lifetime. At least one other person within Soamibagh, Dr. J. N. Hazra, has been so proclaimed, and his circle of followers continues to have a semi-independent status on the outskirts of the Soamibagh colony. Hazra was succeeded by Bibi Rani, the daughter of Madhav Prasad Sinha, after Hazra's death in 1966, and his group is currently led by Santosh Kumar Singh, an Indian Railways employee from Baroda who is said to have an especially large following among the Bengali ladies of the Soamibagh community.[39] But Hazra's group is isolated from the rest of the community, and perhaps Maheshwari's followers feared they would be similarly ostracized if they made their claims openly.

Their fears were warranted. In 1989, Maheshwari's son, Nirmal Das, retired from the Indian Administrative Service in Delhi and moved to Soamibagh, precipitating a crisis of succession. He had stated that the interregnum between gurus "must end, or our religion will die," and prophesied that the new guru would come "soon."[40] His father's small group of Sindhi and Bengali followers embraced him as the legitimate successor of both his father and his father's guru, Madhav Prasad Sinha. The majority of Soamibagh residents, including most of the Gujaratis, quickly rejected his claims; many turned instead to the leadership of Sinha's grandson, Dr. Padam Adhar Sinha, a homeopathic doctor who once owned a foundry company, the Uttam Lauha Udyog. Popularly known as Padam Babu, Sinha is a tall, imposing figure who lives in his grandfather's house in the center of the colony, and has been at the

[38] N. D. Maheshwari et al., *Sant Das Ji*, unpublished manuscript, n.d.

[39] Interview with A. P. Mathur, August 8, 1978. Anukul Thakur's Satsang at Deogarh is yet another split from the Soamibagh line.

[40] Interview with Nirmal Das Maheshwari, New Delhi, December 19, 1986. Another possible successor to Maheshwari is rumored to be Wazir Chand Prabhakar, a Punjabi of Khatri caste who lives at Soamibagh (Interview with P. S. Sharma, August 13, 1985).

forefront of opposition to the pretensions of both Maheshwaris.[41] For years he has been quietly regarded by some as his grandfather's successor.[42] To make matters even more confusing, yet another Soamibagh resident, Jang Bahadur Mathur, has for some years also been giving initiation; he holds services in the meeting room of the last guru's house. Although the Council has not recognized any of these contenders as the official successor—and thus the interregnum formally continues—definite camps of followers have emerged. After forty years in which Soamibagh had virtually no guru, it now potentially has three.

The Spiritual Socialism of "Better-Worldly" Dayalbagh

There are few such controversies across the road in Dayalbagh, for the issue of succession following the death of Gurcharandas Mehta in 1975 was firmly settled in favor of M. B. Lal. Under his leadership the colony has expanded its economic and educational activities, and at Dayalbagh that counts for much. More than in any other Radhasoami community, at Dayalbagh the faith is something that is acted out in a social setting rather than just in private.

From the time of its establishment in 1915 to the present, there has been a broad public interest in what was known as the Dayalbagh experiment, and a parade of government officials and social reformers, from Nehru on down, have made their pilgrimage to Agra. "Dayalbagh products came to my notice," said Nehru. "I came to see with my own eyes the work being done here."[43] What Nehru saw on his visit in 1956 was the efficient use of modern technology by a spiritually dedicated religious community. Other visitors also remarked on this alliance of spiritual and technological power. "What Dayalbagh teaches," a newspaper editor from Lahore exclaimed on visiting Dayalbagh during the 1930s, "is what great miracles can be performed by God force—like other forces of Nature, e.g., steam, electricity, etc.—when building up an ideal structure of human society." The editor went on to state that Dayalbagh was as grand an achievement for the city of Agra in the social realm as the Taj Mahal had been in the architectural.[44] With interests such as these in mind, many

[41] Interview with Dr. Padam Adhar Sinha (Padam Babu), Soamibagh, January 17, 1988. My information on recent developments in Soamibagh comes from telephone interviews with Srivatsa Goswamy, Vrindaban, January 27, 1991; February 9, 1991; and March 1, 1991. He provided additional information by fax on June 14, 1995.

[42] Interview with A. P. Mathur, Agra, August 6, 1978, and with Charan Das (Ray Angona), by telephone, March 5, 1986.

[43] *Souvenir*, pp. 281–82.

[44] Maulana Mohammad Yakub, editorial in *The Light*, December 28, 1936, reprinted in *Huzur Sahabji Maharaj—Sir Anand Sarup—As Others Saw Him*, 2d. ed. (Agra: Radhasoami Satsang Sabha, Dayalbagh, 1966), p. 171.

other progressive Indian politicians over the years have kept up close ties with Dayalbagh; Gandhi himself sent condolences to Dayalbagh at the time of Anand Swarup's death.[45] From 1931 on, annual exhibitions of Dayalbagh goods throughout India were inaugurated by government officials. Through government assistance a hydroelectric substation was established in the colony, and government agencies became large purchasers of Dayalbagh products, especially dairy products from Dayalbagh's model farms. During the Second World War, government officials arranged for American troops stationed in Agra to purchase their milk from Dayalbagh in preference to the Indian military's own dairy.[46] In recent years, Dayalbagh leaders have been proud of their relationship with V. V. Giri, who frequently visited their community during his tenure as president of India.

Despite the curiosity of progressive Indian politicians, what makes Dayalbagh effective as a social and economic organization is not any special technique of administration, but a spirit of collective ownership and a sense of common destiny. The members of the Dayalbagh community are joint owners of the community through a legal trust, but the master ultimately "owns" Dayalbagh; it is he who presides over the property and industry of the community. Individuals live and work there at his behest and partake in its ownership only through their relationship with him. In part for tax reasons, the title to Dayalbagh property has from the beginning been in the name of an administrative society, and since 1937 virtually all of the Radhasoami factories have become limited companies and cooperatives, legally owned by the members of the fellowship who work in them. Yet the directives for administering them come from offices at Dayalbagh. At present the leadership team includes G. D. Sahgal, a former judge in the Allahabad high court, who is president of the society; T. Nath, the general secretary of Dayalbagh; and, of course, M. B. Lal, who, like his predecessors, provides worldly leadership as well as spiritual direction.

The Dayalbagh master is like Plato's philosopher-king, a parallel first drawn by Anand Swarup, the founder, who said, "When I first read Plato's *Republic* I was pleasantly surprised to find . . . many of the ideas I am trying to express here."[47] Swarup's "republic" envisaged a balance between an enlightened constituency and a strong leadership, resulting in great civic pride. Swarup described Dayalbagh's ownership as "trusts to be administered in a religious spirit," and explained the differences between it and the more familiar kind of socialism. Although "the farms and colleges are owned by the community," he said in an interview, the

[45] Ibid., p. 176. The message was sent on June 25, 1937.

[46] *Souvenir*, p. 327.

[47] Brunton, *A Search in Secret India*, p. 237.

concept of joint ownership only extends "to land and houses. . . . Everyone is perfectly free to possess and accumulate whatever money and property he has." Thus Dayalbagh is free from "the tyrannies of socialism." Moreover, Swarup concluded, "Everything is subordinated to our spiritual ideal."[48]

At Dayalbagh, one's salvation is thought to be affected by the quality of one's social relations. Anand Swarup described the Dayalbagh ideal of renunciation as "better-worldliness"—a purified, spiritualized form of worldliness that he depicted as superior to the extremes of crass materialism and otherworldly renunciation. Better-worldliness, he claimed, should be the "aim of man's life on this earth."[49] By participating in better-worldliness, a Dayalbagh devotee was contributing to his or her own destiny and to the destiny of society at large. Involvement in Dayalbagh economic and organizational activities, for example, provided an opportunity for seva on a social scale. The present master reminded a group of his followers who were setting up displays of Dayalbagh products that "the exhibitions are not held for earning profit," but "to inculcate a spirit of cooperation and to work together with love and affection and to earn the Grace of Huzur Radhasoami Dayal."[50]

When Anand Swarup established his first factories, he called them "Model Industries" and intended them to be showplaces of technology and organization. The first product to be manufactured, in 1917, was a simple leather button for British military uniforms. Within ten years Dayalbagh factories were producing surgical instruments, electric fans, textiles, fountain pens, gramophones, and a whole host of leather products.[51] One of the reasons they were successful with leather goods was that Radhasoami residents had no compunction about working with animal hides, thought to be polluting by traditional Hindus, nor were they hesitant about engaging in many other nontraditional areas of work and commerce. After their zenith in the 1930s, Dayalbagh industries went into something of a decline; a steady increase in market competition and alterations in government income tax policies regarding properties owned by religious organizations cut deeply into Radhasoami profits.[52] Under

[48] Ibid., p. 236.

[49] *Souvenir*, p. 313.

[50] *Review of Progress*, p. 12.

[51] *Souvenir*, pp. 314–19.

[52] Ibid., p. 319. In 1942, in an effort to prove that the colony was self-supporting and required its enormous assets for spiritual purposes, Dayalbagh made a ruling prohibiting even its own members from contributing to the organization. Nonetheless, tax officials continued to hound the Dayalbagh offices (Interview with Ram Jadoun, Dayalbagh, November 9, 1973). For a synopsis of Dayalbagh's nineteen-year dispute with the Indian Government's Income Tax Department—from 1935 to 1954—and the several court settlements in Dayalbagh's favor, see *Souvenir*, pp. 345–48.

M. B. Lal's leadership, however, there has been a revival of production and sales of Dayalbagh products. In the first ten years of Lal's administration (1975–1984), the number of Dayalbagh stores throughout India expanded from eleven to fifty-three, and twenty-two new production units were established in the same period, manufacturing handloom cloth, soaps, wash powders, and similar products.[53]

Even more dramatic has been the development of new educational institutions under Lal's regime. Although Dayalbagh established schools and colleges soon after it was founded in 1917, Lal has been keen on expanding yet further this aspect of Anand Swarup's vision, which was

14. Dayalbagh products.

[53] *Review of Progress*, pp. 9–12.

first articulated in one of Dayalbagh's early reports. "Animated by the desire to educate the masses," the report explained, the people of Dayalbagh created schools to "do our little bit in a decent manner."[54] It went on to laud "the kingdom of knowledge, founded, under the aegis of the mighty and unshakeable British Raj, with no selfish motives of any kind."[55] This kingdom of knowledge was explored in cultural evenings at Dayalbagh, in which plays and readings from Shakespeare would enliven the colony's convocations.[56] This heritage has been revived under Lal's leadership. In 1981 the colony persuaded the government of India to authorize a new university to be created at Dayalbagh, based on its existing colleges. The Dayalbagh Educational Institute (DEI) was accordingly created as a "deemed university" by a special charter of the University Grants Commission of the Indian government. As such it is a national university rather than a state institution, a status it shares with the Indian Institute of Science, the Tata Institute of Social Sciences, and the Gandhigram Rural Institute, among others. The head of DEI is Mrs. G. P. Sherry, daughter of the previous master at Dayalbagh, Gurcharandas Mehta.

What makes DEI unusual is its core curriculum of four required courses, intended to inculcate civic values and a sensitivity to the liberal arts. The *Prospectus* for the university describes them as follows:

> 1. Cultural Education (to take pride in the national ethos so that one may not lose one's moorings).
> 2. Comparative Study of Religion: Hinduism, Buddhism, Jainism, Judaism, Christianity, Islam, The "Sant Mat" and modern Religious Movements (to ingrain an attitude of tolerance and a sense of national integration and inculcate moral and spiritual values).
> 3. Scientific Methodology, General Knowledge and Current Affairs (to nurture a scientific temper and be aware of contemporary developments).
> 4. Rural Development: Study of rural society and economy (to foster a fuller understanding of the rural life with a view to appreciate properly the polity and the economy of our country and the social forces at work).[57]

The fourth course also includes a practicum: students must volunteer for participation in a Peace Corps–type rural development project, usually during summer vacation. Also required is participation in physical education classes ("Games") and classes in the arts, such as music, drama,

[54] Radhasoami Educational Institute, *Prospectus for 1918, Report for 1917* (Hyderabad, Sind: R. H. Advani and Co., 1918), p. 3.

[55] Ibid., p. 14.

[56] Interview with J. N. Moudgill, Soaminagar, New Delhi, December 5, 1980.

[57] Dayalbagh Educational Institute, *Prospectus and Application Form*, 1986–1987 session, p. 16.

15. Entrance to the Radhasoami Educational Institute, Dayalbagh.

and dance. All this is in addition to the students' major fields of study, which at DEI are primarily in the sciences and technical fields such as commerce and engineering. Mrs. Sherry claims that through this approach DEI creates better persons, not just better students.[58] M. B. Lal, echoing sentiments first expressed by Anand Swarup, states that the educational institutions of Dayalbagh create an environment where children will become "supermen" able to bring into being a transformed, better-worldly society.[59]

Considering the noisy streets of ordinary Indian cities, Dayalbagh appears to have achieved a transformed society already. Its prosperous tree-lined streets caused one American visitor to describe it as "Westernization with a vengeance."[60] From land that was reclaimed when the Jumna river changed its banks almost a hundred years ago, Anand Swarup and his successors have created a model city of some five thousand residents. Like Soamibagh, the Dayalbagh colony (legally designated a town) is multiregional, and one may find neighborhoods containing Rajasthanis, Punjabis, Biharis, Bengalis, and Tamils as well as people from neighboring Ut-

[58] Interview with Mrs. G. P. Sherry, Agra, December 8, 1986.

[59] Interview with M. B. Lal, Dayalbagh, August 13, 1986. Regarding the "supermen" motif, see also *Review of Progress*, p. 15, and *Souvenir*, p. 358. It is not clear whether Anand Swarup was consciously referring to a similar concept with the same name developed by Friedrich Nietzsche.

[60] Brunton, *A Search in Secret India*, p. 228.

tar Pradesh. This diverse constituency was attracted to Dayalbagh over the years as Anand Swarup and successive masters went on tour. In general there are fewer Gujaratis and Sindhis in Dayalbagh than in Soamibagh, and more devotees from South India and Bengal. The Bengali, Tamil and Telugu languages are taught in Dayalbagh schools, and there is a major branch of Dayalbagh in Andhra Pradesh at Cocanada, established by P. Sitaramayya, an energetic follower of Anand Swarup.[61]

The cosmopolitan, genteel atmosphere at Dayalbagh befits what Anand Swarup envisaged as a socialism of the elite—the "Aris-Demo" ideal, as he called it. Swarup wanted Dayalbagh's residents to "act as if they were a Democratic Community of Aristocrats—Aristocrats, not on account of wealth, etc., but Aristocrats in Spiritualism."[62] Aristocracy was not to mean a life of leisure, however, as Gurcharandas Mehta dramatically showed; he is said to have "denied himself rest and comfort and lived up to the great motto 'Work is Worship.' "[63] At Dayalbagh hard work and a sense of being elite were compatible.

Anand Swarup initially envisaged an ideal city containing not more than twelve thousand residents, the maximum he felt was possible for decent living. Swarup did not want to copy "the monstrous towns of your Western countries; they are overcrowded and therefore breed many undesirable qualities." Instead, he wanted to build "a garden city where people can work and live happily, where they can have plenty of space and air."[64] After completing Dayalbagh, Anand Swarup hoped to create similar model cities all over India, "at least one in each province."[65] With the exception of the colony of Soaminagar near New Delhi, however, his dream remained unfulfilled until 1984, when M. B. Lal embarked on a program of decentralization intended to expand the sales and production units of Dayalbagh industries, and to create new residential colonies at Lucknow, Roorkee, Vishakhapatnam, and Kanpur; others are planned for other cities in Andhra Pradesh, Madhya Pradesh, and Bihar.[66] In a modest way, then, Anand Swarup's plan for the proliferation of Dayalbaghs is being carried out. One English visitor during the time of Anand Swarup thought the Dayalbagh ideal could be replicated throughout India if only there were a hundred leaders of Anand Swarup's quality. Then,

[61] Interview with Ram Jadoun, Dayalbagh, November 9, 1973, and V. Sadyanarayana, Dayalbagh, August 13, 1985.

[62] *Souvenir*, p. 358.

[63] Ibid.

[64] Brunton, *A Search in Secret India*, p. 236.

[65] Ibid.

[66] Interview with G. D. Sahgal, Dayalbagh, August 12, 1985. The new locations are at Kaunool, in Andhra Pradesh; Khandwa, in Madhya Pradesh, and Murar, in Bihar (Interview with G. D. Sahgal, Dayalbagh, December 8, 1986).

he wrote, "how quickly India might become a smiling land, clean, gay, prosperous, dustless and at peace within her borders."[67] The question remains, however, whether even among satsangis, Dayalbagh's experiment with "better-worldliness" is a viable model for social change.

The Spiritual Kingdom of Beas

The only Radhasoami community larger than Dayalbagh is Beas, located near the city of Amritsar in the heart of the Punjab. It has none of the industrial and educational accoutrements of Dayalbagh, but in some ways it is also a social experiment, and like Dayalbagh, it is a city created by and for the master. Sitting by itself on the riverbank at the end of a narrow country road some miles from the nearest railway station, it appears from a distance like a dream city. The towers of the monumental Satsang Ghar float ethereally above the plains, and surrounding it are sturdy brick homes and well-paved, quiet streets. This model city is all the more striking because of the contrast with its rude surroundings. The rough, eroded gullies along the banks of the Beas river that were once

16. Dera Baba Jaimal Singh at Beas, with the Beas River in the background.

[67] Quoted from Yeats Brown, *Lancer at Large*, in *Souvenir*, p. 366. I have not been able to locate Brown's book myself to confirm the accuracy of the quotation.

thought to be inhabited by ghosts became in the 1980s the hideouts of young Sikh terrorists hunted down by the Indian government's armed police. But despite the ghosts and terrorists, many of Beas's visitors think of "this beautiful little dera" as, in the words of one American devotee, "a sacred spot."[68]

As at Dayalbagh, the facilities at Beas are expansive and modern, but even in physical appearance there are substantial differences between the two.[69] Factories and schools dominate the landscape at Dayalbagh, whereas at Beas the Satsang Ghar looms above all else. The offices and product showrooms are the busiest areas at Dayalbagh; at Beas the liveliest quarters are the publications center and the hostels for international guests. At Dayalbagh one is liable to meet only middle-class, merchant-caste Indians, most of them Hindu. At Beas the scene is much more diverse.

The master at Dayalbagh, Dr. Lal-sahib, a widower, lives in a comfortable but modest bungalow in the center of the colony, easily accessible to the rest of the community. At Beas, by contrast, the residence of the master is almost invisible to passersby: only one little room on the third floor and a television antenna peek over the high redbrick walls that surround the manse that Charan Singh shared with his family. During his forty years of leadership, Charan Singh took on an almost regal mien. When he would leave the guarded gate, he would not saunter alone as Dr. Lal-sahib would do at Dayalbagh; in fact, he would not walk at all but would be driven in a small grey car, even when his destination was only the Satsang Ghar a block away. The reason was a sound one, for the crowd hoping to catch a glimpse of his presence would surely make it impossible for him to walk anywhere other than with a phalanx of guards. At Dayalbagh the guru is treated rather like a revered chairman of the board. At Beas he is a spiritual king, and this means that the whole colony at Beas takes on more the appearance of a magical kingdom than does Dayalbagh, especially since it is not burdened with the mundane concerns of running factories and selling products. Almost all of Beas's permanent residents have come to the colony after retirement, and most volunteer their labor on behalf of an organization that has no reason to exist other than to maintain and expand itself. They are proud to serve at a spiritual court. The honorific title given to Charan Singh is in many ways apt, for to many he has been the maharaja of Beas. Like the relationships among friends that anthropologists label "fictive kinships," Beas has produced what might be called a "fictive kingship."

[68] Johnson, *With a Great Master*, p. 99.

[69] My information on the Beas Dera comes from my visits there in 1970–1971, 1973, 1978, 1979, and 1980; interviews with the general secretary, K. L. Khanna, Beas, May 25–26, 1971, and his successor, S. L. Sondhi, Beas, July 12, 1979; and the published reports of the Dera.

As a number of recent films and novels indicate, there is a lingering nostalgia in modern India for the days of the princely states. This is especially true in the Punjab, where until the States Reorganization Act of 1956 small distinctive kingdoms were the dominant form of political organization. Majarajas and maharanis ruled over their dominions with great splendor, leaving the actual administration of the kingdoms in the hands of their chief secretaries, the diwans, whose power was often more palpable than that of the maharajas themselves. It is an interesting fact—perhaps only a coincidence—that Charan Singh and the present master at Beas, Gurinder Singh, are members of the caste from which most of Punjab's princes were drawn; similarly, members of their office staff have come from the castes that supplied the diwans. And indeed, this latter connection is a quite definite one. Daryai Lal Kapur of Beas was known as "Diwan Sahib" because of his role as judge and finance minister in the princely state of Kapurthala.[70] Shyam Lal of Dhara Sindhu Pratap Ashram served the Gwalior princes, and one of his successors, Thakar Mansingh, worked in the court's bureaucracy. Swami Shiv Dayal himself served in the administration of a princely state,[71] and family members of Radhasoami leaders, including the Swami's, have also served in courtly capacities.[72] At Beas and other Radhasoami organizations, these roles are kept alive in a new form.

The kingship model may help to explain several distinctive features of the Beas branch of Radhasoami. One is the special relationship that it has with another branch of the movement located in the nearby town of Tarn Taran. The ties between Beas and Tarn Taran are peculiar in that most branches of Radhasoami have an almost competitive relationship with one another; here, rather, there is a definite kinship. The founder of the Tarn Taran branch, Baba Bagga Singh, was an initiate of Jaimal Singh who established his center some thirty miles from Beas at the time that Sawan Singh became the master.[73] Bagga Singh appealed to people from a different area of the Punjab, and from a different caste: the Ramgarhias, who were traditionally carpenters. Instead of treating him as a rival, Sawan Singh regarded him as a sovereign over an adjoining region, someone

[70] S. L. Sondhi, Preface to Kapur, *Heaven on Earth*, p. xi.

[71] Pratap Singh Seth, *Biography of Soamiji* Maharaj, p. 28.

[72] Ibid. G. D. Sahgal, President of the Dayalbagh Sabha, is the descendent of an administrator in the court of Ranjit Singh, the great nineteenth-century king of Punjab (Interview with G. D. Sahgal, Dayalbagh, August 13, 1985). Thakur Mansingh's ancestors had worked in the Maharaja of Gwalior's administration and served in his army (Interview with Yogesh Sharma, Gwalior, August 21, 1985). For an interesting discussion of the regal aspects of Radhasoami, see Sudhir Kakar, *Shamans, Mystics and Doctors: A Psychological Inquiry into India and Its Healing Traditions* (Boston: Beacon Press, 1982), pp. 136–37.

[73] See Pratap Singh, *Hazur Maharaj Baba Bagga Singh Ji, Janamsakhi* (in Punjabi) (Tarn Taran, Punjab: Radhasoami Tarn Taran, n.d.).

with whom he had a sort of regal alliance. The relationship continues, and even in recent years, during the bhandara festivals at Beas, a recent successor of Bagga Singh, Pratap Singh, has come from Tarn Taran to sit on the dais with Charan Singh.[74]

The kingship model seems also appropriate to the courtly politics of Beas's inner administrative circles. Although the line of command is clearly specified—subcommittee heads report to superiors in higher committees, and the whole structure comes under the review of a general secretary who reports directly to the master—personal relationships count for much. The structure allows some officers to bypass the general secretary: members of the trust committee report directly to the master, as do regional representatives outside of India.[75] During Charan Singh's reign, his personal secretary and staff also were exempt from the general secretary's command, and certain other individuals ignored the formal structure by going directly to the master with their concerns. These included members of prominent old Radhasoami families and distinguished satsangis, such as professors, politicians, and businessmen. Theoretically anyone can speak directly with the master, but access to him is a privilege obtained easily only by a few. Each of these features of Beas's administrative system revives one aspect of the organization of a traditional Indian kingdom.

The Bureaucratization of Beas

In 1990 Beas acquired a new leader. The old-world demeanor of the leaders who have ruled over Beas for most of this century—Sawan Singh, and his grandson, Charan Singh—fit easily into the regal image envisaged by many of their followers, but it is hard to say whether in the long run their current successor will be able to perpetuate this style of leadership, nor if he will want to do so. When Charan Singh died on June 1, 1990, at the age of 73, a will was produced, which he had signed scarcely two days before he passed away, proclaiming his 35-year-old nephew, Gurinder Singh Dhillon, to be the new master. Although it was accepted virtually without dissent, the choice of Gurinder, the son of Charan Singh's sister, surprised many in the Dera's inner circles. Some say it even surprised Gurinder himself. An active man with a degree in commerce, Gurinder

[74] Interview with Pratap Singh, Tarn Taran, November 10, 1980. Deva Singh succeeded Bagga Singh in 1944, and Pratap succeeded him in 1961. After Pratap's death in 1988, the succession has been in dispute. Charan Singh is said to have rejected the claims of the person regarded at Tarn Taran as the successor. Another successor of Deva Singh, Sadhu Singh, established a rival center in Ferozepur.

[75] Interview with K. L. Khanna, Beas, May 26, 1971.

has for some years been living in Spain, working as a businessman in a firm owned by a satsangi in Malaga. He was far from the center of the Dera's politics, and when he came to visit, his friendly manner and informal style of dress seemed slightly out of place in the Dera's solemn halls. It is apt to take some time, therefore, before the transfer of authority becomes complete in the minds of Beas satsangis.

In the meantime, the Beas organization will take care of itself. For many years now, there has been a movement away from the courtly model of the community's politics and a trend towards a more modern, bureaucratic form of organization. This trend began early in Charan Singh's reign. Charan Singh was never very fond of the intrigue that comes with court politics and stated that one purpose in streamlining the administrative structure of the Dera in 1957 was to standardize the process of policymaking and make it less subject to personal influence.[76] He also shifted the legal title to the property at Beas from his own name to a nonprofit trust managed by senior members of the Beas satsang. Other aspects of the administration were turned over to the trust as well, and he hoped that in doing so advancement and influence in its structure would be solely determined by one's abilities.[77] One of Beas's leaders called it "true democracy in action."[78] Charan Singh claimed to have felt a great sense of relief in abdicating his kingly role for a more contemporary one, that of an administrative adviser.[79]

Yet Charan Singh was seen as much more than a policymaker by those who surrounded him, and that fact created some peculiarities in the way his administrative role was defined. The official *Rules and Regulations of the Association* submitted to the government for legal registration in 1957 call him the "patron" of the Dera. It is a happy choice of terms—neither too mechanical nor too pious—for a position that brings with it extraordinary powers. The patron appoints the members of the executive board,[80] determines when they shall meet and what they shall discuss,[81] and has free access to the organization's financial accounts.[82] If he is displeased with the governing structure, he can abolish it altogether.[83] The

[76] Interview with Charan Singh, Beas, August 4, 1979. Other reasons given for establishing the Beas trust were the desire for "more efficient management" of Dera properties and to relieve the master of the time he would otherwise expend in administering them (Kapur, *Heaven on Earth*, p. 413).

[77] Interview with Charan Singh, Beas, August 4, 1979.

[78] K. L. Khanna, written answers to my questions, May 25, 1971.

[79] Charan Singh, *Light on Sant Mat*, pp. 359–60.

[80] Rule 4iii of "Rules and Regulations" in *Memorandum: Rules and Regulations of Association of Radhasoami Satsang, Beas* (Beas: Radhasoami Satsang, Beas, 1968), p. 4.

[81] "Rules and Regulations," pp. 5–6, Rules 8 and 9ii.

[82] Ibid., pp. 7–8, Rule 11.

[83] Ibid., pp. 5, 8–9, Rules 6iii and 21.

patron is patron for life, of course, and if he has not provided for the appointment of a successor before his death, the selection of an organizational successor (but not a spiritual one) is to be made by the leaders of the movement in consultation with the surviving members of his own family.[84] Theoretically, then, the Beas organization could be led for a time by someone who is not a guru, but no one expects such a situation to arise.

The boardroom model of administration is one that seems to be catching on in other Radhasoami branches as well. At Dayalbagh it has been the pattern for some years. Anand Swarup's own leadership style was like that of a committee chairman, and he encouraged his board members to challenge his opinions and enter into debate over administrative—but never spiritual—affairs.[85] Most of the leaders in the Radhasoami organizations are already familiar with this organizational style, since so many of them have served as business and government administrators before coming to the Radhasoami colonies. The present general secretary of Beas was a high-ranking executive in a shipping firm in Bombay; his predecessor was the director of one of India's most prestigious agricultural research institutes. The coordinator of the Sawan-Kirpal Ruhani publications division is chairman of the English department of Delhi University, and his counterpart at Beas was the head of Punjabi University. The supervisor over Beas's volunteer workers was a brigadier general in the Indian army. The office building for these officials at Beas is a model of efficiency, and in it retired administrative officers can do what many of them would like to have done in their earlier careers: run a small and dedicated organization, and run it well.

Maintaining and developing the Dera is one of the Beas organization's main activities. The latest addition is a new hospital, which one newspaper has called "the pride of Beas."[86] Along with the hospital have come more houses, shops and restaurants, all owned and managed by the Dera. Publications provide a second cluster of activities—not just producing and marketing the volumes, but writing and designing them as well. Guests offer the third administrative challenge, for they arrive by the tens of thousands during the bhandara festivals. Thousands also come as patients for the eye camps. During the winter months—when the political situation in the Punjab permits—foreign devotees descend upon the Dera, several hundred at a time. In addition to all of this, there is the fourth area

[84] Ibid., p. 3, Rule 3iv. The spiritual successor is appointed only by the Divine. The requirement to consult family-members has recently been changed.

[85] Although Anand Swarup enjoyed discussing administrative matters, he said that anything he gave as a "proclamation from Radhasoami Dayal" was not to be challenged (Maheshwari, *Truth Unvarnished*, part 1, p. 62).

[86] *The Tribune*, Chandigarh, January 25, 1988, p. 11.

of administration, the one that concerns the affairs of the branch satsangs throughout India and the world.[87] With the exception of the foreign branches, all these administrative areas are coordinated by the general secretary, S. L. Sondhi.

According to Sondhi, his job has the spiritual benefit of keeping the master free from details that would "waste his time."[88] The tasks of administration are acts of service to the master, but like all seva, they are also actions performed on his behalf, as if he were doing them. This notion gives administrators a pious enthusiasm for even the most ordinary task. They are like religious artisans and craftsmen who are given assignments to be creative for the sole purpose of glorifying God; they are unfettered by the mundane standards that normally limit their professions. The Radhasoami administrators are free to create an organization for the sake of its own integrity. For that reason their bureaucracies are usually moral improvements over the worldly institutions that in other ways they mirror. Like artists and artisans, the administrative craftsmen of the Radhasoami centers are involved in a truly creative task: forging order out of the apparent disorder of ordinary reality. So Radhasoami leaders can rightly think of themselves as extending the master's work, helping to make the world a more calm and disciplined place.

Not everyone in the Radhasoami community is pleased with this panoply of organization, however. The American and British devotees are among the most critical, for "organized religion" is one of the unpleasant aspects of their own religious culture that moved them towards the Radhasoami community in the first place. Julian Johnson argued that organization was evil by its very nature, that there should be "no attempt at organizing religion," for the process of organizing it was like "trying to build a cage around an eagle."[89] So Radhasoami administrators share with religious functionaries the world over the problem of theologically justifying their own existence, and in a Hindu milieu the problem is particularly severe. Traditional Hinduism had precious little religious organization, for the whole of India's caste society served as Hinduism's "organization." Perhaps it is significant that the Radhasoami centers have developed in just those places where the old Hindu social order has broken down or is no longer meaningful: in modern cities. There the creation of religious organizations may be seen as an attempt to provide for a new

[87] At the time of the transfer of property to a trust in 1957, the Beas organization held the titles for eighteen branch satsang meeting halls in Delhi, Bombay, Himachal, Pradesh and, of course, the Punjab, in addition to the property at the Dera itself. Since then the number of branch satsang buildings has more than doubled.

[88] Interview with S. L. Sondhi, Beas, July 12, 1979.

[89] Johnson, *With a Great Master*, p. 138.

generation the social stability that earlier generations found in the traditional social order of Hindu castes.

The Multiple Centers of Ruhani Satsang

Perhaps no branch of the Radhasoami family tree has been so well organized, so driven by grand visions of the future, and so subject to organizational disputes, as the Ruhani Satsang, established by Kirpal Singh in 1948. One reason for this is that several masters have succeeded Kirpal Singh, and each has established an ashram of his own. Another reason is the movement's international following, which has produced a number of semi-independent centers abroad. A third reason has to do with the personality of Kirpal Singh himself. He was a charismatic and visionary leader whose ideas energized his followers and sometimes led them into conflicting paths in their attempts to imitate him. From the very beginning his was a community on the move.[90]

When Kirpal Singh came to Delhi in 1948, he was by no means alone. At that time hundreds of thousands of Punjabi refugees were streaming over the border from the newly created Pakistan. Kirpal Singh stayed in Delhi for a time with his son, Darshan Singh, and delivered his first satsang as a spiritual master in the bustling Daryaganj section of the old city. Soon, however, he repaired to the quiet of Rishikesh in the Himalayan foothills, where he and several other disciples of Sawan Singh remained sequestered in a bungalow on the banks of the Ganges for several months. When they returned to Delhi later that year, Kirpal Singh officially established his mission, again holding satsang in Daryaganj. Soon his satsang—and Beas's—had attracted a good number of the refugees who were encamped nearby. A good number of Sawan Singh's other disciples joined his satsang as well. For a time Kirpal Singh lived at Number 1 Kingsway Road, Radio Colony, and rode a bicycle to and from satsang,[91] but in 1951 he purchased a plot of land in the Gurmandi section of Delhi. In time this became the site of Sawan Ashram, named in honor of Kirpal Singh's master.

Sawan Ashram was in a sense Kirpal Singh's Beas, and although it was much smaller in size, its facilities could house several dozen people on a

[90] My information about the Ruhani Satsang is based on interviews with three of Kirpal Singh's successors—Darshan Singh, Thakar Singh, and Ajaib Singh—and with members of their organizations. The most extensive biography of Kirpal Singh is to be found in the anonymous introduction to his *Portrait of Perfection*; there are also useful biographical sections in the Introduction to Kirpal Singh, *The Night is a Jungle* and in the reminiscences in Bhadra Sena, ed., *The Ocean of Grace Divine.*

[91] *Portrait of Perfection*, p. 60.

permanent basis and hundreds more for large events. In the mid-1950s Kirpal purchased a second home, this one in the Himalayan foothills. The masters at Beas also have a mountain retreat; theirs is at Dalhousie. Kirpal Singh's is on Rajpur Road in Dehra Dun. In time this home became more than a retreat; it became an adjunct headquarters, and in 1970 Kirpal Singh purchased enough acreage in the vicinity to launch a model community which he named Manav Kendra, "Humanity Center" or "The Center of Humankind." Within a remarkably few years, Kirpal Singh developed a secure organization and a surprisingly large following. The secret of this accomplishment is that Kirpal Singh went to the people rather than waiting for them to come to him— first the refugees in Delhi; then the urban masses in Delhi, Punjab, Uttar Pradesh, Maharasthra and Rajasthan; and ultimately a young international constituency. It was in nurturing the latter that Kirpal Singh made his movement distinctive. He was one of the first Indian spiritual leaders to respond to the Western interest in Indian religion as it developed from a mild curiosity in the 1950s to a wave of fascination in the 1960s and 1970s.

Kirpal Singh undertook his first international tour in 1955, to fulfill an old request of his master, Sawan Singh.[92] T. S. Khanna, an Indian disciple of the Great Master who had lived in Canada and the United States, also played an important role in this project. When Kirpal Singh returned to America in 1963, the size of the crowds increased several times over, and when he came once more, on his final world tour in 1972, the crowds increased "by a factor of ten."[93] Ultimately Kirpal Singh initiated over eight thousand Westerners, a number that during his lifetime comprised about ten percent of the total membership of Ruhani Satsang.[94] The percentage of revenue gained from their donations was higher than that, and Westerners were visibly present in the leadership circles of Kirpal Singh's ashram; they assisted in publication projects, building programs, and planning for the master's tours. Some of them developed branch organizations of their own. Among them was an American, Russell Perkins, who established the Sant Bani Ashram in 1962 on his farm in Sanborn-

[92] Ibid., p. 77.

[93] Russell Perkins, *The Impact of a Saint: Meetings with Kirpal Singh and Ajaib Singh, 1963–76* (Sanbornton, N.H.: Sant Bani Ashram, 1980), p. 127.

[94] According to records maintained by Kirpal Singh's successors, the total number of initiates in Ruhani Satsang, as of August 4, 1989, is 157,705; over 19,000 of these received initiation outside of India. Of this total, Kirpal Singh initiated 80,446 from the inception of his mission until his death in 1974, 8,643 of them on tours outside India. His son, Darshan Singh, who was Kirpal Singh's major successor, initiated 77,259 (as of the date of his death, May 30, 1989), 10,520 of which were outside of India. (Information supplied in letters to me from J. M. Sethi, Secretary, Sawan Kirpal Ruhani Mission, October 1, 1985; May 7, 1988; May 22, 1988; and November 15, 1988; and Prof. Arthur Stein, August 4, 1989.)

ton, New Hampshire.[95] The farm supported several nonprofit enterprises, including the American edition of the Ruhani Satsang journal, *Sat Sandesh*, established in 1970, and a publishing house for Kirpal Singh's books. Other North American ashrams included Kirpal Ashram in Vermont and the Unity of Man Center (now called Sawan Kirpal Meditation Center) in Bowling Green, Virginia.

Kirpal Singh envisaged his own model community, Manav Kendra, as but the first in a series of five service-oriented colonies, one in the center and one in each of the four directions of India. Each was to be an international community with free education, medical service, and care for the elderly; there were also to be model farms, and schools for teaching the major languages of the world. Only one other colony was started during his lifetime, in 1972, shortly before his death; it was in Baroda, near Bombay, and represented the western outpost.[96] It was never developed, however, and even at the original Manav Kendra only a few buildings were actually constructed.

Kirpal Singh was active on other fronts, however. The response generated by his visits abroad gave the leaders of the Ruhani Satsang the impetus to think of their movement more and more in international terms, and in 1957 Kirpal Singh founded the World Fellowship of Religions, an organization he hoped would bring all religious communities together to work for peace and mutual understanding. It was to include Muslim, Buddhist, Hindu, Christian, and other religious institutions, including the Ruhani Satsang. Kirpal was elected the World Fellowship's first president, and remained so until his death. The organization never really caught on, but for a while it held international multifaith conferences. The largest was "The World Conference on the Unity of Man" held in Delhi in February 1974, scarcely six months before his death; its purpose was to surmount religious differences and celebrate the unity of all persons. It was held on the Ram Lila grounds between the old and new sections of Delhi and attracted a good many public figures, including the prime minister, Indira Gandhi.

On August 1 of that year Kirpal appeared before the Indian parliament, one of the few religious figures to do so, but scarcely three weeks later, on August 21, 1974, he died, and his organization began to unravel. Its problem was in part its success: the movement had grown so rapidly in the 1950s and 1960s that it did not have time to develop the stable infrastructure that would allow the community to maintain itself beyond the death of its leading figure. The infighting after Kirpal Singh's death primarily concerned the issue of where—that is, in whom—the "Master Power," as

[95] Perkins, *Impact of a Saint*, p. 29.

[96] Perkins, Introduction to Kirpal Singh *The Night is a Jungle*, p. xx.

members of Ruhani Satsang call it, had been reincarnated. But it also had to do with property rights and control of the organization; the spiritual and secular issues were linked.

One of Kirpal Singh's disciples and the ashram's chief administrator, Bibi Hardevi, gained control of Sawan Ashram and established Thakar Singh as Kirpal's successor. Most of the other leaders of the movement supported Darshan Singh, Kirpal Singh's son, but since he had been dispossessed of his father's ashram they constructed a new headquarters at 2 Canal Road in Vijay Nagar, in the same suburban area of Delhi where Sawan Ashram is located. They named it the Kirpal Ashram of the Sawan Kirpal Ruhani Mission, and it is today by far the most flourishing of the branches established in Kirpal Singh's name. In addition to claiming eighty-thousand of the followers of his father, Darshan Singh initiated almost that many on his own.[97] In 1986 a new office complex called Kirpal Bagh was completed next to Kirpal Ashram, and following the death of Bibi Hardevi, the old Sawan Ashram was restored to Darshan Singh as well.

Perhaps the most unusual development following the death of Kirpal Singh was the attempt of the American disciple, Russell Perkins, to create support for Ajaib Singh, who prior to being proclaimed a successor of Kirpal had his own small following near Ganganagar in Rajasthan. In a remarkable testimony, *The Impact of a Saint: Seeking and Finding in the World of Today*, Perkins described his disillusionment at witnessing the political maneuvering that followed Kirpal Singh's death—an "overwhelming crashing of competing chords," he called it—and his adventurous search for a new master that ended in the desert of Rajasthan.[98] When he finally met Ajaib Singh, who had first been identified as the new master by one of Perkins's American colleagues, Arran Stephens, he knew "it was Kirpal Singh sitting there, smiling at me."[99] Most of Perkins's ashram in New Hampshire went along with his assessment, and the Sant Bani ashram has virtually separated from the rest of the organization.

The followers of Thakar Singh seem intent on building their own international movement. They have created a new Manav Kendra in Germany in addition to the old Manav Kendra near Dehra Dun, which they received from Bibi Hardevi and which they maintain as Thakar Singh's residence in India. Thakar Singh has established another center in Chandigarh, but most of his followers are in the United States: he maintains an office in New York and has a sizable following on the West Coast. Much of his recruiting is in California, and he is establishing an ashram in Or-

[97] Letter from J. M. Sethi, secretary, Sawan Kirpal Ruhani Mission, May 22, 1988; updated in letters from Prof. Arthur Stein, September 18, 1988 and August 4, 1989.

[98] Perkins, *Impact of a Saint*, p. 147.

[99] Ibid., p. 160.

egon. The momentum of his organization's growth has been stifled, however, by published accounts of his violent assaults on followers thought to be possessed by Kal and of his sexual advances toward female devotees.[100]

A sizable group of foreign initiates led by Reno Sirrine, who had been head of Kirpal Singh's American organization, were unconvinced that the claims of any of the contenders for succession were legitimate, and they proclaimed that an interregnum had occurred. They have created an organization entitled the Divine Science of the Soul, based in Anaheim, California, where they keep the memory of Kirpal Singh alive through publications and presentations of his teachings.

All these groups are splinter organizations, however. The mainstream of the Ruhani Satsang membership in India and abroad solidified under the leadership of Darshan Singh. Many of those who initially followed one of the other successors, including Arran Stephens, the American who discovered Ajaib Singh, came in time to Darshan Singh's camp. Darshan Singh was not quite the conference organizer that his father was; he presided over only one conference of the World Fellowship of Religion—in Delhi, in 1981—and participated in but a single Unity of Man Conference (under a new, gender-inclusive title, "International Human Unity Conference") in November 1988. In general he was less involved in organizational efforts than his father had been. He made no attempt to revive the idea of creating model cities, for example.

In many other ways, however, Darshan Singh proved to be very much his father's son. Most importantly, he gave his movement a stable, continuing home. Beyond that, he greatly expanded the movement's publication program, created a new library in comparative religion, and nurtured his growing following abroad, including a particularly large group in Colombia, South America. A high point in his leadership was a triumphal visit to the United Nations and a conversation with its former assistant secretary-general, Robert Muller. The dialogue was later transcribed and published by the United Nations University for Peace. When he suddenly died on May 30, 1989, in Delhi, shortly before what was to be a tour of Europe and America, his following was profoundly shocked, but most of them soon rallied around Darshan Singh's son, Rajinder, whom he had designated as his successor in his will. Rajinder Singh left his work as an electrical engineer in Chicago to serve as the new bearer of the lineage begun by his grandfather, Kirpal Singh.

[100] See Don Lattin, "The Cloud Over Indian Guru's U. S. Tour," *San Francisco Chronicle*, Saturday, July 23, 1988. For information on Thakar Singh's life, see the introduction to vol. 1 of his *And You Will Fly Up to God* (Kinderhook, N.Y.: Kirpal Light Satsang, 1982).

Coming Home

When there is a crisis in one of the Radhasoami communities, such as the death of a master, attention focuses on the central satsang, whether it be Kirpal Ashram, Beas, Dayalbagh, Soamibagh, Manav Mandir, or one of the others. It is there that the followers come to reaffirm their ties to the community and their commitment to the faith.

In a less dramatic way, such ties and commitments are reaffirmed at least once a year when devotees gather at the centers on bhandara days. In many respects Radhasoami bhandaras are not unlike Hindu pilgrimage events, but there are some striking differences. Traditional Hindu pilgrimage gatherings are only temporary expressions of fellowship, whereas the Radhasoami events convene a community that exists, in diaspora, long before and after the events. For this reason, the Radhasoami collocations are not called *melas* (a crowd that meets and disperses), nor is the journey to a bhandara called a *tirth yatra*, "a journey of crossing over," the term Hindus often use for pilgrimage. The reason is that in Radhasoami the one true spiritual crossing in Radhasoami is considered to be the moment of initiation, and the pilgrimage that matters most is the internal journey of the soul. A trip to the dera is for many a symbolic representation of that internal journey, but the term that is given to the event, *bhandara*, derives from a word meaning storage house or treasury. In modern India the term has also come to mean the opening up of a stockpile of food to supply a feast, especially a meal at a temple following a sacred event. By extension it implies any convocation of spiritually-minded folk, but even when it is used in this more general sense the word retains some of its original emphasis on food and the sharing of wealth.

Given the dull surroundings in which most villagers live, it is no surprise that so many are attracted to these events. But urban people are excited by them as well. Many urban satsangis have forgotten their village origins, and the master's residence gives them a new ancestral home. Radhasoami supplies a familial past as well, and the birth and death dates of the departed fathers and grandfathers of the Radhasoami family provide occasions to gather at the Radhasoami home.

At Beas four great bhandaras are held each year, the largest on the death date of the Great Master. At Kirpal Ashram and other branches of the Ruhani Satsang, the largest bhandara is on the birth date of Kirpal Singh; at Soamibagh, it is on the birth date of Madhav Prasad Sinha; and at Dayalbagh, bhandaras of equal size are held throughout the year on the birth anniversaries of the Dayalbagh masters.[101] Dayalbagh is alone

[101] The regular dates set for bhandaras at each of the centers, and the master honored at each, are as follows: *Soamibagh.* In September, Swami Shiv Dayal is honored; in October,

in restricting its bhandaras: initiates are allowed to attend only one per year, and outsiders are not allowed to enter the bhandara grounds.[102]

These are grand occasions, and even non-satsangis feel the thrill that comes from the sheer spectacle of the events. One outsider, Sudhir Kakar, described his experience in the crowd at Beas as an "assault on the sense of individual identity" which leads to an "altered consciousness."[103] In such a situation, according to Kakar, "the image of one's body becomes fluid and increasingly blurred, controls over emotions and impulses are weakened, critical faculties and rational thought processes are abandoned," and the whole experience is "both forceful and seductive."[104] From a Radhasoami point of view, the force of this experience is caused by a crystallization of spiritual energy, however, rather than by psycho-

---

Brahm Sankar Misra (held in Benares); in November, Madhuv Prasad Sinha (the largest event, some eight to ten thousand attend); in December, Rai Saligram. (Source: interview with P. S. Sharma, Soamibagh, August 13, 1985.)

Mansingh Ashram. The bhandaras correspond with the following Hindu holidays: Deepawali, Holi, Gurupurnam, and Shivratri (the latter also corresponds with the date of Baba Mansingh's death). (Source: interview with Yogesh Sharma, Gwalior, August 21, 1985.)

Peepalmandi. In September, Rai Saligram's death anniversary is celebrated; in November, the birthday of Lalaji (son of Rai Saligram); in December, the birthday of Rai Saligram (the largest event—some five thousand attend). There are also bhandaras on the Hindu holidays of Holi to honor Kunwar-ji, grandson of Rai Saligram, and Janmastami to honor Swami Shiv Dayal. (Source: interview with I. C. Gupta, Peepalmandi, August 10, 1983.)

Dayalbagh. The birth dates of departed masters are celebrated, rather than the death dates. Attendance is limited to those from a particular region for each event. On the Indian holiday of Basant, the birthday of Anand Swarup is celebrated (only Delhi residents may attend); on Holi, Gurcharandas Mehta (for Uttar Pradesh residents); in April, Kamta Prasad Sinha (for residents of the states of Punjab, Jummu and Kashmir, Haryana, and Himachal Pradesh); in August, Swami Shiv Dayal (for Andhra Pradesh, Karnataka, Tamil Nadu, Kerala, Gujarat and Maharashtra); in October, Brahm Sankar Misra (for residents of Bihar, Nepal, West Bengal, Orissa, and Assam); and in December, Rai Saligram (for residents of Madhya Pradesh and Rajasthan). Dayalbagh satsangis from foreign countries may attend any one bhandara in the year. (Source: *Dayalbagh Herald* 63, no. 5 [November 10, 1987], p. 2.)

Beas. The largest bhandara is April 2, the death anniversary of Sawan Singh (several hundred thousand attend); others are held on July 28 for Sawan Singh's birthday, October 27 for Jagat Singh's death anniversary, and December 29 for Jaimal Singh's death anniversary. There are also large monthly satsangs at the Beas dera in February, May, and September. (Source: information card published by Radhasoami Satsang, Beas, n.d.)

Kirpal Ashram. The largest event is on February 6, Kirpal Singh's birthday (twenty-five to thirty thousand attend). Other large bhandaras are on April 2 for Sawan Singh's death anniversary, July 27 for Sawan Singh's birthday (since 1980 celebrated on "Master's Day"), the fourth Sunday of July for Master's Day, August 21 for Kirpal Singh's death anniversary, September 14 for Darshan Singh's birthday (the second largest event). (Source: interview with S. P. Chopra, office secretary, Kirpal Ashram, August 16, 1985.)

[102] Interview with G. D. Sahgal, August 12, 1985.

[103] Kakar, *Shamans, Mystics and Doctors*, p. 130.

[104] Ibid.

logical processes. Everyone who attends a bhandara, for whatever reason, is believed to receive a blessing.

Centering Time: Bhandara Activities

Each of the Radhasoami and Ruhani Satsang centers has evolved its own distinctive style of bhandara, but the general format is the same. The events often last for several days and on each of these a morning satsang begins the day's schedule. This moving account recently published in the *Dayalbagh Herald* highlights some of the special qualities of a bhandara satsang—tinsel wreaths, Holy Photos, and all:

> The day that dawned on the 16th of August was clear, with a pleasant cool breeze. By 4:30 a.m. Satsangi brothers and sisters began to wend their way to the Satsang Hall for *Arati* [worship]. In consonance with the gaiety of the occasion they found the hall gaily bedecked with beautiful tinsel wreaths overhead and wall decorations all over. Large size Photos of Param Purusha Puran Dhani Huzur Soamiji Maharaj, Param Guru Huzur Sahabji Maharaj and Param Guru Huzur Mehtaji Maharaj hung on the wall behind the *Singhasan* [the guru's throne], besides the one on the *Singhasan*. Satsangis came and took their seats in their respective blocks. By 5 a.m. the hall was packed to capacity and the whole congregation sat in the silence of deep concentration waiting to be blessed with the *darshan* [sight] of the Satguru. Gracious Huzur arrived at 5:40 a.m. and paid obeisances to the Holy Photos and took His seat. He then cast His Glances on all sides. It was this precious moment for which everyone had been waiting for. *Arati* on a Bhandara Day is an occasion when the Grace of Huzur Radhasoami Dayal flows forcefully and for this *Arati*, Satsangis try to get the "*Khule nain Darshan*" [open-eyed sight] of the Satguru, creating a subtle spiritual effect that made *Mangalacharan* [a ceremony of invocation] that followed, intensely more meaningful.[105]

At Beas, the crowd is enormous. Tens of thousands participate, more than can be contained within Beas's Satsang Ghar, and services are held in a huge open field behind the building. Despite the size of the crowd, each member of the congregation is able to file past the master and receive the blessings of his darshan directly and close at hand. Given the multitude, this takes quite a while, so a special time is usually allotted for it in the early afternoon. The master arrives after an interlude of privacy and midday rest and seats himself beneath an umbrella on top of a platform ten feet or so above ground level. The congregation has been waiting qui-

[105] *Dayalbagh Herald* 62, no. 47 (September 1, 1987), pp. 1–2. The bhandara was held on August 16, 1987.

etly on canvases that have been stretched over the bare earth, the women on the right and the men on the left. A separate place is left at the very front for foreign devotees.

Darshan is the high point of the spiritual day, a moment of eucharistic participation in which each observer becomes an actor. Kakar, a psychoanalyst, observes that "the transformation of the disciples' faces as their eyes looked into his" was "remarkable," and he likens the "whole transformation" to that experienced by a "nursing infant."[106] At the end of darshan the devotees are nourished even more literally: they receive *prasad*, a gift of food similar to that received in Hindu temples and Sikh gurdwaras, and it also transmits the guru's power. In the granting of darshan and the giving of prasad, a transfer of power is thought to occur, an alchemy by means of which the guru takes in the gross love from his devotees and gives back a spiritual love. As in Hindu and Sikh ceremony, this transfer is mediated through sight and represented by food. Food is an apt metaphor, for once it is ingested it changes from matter to vital energy; the mundane love offered to the master is similarly digested until it assumes a much higher form.

Following darshan comes seva, which in a Beas bhandara means group work, the whole crowd engaged in a single constructive project such as moving dirt to build an elevated road or carrying bricks. As at satsang or darshan the master sits on an elevated place in full view of the proceedings, bathing the whole event in his beneficent gaze. The final event of the day is also a functional one: dinner. It is another occasion upon which an ordinary event is made special by its sheer magnitude: some eight thousand gather at a time in a huge shed in each of the dozen or so shifts required to feed the entire multitude. It is a simple fare of chapattis, vegetables, and lentil soup—and it is free, symbolizing what a bhandara is all about: the opening of the master's largesse to all who wish to receive it.

The four events in a bhandara day—satsang, darshan, seva, and the collective meal—summarize the Radhasoami experience. At the center of each is the master. In the first two events, he presents himself in audible and visible form; in the second two, he allows the devotees to respond, through acts of service and through partaking of his food. Simply by following the routine of any bhandara day, those who are unfamiliar with the Radhasoami faith gain a sense of what it is all about: service, community and the spiritual power of the master. Those who are already satsangis, of course, need not be taught these things again; yet they experience a renewal of the central elements of their faith in the most triumphal of settings, a return to the center, their spiritual home.

[106] Kakar, *Shamans, Mystics, and Doctors*, p. 139.

Part III

SOCIAL CONTEXTS

Eight

A New Community for a New Class

THE OVERWHELMING majority of the leaders of Radhasoami communities come from India's new urban managerial class, and it is their leadership style that one first encounters at the Radhasoami colonies. At Dayalbagh, for instance, one must visit the main office and speak with the general secretary or the president of the association before attending satsang, meeting with the master, or touring the farms and factories. The president of the association, G. D. Sahgal, is a man of stern efficiency who frequently uses the first person singular to talk about the colony's development: "I plan to improve the agricultural areas," he states, and he goes on to describe his plans for developing the publication program with a similar sense of personal authority.[1] A former lawyer who served as a judge on the high court at Allahabad, Sahgal comes from a family of Punjabi Khatris who have been administrators and educators for centuries.

Prior to Sahgal, the chief administrator at Dayalbagh for over forty years was the general secretary, Ram Jadoun, who came from a similar background. Jadoun was born in 1903 into a Rajput family in a small town near Kanpur, and after graduating from Agra College, he taught in schools and colleges in Bihar.[2] For a while he was affiliated with the Arya Samaj, but his parents had been staunch supporters of the Radhasoami faith, so he eventually returned to Agra, where he taught in Radhasoami colleges. He became an official in Radhasoami educational institutions, and in 1939 he was appointed chief administrator of the whole Dayalbagh system, a position he retained until his death in the late 1970s.

To a large extent the character of the Radhasoami community at Dayalbagh is shaped by Jadoun and Sahgal and the many others in leadership roles who come from India's key managerial positions. Yet although such people have embraced the faith in great numbers and are its most influential adherents, one cannot say that Radhasoami simply mirrors the secular life of the managerial class. Radhasoami communities do take on some of the traits of modern culture, but with equal force they reject others, providing an antidote to many of the less happy aspects of contemporary life. This ambivalence towards modernity is echoed in the

[1] Interview with G. D. Sahgal, Dayalbagh, August 13, 1985.

[2] Information about the life of Ram Jadoun comes from my interviews with him on January 10, 1971, and November 9, 1973.

life stories of some of the Radhasoami communities' most important leaders.

The Life and Faith of K. L. Khanna

During the period that Ram Jadoun was at Dayalbagh, his counterpart at Beas, K. L. Khanna, was leaving perhaps an even deeper impression on his community, shaping the voluntary administrators at Beas into a competent organization and superintending Beas's expansion during some of its most active years. Although he was born in a village, Khanna was not a traditional Punjabi. He studied chemistry at the Institute for Agricultural Research in Lyallpur and prepared for a career in agricultural research.[3]

Khanna's chemistry professor was Jagat Singh, a man who became Khanna's mentor in matters extending far beyond the classroom. He brought him to Beas in 1928 to meet the Great Master, but Khanna was not yet ready to seek initiation. The friendship between teacher and student continued, however, and Khanna often visited Jagat Singh long after he left college and joined a government research agency. On several of these occasions he accompanied Jagàt Singh to Beas, but still he did not feel the call to follow him into the Radhasoami faith. The turning point came in 1944, when a great sense of irresolution in his life weighed so heavily upon Khanna that he found it hard to sleep. As he tells the story, he came to a point of desolation on November 1 of that year, when he took leave from his administrative post to seek the counsel of his mentor, who by that time was living in retirement at Beas. When Khanna arrived, Jagat Singh was asleep. He waited beside him the entire night until he awoke. Jagat Singh then embraced him and told him that his difficulties were almost at an end. What he had to offer Khanna, of course, was initiation into the Radhasoami faith. When Jagat Singh became the master in 1948, Khanna served at his side, taking leave from his work as head of one of India's leading agricultural institutes, the experimental Pusa facilities that had been established in Delhi and were later moved to Pusa in the state of Bihar. When Khanna retired from Pusa in 1959, he began a new career as general secretary of the Dera at Beas, a post he held until his death in 1976.

Khanna ran the Beas organization with the same decisive, goal-oriented

[3] Information about K. L. Khanna comes from my interviews with him, including two on May 25–26, 1971, which were later supplemented by written responses to my written questions.

style he had brought to every other administrative task he had undertaken. Yet for him the modern world was inherently vacuous, and although he felt traditional religion had little to offer a scientific mind, he also thought that ordinary science was not capable of plumbing the deepest truths. Khanna's style and his spirituality came together in a Calvinist linkage between administrative virtues, an earnest religiosity, and a theology that was complex and logically satisfying. All these Khanna found in the Radhasoami community and philosophy.

The Dera also replaced what Khanna had lost in childhood—an ancestral home—and it has helped compensate for the fact that his own children lead lives that are widely dispersed. He and his wife Satya have nine children: one became a doctor; others are professors, engineers, administrators. Two of his sons have settled in the United States and a third in Canada. A fourth, Tejendra, whom the family calls Teji, is an official of the Indian government, who has been assigned to the offices of the Punjab state government at Chandigarh.

Teji is a member of the elite Indian Administrative Service (IAS), has a master's degree in political science from the University of California, Berkeley, and before becoming finance commissioner of Punjab, was stationed in Delhi and London. His home in Chandigarh, a spacious new suburban house staffed with a cook, a gardener, and a gatekeeper, is provided by the government. Ordinarily he would also be assigned a chauffeur, but Teji prefers to drive his own car, an Audi, to work. As he drives to and from his office, Teji listens to tape-recorded discourses of Master Charan Singh.

Like his father, Teji weaves into his matrix of Radhasoami spirituality the virtues of a responsible and progressive citizen. Even before the political troubles that imperiled Punjab in the mid-1980s, Teji felt that the greatest danger to modern Indian society was posed by a "collapse of respect for public values" and the moral anomie that he saw enveloping the country. At that time Teji said that he would like to create an Indian organization like the American "Common Cause" to combat these tendencies. Later, after the troubles in the Punjab, he said that before such reforms would be possible, the first moral duty of a civil servant was "the restoration of public order."[4]

Since he and his wife maintain staid Radhasoami habits, they were hardly able to keep up with the pace of Chandigarh's social life. Their social schedule revolves around family affairs and events in the Radhasoami community. They did not participate actively in the Chandigarh satsang, but they are regularly in attendance at Beas and the busy Ra-

[4] Interview with Tejendra Khanna, Chandigarh, July 11, 1979, and January 22, 1988.

dhasoami center in Delhi. At both these places they are surrounded by family and friends from childhood. Since Beas is Teji's family home as well as his spiritual home, Charan Singh and the present master, Gurinder Singh, have been intimate family friends.

Radhasoami Networks in Government and Business

It might appear to the outsider that Teji lives in two worlds, one comprised of government administrators and the other of satsangis; but to some extent they overlap. Quite a few of his colleagues in the administrative service are also satsangis. These have included two occupants of the most important administrative position in the state government: I. C. Puri and Kuldip Singh Narang, who both served as chief secretary of the Punjab administrative service. Now retired, Puri lives in Chicago, where he is vice president of the International Vegetarian Society, and Narang is the chief administrator of the new hospital at Beas. The present head of the Department of Public Administration at Punjab University, Prof. D. R. Sachdeva, is a satsangi, and other adherents of Radhasoami presently serving as IAS officers in the Punjab include Rajan Keshap, a commissioner-rank secretary in the state government. Outside Punjab, Beas satsangis in high administrative positions include Puri's sister, Mona Singla, who serves as an official of the Gujarat government, and Jashwant Rajwade, commissioner of industry in the state of Maharashtra.

One of the most highly placed satsangis in India's administrative system is the recent secretary to the president of India, Prem Kumar, an initiate of Dayalbagh. Among Dayalbagh's members are also the joint secretary of finance of the government of India, Jagmohan Lal Bajaj; the chief secretary of the state of Hariana, P. P. Caprihan; and the general manager of planning for the State Bank of India, A. K. Puri. Across the road from Dayalbagh, in Soamibagh, lives the highest-ranking administrator in Agra, the district commissioner, Anadi Nath Sahgal.

Government agencies have played a major role in the history of Radhasoami communities. It was through the postal system that the brother of Radhasoami's founder came into contact with Rai Saligram: Pratap Singh, Swami Shiv Dayal's brother, was the camp clerk to the postmaster general of the United Provinces and was stationed at Meerut when Saligram, also a postal administrator, visited there on official duties. Other masters who have worked as government servants include Faqir Chand and Kirpal Singh; Darshan Singh retired at the rank of deputy secretary in India's central government. Brahm Sankar Misra and Madhav Prasad Sinha were classmates and later coworkers in the accountant general's office of the state government of Uttar Pradesh. Anand Swarup, Jagat Singh, M. B. Lal, Shyam Lal, I. C. Sharma and A. P. Mathur were professors or teachers, as was Swami Shiv Dayal himself. Kamta Prasad Sinha and Charan Singh were trained as lawyers, and Gurcharandas Mehta and Rajinder Singh were engineers. The military was the point of contact between Jaimal Singh and Sawan Singh, and it is still the case that many leaders of the Beas community are retired army officers.[5]

The teacher-student relationship that prefaced K. L. Khanna's spiritual relationship to Jagat Singh occurs in other branches as well. Former students of M. B. Lal, I. C. Sharma and A. P. Mathur number among their present-day disciples at Dayalbagh, Manavta Mandir and Peepalmandi. Several members of the Agra University faculty joined the Radhasoami fold through Mathur's example when he was head of that institution in the mid-1980s; and Kirpal Singh Narang, who is presently the head of Beas's publications program, set an example for several students and colleagues who joined the Radhasoami community during his tenure as head of Punjabi University in the 1970s. The chairman of the philosophy department at that time, Janak Raj Puri, is now Narang's neighbor in Beas. Puri had no need to be persuaded to join Radhasoami through Narang's influence, however, since Puri comes from an old Radhasoami family; his older brother is the author of a book on Radhasoami teachings. It is his nephew who was once the chief secretary of Punjab and now lives in Chicago.

There are also some significant patterns of Radhasoami association in business and trade, as we have noted in the town of Nabha, where the Radhasoami satsang serves as a sort of cloth merchants' guild. There is similarly a network of satsangis employed in shipping firms in Bombay. In these cases, as in government and education, institutional settings provide the locations in which individuals may adopt the religious affiliation of a friend. Such "faith-adopting" is not common in India, but modern institutions do foster the trend and enable new religious communities such as Radhasoami to flourish. Max Weber has argued that people who come from merchant and artisan professions have "a definite tendency toward congregational religion" and what he calls "a rational ethical religion."[6] Radhasoami provides a new experience of community such as Weber had in mind, not just for business people but for other professionals who associate with occupations that are not organized in traditional Hindu ways, such as government and the army. It is perhaps not surpris-

[5] Jaimal Singh had been a member of the twenty-fourth Sikh Regiment when he was stationed in Agra in 1856 and met Swami Shiv Dayal. Sawan Singh was an engineer with the Military Works Services stationed in the Murray Hills when he met Jaimal Singh there in 1894 (Introduction to Jaimal Singh, *Spiritual Letters*, pp. xix, xx).

[6] Weber, *Economy and Society*, p. 482.

ing that where old patterns of social organization have lost their force, old religious patterns are easily challenged as well.

The Alliances of Kinship

In some cases Radhasoami is able to integrate traditional kinship networks into its own modern style. In 1966, for instance, when Teji Khanna married Uma Mehta, he not only acquired a sparkling and intelligent wife, he also sealed a relationship with a family that had been as active at Beas as his own. Uma's father, R. N. Mehta, the patriarch, is the owner and manager of Mahatta Camera Stores, an old family business that now has its headquarters in Delhi but before India's independence had been

17. R. N. Mehta, head of the Delhi branch of the Radhasoami Satsang, Beas.

located in what is presently Pakistan.[7] ("Mahatta" is simply another way of spelling the Mehta family name.) Originally the family came from Hoshiarpur, where the men in the Mehta family were astute businessmen. They discovered a need for photography studios near British army cantonments and followed the British to the Himalayan foothills, where they established military and government retreats. Mehta and two of his brothers opened shops in the hill towns of Dalhousie, Murray, and Srinagar, and in Rawalpindi, near the Murray hills.

It was in Srinagar that Mehta first became acquainted with the Radhasoami faith. The Great Master, who was on tour in Kashmir, was brought to his studio to be photographed. Later, when Mehta's younger brother developed a stomach ailment, the family remembered that there were doctors among Sawan Singh's retinue, and they sent the younger brother to Beas to be treated by Dr. Julian Johnson, the American disciple of the Great Master who was living there. Mehta received initiation in 1938. After independence and the partition of the Punjab, the Mehta family was forced to flee from Rawalpindi and Kashmir and stayed for a while at Charan Singh's family farm before resettling in Delhi. There they reestablished their photography business on Connaught Circle, where it has become one of New Delhi's most respected commercial institutions.

R. N. Mehta's organizational skills are also highly regarded in the Radhasoami community, for he has developed the Delhi satsang into an enormous institution. It now boasts a cluster of bright, modern-looking buildings in the suburban area of west Delhi. The centerpiece is a large satsang hall that is roughly the size of a basketball gymnasium; it accommodates several thousand for twice-weekly services. More than ten thousand gather on adjacent grounds that compare with a football field in size. These grounds are used for bhandaras and for Sunday gatherings when the crowd is too large to fit inside the hall. Mehta has considerable influence in the Beas central organization and he has been given credit for engineering the meeting that was held between Beas and Dayalbagh leaders in 1978.

When one combines the professional Radhasoami networks with the family ones, the patterns can become quite intricate. There is the Khanna-Mehta-Puri connection, for example: the sister of Uma Khanna (née Mehta) is married to I. C. Puri, the chief secretary of the Punjab government, whose uncle, a former professor of philosophy at Punjabi University, now lives in retirement at Beas.[8] Then there is the Puri-Narang link:

[7] My information about R. N. Mehta and his family comes from my interviews with him in Delhi on December 5, 1980; August 15, 1985; and January 20, 1988.

[8] Uma's other brothers and sisters are similarly well situated. One of her brothers is the present manager of Mahatta; the other is with the 3M Company in the United States. One

I. C. Puri is said to have been an influence on the decision of his successor, Kuldip Singh Narang, to become a satsangi. Kuldip, in turn, influenced the decision of his cousin, Kirpal Singh (K. S.) Narang, to do the same. K. S. Narang was Puri's uncle's superior at Punjab University, and now, in retirement, they continue to work together in the publications office at Beas. To make matters more complicated, another of K. S. Narang's sons, Inder Pal Narang, has married a daughter of the nephew of the Ruhani Satsang founder, Kirpal Singh.[9]

The Merchant-Caste Connection

What unites all these Khannas, Puris, Mehtas, and Narangs, aside from family connections and the similarity in their educational backgrounds, social status, and economic positions, is something that most Indians would immediately detect from their names: the common denominator of caste. They are all Khatris. Many of the masters are also members of the Khatri caste, except at Beas, where they are all Jats.[10] Ruhani Satsang masters have all been Khatris, as have most of the Agra masters, beginning with Swami Shiv Dayal, and including Madhav Prasad Sinha and Gurcharandas Mehta. M. B. Lal is a kindred Kayastha.

Most of the other masters came from similar urban merchant castes: Rai Saligram, Kamta Prasad Sinha, and A. P. Mathur, for example, also Kayasthas, and Anand Swarup was an Ahluwalia. Other gurus have been Aroras and Banias. The priestly caste is scarcely represented at all. Brahma Sankar Misra, the major exception, brought very few of his caste-mates into the fold. Aside from several Brahmans in attendance at the satsangs held at Misra's Radhasoami Bagh in Benares, and an occasional Brahman at the other centers, there are almost no Brahmans in the visible ranks of Radhasoami today. As for leaders, the only other Brahmans to have served as masters were associated with the smaller centers: Faqir Chand and I. C. Sharma at Manavta Mandir, for instance, and Anukul Thakar at Deogarh, Bihar.

Among the merchant-caste members both at Agra and Beas is a significant contingent that comes from Sindh, the region bordering the lower Indus River in what is now Pakistan. At the turn of the century, Rai Saligram initiated a number of satsangis in the Sindhi cities of Hyderabad

---

sister is married to the owner of a chain of movie theaters in Delhi, and another to the owner of a sugar factory (Interview with R. N. Mehta in Delhi, December 5, 1980).

[9] My information on the Puri family comes largely from an interview with Janak Raj Puri, Beas, November 11, 1980. Inder Pal Narang now lives in Alameda, California.

[10] Jaimal Singh was a member of the Gill subcaste of Jats; Jagat Singh was a Klare, Sawan Singh and Charan Singh were Grewals, and Gurinder Singh is a Dhillon.

and Karachi and attracted them to the Agra branch; Brahm Sankar Misra continued to minister to them after Rai Saligram's death.[11] Recently, however, it is the Beas branch that has been recruiting Sindhis, especially those who have settled in Bombay, where Beas maintains a large headquarters. There Charan Singh was sometimes known as the "guru of Sindhis." With the creation of Pakistan in 1947, other Sindhis were scattered to urban centers throughout the world, and Radhasoami's popularity in Indian immigrant communities in Kenya, South Africa, Singapore, England, Canada, and the United States is due in some measure to its being embraced by Sindhis who have settled in those locales.

Many of the descendants of the Sindhis who became Rai Saligram's initiates reside today in Soamibagh. Other Soamibagh residents are Marwaris, members of a merchant-caste community that originated in Jodhpur, a Rajasthani town not far from Sindh. In the nineteenth century there was a great dispersion of Marwaris to cities across north India, and in places such as Calcutta they became leaders of industry.[12] A few, such as the Birlas, have become among India's most wealthy families. Wealth of the Birla magnitude is not represented in Soamibagh, but some of the most common Marwari names, such as Maheshwari and Aggarwal, do appear on its rolls.

Who are these urban merchant castes—the Khatris and Kayasthas and Marwaris—and why do they want to depart from the religious customs of their past? The answer to the first part of the question is problematic, for the classical caste (*varna*) scheme of priests, warriors, merchants, and artisans, followed by untouchables, is imprecise in defining the many existing subcastes (*jatis*) in present-day Indian society. Many Khatris claim that theirs is a Kshatriya (warrior) caste, as the name itself suggests, and a similar claim has been made by Kayasthas.[13] Most scholars disagree, however, and regard such Khatris and Kayasthas as striving for a social status that will befit their considerable economic and educational achievements more than do the merchant-caste categories into which they were born. In the past members of such castes as the Khatris served as shopkeepers, moneylenders, traders, and teachers. Their reputation for mastering knowledge sometimes extended to the spiritual realm: Guru Nanak and the other nine founding gurus of the Sikh tradition were Khatris, members of the Bedi subcaste. In more recent years Khatris have turned to modern business and government organizations, where they have risen to high administrative positions.

[11] Misra, *Solace to Satsangis*, pp. 1–3.

[12] Thomas A. Timberg, *The Marwaris: From Traders to Industrialists* (New Delhi: Vikas Publishing House, 1978), pp. 52–53.

[13] See Karen Leonard, *Social History of an Indian Caste: The Kayasths of Hyderabad* (Berkeley: University of California Press, 1978).

Their rise in social status, however, has not been commensurate with their economic success. Hindu tradition reserves for Brahmans the role of priestly leadership, and the leadership of the Sikh community has changed over the centuries from Khatri to Jat. Jats hold most leadership posts in Sikh religious organizations, in the major Sikh political party, and in the administration of Sikh educational institutions. It is no wonder, then, that members of Khatri castes would be attracted to a new religious community that allows them to rise to levels of leadership and status appropriate to the competence they display in society at large.[14] The Radhasoami community belongs virtually to Khatris alone, and in the Punjab, where Khatris have traditionally been divided between Sikhs and Hindus, the Dera offers a common meeting ground, uniting Khatris of differing religious camps.

The Religion of the Managerial Class

We return to the question raised at the beginning of this chapter as to how much Radhasoami has been stamped by the attitudes and concerns of its urban, merchant-caste constituency, and to what extent it is akin to merchant-caste religious traditions, sects, movements, and denominations elsewhere in India and in the world: the Arya Samaj, for example, or the Vallabhites.[15] Max Weber argued that the merchant-caste values of the Vallabhites made them immune from the "other-worldly" tendencies of Brahmanic Hinduism, and he dubbed their almost Protestant emphasis on the sanctity of hard work and the virtues of an upright life an "inner-worldly asceticism."[16] What made the Vallabha group different from other Hindus, he said, was not just that they were merchants, but that they were merchants on the move: socially mobile and acquisitive. Ordinarily rich businessmen, regardless of cultural setting, have little interest in religion; "skepticism or indifference to religion" has characterized the attitudes of "large-scale traders and financiers."[17] But an exception arises in the case of groups that are involved in "the acquisition of new capital, or more correctly, capital continuously and rationally employed." These

[14] I pursue further the subject of Jat-Khatri relations and its role in the political turbulence of mid-1980s Punjab in my preface to *Religious Rebels in the Punjab: The Social Vision of Untouchables* (Delhi: Ajanta Books International, 1989), the revised Indian edition of my *Religion as Social Vision*.

[15] See Jones, *Arya Dharm*.

[16] Weber, *Religion of India*, pp. 199–201.

[17] Weber, *Economy and Society*, p. 479.

groups, according to Weber, seek a "rational, ethical, congregational religion."[18]

To some extent Weber's description of a merchant caste on the move fits the Khatris, and to some extent his description of a "rational, ethical, congregational religion" fits Radhasoami, but there are some differences on both scores. Khatris, especially the ones in Radhasoami, are not lonely capitalists; they are socially adept managers. And Radhasoami is not quite a community church; it provides not only "worldly" ethical values but the most "otherworldly" of mystical realms. The question, then, is to what degree the inner- and otherworldly characteristics of Radhasoami are consistent with a managerial mentality.

One of the modern, managerial virtues is an emphasis on individual responsibility and achievement. Radhasoami embraces this value in that it provides a community that all, regardless of caste, may enter, and it offers access to salvation unimpeded by the fetters of dharma and caste and achievable in one's own lifetime. The industry and knowledge of techniques that are so highly valued in managerial circles are also praised in the Radhasoami community and given a place in its path to salvation: hard work, craft, and scientific knowledge—even knowledge regarding the "science of the soul"—are the main ingredients of both social and spiritual progress. A third managerial value, a sense of public responsibility, is also consistent with Radhasoami attitudes. Radhasoami colonies provide social wholes, and its theology provides a cosmic whole in which individual members may locate themselves and find their moral and spiritual responsibilities.

Although it would seem at first glance that the Radhasoami tradition does give religious expression to managerial virtues, this conclusion does not entirely jibe with the initiates' own perceptions. For many of them, the Radhasoami path is difficult and unfamiliar, requiring a radical transformation of life. "I had succumbed to the modern world," K. L. Khanna testified, "but I abandoned all interests in personal ambition when I fell at the feet of the master."[19] Although an outsider might interpret Khanna's high position in the Radhasoami satsang as a triumph of personal ambition indeed, from Khanna's point of view his role was only seva, to be exalted no more highly than the work of those who carry baskets of dirt on their heads. The other managerial virtues are similarly qualified: the individualism of Radhasoami's spiritual quest is tempered by the fellowship of satsang; the value placed on religious technique is offset by the assertion that love is a yet more efficacious path; and the sense of responsibility engendered by knowing the whole is belittled by the vastness of

[18] Ibid.

[19] Interview with K. L. Khanna, Beas, May 25, 1971.

the divine responsibility for what cannot be known, the realms beyond human grasp.

It would appear, then, that there are parallel sets of values within the Radhasoami tradition, one confirming the mores of its middle-class constituency—its rational, egalitarian efficiency—and the other transforming those values to produce quite a different vision of the suprarational and social ideal. Both are at odds with traditional Hinduism, but they are also to some extent at odds with each other: the Radhasoami vision of a transformed community and a transcendent authority avoids anomie, rootlessness, aggressive and selfish forms of individualism, and many other moral pitfalls of middle-class modernity. When Baba Ram Jadoun described his participation in the Dayalbagh community as "taking part in the best of the modern world" and then later claimed that his voyage on the Radhasoami path had been "like setting sail in uncharted seas," he was speaking of these parallel tendencies in Radhasoami tradition: one that endorses the better aspects of modernity and one that seeks to transcend the worst of them.[20] These two dimensions of Radhasoami's worldview allow those who possess a modern, managerial outlook to feel confirmed in what they are, but at the same time elevated beyond any worldly identities they know.

[20] Interview with Ram Jadoun, Dayalbagh, November 9, 1973.

Nine

The Faith of Village Untouchables

PARSINI is a village woman in an urban religion. When she goes to the Beas Dera, she does not see the world of K. L. Khanna and the other administrators, except for the products of their labors; that is, the Dera itself and the gala events that provide a sort of theatrical backdrop for her vision of the master. Their world touches but never quite intersects hers.

Parsini spends most afternoons cutting grass in the lowlands outside her village gate to provide fodder for the animals and fuel for the evening meal. Her village is situated in an idyllic setting in the mountain foothills of the Hoshiarpur district, but she lives in the poorest section, a row of simple mud huts. When she returns home, it is to a milk buffalo, a husband who works as a field hand, several grown children and numerous grandchildren, two dark rooms, and a handful of meager possessions.[1] Among them sits a picture of Charan Singh, whom she, like Radhasoami devotees of radically different backgrounds, has revered as master.

Villagers are an anomaly for the Radhasoami tradition as a whole, but the Beas branch has been unusually hospitable to them, and they began to come in large numbers in the 1930s and 1940s. In fact, villagers accounted for a large proportion of the huge increase in membership that Radhasoami saw under the Great Master.[2] Many of them were, like Parsini, Chamars, members of a caste traditionally composed of leatherworkers but today employed as field laborers. They are Untouchables. Most of the villagers who come to the Beas bhandaras are from these

[1] My information about Parsini comes from interviews on October 10, 1971, and August 4–5, 1979, conducted in Hindi and Punjabi. I appreciate the assistance of Mohinder Singh in arranging the interviews and participating in them, and of Devinder Singh in helping to translate. For assistance in transcribing and translating the tape recordings of the interviews, my thanks to Ali Rusum Khan.

[2] The anonymous author of the section entitled "Statistics," included in Jaimal Singh, *Spiritual Letters* (Beas: Radhasoami Satsang, Beas, 1958), states that Sawan Singh initiated "a total of 125,375 souls" whereas Jaimal Singh initiated only 2,343 (pp. xix–xx).

lower classes, as my surveys indicate,[3] and as Charan Singh confirmed.[4] According to traditional Hindu custom, members of these castes could not be touched because their occupations were impure, and they were denied privileges available to others—including the right to enter temples.

When Parsini first heard about the Radhasoami fellowship in the 1940s—she cannot recall the precise year—she did not know whether she would be allowed to join. She thought entry into its community was reserved for Rajputs, in her area the dominant caste, but a cousin who was a satsangi reassured her. She remembers her first trip to the Dera as a grand moment in her life. Parsini stayed there nine days and was initiated by the Great Master. There had been a special urgency in her quest for a master: shortly before, she had lost her only two children through disease. Parsini searched desperately for a holy man who could give her solace, but those she found locally left her unsatisfied. When she met Sawan Singh, "the peace in his eyes" gave her fulfillment, and his powers were confirmed when within two years she gave birth to another child.

The Miraculous Powers of the Master

Punjab's village culture differs in many ways from the high traditions of Hinduism and Sikhism; it includes a strong sense of the vitality of the spirit world. In that world, good and evil beings vie for power. Holy men and women are thought to be in contact with these forces and able to manipulate them to beneficial or harmful effect.[5]

The Radhasoami emphasis on the power of the guru, the force of his gaze, and the efficacy of the charged names fits easily into this traditional village pattern of beliefs about the spirit realm. Parsini uses her picture of Charan Singh as a sort of talisman, placing before it objects symbolizing her concerns, such as the worn shirt of a son whom Parsini wishes to protect, who works in a distant city. At other times she uses the names that were given her at the time of initiation to ward off evil spirits. Once,

[3] My knowledge about village members of Radhasoami comes from my field studies in rural Punjab, including six locales that were the subject of research for a previous book, *Religion as Social Vision* (see pp. 11–21), and an article, "The Cultures of Deprivation: Three Case Studies in the Punjab," *Economic and Political Weekly*, Annual number, February 1979. My comments about village Untouchables in the Radhasoami movement are based on this research and on three additional areas of the Punjab surveyed in August 1979, for this study. One was near the Beas Dera in Gurdaspur district, one in Nabha district, and one in Hoshiarpur.

[4] Interview with Charan Singh, Beas, April 2, 1971.

[5] For a discussion of the village religion of Untouchables, see my *Religion as Social Vision*, pp. 92–106; and G. W. Briggs, *The Chamars* (London: Oxford University Press, 1920), chapter 6.

while returning at dusk from the river where she had been cutting grass, the figure of a woman in a scarlet dress began to approach her, and Parsini was seized with fear. She sensed that the woman was in actuality a demonic spirit. The quick repetition of the five sacred names, however, caused the spirit to vanish into the night.

The gaze of the master also cures illness or wards it off before it strikes. On one occasion Parsini came to Beas with a lingering cough that no doctor had been able to banish. After darshan of the master, the cough disappeared. Since then the cough has come back, and other medical problems have persisted as well, but these things have not caused Parsini to doubt the efficacy of Radhasoami. She reasons that the master is providing her with physical distress to allow her to burn off karmic obligations from the past, or to anticipate them in the future, providing her with a sort of karmic credit.

Not all of Parsini's communications with the master are petitions for relief from distress. There are other benefits to be gained from the link with the master's power: a sense of security, for instance, which she experiences as love. "If you have the love of the master in your heart," Parsini says, "you are strong and unafraid and at peace within." Other religious traditions also supply such assurances, of course, but Parsini has no use for a religion with an absentee Lord, and on that account is unmoved by both Christian and Sikh religiosity. She has often visited an attractive new Sikh gurdwara near her home, but she challenges the Sikh notion of divinity. "Where is their guru?" she asks. "I looked around and didn't see any." At the Beas Dera she is not disappointed.

Acceptance and Entertainment

Even though there are some parallels between her traditional village beliefs and her understanding of Radhasoami, Parsini's initiation was not at first greeted with favor by her family and friends. Her husband feared that she was becoming unbalanced; other villagers made fun of her. They would taunt her by asking, "What new guru do you have today?" Among satsangis, however, she found a great store of personal acceptance, and in time she brought some of her acquaintances into the faith—first her best friend, Shanti, then her husband, then Shanti's, until a circle of about twenty satsangis was created within her own village. If one includes people connected to them by family ties in villages nearby, her Radhasoami network now numbers more than a hundred. Many within this group travel together to the bhandaras. They also hold special satsangs in conjunction with birth celebrations, weddings, and funeral occasions, and they hold satsangs at bhandara times for those who cannot travel to Beas.

Approximately ten miles away in the town of Rupar a plot of land has been purchased by local satsangis and satsang is held every Sunday, but Parsini and her village friends show little enthusiasm for it. "It's mainly for shopkeepers," she explains.

The events at Beas are different, however, and her eyes light up when she describes them. "Everyone goes to the bhandaras," she says. On those occasions she gathers together a group of her friends and they make the entire trip a festive undertaking. The journey takes most of the day, even though Beas is only about forty miles from home. They begin by crowding onto a perilously overloaded scooter-taxi to Rupar, then board an equally crowded bus to Jalandhar, and take another to the stop on the Jalandhar-Amritsar road that is nearest the Dera. They walk the final three miles, although in some instances the driver of a creaking horsecart will urge them to scramble on board for the last stage of their journey. All this is part of the excitement, for in Parsini's mind, the bhandara begins "as soon as we leave the village."

The journey to Beas is the greatest distance Parsini has ever ventured away from her village in the course of her entire life. Punjab's capital, Chandigarh, is scarcely thirty miles away from her home, but she has never visited it; nor has she been to Delhi, 150 miles south. The Dera at Beas supplies every image of the modern world that Parsini possesses. No wonder, then, that she and her friends spend much of their time there simply wandering around, admiring the handsome buildings, and observing everything that fascinates the eye. Parsini is quite eager to believe the many magical stories told about various corners of the Dera, such as the one concerning a spring that mysteriously appeared from the ground, providing a water supply that enabled Jaimal Singh to create the Dera at this location. She is most fond of the version of this story that casts the god Shiva as the agent who made the spring appear; and after hearing the story, one can actually go and see the spring itself. She says that Radhasoami confirms all its stories with things that can be seen by the eye or experienced in one's life.

Of special interest to her at Beas are photographers—she has always been curious about how pictures are made—and foreigners. She explains that her interest is not just curiosity, but an eagerness to receive the spiritual benefit of their darshan. She recalls peering through the entrance gate of the foreigners' guesthouse as a group of Westerners sat at tea in the garden, and receiving a blessing by observing them. The vision was brief, however, for the guard at the gate hurried her on her way. She was not offended, since she assumed he was merely trying to make space for others to come and observe the scene.

Simply being part of the crowd is a great thrill for Parsini. All the attention focused on the master corroborates Parsini's conviction that he is a sacred person, and the size of the crowd gives her a feeling of pride. During darshan, when each person comes to the front of the audience for a brief visual contact with the Lord, she joins her friends in songs of reverence as they move up the crowded aisle to have his gaze directed at them, even for a fraction of a second.

Darshan is not the only moment during the bhandara when Parsini and her friends are singled out: they are also given tasks. To her there is nothing unusual about the seva of moving loads of dirt on her head—whatever lessons of humility are to be learned through this labor were taught to her almost from birth—but at bhandara it is blessed by the presence of the master, members of upper castes and foreigners. And in addition, she and her friends are given special assignments. Several of them have been designated sevadars. Parsini, for instance, works in the kitchen where chapattis are made and lentil soup is cooked to feed the thousands. She spends an hour and a half each day helping to stoke the fires and roll out the chapattis with dozens of other women assigned to that role. Parsini is impressed by the fact that rich women in fancy saris work alongside her with no attention paid to caste or station. The feeling of camaraderie is especially intense at mealtimes, when thousands are seated on the floor in long rows with no regard for social rules against intercaste commensality. "At the Dera when we eat together," Parsini explains, "we are all one family."

The feeling of family responsibility accounts for her and her relations' willingness to work as sevadars without pay. Parsini's son, for instance, mans one of the makeshift tea stalls, and her husband helps superintend the area roped off for parking bicycles, each marked by a tag to identify its owner. These sevadar positions are regarded as honors, and to make certain that they will be assigned the same tasks each year, Parsini and her family come to the bhandara a day early to meet with their respective crews. They are also allowed to stay a day after the end of the bhandara, when they take part in the special satsang for the sevadar community.

Social Change

Although the bhandaras create the impression of a unified family, one might question how realistic Parsini's assessment of Radhasoami's social equality is. Most branches of Radhasoami support equal rights for all castes, and Charan Singh's creation of a single, caste-free dining shed was called a "social revolution."[6] The *Dayalbagh Herald* editorialized that government measures to remove untouchability were unnecessary in the

[6] D. L. Kapur, *Heaven on Earth*, p. 328.

Radhasoami community, since at Dayalbagh all are treated equally "in actual practice."[7] The editor went on to claim that at Dayalbagh "it is difficult to find out who is a Harijan [Untouchable] and who is not. . . . No wonder therefore that the Harijans who have joined this Faith feel that they are as good members of the Satsang as any person of the higher caste."[8] Yet as a practical matter people from the same social backgrounds tend to stick together, and there are very few, if any, marriages in any of the Radhasoami communities between Untouchables and persons of upper castes. Only one member of the Beas executive committee has been recruited from the lower castes, and he had been a member of India's parliament. Some Untouchable leaders from outside the faith have been cynical about what they regard as Radhasoami's easy conquest of lower-caste followers, and one Untouchable activist in nearby Jalandhar characterized the Dera as a "guest house for the rich, where lower castes do the work."[9]

But Parsini does not see it this way. She feels that there have been significant social as well as spiritual changes in her life as a result of her association with the Radhasoami fellowship. She has gained a position of influence among members of her own caste; she associates with people of upper castes on a level of equality when she works as a sevadar at the Dera; through satsang connections she has come to know women of merchant-caste background at Rupar, and her son has developed a friendship with a Rajput man. Moreover, her reputation as a Radhasoami organizer has attracted attention within the upper strata of her village, and recently the wife of a landowner of Gujar caste came to Parsini to inquire about the possibility of joining the satsang. If she did, she would be the first upper-caste person from the village to do so, and that would be a definite credit to Parsini.

In my survey of lower-caste people in village Punjab, I found that Parsini's point of view was consistent with that of other Untouchable satsangis. When I asked to whom they would turn in time of trouble, the Radhasoami respondents said "friends" or "members of their religious group," whereas non-satsangi Untouchables said "the government" or "caste leaders."[10] Sixty percent agreed that caste was not recognized in Radhasoami, while thirty percent said there were some distinctions of caste; only ten percent said there was as much feeling of caste in Radha-

[7] "The Problem of Untouchability," *Dayalbagh Herald*, August 27, 1974, p. 3.

[8] Ibid.

[9] Interview with Lahori Ram Balley, Ambedkar Mission Society, Jalandhar, November 14, 1973.

[10] A statement of the question and a statistical tabulation of the responses to this and the other questions in my survey of approximately 150 upper-caste and lower-caste respondents in six locations in Punjab may be found in an appendix to my "Political Hope."

soami as in Indian society at large. When I asked what sort of social benefits their religious affiliation gave them, the non-satsangi Sikh or Hindu Untouchables listed few, but the satsangi Untouchables mentioned "inner peace," followed closely by "improved social status" and "friendship ties."

Perhaps a listing of "social benefits" is too crass a way to describe the difference Radhasoami has made in the lives of people like Parsini. The main social consequences of her initiation are intangible and consist of differences in the way Parsini and her friends view the world around them and in the way they experience society. Here, too, my survey indicated that their perception was widely shared among their fellow satsangi Untouchables. When I asked, "Who are you?" the answer most frequently given by Radhasoami respondents was that they were satsangis, whereas their non-satsangi castefellows most frequently gave their caste name. Even if the equality of the Beas Dera is only symbolic, the fellowship that Parsini experiences at Beas gives her an image of what society at large might become.

In an earlier generation of Untouchables in the Punjab, similar symbols of equality and hope were provided by the Christian church and a new religion established by the lower castes called Ad Dharm, the "original religion." Many who had initally been attracted to Ad Dharm, Christianity, or the Hindu and Sikh reform movements that opened their doors to lower-caste members early in this century later chose the Radhasoami path.[11] Traditionally the center of support for Ad Dharm and other activist Untouchable organizations, the leatherworkers' neighborhood in the city of Jalandhar has become a center of influence for the Radhasoami movement as well. Several of the more prominent families in this neighborhood have become satsangis, and some of them have been allocated cottages and other facilities at Beas for use during bhandaras. Many of them see their shift from Ad Dharm to Radhasoami as a transfer from one sort of experiment in social equality to another.

The Radhasoami Social Vision

On one level all persons are attracted to Radhasoami for the same reason: the love and grace offered by the master. What satsangis find appealing about the fellowship, however, depends largely upon the social location from which they come. As we observed in the previous chapter, the urban adherents of Radhasoami find at least part of its message and style to be

[11] For a discussion of the relationship between Radhasoami and Ad Dharm, see my "Radhasoami and the Return of Religion," chapter 19 of *Religion as Social Vision*.

a complement to the managerial values of individualism and ingenuity, and they are attracted to a parallel set of communitarian and suprarational values that transcend them. To Parsini and other village Untouchables, this second set of values is quite familiar. She has little difficulty in moving from her traditional rural milieu to a world ruled by a supernatural master to whom one is linked through love and communal associations. What appears strange to a modern urban person—total submission to a holy man—comes relatively easily to village people, especially lower caste villagers, whose traditional beliefs confirm Weber's observation that "the lower the social class the more radical are the forms assumed by the need for a savior."[12]

Yet there are many symbols of power in India, and many saviors. What Parsini and her friends find interesting about the Radhasoami fellowship is that it conveys the other set of values to which we referred, the ones modern Khatris take for granted: the virtues of an individualistic, scientific, and egalitarian society. The Khatris and Untouchables in the Punjab have long had a symbiotic relationship, owing in part to the fact that both of them fear the power of the dominant Jat landowning caste.[13] In the Radhasoami fellowship, members of lower castes can not only align themselves with a Khatri concern but share in the values that Khatris espouse. For Parsini and others struggling to shed the torpor of rural society and the stigma of being regarded as an Untouchable, these notions of equality and technique are what modernity is all about. Radhasoami provides at least a symbol that one has entered the modern world, and in some cases it provides the reality as well.

[12] Weber, *Economy and Society*, p. 487.

[13] For a further discussion of the Khatri-Untouchable alliance, see the preface to my *Religious Rebels in the Punjab*, pp. viii–x.

Ten

A Transnational Culture

THE BIOGRAPHIES of Radhasoami masters often include extensive stories about their colorful British, European, and American followers. Rai Saligram had several American and German devotees.[1] At Soamibagh, one of Madhav Prasad Sinha's most ardent disciples was an American lawyer, Myron Phelps.[2] At Dayalbagh, Anand Swarup showed special delight in his foreign admirers, including a Mr. Pringle from England, Mrs. Cockrain from America, and Mr. Hurst, who was interested in Theosophy and the teachings of Meher Baba, and who gave Anand Swarup practical advice about managing the movement.[3] His favorite, however, was Elizabeth Bruce, whom he described as having "adopted Satsang ways. . . . She squats on the ground . . . and must have been a Hindu in her past life."[4] At Beas, Sawan Singh was surrounded by a host of foreigners. There was a Mr. Landers from South Africa,[5] Dr. Pierre Schmidt from Switzerland,[6] Dr. Julian Johnson from America,[7] and Dr. Randolph Stone, the chiropractor from Chicago who created "polarity therapy."[8] Sawan Singh also had among his followers what appears to be a sizable contingent from the British army, including Col. C. W. Saunders, Sir Colin Garbet, a Colonel Martin, and a Major Litte.[9]

At present, some fifty thousand Westerners have joined one or another of the many branches of the Radhasoami tradition. The largest number in absolute terms is at Beas, but the greatest number in proportion to the

[1] *Souvenir*, p. 60.

[2] Phelps's notes from his stay at Soamibagh have been published as *Notes of Discourses on Radhasoami Faith Delivered by Babuji Maharaj in 1913–14* (Agra: Radhasoami Satsang, Soamibagh, 1947).

[3] Anand Swarup (Sahabji Maharaj), *Diary of Sahabji Maharaj (1930–31)* (Dayalbagh: Radhasoami Satsang Sabha, 1973), p. 179.

[4] Ibid., pp. 109–12.

[5] Charan Singh, *Spiritual Heritage*, p. 125.

[6] Julian Johnson, *Where Masters Walk*, vol. 3, p. 60.

[7] Johnson describes his years at Beas in *With a Great Master in India. Passim.*

[8] Randolph Stone was born in 1890, served as a chiropractor in Chicago most of his life, became initiated in 1945, and died at the Beas dera on December 9, 1981, where he had been living in retirement for the previous eight years. Stone's contribution to Radhasoami literature is his *Mystical Bible* (Beas: Radhasoami Satsang, Beas, 1956). It is a Radhasoami interpretation of Old and New Testament verses.

[9] Charan Singh, *Spiritual Heritage*, p. 125.

total membership belongs to the Ruhani Satsang and Sawan-Kirpal Ruhani organizations.[10] What we will explore in this chapter is why Radhasoami leaders such as Kirpal Singh, Anand Swarup, and Sawan Singh have found Westerners so interesting, and what those foreign satsangis have found so attractive about the Radhasoami way of life.

Such Western satsangis are not, of course, the only foreigners who have taken an interest in Asian religion. Even before 1910, when Dr. and Mrs. H. M. Brock of Port Angeles, Washington, became the first Radhasoami initiates abroad, Americans had displayed a keen interest in India's religious ideas. The writings of Emerson and the Transcendentalists are filled with them, as are the works of many other nineteenth-century authors.[11] It was not until the end of that century, however, when Swami Vivekenanda came to Chicago in 1893 and dazzled the World Parliament of Religions with his presentation of an intellectually respectable Hinduism, that Americans in large numbers began to take seriously the possibility of adopting India's religious concepts as their own.

Yet Hinduism is not an easy faith for foreigners to adopt. It is closely tied to a cultural and social system that is specific to the Indian subcontinent, and only by divorcing its ideas and teachings from this context could it effectively be transported to Western soil. Vivekananda's Vedanta Society, which offered selections from Hindu philosophy taught in a churchlike worship setting, was one attempt to make that transition possible. Other attempts included syncretic movements that brought Hindu ideas and images into a rich intercultural mix.

One of the syncretic movements that involved Hindu ideas and images to a great degree was Theosophy. Founded in 1875 by a Russian expatriate, Madame Blavatsky, and Colonel Olcott, an American, its teachings embraced Hindu notions of karma and reincarnation. At first the headquarters of the movement were located in the United States, but in 1882 they moved to south India. Annie Besant, who had become the major figure in the world Theosophical movement, established her home there as well, and in 1917, after becoming increasingly involved in India's nationalist movement, she became president of the Indian National Con-

[10] These figures are based on Sawan Kirpal Ashram records of 19,179 foreign initiates as of November 15, 1988 (source: personal letters to me from J. M. Sethi, secretary, Sawan Kirpal Ruhani Mission, October 1, 1985; May 7, 1988; May 22, 1988; and November 15, 1988); and Beas statistics of some 30,000 foreign initiates by the end of 1984 (Radhasoami Satsang, Beas: Annual Reports, 1975–1984). These numbers should be increased to include people initiated since those dates and the small number of foreign initiates associated with the other branches of Radhasoami.

[11] See my "Hinduism in America" in Crim et al., *Abingdon Dictionary of Living Religions*, pp. 318–21; J. P. Rao Rayapati, *Early American Interest in Vedanta* (New York: Asia Publishing House, 1973); and Robert S. Ellwood, Jr., *Religious and Spiritual Groups in Modern America* (Englewood Cliffs, N.J.: Prentice-Hall, 1973).

gress. Given their interests in Indian culture it is not surprising that leaders of Theosophy would become aware of new currents in Hinduism, including Radhasoami. How well they knew Radhasoami teachings is not clear, but the first reference to Radhasoami by a writer outside the movement came from a Theosophist,[12] and Rai Saligram was a subscriber to the *Theosophist* magazine.[13] In *Voice of the Silence*, Blavatsky describes the sounds that are linked with the higher spiritual regions, and her description is strikingly similar to the one given by Swami Shiv Dayal.[14] Hervey deWitt Griswold, the first outsider to study Radhasoami in a serious way, was impressed with the similarity between Radhasoami teachings and those of Besant, describing them as "practically identical."[15] Further connections between Radhasoami and Theosophy were established by members of Theosophy who crossed over to Radhasoami membership, including several of the earliest foreign initiates: Myron Phelps, Mr. Hurst, and someone identified by Radhasoami historians only as "a German Theosophist."[16]

One of the reasons such people gave for switching from Theosophy to Radhasoami was their desire to join a movement that seemed to them more authentically Hindu. Even though the leaders of Theosophy borrowed their ideas from Hinduism, and perhaps even from Radhasoami, their movement was essentially Western in its form and interests. The Vedanta Societies also had a strong Western impetus; though their teachings had Hindu roots, they were presented in such a way as to answer to Western philosophic concerns, and a Christian style of worship was adopted. Radhasoami was different: it maintained the same ideas and practices throughout all its outposts, whether in India or the United States. And it was open to all. In fact, Radhasoami was the first religious movement of Hindu ancestry where foreigners had direct and easy access to an original, un-Westernized form of religion. So when the Radhasoami organizations

[12] A. P. Sinnett, *The Occult World* (London: Truebner and Co., 1884), p. 151.

[13] The name of Rai Saligram was included in a list of new subscribers to the *Theosophist* in the issue of January 2, 1882 (vol. 2). I am grateful to Daniel Caldwell, Librarian of the Tucson, Arizona Public Library for locating this reference, and to David Lane for bringing it to my attention.

[14] Blavatsky's description is quoted in Kirpal Singh, *The Jap Ji,* p. 24. It is possible that Blavatsky's references to the sounds of the higher regions come from Nath Yoga writings rather than directly from Radhasoami sources.

[15] Griswold, "Radha Swami Sect In India," p. 193. A connection between Madame Blavatsky's theosophy and Radhasoami teachings is also perceived by Kirpal Singh (*The Jap Ji,* p. 24).

[16] *Souvenir*, p. 60. A more recent connection between Radhasoami and Theosophy is the publication by the Theosophical Society of a book by I. C. Sharma on Edgar Cayce (*Cayce, Karma, and Reincarnation*); Sharma was a devotee of Faqir Chand and some years after writing this book became one of his successors.

opened their doors to foreigners early in this century, they were inaugurating something new: a universal form of Hinduism.

At first foreigners were hardly knocking down the doors to gain admittance. The first members to be initiated abroad belonged to that same small community of mystics and seekers who supplied the clientele for Theosophy. Such people provided the mainstay of the Radhasoami network overseas during the first half of this century, but there were never more than a few hundred of them. In the Beas fellowship, the American initiates of Sawan Singh and Jagat Singh together amounted to only 245.[17] The enormous growth in Radhasoami membership abroad has been recent and has come from two quite different directions.

One period of foreign expansion accompanied the Western interest in Asian religion and in "new religious movements" in the 1960s and 1970s. The masters made triumphant world journeys, and local satsang organizations blossomed throughout North and South America, England and continental Europe, Southeast Asia, and Africa (especially South Africa). Some foreign satsangis established communes, reversing the individualism that characterized the style of many (such as Julian Johnson) in the earlier generations of foreign devotees. For others, their Radhasoami faith was a matter of private practice that was appealing in part because it seemed to be primarily a matter of technique and knowledge rather than piety and dogma, and because Radhasoami teachers were exotic yet accessible. The kind of Hinduism that fascinated Westerners in the sixties was one of meditation practices and communal spirituality, and Hindu yoga was of special interest to those who wished to experiment in world spirituality. Radhasoami's surat shabd yoga was seen as one among several promising styles that Hinduism offered.

Radhasoami teachings were also introduced to Westerners indirectly, through groups that utilized Radhasoami ideas but presented them under their own banner. The Eckankar movement, for example, borrowed directly from the writings of Radhasoami teachers, and its founder, Paul Twitchell, was an initiate of Kirpal Singh.[18] Kirpal Singh had followed his own master, Sawan Singh, in linking the first phrase in Guru Nanak's morning prayer, "eckankar," to the highest level of spiritual consciousness.[19] Twitchell followed suit and made it the name of his

[17] The American initiates of Sawan Singh from 1933 to his death totaled 175, and the initiates of his successor, Jagat Singh, totaled 70 during his three-year reign. From 1951 to 1974 the number of initiates grew dramatically to 5,000 (Letter from Roland G. deVries, American representative of Charan Singh, November 13, 1974). Since then the number has tripled.

[18] See David Christopher Lane, *The Making of a Spiritual Movement: The Untold Story of Paul Twitchell and Eckankar* (Del Mar, Calif.: Del Mar Press, 1983).

[19] Sawan Singh, *Philosophy of the Masters*, vol. 4, pp. 26–29. The term *eckankar* (*ek*

movement. The teachings of the Divine Light Mission, led by the boy guru Maharaj-ji, are essentially those of Radhasoami as well,[20] and other spiritual leaders of the time were also influenced by Radhasoami teachings.[21]

The groundswell of Western interest in Asian religion began to subside in the 1980s, and so did the expansion of Radhasoami membership in Western countries, with the exception of those branches associated with Kirpal Singh. The slack in overseas membership in the Beas branch was soon taken up, however, by a new group of Westerners: members of Indian immigrant families that had settled in the United States, England, and elsewhere abroad. There have been Indian immigrants in the West for most of this century, and some of them, like Kehr Singh Sasmas, the man who brought the Brocks to the faith in 1910, and Bhagat Singh Thind, a teacher of spirituality in Southern California who published twenty books on Radhasoami-related themes in the 1950s,[22] were longtime admirers of Radhasoami thought. The great wave of Indian immigration to

---

omkar) is a central symbol of Sikhism, and literally means "1-Om," although Sikhs themselves often translate it more freely, e.g., "God is unity," or "divine oneness." See Hawley and Juergensmeyer, *Songs of the Saints of India*, p. 65.

[20] For a summary of Maharaj-ji's teachings, see Jeanne Messer, "Guru Maharaj Ji and the Divine Light Mission," in Robert Bellah and Charles Glock, eds., *The New Religious Consciousness* (Berkeley: University of California Press, 1976), pp. 54–55.

[21] Harbhajan Singh Puri, known as Yogi Bhajan, who came from India to found the 3-Ho movement of American Sikhs, is said by some followers of Kirpal Singh to have been an admirer of their master. An American, John-Roger Hinkins, who founded his own religious fellowship after leaving the Eckankar movement, utilizes the teachings of the Radhasoami tradition and refers to Sawan Singh as one of his masters. See Bob Sipchen and David Johnston, "John-Roger," *Los Angeles Times*, August 14–15, 1988; and David C. Lane, "The J. R. Controversy," *Understanding Cults and Spiritual Movements* 1, no. 1 (1984): 1–3.

[22] See, for example, Bhagat Singh Thind, *The Pearl of Greatest Price, or Nam-Rattan* (Hollywood, Calif.: privately published, 1958). Thind describes his form of spiritual practice as "the Living Word, the Holy Nam or Surt-Shabad" (*The Pearl of Greatest Price*, p. vii). Much of his book, *The Radiant Road to Reality* (New York: privately printed, 1939) is borrowed from Julian Johnson's *With a Great Master in India* without acknowledgement. See David Lane, "The Radiant Road to Deception: A Case Study of Dr. Bhagat Singh Thind's Plagiarism," *Understanding Cults and Spiritual Movements* 2, nos. 2–3 (1987), pp. 20–23. Thind, who had come to the University of California at Berkeley as a student in 1913, married an American woman and settled down in southern California, joining the American army in World War I. His name is well known in the history of the South Asian immigrant community in the United States because of his attempt to challenge the American government's restrictive immigration laws. He argued that the rules prohibiting non-Caucasians did not apply to people from India because they were of Aryan descent and were thereby as Caucasian as white Europeans. The "Thind decision" of the U.S. Supreme Court in 1923 rejected Thind's appeal and was a major setback for the liberalization of immigration rules. For a discussion of Thind and the Thind decision, see Joan M. Jensen, *Passage from India: Asian Indian Immigrants in North America* (New Haven: Yale University Press, 1988), pp. 256–58.

the West is relatively recent, however, beginning in Britain when India gained its independence in 1947, and in the United States when changes were made in American immigration regulations in 1965.

Among the recent immigrants were some who had been initiated in India before coming to the West. One of these was T. S. Khanna, the American representative of the Ruhani Satsang masters, who has done much to spread the teachings of Kirpal Singh and Darshan Singh. Khanna was a government administrator who had been assigned to the Indian embassy in Washington and who stayed on after his tour of duty had been completed to work for the U.S. government and to help with the American branches of the Ruhani Satsang organization. Unlike Khanna, however, most recent immigrants who have embraced Radhasoami have done so after arriving in the United Kingdom or the United States, finding in Radhasoami a form of religious community and a kind of spiritual teaching that is congenial to their changed circumstances. Among them is Salina Mansukhani, one of the many Sindhi satsangis abroad, who was chosen Miss India-U.S.A. in 1986. She claims that coming to the Beas Dera, where she stays in the foreigners' guest house, gives her a bit of America in India; and when she is back in the United States, her association with Radhasoami gives her a bit of India in America.[23] These dual characteristics of Radhasoami culture, in fact, appeal to all three groups of Westerners that have been attracted to its membership—the old seekers of a spiritual science, the new followers of gurus, and members of the new immigrant communities from India. In each case Radhasoami provides a community that is both Indian and Western, and a set of teachings that transcends nationality and is easily adapted to any cultural setting.

Julian Johnson and the Spiritual Quest

In Beas and Ruhani Satsang circles, the best-known story of a Westerner's spiritual quest is the one told by Julian Johnson in his published letters, *With a Great Master in India*. This book and his *Path of the Masters* have been best-sellers among English-reading satsangis in India ever since they were issued in the mid-1930s, and they maintain their status in the Beas branch's bookstores even in the 1980s.[24] Johnson's story is idiosyncratic, but it describes a certain kind of Radhasoami seeker from America: fiercely individualistic and skeptical of much of the spirituality of his age,

[23] Interview with Salina Mansukhani, Beas, November 12, 1986.

[24] Interview with Dalat Ram, bookstore manager, Radhasoami-Beas Satsang Hall, Delhi, August 15, 1985.

yet overwhelmingly committed to, and articulately defensive of, his new faith.

"I was born with an irrepressible desire for knowledge," Johnson claimed.[25] After graduating from college in Bolivar, Missouri, and receiving theological training at the University of Chicago and a medical degree from Iowa State, Johnson was still unsatisfied with the promise of Western knowledge. After several careers—as a Baptist minister, a missionary to India, a medical practitioner in the U.S. Navy, and a doctor in private practice in California—he remained personally unfulfilled. He began a spiritual search that led him to "New Thought," as manifested in Christian Science and in "Spiritualism," but "none of these seemed to get at the root of the matter."[26] Johnson came to much the same conclusion after turning to Theosophy and Rosicrucianism. He finally came to "the darkest hour" of his life while visiting southern California's Imperial Valley in the winter of 1928–1929, when "nothing but blank darkness, bitterness of soul and despair settled on me." The only hint that things were to become radically better was a sensation Johnson experienced one morning on waking. He felt he was "floating on an ocean of love."[27]

It was then that he chanced to visit an old friend of his in Ashland, Oregon, an elderly woman who was an initiate of Sawan Singh, and who shared with Johnson her copy of Rai Saligram's *Radhasoami Mat Prakash*. Rai Saligram's use of the phrase "ocean of love" immediately struck a resonant chord with Johnson. He accepted the woman's offer to put him in touch with Dr. H. M. Brock in Port Angeles, Washington, who arranged for his initiation. In 1932 he set sail for India, and upon arriving at the railway station at Jalandhar, an hour or so away from the Beas Dera, he found that the Great Master had come to welcome him. In a letter to the Brocks, Johnson reported that he "would have known he was the Master" even if they had not been introduced. He was rendered speechless, and "a great sense of peace" came into his soul.[28]

Johnson settled down in India, where he became the American in residence at Beas. He did some medical work, but his writing and Dera activities were his real occupations, and they amounted to virtually a full-time job. While in India he came to meet Elizabeth Bruce, the devotee who had so charmed Anand Swarup at Dayalbagh.[29] In time he brought her to Sawan Singh and to Beas, and they were married. As a sort of wedding present, Johnson wrote a biography of her life, entitled *The Unquench-*

[25] Johnson, *With a Great Master*, p. 5.
[26] Ibid., p. 7.
[27] Ibid., p. 11.
[28] Ibid., p. 23.
[29] Ibid., p. 63.

18. Julian Johnson, on the right, at his meditation cave in Beas.

able Flame.[30] At the same time, he continued to travel with the Great Master throughout India, recording his own thoughts and his master's utterances. Johnson described the land on which his master trod as being a special place—neither India nor America, but a different world altogether:

> And now what shall I say? Am I still on earth, or am I in some weird border land? And how shall I estimate the values or describe the situation? It is all so strange, so unlike anything in the homeland. . . . We think of ancient religious

[30] Julian Johnson, *The Unquenchable Flame: Biographical Sketches of Elizabeth Rose Bruce, Sometimes Called "The Woman of Destiny"* (Beas: The Five Rivers Manufacturing Company, 1935).

> teachers who have visited this land and probably stood upon this very spot, including Krishna and Buddha and even Jesus himself. For it is known that he visited here. We try to recall some of the doctrines of the ancient sages, prophets and Mahatmas; and all the while we are conscious of the fact that the greatest of them all sits on a bench here by us at this moment, calmly reading a book. . . . [His] powers far transcend those of the greatest prophets of old; aye, even of the beloved Master of Nazareth and Galilee.[31]

Johnson's story is peculiarly his own, and yet many aspects of it parallel the stories of other seekers from America, England, and Europe. Most Westerners who have found the Radhasoami path came across it after an active search; most found it as an answer to questions that had been troubling them for a long time. A young man from Texas, who reported having had, in connection with a terrifying automobile accident, sensations of leaving his body, hearing remarkable sounds, and seeing dazzling blue and white light, felt he needed assistance in interpreting his experience.[32] A clairvoyant in England also had out-of-body experiences that, from her point of view, needed proper direction. A student in southern California had no such experiences but felt a deep spiritual emptiness that he knew would be fulfilled by a remarkable person. He formulated a set of expectations regarding the perfect teacher and the perfect teachings and went to meetings in the late 1970s to hear touring Indian religious masters.[33] He was determined to find one that would meet his measure, but each seemed limited and unsatisfying. One day while talking to a friend in a restaurant, a passing waiter said, "Just remember 'Radhasoami'." The next day, in a different restaurant, he heard the phrase again, and when he asked the owner what it signified, the owner produced a picture of Charan Singh. As soon as he saw it, the Californian instantly recognized him as the one for whom he had been longing.

The restaurant setting and the mysterious waiter are characteristic of two motifs in stories of this sort: a public location and a chance meeting with an unusual stranger. Another satsangi from California told about his discovery of the faith while walking on the beach. He was confronted by a strange person who seemed to know his inner desires and who suggested that he read books on Radhasoami. The stranger disappeared, but the Californian's interest was piqued, and soon he had the opportunity of meeting a Radhasoami master who was visiting the United States on tour.

[31] Johnson, *With a Great Master*, pp. 37–38.

[32] Interview with Phoenix Salisbury, Beas, November 11, 1980.

[33] Among the less esoteric requirements exacted of this ideal master was that he would be vegetarian, not charge fees for his services, and wear his hair and beard uncut (Interview with David Lane, San Clemente, California, August 14, 1988).

Like other seekers, he reported experiencing a great sense of relief at being saved from his desultory searchings.

A Special Knowledge

At least some of the initial fascination with Radhasoami derives from the fact that it was spawned in a land with a deep and intriguing religious past, a "strange" land, as Johnson put it, "hoary with age and rich in history."[34] The remote and romantic quality of India's landscape evokes biblical images, and the mysteriousness of things Indian is one of the things that makes Radhasoami seem special. At the same time, its ideas are quite accessible. In one of his first letters home, Johnson exclaimed that Radhasoami teachings were "so obviously true" and "so clearly rational." The logic of the faith, he felt, met "all demands of both reason and intuition."[35]

Even today, Westerners at the Dera come less as pilgrims than as students enrolled in an intensive course in Radhasoami theory and practice. On many evenings Charan Singh held question-and-answer sessions solely for his Western guests. New initiates were encouraged to be serious in their study of Radhasoami theology, to "enter the laboratory of the masters" and "sit down before the facts, as a little child, and enquire of them."[36] John Leeming, a scientist from Arizona, claimed in his introduction to an abridged version of the Radhasoami textbook, *Philosophy of the Masters*, that its contents constitute "the key to the laboratory of mind and spirit" and are "no less scientific than the introduction of new tools and references given the scholar as he progresses from general science to physics."[37]

Those Westerners in Radhasoami trained in the physical sciences include doctors, dentists, and chiropractors. The general level of academic attainment among American satsangis in Johnson's time was sufficiently high that he could enumerate the college professors among his colleagues in the Great Master's circle. There continue to be a large number of scientists and academics among the foreign satsangis of the Beas, Ruhani, and Sawan-Kirpal branches, including professors at Claremont, Harvard, the Universities of Hawaii, Rhode Island, and Texas, California State University at San Diego, and Lancaster University in England. Johnson's other profession, that of a clergyman, is also represented among present-

[34] Johnson, *With a Great Master*, p. 37.

[35] Ibid., p. 40.

[36] John H. Leeming, Jr., Foreword to Sawan Singh, *Philosophy of the Masters*, abr. ed., p. xiv.

[37] Ibid., p. xii.

day satsangis. Roland deVries, one of the four representatives of Beas in America, was formerly a Presbyterian minister, and several missionaries to India became themselves converts to Radhasoami. It would seem that those who have some knowledge about Western science and religion are among the most skeptical of their claims to truth, finding replacements for them in Radhasoami's religious science.

Radhasoami knowledge is seen as more than a bridge between religion and science; it fulfills both. "Most religions are built on the experience or 'revelations' of some bygone teacher," John Leeming explained, stating that, unlike Radhasoami, these older religions "offer no scientific way for us to advance in our understanding."[38] Leeming feels that Radhasoami unifies these seemingly irreconcilable approaches to life, and offers an alternative to the "two-culture" dilemma of modern civilization. Paul Brunton began his search in "secret India" determined that it would be scientific:

> I searched through a welter of crass superstitions, incredible impostures and ancient pretensions for those things which are true, which will stand the acid test of thorough investigation. I flatter myself that I could never have done this did I not contain within my complex nature the two elements of scientific scepticism and spiritual sensitivity, elements which usually range themselves in sharp conflict and flagrant opposition.[39]

What Brunton found that so impressed him were forms of spirituality that seemed to be based on knowledge similar—or even superior—to modern science. In a similar vein, Julian Johnson claimed that "religion, or spirituality, as taught and practised by the Masters . . . is a free and exact science," because it is "subject to the same analysis and demonstration as any other science." Since Radhasoami teachings purport to reveal "laws of Nature," it has developed methods "as exact, and . . . results as uniform as in any science known."[40]

This way of thinking betrays a great deal of faith not only in Radhasoami but also in science; it implies that scientific investigation is the major means of authenticating what is true. But there are other moments in which Johnson expressed a certain fatigue with Western rationality, suggesting that Radhasoami's truth is beyond science's grasp. Johnson claimed to have been led astray by science and "modern achievements" in his youth, finding the wisdom of his master far superior.[41] Katherine

[38] Ibid.
[39] Brunton, *A Search in Secret India*, p. 15.
[40] Ibid., p. 138.
[41] Johnson, *With a Great Master*, p. 38.

Wason concurred, saying that Radhasoami ideas came from a "higher consciousness."[42]

This notion that beyond the more accessible, scientific teachings of Radhasoami is a more rarefied truth might explain why there is an air of secrecy about some aspects of Radhasoami teachings and practices. One of the first descriptions of Radhasoami by an outsider, a Christian missionary in India, called it "a semi-secret sect."[43] Some say the reference to Radhasoami teachings as the "secret of secrets" suggests only the intimacy of the truth that is conveyed from master to disciple, not its exclusivity.[44] Even so, the Soamibagh branch has stamped on a manual of meditation practices that "under no circumstances" is it to be shown "to anyone who is not a follower of the Radhasoami Faith."[45] Similarly, the Beas and Ruhani Satsang branches keep their initiatory mantra a secret: satsangis are forbidden to divulge the words whispered to them at the time of their initiation.

The fact that a certain amount of secrecy surrounds Radhasoami teachings and practices means that the Radhasoami knowledge is special, something meant only for a few. "It is an amazing thing," a woman from South Africa remarked to me at the Beas Dera, "to think that this treasury of information is held in the hands of such a small circle as ours. What the world wouldn't give to know what we know!"[46] Knowing what others do not know is indeed an exciting aspect of faith, and this feeling of rare privilege is enhanced, for Western satsangis, by the fact that the truths are to be found in an unusual and distant land. The "strangeness" of India that impressed Johnson at Beas has impressed many seekers of India's spirituality, including Paul Brunton at Dayalbagh. "I feel quite humbly," he wrote, "that I have been privileged to see a remote aspect of India seldom seen and less understood by ordinary travellers."[47] By identifying with Radhasoami's esoteric knowledge, the Westerner forms a personal link with an enduring culture, a fact that is not only aesthetically pleasing but personally reassuring, for an esoteric knowledge ultimately transcends time itself. In the final section of *With a Great Master in India*, Johnson creates a parable of an elegant dance in which the dancers, representing the mass of humanity, fritter away their time in the illusion that the dance will continue forever; meanwhile a fortunate few listen to ex-

[42] Wason, *The Living Master*, p. 12.

[43] Griswold, *Insights into Modern Hinduism*, p. 139.

[44] Darshan Singh, *The Secret of Secrets: Spiritual Talks* (Bowling Green, Va., and Delhi: Sawan Kirpal Publications, 1978).

[45] Rai Saligram, *Jugat Prakash Radhasoami*, title page.

[46] Interview with Emily Sandhurst, Beas, November 12, 1980.

[47] Brunton, *A Search in Secret India*, p. 14.

hortations from a bearded man who urges them to escape from their sham while time remains.[48]

Knowing Someone Important

Those who do escape, and embrace the Radhasoami faith, are linked not only to a special knowledge but also to a special person. For Westerners, such reverence requires a leap of faith. It is not surprising, then, that the words of Western satsangis often take on a biblical luster when they ponder the master's glories. "I sit at the feet of one whose powers are not limited by time or space," Julian Johnson wrote, "whose very glance has in it the power of death or of eternal life; aye, whose commands even the waves of this ancient sea must obey."[49] Another Western satsangi, an African American from Chicago whose three brothers are all Baptist preachers, said that his interest in Radhasoami stemmed from his interest in the Bible: "I had always wanted to live in biblical times," he said.[50]

Gandhi's Christlike attraction for Westerners owed much to his strange combination of familiar and foreign features,[51] and in describing their attraction to the Radhasoami faith, some Westerners have also dwelled on the masters' appearance, especially their distinctive physical characteristics. Brunton, for example, described Anand Swarup as "an alert American mind encased in a brown Hindu body."[52] Johnson, who had a strong anti-semitic streak, was also fascinated by his master's skin color; he claimed he belonged to "the Aryan, the pure white race," and that the color of his skin "is about that of the average American with a good coat of sun tan."[53] Although today there is much less emphasis on the peculiarity of Indian features, still the marvelous beards and turbans of the Beas and Ruhani Satsang masters have a striking appeal to the Western eye.

[48] Johnson, *With a Great Master*, pp. 113–18.

[49] Ibid., pp. 38–39.

[50] Interview with John Price, Beas, November 12, 1980.

[51] See C. F. Andrews's praise of Gandhi's Christlike appearance, quoted in E. Stanley Jones, "The Soul of Mahatma Gandhi," *The World Tomorrow*, December 1924; reprinted in Charles Chatfield, ed., *The Americanization of Gandhi: Images of the Mahatma* (New York and London: Garland Publishing, 1976), p. 652. See also my article, "Saint Gandhi," in John Stratton Hawley, ed., *Saints and Virtues* (Berkeley: University of California Press, 1987), pp. 187–203.

[52] Brunton, *A Search in Secret India*, p. 238.

[53] Johnson, *With a Great Master*, pp. 24–26. Regarding Johnson's anti-Semitism, see also pp. 95–96, 147–48, 168. Johnson claimed that although Jesus' mother was "a Jewess," his father was "a man of pure Aryan blood" (p. 96). This anti-Semitic language is not common to most Western satsangis, however. Some estimate that half of the Beas branch's leaders in the United States have been Jewish (Interview with Roland deVries, Nevada City, California, January 17, 1986).

Even more impressive, of course, is the conviction that behind this physical appearance is an accessible form of God. At the end of the evening sessions that Master Charan Singh held for his Western followers on the second floor of the Beas guesthouse, all would rise and hold their hands prayerfully as he walked down the aisle and down the stairs. As soon as he left the hall, the crowd would scramble to the balcony for one last glimpse of his presence as he crossed through the garden and returned to his own residence. On one of these occasions an American man softly said, "There goes God."[54]

Since people with Christian and Jewish backgrounds are unfamiliar with the concept of semidivine holy men, the master must be fully God, or at least have sufficient spiritual weight to bear the role played by scripture and revelation in biblical traditions. One American satsangi from Georgia said that he was attracted to the Radhasoami tradition because Christian religious teachers lacked a voice of authority and could not give him "straight answers," whereas the Beas masters could.[55] Others are inspired by what appears to them to be the manifestation of Christ in the present day.[56] For those Western satsangis who are more secular, the master's teachings replace older forms of philosophy, explaining "the origin and purpose of life."[57]

In addition to the religious and philosophical reasons for thinking of the master in ultimate terms, there are psychological motivations. Sudhir Kakar points out that the exaggeration of the master's qualities goes hand in hand with the magnification of one's own pride in knowing such a person. These "psychological mechanisms of idealization and identification," he says, "give a newfound centrality to the self."[58] According to Kakar, "the uncritical eulogizing of the guru" is linked to "the disciple's desperate need for idealization and identification with the Master."[59] By enlarging their master's role in the cosmos, some disciples may be magnifying their own, and they see in their master's features the ideal characteristics they hope for in themselves.

An American devotee, Katherine Wason, describes how she was initially attracted to the "kind, beautiful face" of the master because it emanated power and love.[60] Julian Johnson also used the language of love in describing his master, whose heart "holds only loving kindness to all"[61]

[54] This was overheard on a visit to the Dera on November 14, 1980.
[55] Interview with Frank Smith, Beas, November 12, 1980.
[56] Interview with Roland deVries, Nevada City, California, January 17, 1986.
[57] Leeming, Foreword to *Philosophy of the Masters*, p. xi.
[58] Kakar, *Shamans, Mystics, and Doctors*, p. 145.
[59] Ibid., p. 149.
[60] Wason, *The Living Master*, p. 20.
[61] Johnson, *With a Great Master*, p. 25.

and whose voice "is vibrant with love."[62] These words signal what is perhaps the most personal motivation drawing Johnson and other devotees into the master-disciple relationship, the longing for an intimate union. This desire often finds expression in poetry, as in this bit of doggerel composed on the occasion of Charan Singh's visit to the United States:

> It's Master's love that brings Him here—
> To help America bloom,
> To purify the atmosphere
> As Love, for love, makes room.[63]

A Network of Spiritual Associates

When Julian Johnson first arrived at the Beas dera in 1932, he was impressed with the conviviality of its residents: "Their love appears to know no bounds. They treat me as if I were truly their own brother returning from abroad."[64] His description of the Radhasoami community as "a real brotherhood" is echoed by many who come to the Dera and regard it as an Indian home.

Still, satsangis from America and Europe are much more ambivalent about home and family than their Indian counterparts, and this ambivalence is displayed in their attitude toward the Radhasoami fellowship. Some reject the idea that the Radhasoami community is a family, and disdain what they regard as the too-familiar, "country club" atmosphere of the Dera. They regard the relationship with the master as the only one that has any significance and avoid Radhasoami events. One prominent American satsangi refuses to attend bhandaras at Beas because they are too frenetic. "I wouldn't go across the street to attend one of them," he says.[65] When someone as individualistic as Julian Johnson speaks of the Radhasoami "brotherhood," therefore, he is more likely to be embracing a set of associates than a set of relatives. Neither he nor other Westerners of his generation have had any interest in creating separate residential communities modeled after Beas or Dayalbagh.

Most Westerners feel that the only purpose of a separate colony is to live near the master, and that is rarely allowed. Long-term residence by Westerners is discouraged at most Radhasoami centers. The leaders of those centers do not want their communities to be swamped by foreign-

[62] Ibid.

[63] Ross Lionel Williams, "Master's Love Brings Him Here," *R. S. Greetings: North American Sangat*, June 1970, p. 40.

[64] Johnson, *With a Great Master*, p. 26.

[65] Interview with Roland deVries, January 17, 1986.

19. Sawan Singh having tea with two of his British devotees.

ers, and the Indian government's restriction on extending visas to foreigners for lengthy periods of time is an obstacle as well.[66] Only a few Westerners have lived at Radhasoami centers more than a year or so. Among the better-known Western satsangis in residence in India in recent years have been the British novelist, Kate Christy, and her musician husband, Malcolm Tillis, at Sawan Ashram; Paul Hogguel from the Netherlands, who lives near his master, A. P. Mathur, at Peepalmandi in Agra; and Dr. Randolph Stone, the creator of "polarity therapy," who was allowed to set up a house with his niece, Louise Hilger, at Beas.

For Western satsangis, the Radhasoami fellowship provides a network of spiritual comrades throughout the world. When Kate Christy and Malcolm Tillis travel abroad they move from one set of satsangi contacts to another, just as Christian missionaries used to do when they traveled from place to place in foreign lands. Even satsangis who do not travel can come in contact with a far-flung fellowship at Radhasoami rallies and through newsletters and correspondence. The Radhasoami networks in each country have their own activities, and local leaders achieve a certain prominence within them. In the Beas branch, for instance, the four rep-

[66] Charan Singh, *Spiritual Heritage*, p. 131. Visa restrictions apply to American visitors, but not to holders of British or Commonwealth passports. In their cases, presumably, it is Dera rather than government policy that prohibits them from establishing long-term residence at Beas.

resentatives in the United States who have power to administer proxy initiation also superintend the local centers. In recent years these leaders have included H. F. Weekley of Washington, D.C., who has been in charge of the Eastern seaboard; Roy Ricks of Chicago and Gene Ivash, a professor of physics at the University of Texas, who have had jurisdiction over two sections of the Midwest; and Roland deVries, the former Presbyterian minister who is in many ways dean of the American representatives, who has supervised the Western region from his home near Nevada City, California.[67]

Such relationships remind one less of a kinship network than a corporate one, but those who take on the roles often profess a great disdain for the spiritual emptiness of most modern organizations, and organized religion in particular. Julian Johnson was almost vitriolic on the point: "As soon as any religion is settled upon a people in organized form," he claimed, "religion becomes a dead letter, and the priests grow fat."[68] Westerners who despise religious community and those who yearn for it can both be satisfied by the Radhasoami style of organization, in part because it contains an inner contradiction: it is both communal and individualistic. It is similar in this way to a modern bureaucracy, which also contains this tension between individualism and social compliance. Some Western members of the Radhasoami have reconciled the contradiction, however, by taking an individualistic approach to their home cultures but adopting a more communal attitude toward their participation in the transnational community of Radhasoami.

The double identities of such satsangis—an allegiance to the cultures of their birth and to the transnational culture of Radhasoami—is the outward manifestation of an even more important dichotomy in their lives: a split between two levels of reality. At one level lies the world as perceived by the senses and through conventional reason, and at another lie the worlds beyond. The Radhasoami setting permits the soul to begin what Johnson calls "its triumphal journey to distant worlds."[69] It therefore offers more than what Weber called the "instrumental rationality" of modern bureaucratic, industrialized society. It offers an instrumental rationality of its own, with suprarational dimensions, and it offers a universal message framed in distinctly Indian terms. The Radhasoami fellowship is geographically centered and wears India's distinctive cultural garb, but what it ultimately offers to searching, modern Westerners is much more profound than a change of cultural scene.

[67] Interview with Roland deVries, Nevada City, California, January 17, 1986. For many years, prior to Prof. Ivash, the Midwest representative was Col. E. R. Berg, a retired U.S. Air Force Colonel from Minneapolis.

[68] Johnson, *With a Great Master*, p. 137.

[69] Ibid., p. 185.

Conclusion

The Logic of Modern Faith

S. N. EISENSTADT asserts that modernity is not the same in all parts of the world. Because of its distinctive cultural heritage, each society may respond in its own way to new technology and the individualism, skepticism, and social organization that often attend it.[1] This means that such diverse followers of the Radhasoami path as K. L. Khanna, Parsini, and Julian Johnson may perceive the modernity of their faith differently, depending on their respective urban Indian, village Indian, and American points of view. And this means that because the overwhelming majority of the followers are to be found in India, the tradition as a whole reflects a modernity that is more Indian and Hindu than it is Western.

Like other forms of modern religion, the Radhasoami tradition mediates between skepticism and trust, personal affirmation and self-transformation, and individualism and social commitment, and it does so in a form of religion that itself mediates between an orientation to the future and a reliance upon a particular past. According to Ainslie Embree, the "great moment of cultural confrontation" in late nineteenth-century India involved not the East and West, as is often supposed, but "modern scientific culture and traditional religious culture."[2] Radhasoami is a product of this confrontation, and also an attempt to resolve it by raising the encounter to a higher plane, one where a new kind of science and a new kind of religion are compatible.

For that reason those who subscribe to the Radhasoami view of reality regard it as different from traditional secular and religious views in the way that Einstein's physics differs from that of Newton, and in saying so they believe they are speaking in more than a metaphorical way. Their appropriation of scientific language, however, is easily misunderstood. Hervey DeWitt Griswold, the first outsider to write extensively about Radhasoami, regarded this propensity for scientific jargon as one of Radhasoami's more peculiar traits. For Griswold, Radhasoami's fusion of

[1] S. N. Eisenstadt, *Tradition, Change and Modernity* (New York: John Wiley, 1973); *The Origins and Diversity of Axial-Age Civilizations* (Albany: State University of New York Press, 1986); and "Cultural Tradition, Historical Experience and Social Change: The Limits of Convergence," Tanner Lectures at the University of California, Berkeley, May 1989 (unpublished).

[2] Ainslie Embree, *Imagining India: Essays on Indian History* (Delhi and New York: Oxford University Press, 1989), p. 157.

"modern physiological science" with "ancient physiological ideas connected with the yogic doctrine of different centers as 'lotuses' in the body" was "a queer jumbling."[3] Others have been equally put off by Radhasoami analogies of the soul to "kinetic mental ego,"[4] and spiritual transformation to thc chemical changes of gases.

In using the language of science, however, Radhasoami writers do not mean that Radhasoami is a science from a scientific point of view; unlike Christian Scientists, for example, they seldom attempt to employ religious techniques to analyze or alter the obvious aspects of the material world. Yet in another sense they do mean that Radhasoami is equal to science, in that it plays the role that science is sometimes thought to play at the deepest levels of modern consciousness: it reveals the truth and serves as an agent of transformation.

Science and the Perception of Reality

From the Radhasoami perspective, the culprits in our old-fashioned view of reality are the outmoded postulates of Newtonian physics: time and space. In traditional ways of thinking, whether secular or religious, these two dimensions are the bases for understanding almost everything, but adherents of Radhasoami reject them as ultimately static—categories of perception that depend upon limitations and boundaries to be comprehensible. From the Radhasoami perspective, this is one of the central problems with the traditional view of personal existence: limitations on life are what make death possible, and death is the most static condition one can imagine. From a Radhasoami point of view, it is simply untenable to believe that the force of life could disappear.

At the heart of what might be called a Radhasoami physics is a different way of looking at the material world. It is seen as continuous energy expressed in various forms that do not disappear but transmute from one to another. The human task, from a Radhasoami point of view, is to transmute the gross forms of energy manifested in our mortal realities into increasingly rarefied forms. Just as Einsteinian physicists regard their predecessors as obsolete, Radhasoami thinkers view those who cling to all other secular and religious views as seriously outdated. And ignorance is not only unfortunate, it is dangerous. Because time is an illusory concept, it is pernicious. The traditional religions' use of temporal and spatial categories is proof that such worldviews are tools of the negative cosmic agent. In the higher states of consciousness, time, space, and matter are

[3] Griswold, "The Radha Swami Sect in India," p. 183.
[4] Misra, *Discourses*, pp. 216–19.

superseded as the temporal and material orders converge in a more basic form: energy, especially the energy that manifests itself as light and sound. Reality is perceived only in these luminous and beautifully audible forms. To shift one's perception so that one is able to take in such forms is an act of salvation, according to Radhasoami teachings, for it begins the process of refining gross forms of existence into something more vital.

To outsiders it may seem that Radhasoami fails to offer a novel reality; it merely alters one's perception of the familiar. But in the Radhasoami understanding of the way the world works, perception is reality, so to perceive the world differently is to enter a different world. It is like the Escher painting where a frog being drawn becomes a real frog and leaps from the drawing table. The "imaginary" world that one enters in the Radhasoami aesthetic is thought by those who embrace it to be more real than the reality it replaces. Here art does not simply "mirror" reality; it transforms it.

This view of reality changes the Radhasoami believer's notion of the physical world. If perception is everything, the physical world is not as secure and permanent as it appears to be, nor are the boundaries between things and persons and events as discrete as our ordinary senses would lead us to believe. Radhasoami's challenge to ordinary perception inevitably involves a reconsideration of what we know as science and what we know as ourselves.

Therapy and Personal Transformation

From the Radhasoami perspective, the way one thinks about oneself brings the new self into being. For this reason Radhasoami techniques may be thought of as a sort of spiritual therapy. The parallel drawn by Charan Singh is that Radhasoami, like psychotherapy, provides restorative knowledge about oneself.[5] In the Radhasoami view, individuals often have split personalities: there is a tension between their worldly selves and their potentially true selves—a gap that can be bridged by the perceiving consciousness that lies at the intersection of the two. Practitioners of Radhasoami, like patients undergoing psychological therapy, have to become aware of who they are, an awareness that is experienced as liberating.

This view of liberation places great weight on the role of the Radhasoami master as therapist. Both master and therapist represent what the seekers aspire to achieve: a higher state of consciousness that brings calm to one's mind. Followers of Radhasoami idealize and identify with the

[5] Charan Singh, *Light on Sant Mat*, pp. 238–39.

master, as Sudhir Kakar has put it,[6] in order to appropriate his power and bring "peace and direction" to their lives.[7] Kakar goes on to claim, moreover, that the master, like some therapists, enters into "an unconscious collusion with his followers" by exalting himself and infantilizing them.[8] While this may somctimes be the case, the Radhasoami concept of guruship should in theory preclude it, for the master is supposed to surmount any personal feelings of glory in the role and in fact to evince great humility. Of course, the grandiose expectations thrust on a person who is thought to be the guru can easily enlarge that person's sense of importance, but this need not, and theoretically should not, happen. What is important about the Radhasoami master is that he or she is seen as both powerful and accessible, and above all, able to heal. As Kakar observes, those people who had come to Radhasoami with a "severely mauled sense of self-worth" are able through contact with a master to "restore a sense of well-being."[9]

This modern notion of therapeutic personal power is also an ancient one, and the Radhasoami tradition has, in appropriating the sant tradition, revived the notion that one should have an authoritative, personal guide. Like the saints and holy men in the Christendom of late antiquity, India's medieval sants and the modern Radhasoami masters are seen as mortal manifestations of the transformation of material energy. Through them, the guiding, restorative powers of that transformation are conveyed in direct and personal ways.[10]

The Social Transformation of Intimate Authority

The intimate connection of disciples to the master and to one another leads to the creation of fellowships that from one point of view may be seen as spiritual meritocracies: places where, the master willing, people are healed and find salvation through their own individual efforts and their own personal relationships with the master. Modern Indian followers find in Radhasoami's individualism an antidote to what is sometimes perceived as the oppressively communal character of traditional Hindu social organization. Modern Western followers, however, are attracted to

[6] Kakar, *Shamans, Mystics, and Doctors*, p. 145.

[7] Ibid., p. 119

[8] Ibid., p. 150.

[9] Ibid., p. 142.

[10] See Peter Brown, *The Cult of the Saints* (Chicago: University of Chicago Press, 1981); and his article, "The Saint as Exemplar in Late Antiquity," in Hawley, *Saints and Virtues*, pp. 3–14. Other essays in the Hawley volume—those by Babb, Hawley and myself—deal with Hindu notions of sainthood.

what is often lacking in urban European and American societies, except occasionally in religious gatherings: a sense of community. In their critique of American individualism, Robert Bellah and the other authors of *Habits of the Heart* find churches and other religious associations to be among the few vestiges of community in a lonely and alienating society, and even they are often permeated with the acquisitive values of the culture around them.[11] In an earlier work, Bellah argued that those who joined new religious movements in the 1960s and 1970s did so in part as a "repudiation of the tradition of utilitarian individualism."[12]

Those who come to the Radhasoami communities expecting to find a similar repudiation are not wholly disappointed, for the utilitarian aspects of individualism in the Radhasoami communities are softened by bhakti and blended with communalism. This mix is sufficiently interesting to lead observers such as Kakar to regard it as one of the Radhasoami satsang's more remarkable accomplishments,[13] for it defies the common observation that the social world is divided between communities (such as families and ethnic groups) that cohere because of emotional ties, and organizations (typically of an economic or political character) that are held together because they serve to satisfy a plurality of individualistic goals.[14] Radhasoami is both, and would seem to provide the prototype for a new social option.

What holds these two seemingly opposing elements together is a form of leadership that is peculiarly premodern: personal authority. An authority with whom one has an intimate relationship—a parent, a spiritual master, or a divinely anointed monarch—is capable of doing much more than adjudicate between the competing interests of individuals: he or she can awaken conscience, command sacrifice, and engender loyalty and love. In premodern societies the institution of kingship served both individual interests and the cause of communal identity by providing a single figure to whom a large group of people could relate and through whom they could be in touch with one another as well. What made kingship work was a relationship of trust that, as Reinhard Bendix has observed, was virtually always buttressed by religion.[15] The democracies that re-

[11] Robert Bellah et al., *Habits of the Heart*, pp. 219–49.

[12] Bellah, "The New Religious Consciousness and the Crisis in Modernity," in Bellah and Glock, *The New Religious Consciousness*, pp. 333–52; reprinted in Paul Rabinow and William Sullivan, *Interpretive Social Science: A Reader*, p. 346.

[13] Kakar, *Shamans, Mystics, and Doctors*, p. 138.

[14] This is the observation made by Toennies throughout *Community and Society*.

[15] In Bendix's massive study of kingship and the origins of modern democracy in five European and Asian societies, the first generalization made about kings is that their authority "depended on religious sanction" (Reinhard Bendix, *Kings or People: Power and the Mandate to Rule* [Berkeley: The University of California Press, 1978], p. 4). In a different

placed kingships relied upon a different sort of trust for their authority: a trust in reason, due process, and the good will of public-spirited citizens. It is not surprising that when trust in these elements has been eroded, people embrace an earlier form of public authority, such as the spiritual kings of Radhasoami. The personal relationships that Radhasoami followers form with their leaders allow them to restore their faith in social organization, at least in the protected settings of the Radhasoami communities.

Modern Religion

These characteristics of Radhasoami thought—an appropriation of a truth that transcends science, a therapeutic approach to the self, and the reestablishment of personal authority in the social realm—appeal to those who for various reasons have tired of the modern world but are unsatisfied with what the more traditional forms of faith offer as alternatives. These aspects of Radhasoami constitute a form of faith that is modern in a distinctively Indian way, for it is hard to imagine another culture that would have as easy access to the notion of truth as an active force, the self as a fluid, malleable entity, and authority as an element of intimate relationships.

Yet despite the fact that Radhasoami's modernity is distinctively Indian, there are aspects of the Radhasoami tradition that are similar to modern forms of religion throughout the world. Among these are the use of high technology, sophisticated organization and effective publications. Perhaps more important, however, are several modern characteristics of the religious message itself. One of these is the universality of the Radhasoami message and its claim to transcend the particularities of any one cultural tradition. Like the new religious movements in Japan, the Radhasoami teachings relate to dilemmas that are of obvious importance to busy urban lives everywhere: the loss of a sense of personal authority, the insecurity that besets individuals loosed from traditional social moorings, the need for a moral and personal integrity grounded in rational principles, and the desire for a community that conduces to the fulfillment of each individual's potential.

A second feature that the Radhasoami message shares with other forms of modern religion is its orientation toward the future. Like the charismatic preachers of Christian revivalism, the authoritative voices in Radhasoami's tradition come from masters who live in the present but speak

---

vein, Clifford Geertz has remarked that "rulers and gods share certain properties" ("Centers, Kings, and Charisma," p. 152).

on behalf of an even greater authority whose nature is yet to be revealed. The word *Radhasoami* designates a divine terminus of time: the final stage or region towards which all souls seek to travel, the arena in which all existence will finally be fulfilled. What may appear at first to be a Radhasoami form of millennarianism is different from many Christian futurist movements, however, in that it conceives of the future as a process of evolving transformation. Since it does not expect a radical break in human history, it is more like some forms of Christian socialism in attempting to form ideal societies even in the present day.

The integrative logic of Radhasoami is the third feature that it shares with other forms of modern religion. This integrative way of thinking contrasts sharply with the fragmentation of knowledge that has characterized the modern age. Jurgen Habermas, echoing Weber, has said that what he calls the "Enlightenment project" of modern thinkers was intent on separating traditional religious thought into three distinctive modes of reasoning: cognitive-instrumental, moral-practical, and aesthetic-expressive.[16] In reuniting these ways of thinking, Radhasoami and movements like it may be considered not just modern but postmodern, for in repudiating the schisms characteristic of modern thought, they revive important aspects of premodern thinking: the tendency to regard subjective experience and objective reality as related, as in the Sanskrit philosophical systems, or to see all knowledge as part of a single, coherent framework, as in medieval Christian theology.

In both these premodern views, as in Radhasoami's, personal experience was central.[17] In academic circles this notion that "subjective" experience might provide access to "objective" truth has been discredited until recently, when a few scholars have revived the idea that all knowledge is in some sense "personal knowledge," to use Michael Polanyi's words, or "local knowledge," as Clifford Geertz has said—knowledge informed by the way that human subjects perceive what they know.[18] The religious point of view has often clashed with the Enlightenment "project," and although the Reformation was compatible with the Enlightenment in its humanistic attitudes and its detachment from traditional authority, in another sense the Reformation served as the Enlightenment's alter ego. It provided an antidote to the Enlightenment's harsh objectivity

[16] Jurgen Habermas, "Modernity—An Incomplete Project," reprinted in Paul Rabinow and William M. Sullivan, eds., *Interpretive Social Science: A Second Look* (Berkeley: University of California Press, 1987), pp. 148–49.

[17] In medieval physics, for instance, "the entire world of nature was held not only to exist for man's sake, but to be . . . fully intelligible to his mind" (E. A. Burtt, *The Metaphysical Foundations of Modern Science* [Garden City, N.Y.: Doubleday Anchor, 1954], p. 18).

[18] Michael Polanyi, *Personal Knowledge: Towards a Post-Critical Philosophy* (Chicago: University of Chicago Press, 1958); and Geertz, *Local Knowledge*.

by offering a religious view of truth that was personal, intimate and integrative. Modern religious movements throughout the world rejuvenate this Reformation spirit, although often, as in the case of Radhasoami, they look for resources in their own religious past, rather than Europe's. In India this is not difficult to do, for an affirmation of personal knowledge similar to the Reformation's occurred in medieval India in the radical bhakti movement associated with the medieval sants. This Reformation is continued by Radhasoami in the present day.

Many of those who defend the old religious traditions see these new forms of religion as a threat. In India, they see the signs of Radhasoami's vitality—the religious socialism of Dayalbagh, the marble cathedral at Soamibagh, the massive crowds at Beas, the visionary plans of Ruhani Satsang—and fear that the successes of the Radhasoami tradition will spell the end of popular forms of Hinduism and Sikhism. Writing in 1908, Hervey deWitt Griswold despaired that Radhasoami was a "disintegrating and dissolving force" in Indian culture, "continually gnawing at the vitals of old Hinduism."[19] More recently, however, L. A. Babb has placed Radhasoami alongside two other new communities in the Hindu tradition, the Brahmakumaris and the followers of Sathya Sai Baba, and has concluded that rather than gnawing at Hinduism's vitals, these modern forms of religion have helped the tradition to survive. They allow Hinduism to adapt to new conditions in some ways while retaining other, more essential aspects of the Hindu spirit.[20] Raymond Williams makes much the same argument in describing the Swami Narayanan movement in Gujarat as a "new face of Hinduism."[21]

It is obviously true that Radhasoami is in a certain sense a new expression of Hinduism, but as I have tried to argue throughout this chapter and throughout much of this book, it is also a genuinely new religion, a modern religion, a tradition in the making. Its central notions—that truth and authority can be embodied in a person, that transformation of the self occurs through the purification of perception and energy, that love and community can be experienced in dispersion, that social service is based on personal commitment, and that time and place have ultimate centers—each contain features of modern, and in some cases even post-modern, religion. As such, the Radhasoami faith may be a harbinger of the religion of the future, not only in India but elsewhere in the world where modernity is received with a certain amount of suspicion. Many in

[19] Griswold, *Insights into Modern Hinduism*, p. 194. Griswold, a Christian missionary, saw Radhasoami as Hinduism's form of the gnostic heresy, calling it "an old foe in a new dress" (p. 192).

[20] Babb, *Redemptive Encounters*.

[21] Raymond Williams, *A New Face of Hinduism: The Swami Narayanan Movement* (Cambridge: Cambridge University Press, 1984).

both traditional and highly developed areas now seek what the adherents of the Radhasoami communities have found: a pattern of religious expression and experience that allows them to identify with their cultural past without accepting what they see as its superstitious and gaudy excesses, and to embrace modern ways of living without becoming captive to what they perceive as alienating forms of society and sterile forms of thought.

Appendixes

Appendix A

The Radhasoami Family Tree: A Genealogical Outline

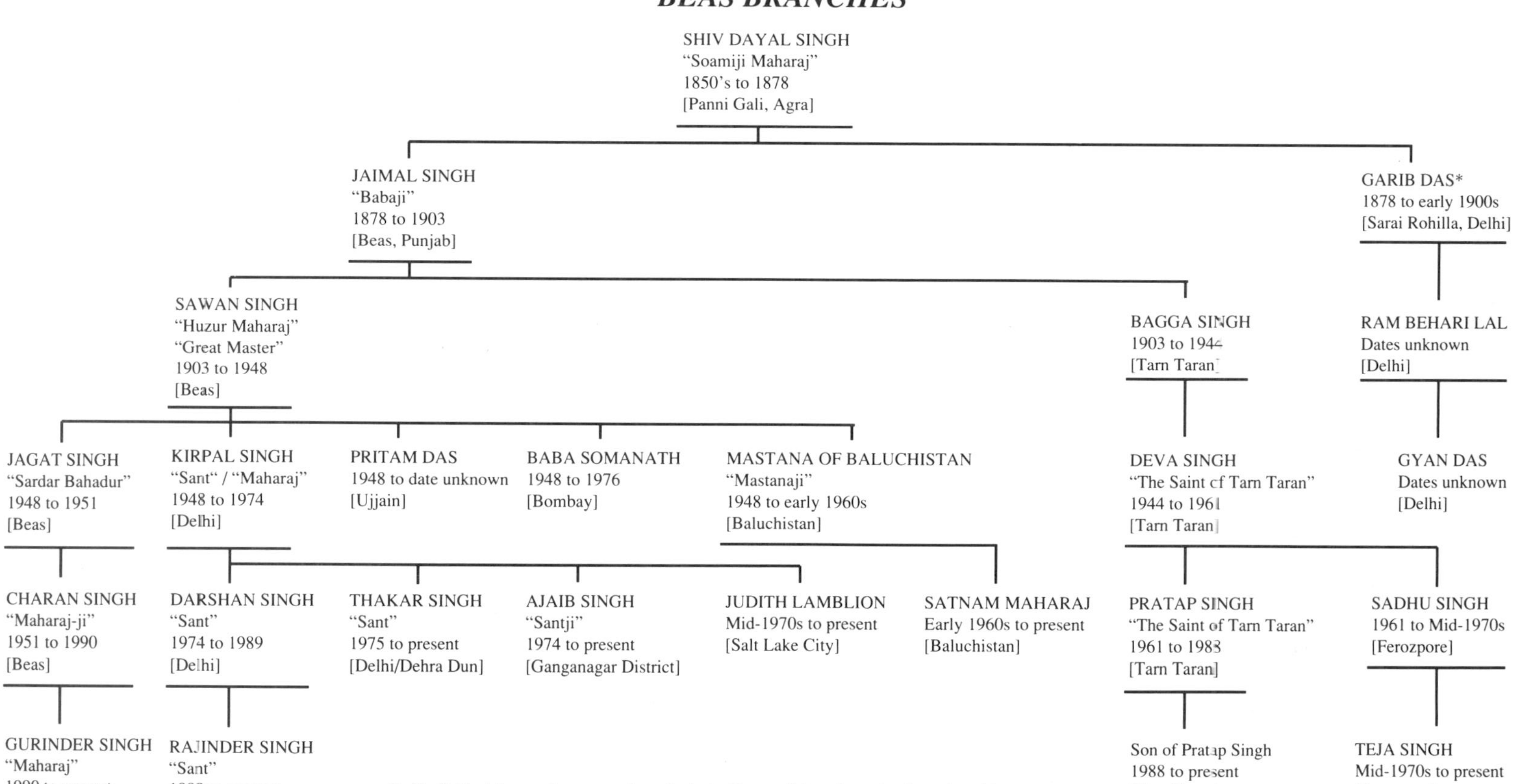

* Garib Das' lineage is separate from both the Beas and Agra branches but, since his group has had close relations with the Beas branches, it is placed among them for convenience.

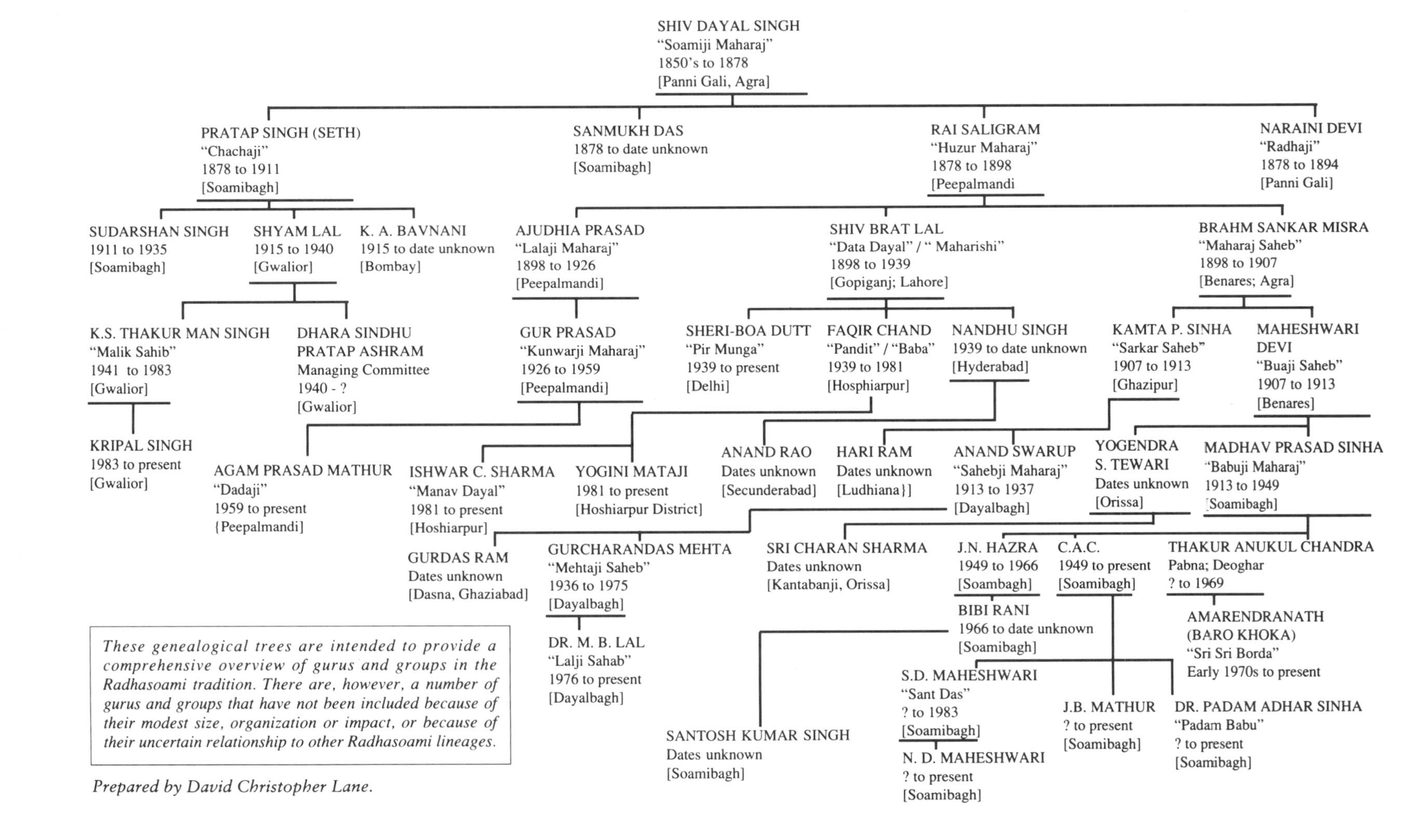

SHIV DAYAL SINGH
"Soamiji Maharaj"
1850's to 1878
[Panni Gali, Agra]
PRATAP SINGH (SETH)
"Chachaji"
1878 to 1911
[Soamibagh]
SANMUKH DAS
1878 to date unknown
[Soamibagh]
RAI SALIGRAM
"Huzur Maharaj"
1878 to 1898
[Peepalmandi
NARAINI DEVI
"Radhaji"
1878 to 1894
[Panni Gali]
SUDARSHAN SINGH
1911 to 1935
[Soamibagh]
SHYAM LAL
1915 to 1940
[Gwalior]
K. A. BAVNANI
1915 to date unknown
[Bombay]
AJUDHIA PRASAD
"Lalaji Maharaj"
1898 to 1926
[Peepalmandi]
SHIV BRAT LAL
"Data Dayal" / " Maharishi"
1898 to 1939
[Gopiganj; Lahore]
BRAHM SANKAR MISRA
"Maharaj Saheb"
1898 to 1907
[Benares; Agra]
K.S. THAKUR MAN SINGH
"Malik Sahib"
1941 to 1983
[Gwalior]
DHARA SINDHU
PRATAP ASHRAM
Managing Committee
1940 - ?
[Gwalior]
GUR PRASAD
"Kunwarji Maharaj"
1926 to 1959
[Peepalmandi]
SHERI-BOA DUTT
"Pir Munga"
1939 to present
[Delhi]
FAQIR CHAND
"Pandit" / "Baba"
1939 to 1981
[Hosphiarpur]
NANDHU SINGH
1939 to date unknown
[Hyderabad]
KAMTA P. SINHA
"Sarkar Saheb"
1907 to 1913
[Ghazipur]
MAHESHWARI
DEVI
"Buaji Saheb"
1907 to 1913
[Benares]
KRIPAL SINGH
1983 to present
[Gwalior]
AGAM PRASAD MATHUR
"Dadaji"
1959 to present
{Peepalmandi]
ISHWAR C. SHARMA
"Manav Dayal"
1981 to present
[Hoshiarpur]
YOGINI MATAJI
1981 to present
[Hoshiarpur District]
ANAND RAO
Dates unknown
[Secunderabad]
HARI RAM
Dates unknown
[Ludhiana}]
ANAND SWARUP
"Sahebji Maharaj"
1913 to 1937
[Dayalbagh]
YOGENDRA
S. TEWARI
Dates unknown
[Orissa]
MADHAV PRASAD SINHA
"Babuji Maharaj"
1913 to 1949
[Soamibagh]
GURDAS RAM
Dates unknown
[Dasna, Ghaziabad]
GURCHARANDAS MEHTA
"Mehtaji Saheb"
1936 to 1975
[Dayalbagh]
SRI CHARAN SHARMA
Dates unknown
[Kantabanji, Orissa]
J.N. HAZRA
1949 to 1966
[Soambagh]
C.A.C.
1949 to present
[Soamibagh]
THAKUR ANUKUL CHANDRA
Pabna; Deoghar
? to 1969
DR. M. B. LAL
"Lalji Sahab"
1976 to present
[Dayalbagh]
BIBI RANI
1966 to date unknown
[Soamibagh]
AMARENDRANATH
(BARO KHOKA)
"Sri Sri Borda"
Early 1970s to present
S.D. MAHESHWARI
"Sant Das"
? to 1983
[Soamibagh]
J.B. MATHUR
? to present
[Soamibagh]
DR. PADAM ADHAR SINHA
"Padam Babu"
? to present
[Soamibagh]
SANTOSH KUMAR SINGH
Dates unknown
[Soamibagh]
N. D. MAHESHWARI
? to present
[Soamibagh]
These genealogical trees are intended to provide a comprehensive overview of gurus and groups in the Radhasoami tradition. There are, however, a number of gurus and groups that have not been included because of their modest size, organization or impact, or because of their uncertain relationship to other Radhasoami lineages.
Prepared by David Christopher Lane.

Appendix B

Radhasoami Studies

WHILE the philosophical and devotional material published by each of the branches of the Radhasoami tradition is voluminous, historical studies by those inside the tradition and objective studies by scholars outside the Radhasoami family have been slow in developing.

The earliest account of the movement is the one given by Rai Saligram in his introduction to *Sar Bachan: Poetry* in 1884. The first independent reference to Rai Saligram and Radhasoami is in A. P. Sinnett, *The Occult World* (1884), p. 151; a reference to an Indian holy man (most likely Rai Saligram) also appears in his *Esoteric Buddhism* (1885). A more extensive discussion of Rai Saligram's life and teachings is to be found in a Vedantic journal, *Prabuddha Bharata*, in May 1898 (pp. 132ff), which is the basis for Max Müller's four-page description of Saligram in *The Life and Sayings of Ramakrishna*, published in 1899. In 1901, the Government of India Census Report published a brief description of the Radhasoami community based on material provided by Brahm Sankar Misra, and in 1902, Pratap Singh, the surviving brother of the original master, published what has become the standard biography of Swami Shiv Dayal. In 1908, Ajudhia Prasad, son of Rai Saligram, published a biography of his father as well.

Many of the other early studies of the movement came from British scholars in India who had originally come to the subcontinent as Christian missionaries. On October 14, 1898, Hervey DeWitt Griswold published an article, "Radha Swami Sect," in a Christian journal, *Nur Afshan* (in Urdu, published in Ludhiana). In 1908 he published another article, "The Radha Swami Sect in India," in the journal *The East and the West*, which was also distributed as a pamphlet by the Christ Church Mission Press; Griswold later used an expanded version of this study as a chapter in his *Insights into Modern Hinduism*, published in 1934. Griswold's primary source of information was an Indian student at Forman Christian College, Lahore, who had formerly been a member of the movement. According to Griswold (*Insights*, p. vii), another missionary-scholar, J. N. Farquhar, relied on Griswold's material for his section on Radhasoami and other movements in *Modern Religious Movements in India,* published in 1914. Even though Farquhar may have borrowed from Griswold for the earlier articles, later accounts of the movement written by Farquhar—including his entry on "Radha Soamis" in Hastings's *Encyclopedia of Religion and Ethics*, published in 1919, and a pamphlet, *Dayal Bagh*, published in 1928—indicate that Farquhar's knowledge of the movement was buttressed by his own visits to Radhasoami sites and interviews with Radhasoami devotees.

As Hindi literature developed as a field of studies, a number of scholars in India included Radhasoami writers in their discussions of the poetry and ideas of writers in the tradition of the medieval sants. There are, for example, sections on Swami Dayal and his writings in P. D. Barthwal, *The Nirguna School of Hindi Poetry*, published in 1936, and in P. Chaturvedi, *Uttari Bharata ki Santa Parampara*, published in Hindi in 1952.

Americans traveling to India in search of spiritual masters earlier in this century provide us with descriptions of the developing Radhasoami communities during those years. The first of these reports, James Bisset Pratt's *India and Its Faiths: A Traveler's Record*, published in 1916, describes the Agra community in the first decade of this century. Julian Johnson gives a book-length account of Sawan Singh and the Beas colony in 1934 in *With a Great Master in India*, and Paul Brunton devotes a chapter to Anand Swarup and Dayalbagh in *A Search in Secret India*, published in 1935. Another traveler, L.S.S. O'Malley, offers a more objective account of Dayalbagh in *Popular Hinduism*, published in 1935.

The wave of interest in Hindu religious movements among Westerners in the 1960s produced a new flood of travelers' accounts of Hindu holy men and their teachings, many of which, in their profiles of modern Hinduism, sketched the lives and teachings of Radhasoami masters. Among these popular and semipopular works are Henry Harper's *Gurus, Swamis, and Avatars* (1972); Khushwant Singh's *Gurus, Godmen and Good People* (1975); Sujan Singh Uban's *The Gurus of India* (1977); Anne Marshall's *Hunting the Guru in India* (1963); and Vishal Mangalawali's *The World of Gurus* (1977).

At the same time a more scholarly approach to the study of the Radhasoami tradition was being aided by the publication of new historical accounts in English (or published simultaneously in English and Hindi) by the Radhasoami communities themselves. These began to appear in the 1950s and in conjunction with centenary celebrations in 1961. The most thorough account is the one published by Dayalbagh, *Souvenir in Commemoration of the First Centenary of the Radhasoami Satsang*. The Soamibagh version of Radhasoami history may be found in S. D. Maheshwari, *Radhasoami Faith: History and Tenets*, published in 1954, and other historical studies are to be found in Kirpal Singh, *A Brief Life Sketch of Hazur Baba Sawan Singh-Ji Maharaj*, published in 1949, and *A Great Saint, Baba Jaimal Singh*, published in 1960. The Beas branch has recently published a history of the Dera by Daryai Lal Kapur, *Heaven on Earth* (1986); and there are historical sections in the introductions to Jaimal Singh's *Spiritual Letters* (1958) and L. R. Puri's *Radha Swami Teachings* (1965), and also in an anonymous pamphlet, *Teachings and Brief History* (1977). A. P. Mathur, great-grandson of Rai Saligram and current master at the Peepalmandi center in Agra, has also written his account of the tradition, *Radhasoami Faith: A Historical Study*, published in 1974.

The latter is also among the first in a series of recent scholarly works on Radhasoami, since in addition to his spiritual duties, Mathur is a historian, and his study of the Radhasoami tradition was originally a Ph.D. thesis for Agra University. Another Ph.D. dissertation written on Radhasoami at Agra University was published as *Radhasvami Sampraday aur Sahitya* (in Hindi) by Oriental Publishers (Delhi, 1971); the author is listed by the single name Saralkumari. Jasmeet Mand, a student in sociology, completed an M.A. dissertation for Punjab University, Chandigarh, on "Social Aspects of Radhasoami Satsang" (1979), which examines the social composition of the Beas branch. A German graduate student, Volker Moeller, did research on Dayalbagh for his Ph.D. dissertation at Tübingen in 1956. In the United States, an M.A. dissertation at the Graduate Theological Union, "Radhasoami Mat: Parampara in Definition and Classification," was completed by David Lane in 1981; and his 1991 Ph.D dissertation in sociology at the University of California, San Diego, was written on the problem of succession in the Radhasoami tradition. Lane has published several articles on Radhasoami-related topics in *The Journal of Transpersonal Psychology*, *Fate*, and other journals, and his booklet, *The Unknowing Sage: The Life and Work of Baba Faqir Chand*, was published in cooperation with Manavta Mandir. A senior thesis for the University of Michigan by M. Aaron Talsky, "The Radhasoami Tradition: Charismatic Routinization and Its Doctrinal Consequences" (1986) focuses on the early successors to Swami Shiv Dayal. A Ph.D. dissertation for the Divinity School of the University of Chicago by Daniel Gold, "The Lord as Guru in North Indian Religion: Hindi *Sant* Tradition and Universals of Religious Perception" (1982), which includes a discussion of several Radhasoami masters and their teachings, has been published, in revised form, as *The Lord as Guru* (New York: Oxford University Press, 1987). An article based on this dissertation is included in K. Schomer and W. H. McLeod, eds., *The Sants: Studies in a Devotional Tradition of India* (1986).

Other scholarly works on Radhasoami include a chapter by a historian of religion, Philip Ashby, in his *Modern Trends in Hinduism* (1969) and a study of Radhasoami therapy by a psychoanalyst, Sudhir Kakar, in his *Shamans, Mystics and Doctors* (1982). An anthropologist, Lawrence A. Babb, has published an excellent article on Radhasoami cosmology ("The

Physiology of Redemption") in the journal *History of Religions*, and he also has an extensive section on Radhasoami in his *Redemptive Encounters* (1987). Kakar's study is based on visits to the Beas Dera, and Babb's work is based on considerable field study at Soamibagh. My own work on Radhasoami, based on field studies at Beas, Agra, Benares, Delhi, Hoshiarpur, Gwalior, and elsewhere from 1970 to 1991 has led to several publications prior to this book, including an article, "Radhasoami as a Trans-National Movement" in J. Needleman and G. Baker, eds., *Understanding the New Religions* (1979); a chapter, "Radhasoami and the Return of Religion," in my *Religion as Social Vision* (1982); an article, "The Radhasoami Revival of the Sant Tradition" in Schomer and McLeod, eds., *The Sants* (1986); an article, "Patterns of Pluralism: Sikh Relations with Radhasoami," in Joseph T. O'Connell, et al., eds., *Sikh History and Religion in the Twentieth Century*; and entries on "Radhasoami Satsang" in *The Encyclopedia of Asian History* (1988), and in the forthcoming editions of the *Harper Dictionary of Religions* and *Encyclopedia Britannica*. The latter will replace an entry on Radhasoami written by Khushwant Singh which appeared in earlier editions of the Encylopedia.

Appendix C

How Many Initiates Are There?

SECURING a number for the total membership of the Radhasoami communities is not an easy matter. Members of Radhasoami's residential communities comprise a relatively stable population, but of course the wider membership—those who attend satsang in the local branches—fluctuates greatly over time. The only reliable figure is the number of those who have actually received initiation, and fortunately records have been kept in most branches of Radhasoami of those who have been officially received into the fellowship. It should be kept in mind, however, that while Radhasoami officials keep records of initiations, they do not keep track of what happens to the initiates later on and thus do not record the numbers of those who later leave the fellowship or die. Part of the reason for this administrative neglect is doctrinal: after a soul has been united with a master, according to Radhasoami thought, such mundane matters as the initiate's death or lapsed commitment cannot sever this relationship. Their souls remain united with the master regardless of the disposition of the physical body. Thus it is theologically impossible to subtract anyone from a list of initiates once he or she has been placed on it. Moreover, Radhasoami theology also allows for the possibility of "secret" initiations, ones that the master chooses to make without revealing them to the organization's officials. Therefore, the record-keepers stress that their lists are only of "recorded initiations," and that there may be others who "are not recorded, but have been blessed with the divine gift" (letter from J. M. Sethi, Sawan Kirpal Ruhani Mission, October 1, 1985).

In discussing the problem of numbers with Roland deVries, the American representative of Charan Singh, he suggested that a realistic estimate of the active American membership should be gauged not by the roll of initiates (some 10,000 in the United States) but by the number of subscribers to the American newsletter of the community. There are 2000 of these, and if one could assume that the magazine was read by at least two Radhasoami initiates per household, this would place the number of active members in the United States at 4000. This seems to me to be a sensible method of calculation, and by extending it, one would come up with a conservative estimate of the actual number of active members in all branches of Radhasoami throughout the world as perhaps 40 percent of the official total. This would make the current active membership at a bit more than a half million people—an impressive number for a new religious tradition, but something considerably less than the almost two million recorded as initiates by the various branches themselves (see below).

The earliest estimates of the initiates of Swami Shiv Dayal is 8–10,000 over a seventeen-year period (*Biography of Soamiji Maharaj*, p. 51). The 1901 Census of India indicated that there were around 15,000 persons in the United Provinces who returned their religion as Radhasoami Satsang, and Hervey DeWitt Griswold estimated 30,000 members in 1908 (p. 192). In 1928, Griswold revised his figures dramatically, claiming that the combined followers of all Agra branches numbered 100,000 (Griswold, *Insights into Modern Hinduism*, p. 139). In 1935, Julian Johnson estimated a total number of 250,000 members throughout India, including 100,000 at Dayalbagh, which he describes as the largest center, and 30–40,000 at Allahabad.

More recent figures, supplied by the Radhasoami centers, are as follows:

Beas: 1,427,408 as of July 6, 1990.

Specific figures for each master at Beas are as follows:

Initiates of Jaimal Singh: 2,343 (source: "Statistics" in Jaimal Singh, *Spiritual Letters*, p. ixx).

Initiates of Sawan Singh: 125,375 (source: *Spiritual Letters,* p. xx; D. L. Kapur, *Call of the Great Master*, lists the number as 126,000, and K. L. Khanna, in written answers to my questions, [May 25, 1971] lists the number as 124,000).

Initiates of Jagat Singh: 18,000 (source: J. M. Lal, "Preface" to Julian Johnson, *With a Great Master in India*).

Initiates of Charan Singh: 1,281,690 (source: the official announcement of Charan Singh's death given by the Beas Dera, July 6, 1990). The official records of Beas for 1974, 1975, 1976 and 1977 give the following figures for new initiations during each of those years: 22,271; 27,717; 33,052; 47,072. These figures are in line with those given to me informally in 1986, which yielded a total of over 700,000 initiates. In later years, Charan Singh held mass initiations, yielding tens of thousands of new members at each event.

Ruhani Satsang/ Sawan Kirpal Ruhani Mission: 157,705 as of August 4, 1989 (source: letters to me from J. M. Sethi, general secretary, October 1, 1985; May 7, 1988; May 22, 1988; November 15, 1988; and from Art Stein, August 4, 1989).

The initiations were made by the following masters:

Initiates of Kirpal Singh: 80,446 (source: J. M. Sethi). One of the Ruhani Satsang publications listed the number as 90,000 (source: Introduction to Kirpal Singh, *A Great Saint: Baba Jaimal Singh*, p. iii).

Initiates of Darsan Singh: 77,259 as of May 30, 1989 (source: J. M. Sethi and Art Stein).

No exact figures are available for the initiates of Ajaib Singh and Thakar Singh, but there are at least several thousand each. Thakar Singh initiates virtually all the members of the audiences who remain following his public speeches.

Dayalbagh: 200,000 (source: interview with G. D. Sahgal, general secretary of the organization on August 10, 1983). The Dayalbagh organization does not make public the number of its initiates. The only published figure is 110,000 (source: Anand Swarup, quoted in Paul Brunton, *A Search in Secret India* [1935], p. 235). A rival of the Dayalbagh leaders estimated 60,000 (S. D. Maheshwari, *Truth Unvarnished,* part 1, p. 251).

Soamibagh: 100,000 (source: S. D. Maheshwari, *Truth Unvarnished,* part 1, p. 251; his calculation is based on sales figures for books aimed exclusively at followers, multiplied by a factor of six, the number of members Maheshwari assumes would be part of each household possessing the book). The Soamibagh Council does not make public the number of its initiates. A current resident of Soamibagh, P. S. Sharma, estimates the present number of active satsangis in the branch at 40,000 (source: interview with P. S. Sharma, Soamibagh, August 13, 1985). Sharma claims that there were 20,000 in attendance at the large centennial celebrations of the colony and estimates that an equal number were not able to attend.

Peepalmandi: 15,000 (source: estimates based on interviews with A. P. Mathur and his associates, August 12, 1983).

Sant Mansingh Mandir, Gwalior: 500 throughout India (source: Yogesh Sharma, Gwalior, August 21, 1985).

Bibliography

A. Theoretical Considerations

Bell, Daniel. *The Coming of Post-Industrial Society*. New York: Basic Books, 1973.

———. *The Cultural Contradictions of Capitalism*. New York: Basic Books, 1976.

Bellah, Robert N. *Beyond Belief: Essays on Religion in a Post-Traditional World*. New York: Harper and Row, 1970.

———, ed. *Religion and Progress in Modern Asia*. New York: The Free Press, 1965.

Bellah, Robert N. et al. *Habits of the Heart: Individualism and Commitment in American Life*. Berkeley: University of California Press, 1985.

Bellah, Robert N. and Charles Glock, eds., *The New Religious Consciousness*. Berkeley: University of California Press, 1976.

Ben-David, Joseph and Terry Nichols Clark. *Culture and Its Creators: Essays in Honor of Edward Shils*. Chicago: University of Chicago Press, 1977.

Bendix, Reinhard. *Kings or People: Power and the Mandate to Rule*. Berkeley: University of California Press, 1978.

———. "Tradition and Modernity Reconsidered." *Comparative Studies in Society and History* 9 (1966–1967): 292–346.

Brown, Peter. *The Cult of the Saints*. Chicago: University of Chicago Press, 1981.

———. "The Saint as Exemplar in Late Antiquity." In John Stratton Hawley, ed., *Saints and Virtues*, pp. 3–14. Berkeley: University of California Press, 1987.

Burtt, E. A. *The Metaphysical Foundations of Modern Science*, Garden City, N.J.: Doubleday Anchor, 1954.

Bynum, Caroline Walker, et al., eds. *Gender and Religion: On the Complexity of Symbols*. Boston: Beacon Press, 1986.

Douglas, Mary. "The Effects of Modernization on Religious Change." *Daedalus* 111, no. 1 (Winter 1982): 1–19.

Eisenstadt, S[hmuel] N[oah]. "Cultural Tradition, Historical Experience and Social Change: The Limits of Convergence." The Tanner Lectures at the University of California, Berkeley, May 1989.

———. *The Origins and Diversity of Axial-Age Civilizations*. Albany: State University of New York Press, 1986.

———, ed. *The Protestant Ethic and Modernization: A Comparative View*. New York: Basic Books, 1968.

———. *Tradition, Change, and Modernity*. New York: Wiley, 1973.

Erikson, Erik. *Identity and the Life Cycle*. New York: Norton, 1980. Orig. pub. as "Identity and the Life Cycle: Selected Papers." *Psychological Issues* 1, no. 1 (1959): 1–166.

Foucault, Michel. *The Archeology of Knowledge*. Trans. A. M. Sheridan Smith. New York: Harper and Row, 1976.

———. *Language, Counter-Memory, Practice; Selected Essays and Interviews*. Trans. Donald F. Boudard and Sherry Simon. Ithaca: Cornell University Press, 1977.

Geertz, Clifford. "Centers, Kings, and Charisma: Reflections on the Symbolics of Power." In Joseph Ben-David and Terry Nichols Clark, eds. *Culture and its Creators: Essays in Honor of Edward Shils*, pp. 150–67. Chicago: University of Chicago Press, 1977.

———. *Interpretation of Cultures*. New York: Basic Books, 1973.

———. *Local Knowledge: Further Essays in Interpretive Anthropology*. New York: Basic Books, 1983.

———, ed. *Old Societies and New States: The Quest for Modernity in Asia and Africa*. New York: Free Press, 1963.

Green, Ronald. *Religion and Moral Reason: A New Method for Comparative Study*. New York: Oxford University Press, 1988.

———. *Religious Reason: The Rational and Moral Basis of Religious Belief*. New York: Oxford University Press, 1978.

Habermas, Jurgen. "Modernity—An Incomplete Project." In Paul Rabinow and William M. Sullivan, eds., *Interpretive Social Science: A Second Look*, pp. 147–59. Berkeley: University of California Press, 1987.

Hammond, Phillip E., ed. *The Sacred in a Secular Age*. Berkeley: University of California Press, 1985.

Heidegger, Martin. *On the Way to Language*. Trans. Peter D. Hertz. New York: Harper and Row, 1971.

Honko, Lauri, ed. *Science of Religion, Studies in Methodology*. The Hague: Mouton, 1979.

Kitagawa, Joseph. "The History of Religion in America." In Mircea Eliade and Joseph Kitagawa, eds., *History of Religions: Essays in Methodology*. Chicago: University of Chicago Press, 1959.

Lawrence, Bruce. *Defenders of God: Fundamentalist Movements in Christianity, Judaism, and Islam*. San Francisco: Harper and Row, 1989.

Lindbeck, George. *The Nature of Doctrine: Religion and Theology in a Post-liberal Age*. Philadelphia: Westminster Press, 1984.

Marty, Martin E. *What is Modern About the Modern Study of Religion?* Tempe, Ariz.: Department of Religious Studies, Arizona State University, 1985.

Polanyi, Michael. *Personal Knowledge: Towards a Post-Critical Philosophy*. Chicago: University of Chicago Press, 1958.

Reynolds, Frank and Earle H. Waugh, eds. *Religious Encounters with Death: Insights from the History and Anthropology of Religions*. University Park, Pa.: Pennsylvania State University Press, 1977.

Ricoeur, Paul. *Interpretation Theory: Discourse and the Surplus of Meaning*. Fort Worth: Texas Christian University Press, 1976.

Schleiermacher, Friedrich. *On Religion*. Trans. Terrence N. Tice. Richmond: John Knox Press, 1969.

Shils, Edward. *Center and Periphery: Essays in Macrosociology*. Chicago: University of Chicago Press, 1975.
Smart, Ninian. *Worldviews: Crosscultural Explorations of Human Beliefs*. New York: Charles Scribner's Sons, 1983.
Smelser, Neil. *A Theory of Collective Behavior*. New York: Free Press, 1962.
Smith, Jonathan Z. *Imagining Religion: From Babylon to Jonestown*. Chicago: University of Chicago Press, 1982.
Smith, Wilfred Cantwell. "Comparative Religion: Whither—and Why?" In Mircea Eliade and Joseph Kitagawa, eds. *History of Religions: Essays in Methodology*. Chicago: University of Chicago Press, 1959.
———. *The Meaning and End of Religion*. New York: Harper and Row, 1962.
———. "Philosophia as One of the Religious Traditions of Humankind." In *Différence, Valeur, Hiérarchie*, pp. 265–75. Paris: Éditions de l'École des Haute Études en Sciences Sociales.
———. *Towards a World Theology: Faith and the Comparative History of Religion*. Philadelphia: Westminster Press, 1981.
Staal, J. Frits. *Rules Without Meaning: Ritual, Mantras, and the Human Sciences*. New York: Peter Lang, 1989.
Toennies, Ferdinand. *Community and Society*. Trans. and intro. Charles P. Loomis. East Lansing: Michigan State University Press, 1957.
Tracy, David. *The Analogical Imagination: Christian Theology and the Culture of Pluralism*. New York: Crossroads, 1981.
Troeltsch, Ernst. *The Social Teachings of the Christian Churches*. Trans. Olive Wyon. Intro. H. Richard Niebuhr. New York: Harper and Row, 1960.
Waardenburg, Jacques. *Reflections on the Study of Religion*. The Hague: Mouton, 1978.
Weber, Max. *Economy and Society*. Ed. Guenther Roth and Claus Wittich. Berkeley: University of California Press, 1978.
———. *The Sociology of Religion*. Trans. Ephraim Fischoff. Boston: Beacon Press, 1963.
Werblowsky, R. J. Zwi. *Beyond Tradition and Modernity: Changing Religions in a Changing World*. London: Athlone Press of the University of London, 1976.
Wilson, Bryan. *Religion in Secular Society: A Sociological Comment*. London: Watts, 1966.
———. *Religion in Sociological Perspective*. New York: Oxford University Press, 1982.
———. *Sects and Society*. Berkeley: University of California Press, 1961.
Yinger, J. Milton. "Pluralism, Religion and Secularization." *Journal for the Scientific Study of Religion* 6 (1967): 17–30.
Zaleski, Carol. *Otherworld Journeys: Accounts of Near-Death Experience in Medieval and Modern Times*. New York: Oxford University Press, 1987.

B. Religion and Society in India

Adi Granth: Selections from the Sacred Writings of the Sikhs. Trans. Trilochan Singh. London: Allen and Unwin, 1960.

Ashby, Philip. *Modern Trends in Hinduism*. New York: Columbia University Press, 1969.

Babb, Lawrence A. *Redemptive Encounters: Three Styles in the Hindu Tradition*. Berkeley: University of California Press, 1987.

Banerjea, A. K. *Philosophy of Gorakhnath*. Gorakhpur: Mahant Dig Vijai Nath Trust, 1961.

Barthwal, Pitambar Datta. *The Nirguna School of Hindi Poetry: An Exposition of Medieval Indian Santa Mysticism*. Benares: Indian Book Shop, 1936.

Bhardwaj, Surinder Mohan. *Hindu Places of Pilgrimage in India: A Study in Cultural Geography*. Berkeley: University of California Press, 1973.

Blavatsky, Madame Helena P. *The Voice of Silence and Other Chosen Fragments*. Los Angeles: Theosophy Book Co., 1928.

Bly, Robert. *The Kabir Book*. Boston: Beacon Press, 1971.

Briggs, George W. *The Chamars*. London: Oxford University Press, 1920.

———. *Goraknath and the Kanphata Yogis*. Delhi: Motilal Banarsidass, 1973. Orig. pub. 1938.

Brunton, Paul. *A Search in Secret India*. New York: S. Weiser, 1970. Orig. pub. 1935, by E. P. Dutton.

Chatfield, Charles, ed. *The Americanization of Gandhi: Images of the Mahatma*. New York and London: Garland Publishing, 1976.

Chaturvedi, P. *Uttari Bharata ki Santa-Parampara* (in Hindi). Prayag: Bharati-Bhandara, 1952.

Das Gupta, Shashibhusan. *Obscure Religious Cults*. Calcutta: Firma K.L.M Private, 1976. Orig. pub. 1946.

Dumont, Louis. *Homo Hierarchicus: The Caste System and Its Implications*. Chicago: University of Chicago Press, 1970. Rev. English ed. Trans. Mark Sainsbury, Louis Dumont, and Basia Gulati. Delhi: Oxford University Press, 1988.

———. "World Renunciation in Indian Religions." Appendix B of *Homo Hierarchicus: The Caste System and Its Implications*. Rev. English ed., trans. Mark Sainsbury, Louis Dumont, and Basia Gulati. Delhi: Oxford University Press, 1988.

Dwivedi, Hari Prasad. *Kabir*. Allahabad: Hindustani Academy, 1955.

Dwivedi, Hari Prasad. *Natha-sampradaya* (in Hindi). Allahabad: Hindustani Academy, 1950.

Eck, Diana. *Benares: City of Light*. New York: Knopf, 1982.

———. *Darsan: Seeing the Divine Image*. Chambersburg, Pa.: Anima Press, 1982.

Eliade, Mircea. *Yoga: Immortality and Freedom*. Trans. Willard R. Trask. Princeton: Princeton University Press, 1969.

Ellwood, Robert S., Jr. *Religious and Spiritual Groups in Modern America*. Englewood Cliffs, N.J.: Prentice-Hall, 1973.

Embree, Ainslie T. *Imagining India: Essays on Indian History*. Delhi: Oxford University Press, 1989.

———. *Utopias in Conflict: Religion and Nationalism in Modern India*. Berkeley: University of California Press, 1990.

———, ed. *Sources in Indian Tradition.* New York: Columbia University Press, 1987.

Ezekiel, Isaac A. *Kabir, the Great Mystic.* 3d ed. Beas: Radhasoami Satsang, Beas, 1978. Orig. pub. 1966.

Farquhar, J. N. *Modern Religious Movements in India.* Delhi: Munshiram Manoharlal, 1977. Orig. pub. 1914.

Gold, Daniel. *The Lord as Guru: Hindi* Sants *in the Northern Indian Tradition.* New York: Oxford University Press, 1987.

———. "The Lord as Guru in North Indian Religion: Hindi *Sant* Tradition and Universals of Religious Perception." Ph.D. dissertation, Divinity School, University of Chicago, 1982.

Grewal, J. S. *Guru Nanak in History.* Chandigarh: Punjab University, 1969.

———. "A Perspective on Early Sikh History." In Mark Juergensmeyer and N. Gerald Barrier, eds., *Sikh Studies: Comparative Perspectives on a Changing Tradition.* Berkeley: Berkeley Religious Studies Series, 1979.

Griswold, Hervey DeWitt. *Insights into Modern Hinduism.* New York: Henry Holt and Co., 1934.

Hawley, John Stratton. *At Play with Krishna: Pilgrimage Dramas from Brindavan.* Princeton: Princeton University Press, 1981.

———. "The Sant in Sur Das." In Karine Schomer and W. H. McLeod, eds., *The Sants: Studies in a Devotional Tradition of India,* pp. 191–211. Berkeley: Berkeley Religious Studies Series; Delhi: Motilal Banarsidass, 1987.

———. *Surdas: Singer, Poet, Saint.* Seattle: University of Washington Press, 1984.

———, ed. *Saints and Virtues.* Berkeley: University of California Press, 1987.

Hawley, John Stratton, and Mark Juergensmeyer, trans. *Songs of the Saints of India.* New York: Oxford University Press, 1988.

Hawley, John Stratton, and Donna Wulff, eds. *The Divine Consort: Radha and the Goddesses of India.* Berkeley: Berkeley Religious Studies Series; Delhi: Motilal Banarsidass, 1982.

Hess, Linda, and Shukdev Singh. *The Bijak of Kabir.* San Francisco: North Point Press, 1983.

Jensen, Joan M. *Passage from India: Asian Indian Immigrants in North America.* New Haven: Yale University Press, 1988.

Jones, Kenneth W. *Arya Dharm: Hindu Consciousness in 19th-Century Punjab.* Berkeley: University of California Press, 1976.

Juergensmeyer, Mark. "The Cultures of Deprivation: Three Case Studies in the Punjab." *Economic and Political Weekly.* Annual number, February 1979, pp. 255–62.

———. "Hinduism in America." In Keith Crim, et al., eds., *Abingdon Dictionary of Living Religions,* pp. 318–21. Nashville: Abingdon Press, 1981.

———. "Political Hope: Social Movements of North India's Untouchables." Ph.D. dissertation, Department of Political Science, University of California, Berkeley, 1974.

———. *Religion as Social Vision: The Movement Against Untouchability in 20th Century Punjab.* Berkeley: University of California Press, 1982. Rev. ed. pub.

as *Religious Rebels in the Punjab: The Social Vision of Untouchables*. Delhi: Ajanta Books, 1988.

Juergensmeyer, Mark, and N. G. Barrier, eds. *Sikh Studies: Comparative Perspectives on a Changing Tradition*. Berkeley: Berkeley Religious Studies Series, 1979.

Kabir. *Kabir Sahab ka Anurag Sagar*. Allahabad: Belvedere Printing Works, 1975. Trans. Raj Kumar Bagga, Partap Singh, and Kent Bicknell, as *The Ocean of Love*. Sanbornton, N.H.: Sant Bani Ashram, 1982.

Kakar, Sudhir. *Shamans, Mystics and Doctors: A Psychological Inquiry into India and Its Healing Traditions*. Boston: Beacon Press, 1982.

Khane, R. S. *Food, Society and Culture*. Durham, N.C.: Carolina Academic Press, 1986.

Kopf, David. *The Brahmo Samaj and the Shaping of the Modern Indian Mind*. Princeton: Princeton University Press, 1979.

Leonard, Karen. *Social History of an Indian Caste: The Kayasths of Hyderabad*. Berkeley: University of California Press, 1978.

Lorenzen, David. "The Kabir Panth and Social Protest." In Karine Schomer and W. H. McLeod, eds., *The Sants: Studies in a Devotional Tradition of India*, pp. 281–303. Berkeley: Berkeley Religious Studies Series; Delhi: Motilal Banarsidass, 1987.

———. "Traditions of Non-Caste Hinduism: The Kabir Panth." *Contributions to Indian Sociology* 21, no. 2 (1987): 263–83.

McLeod, W. H. *The Evolution of the Sikh Community*. Oxford: Clarendon Press, 1976.

———. *Guru Nanak and the Sikh Religion*. Oxford: Clarendon Press, 1968.

———. "The Meaning of 'Sant' in Sikh Usage." In Karine Schomer and W. H. McLeod, eds., *The Sants: Studies in a Devotional Tradition of India*, pp. 251–63. Berkeley: Berkeley Religious Studies Series; Delhi: Motilal Banarsidass, 1987.

———. *Textual Sources for the Study of Sikhism*. Manchester: Manchester University Press, 1984.

Madan, T. N. *Non-Renunciation: Themes and Interpretations of Hindu Culture*. Delhi: Oxford University Press, 1987.

Malik, S. C., ed. *Indian Movements: Some Aspects of Dissent, Protest and Reform*. Simla: Indian Institute of Advanced Study, 1978.

Misra, B. B. *The Indian Middle Classes: Their Growth in Modern Times*. London: Oxford University Press, 1961.

Müller, Max. *Ramakrishna—His Life and Sayings*. London: Longmans Green and Company, 1898; New York: Charles Scribner's Sons, 1899.

Nayar, Kuldip, and Khushwant Singh. *Tragedy of Punjab*. New Delhi: Vision Books, 1984.

Needleman, Jacob, and George Baker, eds. *Understanding the New Religions*. New York: Seabury, 1979.

O'Connell, Joseph et al., eds. *Sikh History and Religion in the Twentieth Century*. Toronto: Centre for South Asia Studies, University of Toronto, 1988.

O'Flaherty, Wendy Doniger. *Siva: The Erotic Ascetic*. Oxford: Oxford University Press, 1973.

———. *Women, Androgynes, and Other Mythical Beasts*. Chicago: University of Chicago Press, 1980.

Oman, John Campbell. *The Mystics, Ascetics, and Saints of India*. London: T. Fisher Unwin, 1903.

Prasad, Bhagwan. *Socio-Economic Study of Urban Middle Classes*. Delhi: Sterling Publishers,1968.

Puri, Janak Raj. *Guru Nanak: His Mystic Teachings*. Beas: Radhasoami Satsang, Beas, 1982.

Raghavan, V. *The Great Integrators: The Saint-Singers of India*. Patel Memorial Lectures. New Delhi: Publications Division, Ministry of Information and Broadcasting, Government of India, 1966.

Rayapati, J. P. Rao. *Early American Interest in Vedanta*. New York: Asia Publishing House, 1973.

Rudolph, Lloyd I. and Susanne Hoeber Rudolph. *The Modernity of Tradition: Political Development in India*. Chicago: University of Chicago Press, 1967.

Sarkar, Benoy Kumar. *The Folk Elements in Hindu Culture: A Contribution to Socio-Religious Studies in Hindu Folk-Institutions*. New Delhi: Cosmo Publications, 1981. Orig. pub. 1917.

Schomer, Karine and W. H. McLeod, eds. *The Sants: Studies in a Devotional Tradition of India*. Berkeley: Berkeley Religious Studies Series; Delhi: Motilal Banarsidass, 1987.

Sen, Kshitimohan M. *Medieval Mysticism of India*. Trans. Manomohan Ghosh. New Delhi: Oriental Books Reprint Corporation, 1974. Orig. pub. in 1929.

Sethi, V. K. *Kabir: The Weaver of God's Name*. Beas: Radhasoami Satsang, Beas, 1984.

Sharma, I. C. *Cayce, Karma, and Reincarnation*. New York: Harper and Row, 1975.

———. *Ethical Philosophies of India*. Ed. and rev. Stanley M. Daugert. London: Allen and Unwin, 1965. Reprint New York: Harper and Row, 1970.

———. *India's Democracy and the Communist Challenge*. Lincoln, Neb.: Johnson Publishing Co., 1967.

Shobha, Savitri Chandra. *Social Life and Concepts in Medieval Hindi Bhakti Poetry*. Meerut: Chandrayan Publications, 1983.

Silburn, Lilian. *Kundalini: Energy of the Depths*. Trans. Jacques Gontier. Albany: State University of New York Press, 1988.

Singer, Milton. *When a Great Tradition Modernizes*. New York: Praeger, 1972.

Sinnett, A. P. *The Occult World*. London: Truebner and Co., 1884.

Smith, Donald E. *India as a Secular State*. Princeton: Princeton University Press, 1963.

———, ed. *Religion and Political Modernization*. New Haven: Yale University Press, 1974.

Srinivas, M. N. *Caste in Modern India and Other Essays*, Bombay: Asia Publishing House, 1962.

Srinivas, M. N. *Social Change in Modern India*. Berkeley: University of California Press, 1968.

Tagore, Rabindranath. *Songs of Kabir*. New York: Macmillan Publishing Co., 1915.

Thrasher, Allen W. "Magical Journeys in Classical Sanskrit Literature." Paper presented to the annual meeting of the American Academy of Religion, San Francisco, December 1977.

Timberg, Thomas A. *The Marwaris: From Traders to Industrialists*. New Delhi: Vikas Publishing House, 1978.

Upadhyaya, K. N. *Dariya Sahib: Saint of Bihar*. Beas: Radhasoami Satsang, Beas, 1987.

Vaudeville, Charlotte. *Kabir*. Oxford: Clarendon Press, 1974.

Weber, Max. *Religion of India: The Sociology of Hinduism and Buddhism*. Trans. Hans H. Gerth and Don Martindale. New York: The Free Press, 1958.

Wescott, G. H. *Kabir and the Kabir Panth*. Varanasi: Bhartiya Publishing House, n.d. Orig. pub. 1907.

Wilkins, W. J. *Modern Hinduism*. Delhi: B. R. Publishing Corporation, 1975. Orig. pub. 1887; rev. in 1900.

Williams, Raymond. *A New Face of Hinduism: The Swami Narayanan Movement*. Cambridge: Cambridge University Press, 1984.

C. Writings Related to Radhasoami

Ashby, Philip. "Popular Esoteric Religion: Radha Soami Satsang." In *Modern Trends in Hinduism*, pp. 71–90. New York: Columbia University Press, 1969.

———. "The Radhasoami Satsang and Sikhism." *Illustrated Weekly of India* 90, no. 46 (November 16, 1969): 14.

Babb, Lawrence A. "The Physiology of Redemption." *History of Religions* 22, no. 4 (May 1983): 293–312.

———. *Redemptive Encounters: Three Styles in the Hindu Tradition*. Berkeley: University of California Press, 1987.

Barthwal, Pitambar Datta. *The Nirguna School of Hindi Poetry: An Exposition of Medieval Indian Santa Mysticism*. Benares: Indian Book Shop, 1936.

Brace, Kerry. *The Living Ideal* (Biography of Shree Shree Thakur Anakulchandra). Hartford, Conn.: Jeffrey Renert, publisher, 1977.

Brunton, Paul. *A Search in Secret India*. New York: E. P. Dutton, 1959. Orig. pub. 1935.

Dayalbagh Educational Institute (Dayalbagh, Agra). Prospectus and Application Form, 1986–1987 session.

Dhir, Mata Sheila. "How the Master Revealed Himself." In Bhadra Sena, ed., *The Ocean of Grace Divine*, pp. 31–36. Delhi: Ruhani Satsang, 1976.

Farquhar, J. N. *Dayal Bagh*. N.p. 1928.

———. "Radhasoami Satsang." In James Hastings, ed., *Encyclopedia of Religion and Ethics* (1919).

———. "The Radha Soami Satsang." In *Modern Religious Movements in India*. Delhi: Munshiram Manoharlal, 1977. Orig. pub. 1914.

Garbett, Sir Colin. *The Ringing Radiance*. Beas: Radhasoami Satsang, Beas, 1968.

Gill, Hilda, ed. *Glimpses of the Great Master*. Hong Kong: Cami Moss, 1986. Pub. with the permission of Radhasoami Satsang, Beas.

Gold, Daniel Richard. "Clan and Lineage among the Sants: Seed, Service, Substance." In Karine Schomer and W. H. McLeod, eds., *The Sants: Studies in a Devotional Tradition of India*, pp. 305–27. Berkeley: Religious Studies Series; Delhi: Motilal Banarsidass, 1986.

———. *The Lord as Guru: Hindi* Sants *in North Indian Tradition*. New York: Oxford University Press, 1987.

———. "The Lord as Guru in North Indian Religion: Hindi *Sant* Tradition and Universals of Religious Perception." Ph.D. dissertation, Divinity School of the University of Chicago, 1982.

Government of India. "Radhasoami Satsang." In *Government of India Census Report*. Delhi: Government of India, 1901.

Griswold, Hervey DeWitt. *Insights into Modern Hinduism*. New York: Henry Holt and Company, 1934.

———. *Radha Swami Sect*. Cawnpore: Cawnpore Mission Press, 1907.

———. "The Radha Swami Sect" (in Urdu). In *Nur Afshan*. Ludhiana: n.p., n.d.

———. "Radha Swami Sect in India." In *The East and the West* (1908).

Harper, Henry. *Gurus, Swamis, and Avatars*. Philadelphia: Westminster Press, 1972.

Hauserman, Ray A., Jr., and Constance Loveland. *Ocean in a Teacup: The Story of Sree Sree Thakur Anukul Chandra*. New York: Harper and Row, 1962.

Hit Ki Bat (in Hindi). Gwalior: Shabd Pratap Satsang, n.d.

Hummel, Reinhart. *Indische Mission und neue Frömmigkeit im Westen*. Stuttgart: Kohlhammer, 1980.

Huzur Data Dyal: Pavitra Jivan Charitra. (in Hindi). Gwalior: n.p., n.d. Anonymous biography of Sham Lal.

Irwin, Sudha. "Work and Worship Fill Days in Dera." *National Georgraphic School Bulletin* 53, no. 12 (November 25, 1974): 179–83.

Johnson, Julian. *The Call of the East: The Autobiography of an American Surgeon*. Beas: The Sawan Service League, 1936.

———. *The Path of the Masters: The Science of Surat Shabd Yoga*. Beas: Radha Soami Satsang, Beas, 1975. Orig pub. 1939.

———. *The Unquenchable Flame: Biographical Sketches of Elizabeth Rose Bruce, Sometimes Called "The Woman of Destiny."* Beas: The Five Rivers Manufacturing Company, 1935.

———. *With a Great Master in India*. Beas: Radhasoami Satsang, Beas, 1971. Orig. pub. 1934.

Jones, Kenneth W. *Socio-Religious Reform Movements in British India* (The New Cambridge History of India, vol. 3:1). Cambridge: Cambridge University Press, 1989, pp. 72–77, 189–92.

Judgement in Civil Suit No.1 of 1943 (Agra) Delivered by Shri Prakash Chandra, P.C.S. 2nd. Addl. Civil Judge, Agra. Agra: Radhasoami Satsang Sabha, Dayalbagh, 1961.

Juergensmeyer, Mark. "Patterns of Pluralism: Sikh Relations with Radhasoami." In Joseph T. O'Connell, et al., eds., *Sikh History and Religion in the Twentieth Century*. Toronto: Centre for South Asian Studies, University of Toronto, 1988, pp. 52–69.

———. "Political Hope: Scheduled Caste Social Movements in the Punjab, 1900–1970." Ph.D. dissertation, Department of Political Science, University of California, Berkeley, 1974.

———. "Radhasoami and the Return of Religion." In *Religion as Social Vision: The Movement Against Untouchability in 20th Century Punjab*. Berkeley: University of California Press, 1982.

———. "Radhasoami as a Trans-National Movement." In Jacob Needleman and George Baker, eds., *Understanding the New Religions*, pp. 190–200. New York: Seabury, 1979.

———. "The Radhasoami Revival of the Sant Tradition." In Karine Schomer and W. H. McLeod, eds., *The Sants: Studies in a Devotional Tradition of India*, pp. 329–55. Berkeley: Berkeley Religious Studies Series; Delhi: Motilal Banarsidass, 1986.

———. "Radhasoami Satsang." In *The Encyclopaedia Britannica*. Chicago: Encyclopedia Britannica, 15th edition, 1986, Micropeadia, vol. 9, p. 885.

———. "Radhasoami Satsang." In *Encyclopedia of Asian History*. New York: Macmillan, 1988, vol. 3, p. 317.

Kakar, Sudhir. "The Path of the Saints." In *Shamans, Mystics and Doctors*, pp. 119–50. Boston: Beacon Press, 1982.

———. "Psychoanalysis and Religious Healing: Siblings or Strangers?" *Journal of the American Academy of Religion* 53, no. 4 (December 1985): 841–53.

Kamal, B. R., ed. *The Master Speaks to the Foreigners: Seekers from Abroad*. Hoshiarpur: Faqir Library Charitable Trust, n.d. (c. 1979).

Kapur, Daryai Lal. *Call of the Great Master*. 5th ed. Beas: Radhasoami Satsang, Beas, 1978. Orig. pub. in 1964.

———. *Heaven on Earth*. Beas: Radhasoami Satsang, Beas, 1986.

Kaur, Harbhajan. "The Sound of Naam." *Ruhani Newsletter*, September–October 1975, pp. 50–52.

Khanna, Radha Krishna. "At the Feet of the Great Hazur." *Sat Sandesh*, April 1978 and July 1978.

———. "The Master's Master." *Sat Sandesh*, July 1978.

———. *Truth Eternal: The True Nature of Soamiji's Teachings on Sant Mat, the 'Radhasoami Faith'*. New Delhi: privately published, 1961.

Lane, David Christopher. "The Enchanted Land, Part I." *Fate*, October 1984, pp. 66–73.

———. "The Hierarchical Structure of Religious Visions." *Journal of Transpersonal Psychology* 15, no. 1 (1983): 51–60.

———. *The Making of a Spiritual Movement: The Untold Story of Paul Twitchell and Eckankar*. Del Mar, Calif.: Del Mar Press, 1983.

———. "The Politics of Guru Successorship." Ph.D. dissertation, Department of Sociology, University of California, San Diego, 1991.

———. "Radhasoami Mat: Parampara in Definition and Classification." M.A. dissertation, Graduate Theological Union, 1981.

———. "The Radiant Road to Deception: A Case Study of Dr. Bhagat Singh Thind's Plagiarism." *Understanding Cults and Spiritual Movements* 2, nos. 2–3 (1987), pp. 20–23.

———. "The Reluctant Guru: The Life and Work of Baba Faqir Chand." *The Laughing Man* 3, no. 1, pp. 70–77.

———. *The Unknowing Sage: The Life and Work of Baba Faqir Chand.* Hoshiarpur: Manavta Mandir, 1989.

Lattin, Don. "The Cloud Over Indian Guru's U. S. Tour." *San Francisco Chronicle*, July 23, 1988.

Leeming, John M. Jr. Foreword to Sawan Singh (Huzur Maharaj-ji), *Philosophy of the Masters.* Abr. Beas: Radhasoami Satsang, Beas, 1973. Orig. pub. 1943.

———. *Yoga and the Bible: The Yoga of the Divine Word.* Beas: Radhasoami Satsang, Beas, 1963.

Maheshwari, Nirmal Das, et al. *Sant Das Ji* (in Hindi). Unpublished manuscript. n.d.

Maheshwari, Sant Das. *Bhaktmal of the Radhasoami Faith.* Agra: Radhasoami Satsang, Soamibagh, 1979. Orig. pub. in Hindi, 1949.

———. *Biography of Babuji Maharaj.* Agra: Radhasoami Satsang, Soamibagh, 1971.

———. *Biography of Buaji Saheba.* Agra: Mrs. S. D. Maheshwari, Publisher, 1983.

———. *Biography of Huzur Maharaj.* Agra: Radhasoami Satsang, Soamibagh, 1971.

———. *A Brief Description of Radhasoami Faith and a Short Note on the Holy Samadh of Soamiji Maharaj, The August Founder of the Faith, Under Construction.* 3d ed. Agra: Radhasoami Satsang, Soamibagh, 1978.

———. "Correspondence Exchanged Between the Secretary, Soamibagh, Agra (India) and a Follower of the Beas Group, Mr. Harvey H. Myers, California, U.S.A." In Shiv Dayal Singh et al., *Holy Epistles and Other Sacred Writings*, vol. 1, pp. 384–415. Ed. and transl. S. D. Maheshwari. Agra: Radhasoami Satsang, Soamibagh, 1964.

———. *Correspondence with Certain Americans During Interregnum Following the Departure of Babuji Maharaj.* 6 vols. Agra: Radhasoami Satsang, Soamibagh, 1960 (vols. 1–5), 1985 (vol. 6).

———. *Glossary of Radhasoami Faith.* Agra: Radhasoami Satsang, Soamibagh, 1967.

———. *Let Them Speak the Truth: Some Questions Addressed to the Dayalbagh Group of the Radhasoami Faith with a View to Bringing Out Self-Contradictions and Inconsistencies in Their Teachings of the Faith as Well as Distortions of and Deviations from the Original Teachings.* Agra: Radhasoami Satsang, Soamibagh, 1982.

———. *Param Sant Tulsi Saheb.* Agra: Radhasoami Satsang, Soamibagh, 1979.

———. *Radhasoami Faith: History and Tenets.* Agra: Radhasoami Satsang, Soamibagh, 1954.

Maheshwari, Sant Das. *Sants, Sadhs, Mahatmas and Devotees of the Past (Their Short Biographical Sketches)*. Agra: Radhasoami Satsang, Soamibagh, 1980. Orig. pub. as *Nutan Bhaktmal* (in Hindi), 1950.

———. *Radhasoami Faith: History and Tenets*, Agra: Radhasoami Satsang, Soamibagh, 1954.

———. *Thesis on a Thesis*. Agra: Radhasoami Satsang, Soamibagh, n.d.

———. *Truth Unvarnished*. 2 vols. Agra: Radhasoami Satsang, Soamibagh, 1970.

Mand, Jasmeet. "Social Aspects of Radhasoami Satsang." M. A. dissertation, Department of Sociology, Punjab University, Chandigargh, 1979.

Mangalawali, Vishal. *The World of Gurus*. New Delhi: Vikas Publishing House 1977.

Marshall, Anne. *Hunting the Guru in India*. London: Victor Gollancz, 1963.

Mathur, Agam Prasad. (Dada-ji Sahib). *Jivan Charitra, Param Purush Paran Dhani Lala Ji Maharaj Rai Ajudhia Prasad Ji Sahib* (in Hindi). Agra: Huzuri Bhavan, Peepalmandi, 1967. Biography of Ajudhia Prasad.

———. *Radhasoami Faith: A Historical Study*. Delhi: Vikas Publishing House, 1974.

Mehta, Gurcharandas. Introduction to Anand Swarup, *Yathartha Prakash*. Agra: Radhasoami Satsang, Dayalbagh, 1954.

Misra, Pitambar. *Divya Charitamrit* (in Hindi). New Delhi: Architect Sudarshan Kumar Chopra, 1973.

Moeller, Volker. "Der Rādhāsvāmī-Satsang und die Mystik der Gottestöne." Ph.D. Diss., Tübingen, 1956.

Müller, Max. *The Life and Sayings of Ramakrishna*. New York: Charles Scribner's Sons, 1899.

O'Malley L.S.S. *Popular Hinduism: The Religion of the Masses*. London: Cambridge University Press, 1935.

Patanjali, V. "The Radhasoami." *Illustrated Weekly of India* 90, no. 46 (November 16, 1969): 8–13.

Pavitra Jivan Charitra: Param Parush Dhani Sant Sangam Hazur Data Dyal (in Hindi). Gwalior: Shabd Pratap Satsang, 1944. Sacred life history of Shyam Lal Gupta.

Perkins, Russell. *The Impact of a Saint: Meetings with Kirpal Singh and Ajaib Singh, 1963–76*. Sanbornton, N.H.: Sant Bani Ashram, 1980.

———. Introduction to Kirpal Singh, *The Night is a Jungle and Other Discourses*. Sanbornton, N.H.: Sant Bani Ashram, 1974.

———. Introduction to *The Ocean of Love: The Anurag Sagar of Kabir*. Trans. Raj Kumar Bagga. Ed. Russell Perkins. Sanbornton, N.H.: Sant Bani Ashram, 1982.

Pfeifer, Netta. *A Soul's Safari*. 2d ed., enl. Beas: Radhasoami Satsang, Beas, 1981. Orig. pub. 1978.

Phelps, Myron H. *Notes of Discourses on Radhasoami Faith Delivered by Babuji Maharaj in 1913–14*. Agra: Radhasoami Satsang, Soamibagh, 1947.

Prasad, Ajudhia. *Jivan Charitra: Param Purush Puran Dhani Huzur Maharaj Sahib Radhaswami Dayal Ali Janab Rai Saligram Sahib Rai Bahadur* (in Hindi),

Agra: Agam Prasad [Mathur], Huzuri Bhavan, Peepalmandi, n.d. orig. pub. 1908. Biography of Rai Saligram.

Pratt, James Bisset. "Radhasoamis and Theosophists." In *India and Its Faiths: A Traveler's Record*. London: Constable and Co., 1916.

Puri, Janak Raj. *Tulsi Sahib: Saint of Hathras*. Beas: Radhasoami Satsang, Beas, 1978.

Puri, Lekh Raj. *Mysticism: The Spiritual Path*. 2 vols. 4th ed. Beas: Radhasoami Satsang, Beas, 1974.

———. *Radha Swami Teachings*. 2d ed. Beas: Radhasoami Satsang, Beas, 1972. Orig. pub. 1965.

———. *Teachings of the Gurus*. 2d ed. Beas: Radhasoami Satsang, Beas, 1978. Orig. pub. 1973.

Radhasoami Educational Institute. *Prospectus for 1918, Report for 1917*. Hyderabad, Sind: R.H. Advani and Co., 1918.

Radhasoami Satsang, Beas. Annual Reports, 1963–1984.

———. *Eye Camp Administrative Instructions*. Beas: Radhasoami Satsang, Beas, 1973, 1975.

———. *Memorandum: Rules and Regulations of Association of Radhasoami Satsang, Beas*. Beas: Radhasoami Satsang, Beas, 1968.

———. *Radha Soami Satsang, Beas: Origin and Growth*. Beas: Radhasoami Satsang, Beas, n.d. (c. 1972).

———. *Teachings and Brief History*. Beas: Radhasoami Satsang, Beas, 1977.

Radhasoami Satsang, Dayalbagh. *Dayalbagh (Agra): A Brief Description of the Origins, Early History and Development of the Colony and its Institutions*. Agra: Radhasoami Satsang, Dayalbagh, 1984. Orig. pub. 1928.

———. *Huzur Sahabji Maharaj—Sir Anand Sarup—As Others Saw Him—A Collection of Opinions about the Personality and Work of His Holiness Huzur Sahabji Maharaj by Individuals and Newspapers, etc.* 2d ed. Agra: Radhasoami Satsang Sabha, Dayalbagh, 1966.

———. *Review of Progress Made by Satsang Institutions During the Last Ten Years (1975–1984)*. Supplement to the *Dayalbagh Herald*, August 13, 1985.

———. *Sahabji Maharaj As Others Saw Him*. Agra: Radhasoami Satsang Sabha, Dayalbagh, 1969. Personal Accounts of Anand Swarup.

———. *Souvenir in Commemoration of the First Centenary of the Radhasomi Satsang (1861–1961)*. Agra: Radhasoami Satsang Sabha, Dayalbagh, 1962.

Radhasoami Satsang Sabha, Ghazipur. *Constitutional Principles Underlying the Inauguration of the System of Administration of the Radhasoami Satsang Affairs by an Elected Council*. Ghazipur: Radhasoami Satsang Sabha, Ghazipur, 1910.

Ram, Rai Sahib Munshi. *With the Three Masters*. 3 vols. Beas: Radhasoami Satsang, Beas, 1967.

Rasulpuri, Ram Rijhand. *Yug Purush aur Yug Dharam* (in Hindi). Muzufurnagar: Swastiprakashand, 1956.

Sanders, C. W. *The Inner Voice*. 8th ed., rev. Beas: Radhasoami Satsang, Beas, 1983. Orig. pub. 1948.

Saralkumari. *Radhasvami Sampraday aur Sahitya* (in Hindi) Delhi: Oriental Publishers, 1971.

Sasmas, Kehr Singh. "The Dawn of Spirituality in the West." Trans. and intro. Bhadra Sena. *Sat Sandesh*, April 1977, pp. 23–31.

Science of Spirituality: Sawan Kirpal Ruhani Mission. Bowling Green, Va.: Sawan Kirpal Publications, n.d.

Sena, Bhadra, ed. *Sant Kirpal Singh Ji Maharaj—The Ocean of Grace Divine*. Trans. Vinod Sena. Delhi: Ruhani Satsang, 1976.

Seth, Pratap Singh. *Biography of Soamiji Maharaj*. Agra: Radhasoami Satsang, Soamibagh, 1978. Orig. pub. in Hindi, 1902.

———. *Hazur Maharaj Baba Bagga Singh Ji, Janamsakhi*, (in Punjabi), Tarn Taran, Punjab: Radhasoami Tarn Taran, n.d. Life story of Bagga Singh.

Sethi, Shanti. *Message Divine*. Beas: Radhasoami Satsang, Beas, 1973.

Sharma, Ishwar Chandra. *Sidha Satpurusha Faqir Baba* (in Hindi; biography of Faqir Chand). Hoshiarpur: Manavta Mandir, 1985.

Singh, Khushwant, ed. *Gurus, Godmen, and Good People*. Bombay: Orient Longman, 1975.

———. "Radhasoami Satsang." In *Encyclopedia Britannica*. Chicago: University of Chicago Press, 1980.

Singh, Kirpal. *A Brief Life Sketch of Hazur Baba Sawan Singh-Ji Maharaj*. New Delhi: Ruhani Satsang, 1949.

———. *A Great Saint, Baba Jaimal Singh: His Life and Teachings*. New Delhi: Ruhani Satsang, 1960.

Singh, [Lala] Pratap. *Biography of Soamiji Maharaj*. Trans. S. D. Maheshwari. Agra: Radhasoami Satsang, Soamibagh, 1968. Orig. pub. in Hindi, 1902.

Sinnett, A. P. *Esoteric Buddhism*. San Diego: Wizard's Bookshop, 1981. Orig. pub. 1885.

Sinnett, A. P. *The Occult World*. London: Truebner and Co., 1884.

Sipchen, Bob, and David Johnston, "John-Roger." *Los Angeles Times*, August 14–15, 1988.

Srivastava, Kuber Nath. *Realisation of "The Reality."* Hoshiarpur: Manavata Mandir, 1978.

Stone, Randolph. *Mystic Bible*. Beas: Radhasoami Satsang, Beas, 1956.

Talsky, M. Aaron. "The Radhasoami Tradition: Charismatic Routinization and Its Doctrinal Consequences." Unpublished senior thesis, University of Michigan, 1986.

Thind, Bhagat Singh. *The Pearl of Greatest Price, or Nam-Rattan*. Hollywood, Calif.: published by author, 1958.

———. *The Radiant Road to Reality*. New York: published by author, 1939.

Tillis, Malcolm. *Emergence of a New Master, Darshan Singh*. Delhi: Kirpal Printing Press, 1975.

Tillis, Malcolm and Cynthia Giles, eds. *Turning East: New Lives in India, Westerners and Their Spiritual Quests*. New York: Paragon House, 1989.

Tulsi Sahib. *Ghat Ramayana* (in Hindi). Allahabad: Belvedere Press, 1911.

———. *Tulsi Sahib Hatras Wale-ki Shabdwali aur Jivan-Charitra* (in Hindi). 2 vols. Allahabad: Belvedere Press, 1903.

———. *Tulsi Sahib—Saint of Hathras.* Trans. Janak Raj Puri. Punjab: Radhasoami Satsang Beas, 1978.

Uban, Sujan Singh. *The Gurus of India.* London: Fine Books Oriental, 1977.

Wason, Katherine. *The Living Master.* 4th ed., Beas: Radhasoami Satsang, Beas, 1979. Orig. pub. 1966.

White, Stanley. *Liberation of the Soul.* 3d rev. ed., Beas: Radhasoami Satsang, Beas, 1975.

D. Writings of the Radhasoami Masters

[Note: This listing includes only works by acknowledged Radhasoami masters, in English translation when available, written during their tenures of office. Writings about them, interviews with them, writings by them before they assumed office, and writings by them in a nonspiritual capacity are included in the general listing of books on Radhasoami.

Chand, Faqir (Dayal Faqir). *Be Man.* Aligarh: Faqir Sahitya Praka shan, 1956.

——— (H. H. Param Dayal Faqir Sahibji Maharaj). *Independence Day Messages from 1947 to 1962.* Ed. M. L. Govila Vishwa Premi. Aligarh: Be Man Hindi Monthly Magazine, Dayal Compound, 1963.

——— (His Holiness Param Sant Param Dayal Pandit Faqir Chand Ji Maharaj). *Jeevan Mukti (Liberation in Life).* Trans. B. R. Kamal. Hoshiarpur: Faqir Library Charitable Trust, n.d.

———. *Key to Freedom by a True Faqir.* Trans. R.S.S.N. Mathur. Aligarh: Be Man Hindi Monthly Magazine, Dayal Compound, 1963.

———. *Manavta: The True Religion.* Trans. B. R. Kamal. Hoshiarpur: Faqir Library Charitable Trust, n.d.

———. *The Master Speaks to the Foreigners, Seekers from Abroad.* Ed. B. R. Kamal. Hoshiarpur: Faqir Library Charitable Trust, 1978.

——— (His Holiness Param Sant Param Dayal Pandit Faqir Chand Ji Maharaj). *The Secret of Secrets.* Trans. B. R. Kamal. Hoshiarpur: Faqir Library Charitable Trust, n.d.

———. *Truth Always Wins—Satyameva Jayte.* Ed. B. R. Kamal. Hoshiarpur: Manavta Mandir, 1974.

——— (His Holiness Param Sant Param Dayal Pandit Faqir Chand Ji Maharaj). *A Word to Americans.* Ed. I. C. Sharma. Hoshiarpur: Faqir Library Charitable Trust, n.d.

——— (His Holiness Param Sant Param Dayal Pandit Faqir Chand Ji Maharaj). *A Word to Canadians.* Ed. P. N. Roy. Hoshiarpur: Faqir Library Charitable Trust, n.d.

Lal, Shyam (Lala Shyam Lal Ji Sahib). *Retransformation of Self.* 2d ed., rev. Gwalior: Shabda Pratap Satsang, 1957. Orig. pub. 1927.

Lal, Swami Ram Bihari. *The Way Out—Is In.* Oak Grove, Calif.: Grove Press, 1958. Orig. pub. as *True and Practical Divine Knowledge.* Delhi: Sarai Rohilla, n.d.

Mathur, Agam Prasad (Dada-ji Sahib). *Amrit Bachan Radhasoami* (in Hindi). Transcribed by I. C. Gupta. Agra: Huzuri Bhavan, Peepalmandi, 1980.

Mehta, Gurcharandas (Param Guru Huzur Mehtaji Maharaj). *Selected Bachans.* Agra: Radhasoami Satsang Sabha, Dayalbagh, 1984.

Misra, Brahm Sankar (Maharaj Sahib). *Discourses of Maharaj Saheb.* Trans. S. D. Maheshwari. Agra: Radhasoami Satsang, Soamibagh, 1978.

——— (Maharaj Sahib). *Discourses on Radhasoami Faith.* 5th ed. Agra: Radhasoami Satsang, Dayalbagh, 1973. First English ed. 1960.

——— (Maharaj Sahib). *A Solace to Satsangis: Being a Collection of Letters of Consolation and Advice Written By Maharaj Sahib to Outstation Satsangis after the Departure of Huzur Maharj.* 2d ed. Agra: Radhasoami Satsang, Soamibagh, 1952.

Saligram, Rai (Param Purush Puran Dhani Huzur Maharaj). *Catechism on Sant Mat or Radhasoami Faith.* Trans. S. D. Maheshwari from notes taken by an anonymous satsangi and approved by Rai Saligram. Agra: Radhasoami Satsang, Soamibagh, 1969.

Saligram, Rai (Huzur Maharaj). *Guru Updesh.* Trans. S. D. Maheshwari. Agra: Radhasoami Satsang, Soamibagh, 1969.

——— (Huzur Maharaj). *Jugat Prakash Radhasoami—A Guide for the Practitioners of Surat Shabd Yoga of the Radhasoami Faith.* Trans. S. D. Maheshwari. Agra: Radhasoami Satsang, Soamibagh, 1964.

——— (Param Purush Puran Dhani Huzur Maharaj). *Nij Updesh Radhasoami.* Trans. S. D. Maheshwari, Agra: Radhasoami Satsang, Soamibagh, 1969.

——— (Huzur Maharaj). *Param Sant Tulsi Saheb (of Hatras): His Short Biographical Sketch and The Inner Meaning of His Hymns and Portions of His Ghat Ramayan Given at the End of Prem Patra Rahasoami vol. VI.* Trans. S. D. Maheshwari. Agra: Radhasoami Satsang, Soamibagh, 1979.

——— (Huzur Maharaj). Preface to Shiv Dayal Singh (Radhasoami Saheb), *Sar Bachan Radhasoami: Poetry.* Trans. S. D. Maheshwari. Agra: Radhasoami Satsang, Soamibagh, 1970. Orig. pub. in Hindi. Allahabad: Prayag Press Company, 1884.

——— (Param Purush Puran Dhani Huzur Maharaj). *Prem Bani Radhasoami.* 4 vols. Trans. S. D. Maheshwari. Agra: Radhasoami Satsang, Soamibagh, 1980.

——— (Param Purush Puran Dhani Huzur Maharaj). *Prem Patra Radhasoami.* Trans. S. D. Maheshwari. Agra: Radhasoami Satsang, Soamibagh, 1960.

——— (Param Purush Puran Dhani Huzur Maharaj). *Prem Updesh Radhasoami ("Radhasoami's Message and Teaching of Love"), Being Extracts from Letters Written by Huzur Maharaj to Satsangis During the Interregnum Following the Departure of Soamiji Maharaj in 1878.* Trans. S. D. Maheshwari. Agra: Radhasoami Satsang, Soamibagh, 1963.

——— (Huzur Maharaj). *Radhasoami Mat Prakash or A Brief View of Radhasoami Faith—Being a Message of Eternal Peace and Joy to All Nations.* 5th ed. Agra: Radhasoami Satsang, Soamibagh, 1959.

——— (Param Sant Sat Guru Huzur Maharaj). *Sant Sangrah* (A collection of sants). 2 vols. Trans. S. D. Maheshwari. Agra: Radhasoami Satsang, Soamibagh, 1971.

——— (Param Purush Puran Dhani Huzur Maharaj). *Sar Updesh Radhasoami.* Trans. S. D. Maheshwari. Agra: Radhasoami Satsang, Soamibagh, 1969.

Singh, Charan (Maharaj Charan Singh Ji). *Light on Saint Matthew*. Beas: Radhasoami Satsang, Beas, 1978.

——— (Maharaj Charan Singh Ji). *Light on Sant Mat*. 4th ed. Trans. Jagmohan Lal, Janak Raj Puri, and Sardar Daryai Lal. Beas: Radha Soami Satsang, Beas, 1974.

——— (Maharaj Charan Singh Ji). *The Master Answers to Audiences in America*. 3d. ed., rev. Beas: Radhasoami Satsang, Beas, 1973. Orig. pub. 1966.

——— (Maharaj Charan Singh Ji). *The Path*. 2d ed., Beas: Radhasoami Satsang, Beas, 1983. Orig. pub. 1969.

——— (Maharaj Charan Singh Ji). *St. John, The Great Mystic*. Beas: Radhasoami Satsang, Beas, 1970.

——— (Maharaj Charan Singh Ji). *Spiritual Heritage*. Beas: Radhasoami Satsang, Beas, 1983.

Singh, Darshan. *The Challenge of Inner Space*. Bowling Green, Va.: Sawan Kirpal Publications, 1984.

———. *The Cry of the Soul: Mystic Poetry*. Bowling Green, Va.: Sawan Kirpal Publications, 1977.

———. Introduction to *Portrait of Perfection: A Pictorial Biography of Kirpal Singh*. Bowling Green, Va. and Delhi: Sawan Kirpal Publications, 1981.

———. *The Secret of Secrets: Spiritual Talks*. Bowling Green, Va., and Delhi: Sawan Kirpal Publications, 1978.

———. *Spiritual Awakening*. Bowling Green, Va.: Sawan Kirpal Publications, 1982.

———. *Talash-i Nur* (The search for light; in Urdu). New Delhi: Sawan Kirpal Ruhani Mission, 1980. Orig. pub. 1965.

———. *A Tear and a Star*. Bowling Green, Va.: Sawan Kirpal Publications, 1986.

Singh, Darshan, and Robert Muller. *Ambassadors of Peace: A Dialogue at the United Nations between Dr. Robert Muller and Sant Darshan Singh*. Ed. Arthur Stein. Costa Rica: University for Peace, 1988.

Singh, Jagat (Maharaj Sardar Bahadur). *Science of the Soul*. Beas: Radhasoami Satsang, Beas, 1972

Singh, Jaimal (Baba Ji Maharaj). *Spiritual Letters from Jaimal Singh Ji Maharaj*. 4th ed. Trans. Jagmohan Lal. Beas: Radhasoami Satsang, Beas, 1958.

Singh, Kirpal. *A Brief Life Sketch of Hazur Baba Sawan Singh-Ji Maharaj*. New Delhi: Ruhani Satsang, 1949.

———. *The Crown of Life—A Study in Yoga*. 3d ed. Anaheim, Calif.: Ruhani Satsang, Divine Science of the Soul, 1980. Orig. pub. Delhi, 1961.

———. *Godman: Finding a Spiritual Master*. New Delhi: Ruhani Satsang, 1971.

———. *A Great Saint, Baba Jaimal Singh: His Life and Teachings*. Delhi: Ruhani Satsang, 1973.

———. *Heart-to-Heart Talks*. 2 vols. New Delhi: Ruhani Satsang, 1975, 1976.

———. *Instructions for Holding Satsang*. Circular Letter no. 4, December 1956.

———. *The Jap Ji: The Message of Guru Nanak*. 2d. ed. Delhi: Ruhani Satsang, Sawan Ashram, 1964.

———. *Man, Know Thyself: Being a Talk Given by Sant Kirpal Singh Ji for Seek-*

ers After Truth. Bowling Green, Va.: Sawan Kirpal Publications, 1980. Orig. pub. in 1954.

———. *Morning Talks, 1967–68*. 4th ed., Bowling Green, Va.: Sawan Kirpal Publications, 1981. Orig. pub. 1970.

———. *Naam or Word*. Bowling Green, Va.: Sawan Kirpal Publications, 1981. Orig. pub. 1960.

———. *The Night Is a Jungle, and Other Discourses*. Sanbornton, N.H.: Sant Bani Ashram, 1974.

———. *Portrait of Perfection: A Pictorial Biography of Kirpal Singh*, Bowling Green, Va. and Delhi: Sawan Kirpal Publications, 1981. A collection of writings, transcribed utterances, and photographs.

———. *Prayer: Its Nature and Technique*. 4th ed., Bowling Green, Va.: Sawan Kirpal Publications, 1981. Orig. pub. 1959.

———. *Spiritual Elixir*. Delhi: Ruhani Satsang, 1972.

Singh, Kirpal. *Spirituality: What It Is*. 5th ed., Bowling Green, Va.: Sawan Kirpal Publications, 1982. Orig. pub. 1959.

———. *The Teachings of Kirpal Singh: 3 Volumes Complete in 1 Book*. Bowling Green, Va.: Sawan Kirpal Publications, 1981. Part 1 orig. pub. as *The Holy Path*, 1974; Part 2 as *Self-Introspection and Meditation*, 1975; Part 3 as *The New Life*, 1976.

———. *The Way of the Saints, Sant Mat: Collected Short Writings of Kirpal Singh*. Sanbornton, N.H.: Sant Bani Ashram, 1976.

———. *The Wheel of Life and the Mystery of Death: Two Books by Kirpal Singh*. Kinderhook, N.Y.: Kirpal Light Satsang, 1986.

Singh, Sawan (Huzur Maharaj). *Discourses on Sant Mat*. 2d. ed. Beas: Radhasoami Satsang, Beas, 1970.

——— (Huzur Maharaj). Introduction to Jaimal Singh, *Spiritual Letters from Jaimal Singh Ji Maharaj, 1896–1903*, Beas: Radhasoami Satsang, Beas, 1958.

——— (Huzur Maharaj). *My Submission*. 2d ed. Beas: Radhasoami Satsang, Beas, 1977.

——— (Huzur Maharaj). *Philosophy of the Masters*. 5 vols. Beas: Radhasoami Satsang, Beas, 1977. Orig. pub. in Hindi, 1943.

——— (Huzur Maharaj). *Philosophy of the Masters*. Abr. John H. Leeming Jr. Trans. R. D. Ahluwalia, T. C. Aggarwal, et al. Punjab: Radhasoami Satsang, Beas, 1973. Orig. pub. in 1943.

——— (Huzur Maharaj). *Spiritual Gems—Extracts from Letters to Seekers And Disciples*. 3d. ed. Punjab: Radhasoami Satsang, Beas, 1976.

——— (Huzur Maharaj Ji). *Tales of the Mystic East*. 4th ed. Trans. Joseph Leeming and K. L. Khanna. Punjab: Radhasoami Satsang, Beas, 1977.

Singh, Shiv Dayal (Soamiji Maharaj). *Elucidation of Japji*. Trans. S. D. Maheshwari. Agra: Radhasoami Satsang, Soamibagh, 1975. Orig. pub. 1960 in Hindi, from notes said to have been dictated in 1877.

——— (Param Purush Puran Dhani Huzur Soamiji Maharaj). *Sar Bachan Radhasoami: Poetry* (in Hindi). 2 vols. Ed. Rai Saligram (Huzur Maharaj). Allahabad: Rayag Press Company, 1884. Trans. S. D. Maheshwari. Agra: Radhasoami Satsang, Soamibagh, 1970.

——— (Param Purush Puran Dhani Huzur Soamiji Maharaj). *Sar Bachan Radhasoami: Prose* (in Hindi). Allahabad: Rayag Press Company, 1884. Trans. S. D. Maheshwari (Agra: Radhasoami Satsang, Soamibagh, 1958), Sewa Singh (Beas: Radhasoami Satsang, Beas, 1934, rev. 1955), and an anonymous translator (Agra: Radhasoami Satsang Sabha, Dayalbagh, 1959).

Singh, Shiv Dayal (Soamiji Maharaj), and Rai Saligram (Huzur Maharaj). *Last Discourse of Soamiji Maharaj, and Letters of Soamiji Maharaj and Huzur Maharaj.* Trans. S. D. Maheshwari, Agra: Radhasoami Satsang, Soamibagh, 1960.

——— (Soamiji Maharaj), and Rai Saligram (Huzur Maharaj). *Niyamawali—Containing Shabds (Hymns) from Sar Bachan Radhasoami (Poetry) and Prem Bani Radhasoami.* Trans. S. D. Maheswari. Agra: Radhasoami Satsang, Soamibagh, 1969.

Singh, Shiv Dayal (Soamiji Maharaj), Rai Saligram (Huzur Maharaj), Brahm Sankar Misra (Maharaj Saheb), and Madho Prasad Sinha (Babuji Maharaj). *Holy Epistles and Other Sacred Writings.* 2 vols. Ed. and trans. S. D. Maheshwari. Agra: Radhasoami Satsang, Soamibagh, 1964.

Singh, Thakar. *And You Will Fly Up To God: A Collection of Talks.* Kinderhook, N.Y.: Kirpal Light Satsang, 1982.

———. *Gospel of Love.* Delhi: Ruhani Satsang, 1984.

Sinha, Kamta Prasad (Sarkar Sahab). *Four Letters from the Pen of His Holiness Huzur Sarkar Sahab.* Agra: Radhasoami Satsang Sabha, Dayalbagh, 1983. Orig. pub. 1938.

Sinha, Madhav Prasad (Babuji Maharaj). *Discourses of Babuji Maharaj.* 5 vols. Trans. S. D. Maheshwari. Agra: Radhasoami Satsang, Soamibagh, 1974–1978.

——— (Babuji Maharaj). *Notes of Discourses on Radhasoami Faith Delivered by Babuji Maharaj in 1913–1914 as Taken by a Satsangi, Mr. Myron H. Phelps.* 2d ed. Agra: Radhasoami Satsang, Soamibagh, 1947.

——— (Babuji Maharaj). "Questions and Answers." In *Holy Epistles and Other Sacred Writings*, vol. 1, pp. 465–76. Trans. S. D. Maheshwari. Agra: Radhasoami Satsang, Soamibagh, 1964.

——— (Param Purush Puran Dhani Babuji Maharaj). *Teachings of Radhasoami Faith Based on Babuji Maharaj's Discourses.* Trans. S. D. Maheshwari. Agra: Radhasoami Satsang, Soamibagh, 1960.

Swarup, Anand (Sahabji Maharaj). *Diary of Sahabji Maharaj (1930–31).* 2 vols. Dayalbagh: Radhasoami Satsang Sabha, Dayalbagh, 1973.

——— (Sahabji Maharaj). *Radhasoami Mat Darsana (Exposition of the Radhasoami Faith).* Trans. under the authority of the Radhasoami Satsang Sabha, Dayalbagh. Agra: Radhasoami Satsang Sabha, Dayalbagh, 1960.

——— (Sahibji Maharaj). *Table-Talk of Param Guru Huzur Sahabji Maharaj.* Trans. under the authority of the Radhasoami Satsang Sabha, Dayalbagh. Agra: Radhasoami Satsang Sabha, Dayalbagh, 1983. Orig. pub. 1930.

——— (Sahibji Maharaj). *Yathartha Prakasa.* Trans. under the authority of the

Radhasoami Satsang Sabha, Dayalbagh. Agra: Radhasoami Satsang Sabha, Dayalbagh, 1954.

E. *Radhasoami* Journals and Newspapers

Dayalbagh Herald. Weekly publication of the Dayalbagh Press, Agra.

Harbinger. Quarterly journal of the Radhasoami Satsang Association of North America (Dayalbagh).

Prem Patra. Fortnightly periodical published under the leadership of Rai Saligram.

Radhasoami Greetings (previously published as *R. S. Greetings* by Seva Trust and R. S. Books, Oak Park, Illinois). Quarterly publication of the North American Sangat, Radhasoami Satsang, Beas, in Washington, D.C. No volume numbers listed.

Sat Sandesh. Published monthly in Urdu and Hindi by Sawan Kirpal Publications, Delhi, and in English by Sawan Kirpal Publications, Bowling Green, Va. No volume numbers listed.

Where Masters Walk. Series of brochures published by the South African Sangat of the Radhasoami Satsang, Beas, in Durban, South Africa (no date; c. 1979).

F. Interviews and Correspondence

Balley, Lahori Ram, Ambedkar Mission Society. Jalandhar, November 14, 1973.

Bhatnagar, G. S., devotee of Radhasoami Satsang, Dayalbagh. Dayalbagh, August 13, 1985.

Bhatnagar, Sudhir, member of Radhasoami Satsang, Soamibagh. San Jose, California, August 9, 1987.

Chand, Faqir, master of Manav Mandir. Hoshiarpur, August 19, 1978.

Chopra, S. P., office secretary, Kirpal Ashram. New Delhi, August 16, 1985.

Das, Baba Abhya, sadhu at Peepalmandi Ashram. Agra, August 12, 1985.

Das, Charan (Ray Angona), former resident of Soamibagh. By telephone, March 5, 1986.

Das, Sant Prakash, present master of Tulsi Sahib's ashram. Hathras, August 9, 1978.

deVries, Roland, representative of Master Charan Singh in the United States. Menlo Park, California, August 22, 1972; Nevada City, California, January 17, 1986; correspondence on November 13, 1974.

Goswamy, Srivatsa, spiritual leader of Jai Singh Ghera, Vrindaban. By telephone, January 27, 1991; February 9, 1991; March 1, 1991.

Gupta, B. L., leader of Dhara Sindhu Pratap Ashram. Gwalior, August 21, 1985.

Gupta, I. C., office manager, Huzuri Bhavan, Peepalmandi, Agra, August 10, 1983.

Harris, Shiela, devotee at Dera Baba Jaimal Singh. Beas, November 12, 1980.

Hogguel, Paul, resident of Huzur Bhavan Ashram, Peepalmandi. Agra, December 6, 1980.

Jadoun, Baba Ram, general secretary of Radhasoami Satsang Sabha, Dayalbagh. Agra, November 9, 1973.

Kapur, C. L., president of the Punjabi Bagh Satsang Ghar (a local branch of the Radhasoami Satsang, Beas). Delhi, November 29, 1986.

Kaur, Harbhajan, wife of Master Darshan Singh. Alexandria, Virginia, July 22, 1986.

Khanna, K. L., general secretary of Radhasoami Satsang, Beas. Dera Baba Jaimal Singh, Beas, May 25, 1971; May 26, 1971; written responses to my questions, May 25, 1971.

Khanna, Tejendra, Officer in the Indian Administrative Service and member of Radhasoami Satsang, Beas. Chandigarh, July 11, 1979, and January 22, 1988.

Lal, M. B., Master of Radhasoami Satsang, Dayalbagh. Agra, August 9, 1978; December 5, 1980; August 10, 1983; August 12, 1985; August 13, 1985.

Lane, David, San Clemente, California, August 14, 1988.

Maheshwari, Nirmal Das, officer in the Indian Administrative Service and son of Sant Das Maheshwari. New Delhi, December 1986.

Maheshwari, Sant Das, former secretary to Madhav Prasad Sinha and director of the Publications Office, Soamibagh. Soamibagh, Agra, July 14, 1978.

Mansukhani, Salina, former Miss India-USA and member of Radhasoami Satsang, Beas. Beas, November 12, 1986.

Mathur, Agam Prasad, professor of history, Agra College, and master of the Radhasoami Satsang, Huzuri Bhavan, Peepalmandi. Agra, August 8, 1978; December 6, 1980; August 10, 1983; August 12, 1985; August 13, 1985.

Mehta, R. N., head of the Delhi branch of the Radhasoami Satsang, Beas. Delhi, December 5, 1980; August 15, 1985; and January 20, 1988.

Moudgill, J. N., resident of Soaminagar. New Delhi, December 5, 1980.

Mukerji, S. C., manager of Radhasoami Bagh, Benares, August 19, 1985.

Nam, Grindhmuni, master of the Dharamdasi Order of Kabirpanthis. Raipur, August 23, 1985.

Narang, Kirpal Singh, head of Publications Office, Radhasoami Satsang, Beas. Beas, November 12, 1980.

Narang, Surjit Singh, professor of political science, Guru Nanak Dev University. Amritsar, August 10, 1979; January 13, 1991.

Naryanan, Kripal, devotee of the Radhasoami Satsang, Dayalbagh. Agra, August 13, 1985.

Nath, T., general secretary, Radhasoami Satsang Sabha, Dayalbagh. Agra, August 12, 1985.

Parsini, member of Radhasoami Satsang, Beas. Village Nalla, Ropar district, Punjab, October 10, 1971; August 4–5, 1979.

Prabhakar, Wazir Chand, resident of Soamibagh. Agra, August 10, 1983.

Price, John, guest at Dera Baba Jaimal Singh, Beas. Beas, November 12, 1980.

Puri, Janak Raj, Publications Office, Radhasoami Satsang, Beas. Beas, November 4, 1980.

Ram, Dalat, manager of Book Sales, Radhasoami Satsang, Beas, Delhi branch. New Delhi, August 15, 1985.

Ram, Sundar, head of Radhasoami Satsang, Beas, Nabha branch. Nabha, August 15, 1983.

Sadyanarayana, V., devotee of Radhasoami Satsang Sabha, Dayalbagh. Agra, August 13, 1985.

Sahgal, G. D., president, Radhasoami Satsang Sabha, Dayalbagh. Agra, August 6, 1985; August 12, 1985.

Salisbury, Phoenix, guest at Dera Baba Jaimal Singh, Beas. Beas, November 11, 1980.

Sandhurst, Emily, guest at Dera Baba Jaimal Singh, Beas. Beas, November 12, 1980.

Sethi, J. M., secretary, Sawan Kirpal Ruhani Mission. Correspondence on October 1, 1985; May 7, 1988; May 22, 1988; November 15, 1988.

Sharma, P. S., resident of Soamibagh. Agra, August 13, 1985.

Sharma, Yogesh, resident of Thakar Mansingh Ashram. Gwalior, August 21, 1985.

Sherry, Mrs. G. P., head of Dayalbagh Educational Institute. Agra, December 8, 1986.

Singh, Brajendra, private secretary to A. P. Mathur, Peepalmandi. Agra, August 12, 1985.

Singh, Charan, master of Radhasoami Satsang, Beas. Beas, August 4, 1978; August 11, 1979; November 11, 1980.

Singh, Darshan, master of Kirpal Ashram. New Delhi, August 16, 1985.

Singh, Pratap, master of Radhasoami Satsang, Tarn Taran. Tarn Taran, Punjab, November 10, 1980.

Singh, Sukhdev, professor of Hindi literature, Benares Hindu University. Benares, August 19, 1985.

Singh, Shri Ram, devotee at Radhasoami Satsang, Dayalbagh. Agra, August 13, 1985.

Sinha, Dr. Padam Adhar (Padam Babu), resident of Soamibagh and son of Madhav Prasad Sinha. Agra, January 17, 1988.

Sitaramayya, P., resident of Dayalbagh. Agra, August 13, 1985.

Smith, Frank, guest at Dera Baba Jaimal Singh. Beas, November 12, 1980.

Sondhi, S. L., general secretary of Radhasoami Satsang, Beas. Beas, July 12, 1979.

Stein, Arthur, editor of *Sat Sandesh*. Correspondence on August 4, 1989.

Tillis, Kate and Malcolm, member of Ruhani Satsang and Sawan Kirpal Ruhani Mission. Landaur, India, October 24, 1980; October 28, 1980; November 20, 1980; and correspondence, February 4, 1982.

Index